RV Vacations

6th Edition

by Dennis C. Brewer

for dummies®
A Wiley Brand

RV Vacations For Dummies®, 6th Edition

Published by **John Wiley & Sons, Inc.,** 111 River Street, Hoboken, NJ 07030-5774, www.wiley.com

Copyright © 2020 by John Wiley & Sons, Inc., Hoboken, New Jersey

Media and software compilation copyright © 2020 by John Wiley & Sons, Inc. All rights reserved.

Published simultaneously in Canada

For general information on our other products and services, please contact our Customer Care Department within the U.S. at 877-762-2974, outside the U.S. at 317-572-3993, or fax 317-572-4002. For technical support, please visit www.wiley.com/techsupport.

Wiley publishes in a variety of print and electronic formats and by print-on-demand. Some material included with standard print versions of this book may not be included in e-books or in print-on-demand. If this book refers to media such as a CD or DVD that is not included in the version you purchased, you may download this material at http://booksupport.wiley.com. For more information about Wiley products, visit www.wiley.com.

Library of Congress Control Number: 2019954069

ISBN: 978-1-119-56017-3

ISBN (ePDF): 978-1-119-56019-7; ISBN (ePub): 978-1-119-56018-0

Manufactured in the United States of America

Table of Contents

Introduction

Congratulations! After looking at all those recreation vehicles (RVs) rolling down the highway and wondering what driving one would be like, you decided it is time to find out. You're probably like us:

Whether you want to travel on vacation for a few weeks, catch a long weekend in the mountains, enjoy your favorite fishing hole, or get on the road full time to fulfill a lifelong dream, you can do no better than to experience it all in an RV. When you travel by RV, you can be close to the ones you love or find a place full of peace and quiet you can have to yourself. RVs provide a wealth of self-sufficiency and control over your life on the road. That is just the beginning of the list of benefits traveling by RV will give you.

On the road, we meet families with children, independent young couples who bring their offices along and work on the road, pet owners who don't want to leave their animals behind, retirees who've been planning for years to discover America gradually, fussy diners who don't want to down *another* fast-food meal, sleepers who don't like to wonder who slept in their bed the night before, and those with disabilities or those with dietary restrictions who know that their specialized adjustments in the RV enable them to travel safely and securely, and on their own terms.

About This Book

In the first chapters of this book, we tell you just about everything you ever wanted or needed to know about RVing, tempered by our own experiences with tents, vans, trailers, Class C, and class A motor homes, with over eight years of that full-time living in one for travel, work, and play.

Then, we give you an insider's look at some all-time favorite preplanned route suggestions, particularly suited for RVs, in what we think is the most diverse, beautiful, and exciting travel venue in the world — the North American Continent, from Florida across parts of Canada to Alaska. And, finally, we offer some practical tips that make all this travel easier on the mind and budget.

Throughout the book's suggested travel routes — 16 in total — we give you the information you need to find your way and point out popular highlights. We share some favorite campground locations with you, and because, in most cases, you're carrying your own kitchen, we steer you to places where you can pick up local produce, regional farm to table foods, or one-of-a-kind takeout meals to pick up and eat later.

There are a few ways to use *RV Vacations For Dummies* as a reference guide. You can start at the first page and read all the way through. If you're a more experienced RVer, you can flip to a favorite travel route, and start checking out the recommended destinations and campgrounds. You can move from chapter to chapter, picking and choosing information that interests you most.

You won't find much in this book about repairing a malfunctioning RV. We learned to leave that to the experts. That said, through the years, we've acquired a few handy preventive maintenance routines, which we pass on to help you and your RV stay in shape and cut down on repair bills.

Please be advised that travel information is subject to change at any time — this is *especially* true of prices. And with an RV, any noticeable change in the cost of gas will make an equally noticeable difference in your budget — your home on wheels has a particularly large appetite for petroleum! We, therefore, suggest that you write or call ahead for confirmation when making your travel plans. The authors, editors, and publisher can't be held responsible for the experiences of readers while traveling.

Your safety is important to us, so we encourage you to stay alert and be aware of your ever-changing surroundings. Keep a close eye on cameras, smartphones, purses, and wallets, all favorite targets of thieves and pickpockets. And always lock your vehicle in or out of campgrounds.

Conventions Used in This Book

To keep this book from being longer than the *Great Expectations* tome, we use a number of abbreviations in the driving chapters.

Campground amenities are abbreviated as follows:

CATV: Cable TV hookup

SATV: Satellite TV hookup

Wi-Fi: Wireless Internet connection

Here are the abbreviations for credit cards:

AE: American Express

DISC: Discover

MC: MasterCard

V: Visa

And we use the following abbreviations for road names:

I-#: Interstate highway

SR #: State road

CR #: County road

FM #: Farm-to-market road

We use some general pricing information to help you as you decide where to camp. The following system of dollar signs is meant to be a guideline only and denotes the range of costs for one night in a campground.

Cost	Campground
$	$10 or less
$$	$11 to $20
$$$	$21 to $30
$$$$	$31 to $40
$$$$$	$41 or more

Foolish Assumptions

As we wrote this book, we made some assumptions about you and your needs as an RVer. Here's what we think might be true about you:

» You may be an inexperienced RVer looking for insight and advice about what RVing is all about.

» You may be an experienced RVer looking for new experiences, new attractions, or new roads to travel, and you don't want to miss a good bet.

» You're not looking for a directory that provides lists of every campground, attraction, or food venue available to you. Instead, you're looking for a book that focuses on the most important information and integrates that information into the best or most unusual experiences as you travel the highway.

» You may be an inexperienced RVer seeking to learn information and discover patterns that help your plan your own future adventures.

If you fit any of these criteria, *RV Vacations For Dummies*, 6th Edition, gives you the information you're seeking!

How This Book Is Organized

Although divided into six parts, the book consists of three major sections. Parts 1 and 2 provide the how-to info that you need to get started before you hit the road. Parts 3, 4, and 5 include 16 wonderful trip suggestions, each in a different area of the United States and Canada. And, finally, Part 6 gives you some interesting and out of the way attractions for RVers who want to set up to explore some locations beyond the planned trips in this book and some ten of the bring-along items you will want to have with you.

Part 1: Getting Started

What is an RV and what is RVing? You find out in this part, and you see why we think it's the greatest thing since the invention of the wheel. We tell you where to consider traveling and when, give you helpful tips, fill you in on some best features of RVing, and debunk some RV myths.

Part 2: Paying Attention to the Details

Here you discover the how to budget for a trip. This part includes tips for getting started — what to plan for, how to prepare, and what you need to know about choosing and using campgrounds, accommodating special needs, and more.

Part 3: Exploring the East

In Chapters 8 through 12, we explore parts of the eastern United States by RV. The driving routes in each chapter offer a variety of scenery and activities, and includes scenic roadways, sightseeing attraction, or national parks. Two routes — The Coast of Maine: Lobster Land and The Gulf Coast: Tallahassee to New Orleans — follow along the sea. The Blue Ridge Mountains: Skyline Drive and Blue Ridge Parkway brings together two great American roadways with the Great Smoky Mountains National Park — all without the hassle of commercial traffic. Western New York: Cooperstown to Niagara Falls lets you see a museum for baseball greats and witness the grandeur of

Niagara Falls. The Natchez Trace: Natchez to Nashville, takes you through the old and new South, past the birthplaces of such icons as Elvis, and other famous folks from the south. And, of course, we share popular campgrounds and cafes to find along the way.

Part 4: Discovering Mid-America

Chapters 13 through 17 take you through the middle of North America with a choice of five itineraries, at least one of which should be within a reasonable driving time from a Midwestern home base. Texas Hill Country: Bluebonnets and Barbecue tells you about natural wildflower shows and where to find the best barbecue. The Heart of Ohio: A Circle around Circleville carries you on a loop from aviation history to rock-'n'-roll, with a pause in the world's largest Amish community. Northern Minnesota: Paul Bunyan Country visits a classic American icon that delights kids of all ages, takes you to the start of the great Mississippi River, and leads you to North America's largest shopping mall. Lake Superior Circle Tour takes you around the largest surface area of fresh water in the Western Hemisphere and across the border to Canada and back. The Ozarks and Branson: Hot Springs to Springfield lets you in on how to get good deals in an area that is a very popular travel destination for music lovers from North America and from all over the world.

Part 5: Seeing the West

In Chapters 18 through 23, we follow the trail of American icons through some of the world's most incredible scenery. Montana and Wyoming: Tracking Buffalo Bill follows the famous showman through Yellowstone National Park and to the town of Cody, Wyoming, which is named for him. New Mexico: Billy the Kid Meets E.T. lets you visit a notorious real-life cowboy and the alien visitor from the film E.T. (whose space-alien relatives are said to have dropped in on Roswell, New Mexico). The Oregon Coast: California to Washington combines scenery with seafood, taking you beachcombing, kite-flying, and wine-tasting, while California's Central Coast: Malibu to Monterey explores what some people think is the most beautiful place on earth. Route 66: OK to L.A. follows the remnants of the famous road and digs out some little-known and big-name landmarks along the way. ALCAN Trip: Seattle to Fairbanks takes you through some of the most magnificent scenery in Western Canada and into Anchorage, Alaska as a stayover location for some unforgettable day trips.

Part 6: The Part of Tens

The Part of Tens highlights campgrounds and destinations beyond the itineraries in this book. We know that after RVers get started, they soon want to travel more and more and discover new destination and attractions on their own. This part includes our choices for one of ten best out of the way, hard to find, or often overlooked destinations in every U.S. state and Canadian province. This part ends with the listing of Ten Greatest Travel Gadgets to have along on any trip to improve safety, keeping in touch, and enjoying the stays wherever they may be.

Appendix: Quick Concierge

Here find facts you need to know to complete the last details for your RV vacation, some toll-free telephone numbers and a few websites to explore. We include a list of common RV and campground terms to help with budget planning and choosing a campground.

Icons Used in This Book

In the margins of this book are helpful icons. They are intended to focus attention to certain kinds of information. Here's what the icons mean:

BARGAIN ALERT

This icon pegs the bargains and money-saving tips for your RV vacation, from where to purchase groceries to campgrounds that represent a good value.

KID FRIENDLY

This icon flags when something is of interest to the younger travelers.

REMEMBER

This icon highlights information worth remembering.

TIP

For hints, tips, or insider advice to make your trip run smoother, look for this icon. Although the point of a travel guide is to serve as one gigantic tip, this icon singles out nuggets of information that may be new to you.

WARNING

Accompanying this icon are special warnings for RVers, whether you face a low bridge ahead or a difficult parking situation.

Beyond the Book

There is never enough room to cover everything in a book like this. To help fill in the whole picture we render up some more tips for readying the RV for travel. For each region and outdoor environment there are some suggested precautions to follow and details to pay particular attention to. Finally, some low-tech hacks and routine items worth making into pre-travel and travel habits. To access the Cheat Sheet for this book, visit www.dummies.com, enter **RV Vacations For Dummies Cheat Sheet** in the Search box on the website, and click the link that appears in the search results.

Where to Go from Here

It's time to enjoy the freedom of the open road! How you use this guide is up to you. You can start from the beginning and read straight through, or dip into the middle and extract information of interest. Think of us as an interested, experienced guide full of helpful suggestions. The information can help you with choices for stocking up with your favorite supplies and deciding when and where to travel. With your RV as home and all the highways of North America on the other side of the windshield, you can feel like the king or queen of the road.

1
Getting Started

Chapter **1**

All the Best Reasons to Take an RV Vacation

When we discovered RVing, we couldn't believe how perfectly the experience fit our personality and desire to live a down-sized lifestyle, how comfortable and convenient it is, and how liberating it makes traveling while savoring the rewards of new experiences and meeting new people. There are many reasons why traveling and vacationing by RV is more convenient and pleasant than other methods. Perhaps as you read this book, you'll discover some of your own reasons to add to our list of the best reasons to RV anywhere or everywhere.

To help with my first RV experience, I looked for a book like this one. Because I couldn't find one, I wrote this book for you.

Counting the Reasons to RV

Freedom! If you want to sum up RV travel in one word, that's it. *Freedom.* An RV vacation carries with it a great many benefits, more than you'd get from paying years ahead to take a trip around the moon (if you have enough money) or taking a cruise down the Mississippi River. A few obvious and not-quite-so-obvious-benefits of traveling by RV are a wee bit different from those of other types of travel.

Containing costs

Some budget choices are yours, such as eating on the road versus dining in, or paying $6 for an overnight stay at a city-run no-frills campground versus paying nearly $100 a night at Disney's Fort Wilderness Resort and Campground. You have little control of fuel prices, however.

My current motor home is a gas-burning big-block V-8 of the highest order; it's called the Workhorse, and it's exactly that. To do its work of pulling my 36-foot Class A motor home and towed car, it delivers an average 7.1 miles per gallon on flat land. Some of the smaller four-cylinder class B and C diesel rigs hit 12 to 18 miles per gallon.

TIP

You can do a few things to economize on fuel. Keep your speed a bit below the speed limit, make sure that your tire pressures are correct, and go easy on the throttle when you're starting again from a stop.

Aside from fuel, you can control just about everything else involving your RV vacation. How far you go, how long you stay, whether to choose a state campground or luxury RV resort, and what you'll eat and drink are cost variables to a large extent. Sometimes, a hot dog and fixings can be as pleasurable an eating experience as an Angus steak-and-lobster dinner, as long as you're eating the hot dog on a nice day in one of your favorite places on the planet. Your RV vacation can take you to the places you most want to be.

Enjoying maximum convenience

When you, your traveling companions, or the children need to use the restroom in an airplane or on the train, the queue can easily get the best of you in terms of inconvenience. On the rare occasions when roadblocks occur while you're traveling in a motor home, convenience is no problem. The restroom is right there; the generator can be turned on to heat a TV dinner in the microwave or brew a cup of coffee, and the fridge is always stocked with a cold drinks and healthy snacks. Convenience is just a few steps or an arm's reach away. Frustration becomes a zero as long as everything you need is at hand.

Controlling the destination

Freedom translates to being in control of your own direction and destiny. Vacationing or living full-time in an RV delivers on the freedom promise in multiple ways. If you like out-of-the way places, some off-the-grid public lands allow you to boondock (that is, dry-camp meaning no hookups of any kind), offering such permits at low cost. Conserving on resources such as fresh water during a four-day stay near your favorite trout stream is in the realm of possibility with an RV vacation; you and your companion have nothing to distract you from catching trophy trout. If out-of-the-way living is your thing, RVing should be your ticket there, while there, and back again. Should you prefer big-city crowds and live theater, getting there in your RV can be as easy as getting to that trout stream.

Whether you're going to the beach, a museum, or the golf course, or taking the kids to their travel-team soccer matches, there's no better way to get to your destination for the day or weekend than an RV. An RV offers comfort and convenience, and you control the route and the way points. Want to see the Cadillac Ranch on the way to Amarillo or the World's Largest Ball of Sisal Twine in Kansas? If so, your RV will let you pass by those spots on your way to where you're going. You can see all the sights you have time for along the road. You control the route, the way points, and the destinations when you travel in an RV.

Finding your rhythm on the road

RV travel can help you leave the rush-rush of the everyday world behind the minute you turn the key on. Some folks who travel in RVs consider driving 300 miles a day to be enough; others take 600 miles or more in stride. Your route, days for travel, and temperament all come into play when you get on the road. It's a good idea to know thyself when making your travel plans.

It's also good to know your travel companions' taste or tolerance for road miles before you begin your journey. Often, I break a long trip into legs that vary in distance and time. Think in terms of short, long, and medium road legs for each day on the road. You usually have enough to do the night before the journey or on the morning of departure that making the first day's ride a short one often makes sense. Planning your travel tempo can also eliminate the urge to rush.

TIP

When you're making your plan, pay attention to speed limits. Following historic U.S. 41 to Florida is probably going to take much more time than traveling Interstate 75. Always allow enough travel time to stay alert and be safe.

Having room for lug-along stuff

You have to pay attention to gross vehicle weight in an RV, and it's up to you to decide what will roll down the road with you. The only baggage handler involved is you; no tipping or extra fees are required. If you want to take along an extra little black dress for a Saturday night out or a set of golf clubs in case you get a tee time in the off hours, you can probably find places to put them in the RV.

Manufacturers pay close attention to designing to include storage space and making available some weight allowance for necessary goods and toys. Choose your take-along items wisely, and you should have room for the few extras that can enhance your vacation time.

Being close to events

Airplanes and trains get you to the event city, but the right-size RV gets you to the team's tailgate party, with all the comforts of home a few steps away. Whether you're going to a NASCAR race, an NFL football game, college sporting events, the racetrack, or a family reunion at the beach, an RV is a great way to get there and get up close while being "at home" in your own space.

If you or a companion is physically challenged, the ability to get an RV close to whatever's happening is one of many benefits of traveling to events by RV.

Bringing your pets for free

If you prefer to take your puppy on the trip because there are no decent kennels in your neighborhood, or if your cat sitter called in sick, traveling by RV means that your pets can easily go with you. If you simply can't bear to be without them, the right RV will have room for your favorite pet's travel needs.

REMEMBER

Some parks and campgrounds have pet limits and rules that prohibit aggressive dog breeds and wolf hybrids; other resorts limit how many members of your canine family can be with you. But parakeets, parrots, and other caged pets are welcome at many campgrounds. Check the leash, clean-up, and approved-pet rules before you reserve your overnight stays.

Changing your mind if you want to

Not too long ago, while traveling south on Interstate 25 south of Albuquerque on our way to the Rio Grande Valley, I stopped to have lunch at a roadside rest stop. About halfway through lunch, I decided to go to Tucson instead. Changing your mind is as easy as taking a right turn instead of a left turn at the next intersection when you're vacationing by RV. The same thing is difficult and not recommended when you're flying at 30,000 feet or traveling by train.

Keeping it clean

Sure, it can be nice to be in a five-star hotel where all the work is done for you, yet even the best hotels occasionally slip up on maintaining cleanliness to your own acceptable standards. You're the housekeeping department when you're vacationing in your RV, and the cleanliness chores are yours to perfect. Your own cleaning standards prevail, and the ecofriendly supplies are yours to choose. You know with certainly that the sheets on the bed are clean at night and there are no bedbugs to bite you or the kids.

Cleaning, meal preparation, and normal housekeeping tasks such as vacuuming, dusting, and shaking out the rugs might take an average 20 minutes a day in an RV. Maintaining your space to your high standards can make all the difference in your quality of life on the road.

Reaping the scenic rewards of driving

Seeing the USA when you break free of the expressways and taking some historical routes across the country bring to life history, geography, archeology, architecture, engineering feats, and monuments, as well as the natural beauty of whatever state, province, or nation you're traveling through. Some of those majestic sights, sounds, and smells will burn their way into your memory forever. The roar and mist of Niagara Falls (on either side of the U.S.–Canada border) or Tahquamenon Falls in upper Michigan aren't easily forgotten. Getting out of your rig and walking to the first overlook at the Grand Canyon in Arizona can make your heart skip a beat.

One of my favorite things on every drive is crossing rivers and natural divides on the engineering marvels we call bridges, first perfected by the Romans. The United States has some 600,000 highway bridges you could cross; some of them qualify as works of engineering art. Some favorite bridges crossover the Mississippi River and the many rivers along the Pacific Coast in Oregon. Another favorite is the mighty Mackinaw Bridge in upper Michigan.

Often unlikely beauty is found on the road. Driving toward Tucson on U.S. 10 from the east gives you a glimpse of the earth's violent past when you see what I call "boulder row" near Texas Canyon. The biggest boulders I have ever seen are precariously perched alongside the expressway creating quite a site to see.

Keeping the kids entertained

Taking my boys to a vacation or weekend destination by car always meant hearing "Are we there yet, Papa Smurf?" Hearing it was always fun the first time because it meant that they were excited about the destination; by the third time, it was old news. When you travel with young children by RV, bring some games or craft projects that are safe for them to play with while they're buckled up at the dinette.

Discovering Something for Everyone

KID FRIENDLY

For families with children, drives include a wealth of show-and-tell and how-I-spent-my-summer-vacation material, from discovering how baseball was invented at the National Baseball Hall of Fame in Cooperstown, New York (Chapter 9); to seeing curious underground rock formations at Carlsbad Caverns National Park in Carlsbad, New Mexico (Chapter 19); and finding out at the McKinley Museum in Canton, Ohio (Chapter 14), why President William McKinley always wore a red carnation. Kids remember the McKinley story because they hear it from the animatronic version of the man himself.

Hikers and bikers can pinpoint state or national parks with great walking and bicycle trails. Oregon Dunes National Recreation Area (Chapter 20) is just one of many parks in that state with hiking trails that skirt the coast. Cyclists can take advantage of 45 miles of carriage roads in Maine's Acadia National Park (Chapter 8) or wooded roads that are regularly closed to traffic in Great Smoky Mountains National Park (Chapter 10) on the Tennessee–North Carolina border. Best of all, after a day of breaking a sweat, you can return to a hot shower and comfortable RV bed instead of an air mattress on the ground.

Do you want to settle into the driver's seat and just cruise? I have the roads for you. Scenic highways such as the Blue Ridge Parkway and Skyline Drive (Chapter 10), Natchez Trace (Chapter 12), and California's Pacific Coast Highway (Chapter 21) were built for slow, easy driving and frequent stops to admire the view or set out a picnic. For a slice of Americana, drive what remains of old Route 66 between Oklahoma and California (Chapter 22).

For more of what makes America unique, look no farther than the country's colorful icons. New Mexico brings Billy the Kid to life again along the Billy the Kid National Scenic Byway (Chapter 19), while Buffalo Bill Center in Cody, Wyoming, celebrates yet another figure from the American West (Chapter 18). From folklore and the imagination come Minnesota's Paul Bunyan (Chapter 15), who pops up in living color by the side of the road in Bemidji and Akeley.

For delicious tastes of America, sample fresh-from-the-sea Maine lobster with melted butter (Chapter 8), Texas barbecued brisket smoky from the grill (Chapter 13), Santa Maria barbecue along California's Central Coast (Chapter 21), succulent shrimp and oysters around the Gulf Coast (Chapter 11), Virginia country ham on a fresh-baked biscuit (Chapter 10), or New Mexico's spicy chili dishes (Chapter 19).

Music lovers can tap their toes to the rich sounds of America. Enjoy authentic mountain music at the Ozark Folk Arts Center or pop/country music productions in Branson, Missouri (Chapter 17); hear funky blues and soul at the Alabama Music Hall of Fame, or visit the birthplaces of W. C. Handy and Elvis Presley (Chapter 12); and listen to rock in all its forms at Cleveland's Rock and Roll Hall of Fame and Museum (Chapter 14).

Sports fans find great entertainment in the National Baseball Hall of Fame in Cooperstown, New York (Chapter 9), which has the gloves, bats, and uniforms of famous players from the past; the Mississippi Sports Hall of Fame and Museum (Chapter 12), where you can make like a sports announcer and tape your own play-by-play commentary; and the a Hockey Hall of Fame (Chapter 15), where you can take shots at an electronic goalie.

Professional or amateur photographers will marvel at the sunsets over Lake Superior from the shoreline at McClain State Park (Chapter 16) or be awestruck by sunrise at Whitefish Point at the Great Lakes Shipwreck Museum (Chapter 16).

Saving Money in a Campground

RVing can be a very cost-effective way to travel, but opportunities to make your dollar go farther are around every bend. Here are my recommendations of ways to save money in a campground:

» **Never pay for more park than you'll use.** Posh campgrounds with swimming pools, spas, and tennis courts are usually pricier than simple, clean, mom-and-pop campgrounds. The latter are adequate for an overnight stay. If there's a charge per hookup, take the electric and water hookup, and forgo the sewer unless you really need it.

» **Camp without hookups.** You can do this comfortably for several nights as long as you don't insist on using the RV's air conditioner or microwave, both of which require an electrical hookup or generator. Read a book or listen to music on a portable player for entertainment and cook on your gas cooktop or outdoors on a grill. You'll have on-board running water, lights, refrigeration, heat, and hot water for washing dishes and showering.

» **Watch out for campground surcharges.** Some campgrounds charge extra fees for running your air conditioner or hooking up to cable TV, a surcharge for 50-amp electricity, or "extra person" charges for more than two people when you're traveling with your kids or friends. Some of the campgrounds that accept pets may also levy a fee for pets.

» **Join membership clubs that offer discounts at campgrounds.** KOA and Good Sam usually offer discounts of 10 percent. KOA promises the discount whether you pay by cash or credit card; some Good Sam campgrounds grant the discount only if you pay cash. In most cases, you can join up at the campground when you register.

» **Take advantage of age or veteran status.** If you or a companion is 62 or older, you should apply for a free America the Beautiful Pass–The National Parks and Federal Recreational Lands Annual Pass (now *that's* a mouthful!), which replaces the Golden Age Passport. With this $80 for a lifetime (free for US Military) pass and proof of age at a national park's visitor center, you and your vehicle enter the park, national monument, recreation area, or wildlife refuge with the pass and can get a discount on camping areas administered by the federal government.

U.S. military, eligible veterans and/or retirees, active-duty members, and reservists can find FAM-CAMPS at many military bases. Short stays are available for reasonable rates.

» **Look for free campgrounds.** These campgrounds include those in the Southwestern desert that are administered by the Bureau of Land Management.

» **Get a current campground guide.** You can request a state tourism office's free campground guide. County, city, and national forest campgrounds range from free to considerably less expensive than most privately owned campgrounds, although they may not offer the luxury of hookups.

» **Ask for discounts.** If you arrive late at a campground, some campground owners will give you a discount if you stay overnight on a self-contained basis in an overflow area; others won't.

Stay longer than a week, and you can negotiate discounts of 10 to 20 percent or more, depending on the season and length of stay. Some owners offer one free day for every six you pay for.

» **Consider volunteering as a campground host.** If you're interested in staying a long time in one area, you can camp free and may even pick up a bit of pocket change for performing specified duties on the premises. (See the nearby sidebar "Becoming a campground host" for more information.)

BECOMING A CAMPGROUND HOST

You can find host jobs in many campgrounds, both public and privately owned; they double as troubleshooters when the office is closed or the rangers are off duty. They're usually camped in a conspicuous spot near the entrance with a sign indicating that they're your hosts.

In theory, being a campground host is a great idea. You live in your RV in a lovely campground with free hookups, maybe even with your choice of sites. In practice, however, veterans of the job seem to love it or hate it. Some mutter darkly about being underappreciated; others describe the experience as a highlight of their lives. Much depends on how thoroughly you check out the opportunity and campground management ahead of time, as well as how realistic you are about doing hard and sometimes unpleasant chores, such as cleaning toilets and showers or telling noisy campers to turn down their radios.

If you already have a specific campground in mind, send a résumé that includes personal and business references; you also may be asked for a recent photo and a photo of your RV. Many campgrounds prefer a couples to a single host, or they require a single person to work 30 to 40 hours a week, compared with 15 or 20 hours each for a couple.

If you want to volunteer in a national park or forest service campground, contact the National Forest Service directly or the National Parks Service.

Two websites that list working-camper opportunities are https://www.work-for-rvers-and-campers.com and https://www.workamper.com.

Finding Top Locations around the USA

When it comes to choosing where to stay it could be as simple as good, better, or best or simply selecting between two choices from what is available in smaller less popular areas. Any campground offers a place to turn off the engine and sleep for a few hours and sometimes that is enough. Over time you will develop your own criteria. In this section, find a few ideas to get you started.

Choosing some of the best campgrounds

» **AAA Midway RV Park,** Coos Bay, Oregon (☎ 541-888-9300; www.midwayrvparkcoosbay.com): Three blocks from the ocean and convenient to town, this park has 59 full hookups, Wi-Fi, and easy access to great seafood restaurants and markets. Cost: $45 to $90 per night.

» **The Campsites at Disney's Fort Wilderness Resort,** Lake Buena Vista, Florida (☎ 407-939-2267; https://disneyworld.disney.go.com/resorts/campsites-at-fort-wilderness-resort): Fort Wilderness has 694 full hookups near the Disney World action, with transportation to the park. The lake offers boating and fishing, or you can golf or relax in the pool. Cost: $57 to $184.

» **The Great Outdoors RV, Nature & Golf Resort,** Titusville, Florida (☎ 800-621-2267; https://www.tgoresort.com): Here, you find 150 full hookups, a lake for fishing, a spa, an 18-hole golf course, tennis courts, and a heated pool. Cost: $70.

» **Harbortown RV Resort,** Monroe, Michigan (☎ 734-384-4700; https://www.harbortownrv.com): Harbortown has 248 paved sites; 130 of them are full hookups, some with 50-amp electricity. It also has an 18-hole golf course; fishing; and a kids' fun center with miniature golf, an arcade, go-karts, and batting cages that augment the heated pool. Cost: $48 to $61.

» **Traverse Bay RV Resort,** Acme, Michigan (☎ 231-938-5800; http://traversebayrv.com): Traverse Bay has 157 extra-wide, paved sites with patios and full hookups. The park is restricted to motor homes and fifth-wheels that are 28 feet or longer and not older than ten years. Cost: $69 to $95.

Seeing museums that are well worth the visit

» **Admiral Nimitz Museum and National Museum of the Pacific War,** Fredericksburg, Texas (see Chapter 13): Extensive coverage of World War II battles in the Pacific is located in the restored Nimitz Steamboat Hotel and Gardens.

» **Alabama Music Hall of Fame,** Tuscumbia, Alabama (see Chapter 12): Although the museum contains only the work of musicians who were born or lived in Alabama, the list is extensive, including Nat King Cole, Dinah Washington, Lionel Richie, and Toni Tennille. It's a seeing-and-listening museum.

» **Biltmore Estate,** Asheville, North Carolina (see Chapter 10): This museum is pricey but worth the expenditure. The massive 250-room Biltmore mansion and gardens give an extensive picture of how the other half once lived.

» **Buffalo Bill Center,** Cody, Wyoming (see Chapter 18): Five museums are set in a sprawling complex containing the Buffalo Bill Museum, the Plains Indian Museum, the Whitney Gallery of Western Art, the Cody Firearms Museum, and the Draper Museum of Natural History. You easily can spend an entire day (or more) here.

» **Farnsworth Art Museum,** Rockland, Maine (see Chapter 8): This complex of consists of the Farnsworth Art Museum and the Wyeth Center in town, and the Olson House (celebrated in Andrew Wyeth's painting *Christina's World*) in the nearby countryside.

» **Hearst Castle,** San Simeon, California (see Chapter 21): Built from 1919 to 1947, the building was never finished. Four different tours cover the interior and exterior of "The Ranch," as William Randolph Hearst dubbed his castle by the sea.

» **Museum Center at Union Terminal,** Cincinnati, Ohio (see Chapter 14): The restored 1933 Art Deco railway station is now home to three excellent museums: the Cincinnati History Museum, the Museum of Natural History, and the hands-on Children's Museum.

» **National Baseball Hall of Fame,** Cooperstown, New York (see Chapter 9): Baseball fans can spend several days perusing artifacts ranging from Ty Cobb's sliding pads to bats used by Mickey Mantle and Mark McGwire.

- » **Ozark Folk Arts Center,** Mountain View, Arkansas (see Chapter 17): The center was created in 1973 to preserve the music, dance, handicrafts, and folkways of the Ozarks. Wander among artisans and craftsmen at work and eat some down-home Ozark food.

- » **The Rock and Roll Hall of Fame and Museum,** Cleveland, Ohio (see Chapter 14): A modern glass building designed by I. M. Pei houses a huge collection of artifacts, such as life-size mannequins of John Lennon, Alice Cooper, and Michael Jackson, plus many of their instruments.

Stopping in national parks along the way

- » **Acadia National Park,** Maine (see Chapter 8): This park has a 27-mile Park Loop Road, which makes a circle out of Bar Harbor and offers a good overview of the gardens, beaches, cliffs, and Cadillac Mountain.

- » **Carlsbad Caverns National Park,** New Mexico (see Chapter 19): A variety of caverns offers exciting, colorful underground tours. Join the evening crowd to watch 300,000 bats soar out of the cave for their evening meals.

- » **Grand Canyon National Park,** Arizona (see Chapter 22): This spectacular attraction can be crowded in summer. A good way to visit is to take the Grand Canyon Railway for a round-trip train ride out of Williams, Arizona.

- » **Great Smoky Mountains National Park,** North Carolina and Tennessee (see Chapter 10): Located at the end of the Blue Ridge Parkway, the park has an 11-mile, loop road off Newfound Gap Road that's a must-see.

- » **Lyndon B. Johnson National Historical Park,** Texas (see Chapter 13): Visitors see the birthplace, home, ranch, and final resting place of the former president. The park has two parts: Johnson City, which has the visitor center, and the LBJ Ranch.

TEN PERSONALITIES THAT ARE IDEAL FOR RVING

So is RVing for you? See whether you fit any of these personality types:

- **Garbo gourmets:** Alone together, luxuriating in the best that life can offer, these epicures carry their own wines and food, sleep in their own beds, and select their own surroundings by serendipity.

- **Sportsmen and sportswomen:** Skiers, fishermen, surfers, golfers, and mountain bikers get into the heart of the action with all the comforts of home a few steps away.

- **Weekenders:** The stressed-out get out of the rat race and into the countryside to leave behind the pressures of the workweek.

- **Families on vacation:** Families think of their motor homes as a budget hotel and round-the-clock self-serve restaurants. For the kids, RVing means no more "Are we there yet?" or "I have to go potty!" or "I'm hungry!" Everything is here.

- **Ecotourists:** Getting back to nature the easy way, ecotourists bird-watch at dawn and spot for wildlife at twilight. Photography and hiking lay very few burdens on Mother Earth.

- **Ultimate shoppers:** Hitting all the antiques shops, all the estate sales, and the world's biggest swap meets, shoppers enjoy comfort and style with room to take home all their treasures in the RV.

- **Pet lovers:** Taking Fifi and Fido along for the ride and enjoying their company, animal lovers avoid facing rebellious and destructive pets after a spell of boarding them in a kennel.

- **Travelers with disabilities:** A customized RV can open up the world with familiar and accessible surroundings.

- **Special-events attendees:** Tailgating for a football game or hitting a jazz or arts festival on the spur of the moment, RVing fans sidestep overbooked hotels and restaurants and can invite friends in for a meal.

- **Relatives:** While visiting relatives and friends, RVers can take along their own beds and bathrooms. When parked at home, RVs provide an extra guest room with a bathroom.

- » **Petrified Forest National Park and Painted Desert,** Arizona (see Chapter 22): Stop in the visitor center at the entrance to the Petrified Forest to get a map to use a loop road through both areas.

- » **Shenandoah National Park,** Virginia (see Chapter 10): Skyline Drive begins in this park and heads south into the Blue Ridge Parkway. Three RV campgrounds are located within the park.

- » **Vicksburg National Military Park,** Mississippi (see Chapter 12): This park is the site of one of the most decisive battles of the Civil War. A 16-mile auto tour runs through the park and its monuments.

Chapter 2

Making Destination Decisions

The 16 RV vacation drives presented in this book explore different regions of the contiguous United States and some parts of Canada, with their diverse four-season weather, so certain drives are best during certain seasons. In this chapter, we suggest criteria to use for deciding the best season for each drive and how much time to schedule.

Revealing the Secrets of the Seasons

Summer is the most popular vacation time for families because in most regions, the kids are out of school for longer periods. But for RVers who are looking for more solitude and milder weather, spring and fall may be preferable. In the southernmost parts of the United States, winter is best for its mild, sunny weather, but in resort areas, prices can climb with popularity, peaking between Christmastime and the weekend of Presidents' Day.

In RV parlance, retirees from Northern regions fleeing winter weather are known as *snowbirds*, and they're warmly welcomed in the South, particularly southern Texas along the Rio Grande, along the Gulf of Mexico from Florida to Louisiana, in southern Arizona and New Mexico, and in the California deserts. Snowbirds usually flee the Northeast, Midwest, or Northwest when the first cold weather hits, spend the winter months in the sun, and head back home in the spring.

Summer is prime time almost everywhere in the North, but it's too hot for optimum comfort in the snowbird winter retreats of the South.

Off season means smaller crowds and lower prices, but it also can mean that some campgrounds, restaurants, and shops are closed or on reduced hours. In each driving chapter, I list what are currently known opening and closing dates for seasonal campgrounds and attractions, so pay close attention if your trip is scheduled during a transitional month such as April or October.

TIP

Traffic is almost always heavy on the interstate highways, no matter what the season. On the first and last days of a holiday weekend, the highways — and even some back roads — are more crowded than usual. Smart RVers often opt to stay an extra night or two at the campground and then drive home after most people have returned to work. Routes through major cities are nearly always busy, particularly during business hours during the work-week, and every city experiences morning, afternoon, and evening traffic peaks, so timing is everything when you're planning routes through or around the biggest cities in every state. You improve your chance of missing the peaks from approximately 9:30 to 11 a.m., 1:30 to 2:45 p.m., and 6:45 to 8:30 p.m. Traffic at these times isn't guaranteed but is likely to be lighter in most major cities.

TIP

If you'll be passing through a large city on an expressway or toll road, check a good map to set your expectations. Calculate the distance you need to travel to get though the cities and how long the trip will take, using an average speed of, say, 45 mph.

Scoping Out Your Perfect RV Vacation

I had trouble narrowing my favorite RV drives to the 16 in this book, so I know that you may have trouble choosing among them too. The following sections offer a rundown of things to consider for each drive, including what you can see, the best times to go, who should go, who *shouldn't* go, and how much time to allow. In the "Getting There" sections of each drive detailed in Chapters 8 to 23, I suggest a starting point, and distance references begin there, but you can jump in at any point along the drive and do what you please.

TIP

Some geographic areas that I describe are closer to you than others, of course, so if you plan to rent an RV for your vacation, take note that you don't have to rent one close to home. Nation-wide rental companies mean that you can fly to another part of the country and rent your RV there (see the appendix).

TIP

Regardless of your starting point, consider planning a route that enables you to visit friends or relatives along your drive. They'll be glad to see you, not least because you're carrying your own bedroom and bathroom!

Consider using these criteria for every one of the detailed drive chapters in the book, the one-off places, and frankly any RV trip you plan to take anywhere in the future.

» **Best time to go:** Selecting the best time to go to a location, take a trip, see a destination, state province, or visit an area is a function of geography, weather, seasonal crowding or closing, safety concerns, and traffic.

Geography impacts what you will encounter in coastal areas, the plains, desert areas, and mountain ranges. Mountain states and locations can get very cold in the late fall and stay that way until early spring. Coastal areas can be prone to fog any time of the year but particularly in the fall and spring.

Weather: Weather patterns and temperatures drastically change as the seasons change. Northern states and provinces should be visited when the risk of snow is none or low.

Seasonal crowding or closing: Many, if not all, of the attractions and most of the campgrounds are closed in the winter in the northern tiers of the continent and the reverse is true in the heat of the desert regions of the country. Late spring and early autumn are less crowded in most seasonal locations in the north and south.

Safety concerns: There are places in mountainous regions where roads are closed in winter on short notice due to snow and ice fall and in places like Wyoming. Heavy fogs and sometimes-icy roadways can be dangerous in northern coastal areas also. Desert destination can get too hot for the uninitiated in the summer months. Asses the challenges you might face and evaluate your tolerance for them before you go.

Traffic: Busy holidays and holiday weekends are rarely the best times to be on the road. A day or two ahead or a day or two after might be the wiser choice for when to go somewhere.

» **Who should go:** This section amount to a matching game. The list is long and the trips are varied. It comes down to how do you define yourself, your likes and dislikes, your hobbies, what makes you into you? Your answers should and will be a huge factor in the trip choices that you make. There is something for just about everyone in the trip chapters. The two universal reasons to go on an RV trip are to have a new experience and to build new memories. If that works for you, then so will any trip in the book.

» **Who shouldn't go:** RV adventures and trips are all about getting out of one's own comfort zone and familiar setting and getting behind the wheel or passenger seat and finding a sense of adventure so just about everyone should be willing to consider giving it a go. There are real issues, though, for some. Health considerations and allergies may be reasons not to travel or visit a particular area or go during the heavy pollen season. Too much heat or extreme cold weather is another reason to not find a particular trip or destination desirable. Otherwise not going to certain attractions or particular areas simply comes down to personal preferences and when that is the case, not going is the adult choice to make. For some, budget will be a valid reason to make another choice or lack of tolerance for long travel distances. If one can get past those factors then go, by all means; if not, make another choice.

» **How far/how long:** Deciding how far the trip is simply requires applying a formula and a little math on the back of an envelope to get to how long you should plan for being on each new trip.

The calculations presented in Chapters 8 to 23 are an adequate amount of time for most travelers to take in the sights and locations presented. To cut them or ad lib a trip of your own, use the calculations presented below.

Begin the calculation by determining the total length of the trip and side trip in road miles or kilometers. To determine the windshield time (driving time) needed, divide the distance by an average of 55 miles per hour or to find driving hours. Based on your willingness to spend time each day driving, take the hours from the last step by your comfort number for driving, say, 6 hours per day. You now have the days of driving time needed and the number of nightly campgrounds stops you will need. For each major visit or destination or activity you will visit on the trip, such as a museum or event, add a day or two for the event. Add at least one day of rest on longer trips for each major leg of the trip and another day or two for weather considerations.

» **Scenery:** Scenery for an RV traveler is what you see mostly through the windows of the RV or statically from a roadside park or turnoff. Scenery is the breathtaking vistas and panoramas presented to you along the way just because you embarked on a trip using a particular route. If mountains impress you, then take on a trip from this book that gets you to or crosses over mountains. If you love to see the ocean with sandy or rocky shores or take in a sunrise or sunset over the water, then a coastal trip should be your priority choice. Once you get to a destination, then scenery morphs into sightseeing, then scenery presents itself again as you return or finish the loop.

» **Sightseeing:** This book is all about sightseeing. Sightseeing is what you do when you reach a waypoint or a destination. It is an art museum, a restaurant, a challenging golf course, a theater, a place to eat, a place to learn. It is the focus of taking a trip in an RV or living in one full time. What should you go to see? How do you decide among the trips in this book or other destination you know about? For us, it is simple: Ask what is your passion; where have you not been before; what can you see there; what might you learn or learn about once there? On top of all that, ask what pleasant surprise might come to you from making this trip? Ask and answer these questions and the first trip and the next trip and every trip you take will be an easy choice to make.

» **Food:** Access to good food is near ubiquitous in all states and provinces and in most of them you do not have to travel far to find a store or restaurant. I dare to suggest you can find a hamburger in every state and province even if one of them only serves moose burgers. Fresh caught fish are air freighted or flash frozen and shipped from all over to all over the world to the continent where there is a demand. Fresh fruit and vegetables travel east and west and north and south across the planet to local markets every day. Sometimes a product is traveling in all those directions at the same time. Traveling by RV will generally not present the traveler with a challenge to find something to eat.

The whole idea or challenge behind traveling by RV to find food is to find and try local, fresh, ethnic, unfamiliar, and regionally unique foods that are better from the sources along the way than you can get or make at home. Trying something new or different is a benefit afforded and accommodated very well with RV travel. Of course, a personal willingness to taste something like a fried dill pickle on your first trip to Florida is necessary. Keep an open mind and an open palate when you travel. Be willing to try just about any food once and culinary travel adventures are yours for the tasting.

» **Shopping:** Everybody loves to shop except those who don't. One thing you can count on when traveling by RV there will be new and different places to shop. Some are listed in the "drive" chapters of this book. It would be rare for someone to take an RV trip just to shop, yet I am sure it happens. It must come down to this: Is the destination on this trip likely to take me to the things and bits I like to shop for? If yes, then this must be the place to go. Bring your wallet.

» **Offbeat:** There are many places suggested in this book that qualify as offbeat. If the offbeat is your beat, then pick that trip and go for it. There is no logic behind picking among the offbeat; that is done just for fun.

2

Paying Attention to the Details

Chapter **3**

Building Your Travel Budget

B udgeting for a trip in an RV has a few different wrinkles from a vacation on which you're not driving your accommodations around. In this chapter, I provide some basic information, tips, and instructions on planning the budget for your upcoming RV trip.

Adding It Up: Your Vacation Budget

You won't be able to figure out to the last cent how much you'll be spending, but the Cheat Sheet for this book and the information in this chapter can help you develop some reasonable estimates for building your travel budget. You can find the Cheat Sheet by visiting www.dummies.com and entering **RV Vacations For Dummies Cheat Sheet** in the Search box.

Transportation

Transportation — renting or buying and maintaining an RV and then filling the gas tank — is the biggest chunk of your budget. For information on renting and buying, see "Testing the Waters: RV Rentals" and "Taking the Plunge: RV Purchases" later in this chapter.

Even after you own an RV, you must pay attention to the cost of filling the gas tank and maintaining the vehicle in top working order. You'll want to prorate your annual maintenance costs, insurance, license, scheduled maintenance, and minor repairs on a per-mile or per-month basis.

The total cost of fuel depends on how much time you plan to spend on the road. Your gas price per day goes down considerably if you spend some days hiking, fishing, or doing local sightseeing. To get an estimate, drive mentally through your trip, adding up the mileage as you go based on the estimates in this book. You can confirm the mileage online at sites such as Google Maps (https://www.google.com/maps) and MapQuest (https://www.mapquest.com).

Next, settle on an expected average per-gallon price for gas. You can take an average figure per gallon from the signs at your local service station. Knowing the exact price of gas in the future or even two or three states down the road is impossible, but GasBuddy (https://www.gasbuddy.com/GasPriceMap) can give you current retail prices throughout the country, including the lowest prices in a particular area. Divide the daily or total trip mileage by the estimated miles per gallon that your RV gets, and you can get a good idea of how many gallons you'll use per day or for the entire drive. For tips on saving money on fuel costs, see Chapter 4.

Maintenance costs vary according to the type of RV you have. A towable has fewer motor-related costs than a motor home, of course, but your towing vehicle may require some maintenance. A rental unit should be in tip-top condition when you pick it up, so maintenance costs will be minimal. If you own the RV, you face unexpected road risk costs; roofs can peel off, flying debris can shatter windows, and tires can fail. Your warranty or RV insurance may cover such incidents.

TIP

Along with regular engine and vehicle upkeep on a long haul, spend that little bit of extra money on RV service when necessary. If you own your RV, it's a good idea to get an annual multipoint checkup at your dealership, performed by a qualified RV technician. The added expense can save money in the long run.

REMEMBER

Be aware that when you travel on back roads, you not only drive slower (not a bad idea when sightseeing), but also avoid the toll roads that charge fees based on the number of axles on your rig. Parking charges may double or triple for RV drivers. My 36-foot motor home takes up two parking meters (three or four with the tow car), and all those meters must be fed. Parking lots may charge additional fees depending on the size of your rig. Always be mindful of your overhead-clearance requirements when attempting to use pay-for-parking lots.

RV and camping supplies

You can purchase most RV and camping supplies at your local supermarket. Specialty items such as storage-tank deodorizers, biodegradable toilet paper, and other RV items are available in RV stores and auto-supply shops. For a list of what I consider to be essential supplies, check out the RV Vacations For Dummies Cheat Sheet. You can access the Cheat Sheet by visiting at www.dummies.com and entering **RV Vacations For Dummies Cheat Sheet** in the Search box.

Campgrounds

A family of four can often vacation in a family campground for as little as $250 per week, and a snowbird can spend the entire winter season in a full-service, warm-climate resort for $1,800 to $3,200. To determine your expenses, add up the campground fees for each night you're spending on the road.

Food

RVs have one great money-saving feature: You can buy your own groceries and prepare your own meals instead of eating out. Even buying takeout lunches or making picnics at rest stops is less expensive than eating in a restaurant. Figure on spending one fourth to one third more than you'd spend for food at home, allowing for splurges and snacks on the road. Making your own meals is a great benefit when anyone in the travel party has food allergies or ingrained preferences for or against particular foods.

Attractions and activities

I list current admission fees for attractions and activities throughout this book. You can easily include the must-sees and maybes in your budget and leave out the ones that don't interest you as much. I also recommend free attractions that you can visit without adding to the bottom line.

Shopping and entertainment

Budgeting for something as personal as shopping is difficult unless, of course, you're honest about your own weaknesses. I buy only what I really need, plus some discounted items such as candies from the factories that make them or one-of-a-kind artworks. You'll figure out your budget based on your own idea of what's a bargain and what's a great souvenir. The good thing about a large RV — the fact that it can accommodate large souvenirs — can also be the bad thing.

Because I like to sightsee during the day and spend evenings in the campground, my entertainment costs are minimal. Many campgrounds offer free movies or live music during the summers. If you're taking the Ozarks and Branson drive in Chapter 17, however, factor in the cost of buying tickets to one of the shows — the highlight of that itinerary. I list some average show prices in that chapter. Matinees usually are less expensive than evening shows, although ticket prices in Branson generally aren't as high as those for other major venues nationally.

Testing the Waters: RV Rentals

My family's first RV experience was snowbirding in a used 24-foot motor home for two seasons. As we traveled, we frequently saw rental RVs (other class Cs in particular) from a few major national RV rental companies. Renting presents a great opportunity to try the RV experience before you buy into it fully. Trying different styles of RVs by renting them first has the potential to help you make the best purchase decision if you're on a path to buy one. Renting an RV every summer for vacation is another alternative to buying; you get all the benefits of going on vacation in an RV without the added responsibilities of ownership.

After testing personal compatibility with RV living in a 24-foot class C, I decided to purchase a new gas Class A. Now I own a 36-foot motor home with three slide outs with a bath and a half and all the comforts and amenities of home.

When to rent

If you don't own an RV, you need to rent or buy one for your trip. How do you decide which to do? In the following circumstances, renting an RV makes more sense when

» You're setting out on your first RV journey.

» You're thinking about replacing your current RV with a different type.

» Your family takes a two-week vacation every year and wants to do so in an RV. That way, you can test-drive different models each year, and when the time comes to buy, you'll know what you want.

» You want to travel for several weeks in a location far from home. Fly-and-drive packages are available from several rental companies.

» You want to drive a rough or rugged stretch of road without subjecting your own RV to wear and tear.

» You want to travel a long haul (such as Route 66) in only one direction.

How to rent

Several companies rent RVs. To find one near you, go to the Recreational Vehicle Rental Association (RVRA) website (www.rvda.org/RVDA/Find_A_Dealer/RV_Rentals_On_The_Rise.aspx), or look in your local telephone directory.

TIP

Make reservations for your RV about three months in advance, especially for holiday periods and peak travel seasons, when tourists from Europe, Australia, and New Zealand who like to rent them for visits to national parks or drives along the California coast. During the off season, however, you may be able to book a spur-of-the-moment rental for a few days or a week, especially from a nearby dealer.

The most common rental unit available is the motor home — the Type C mini motor home — which accounts for 90 percent of all rentals.

Prices begin at around $1,000 per week plus a fee for miles driven. For tips on negotiating a rate, see "How to get the best rate" later in this chapter. Keep in mind, however, that your rental rate doesn't include

» **The use of the generator:** You need the generator for operating the ceiling air conditioner, microwave oven, and TV in places that don't have electrical hookups. When you return the RV, the dealer reads the generator counter (usually located near the on/off switch) to determine the use-time you logged.

» **Certain furnishings and utensils:** Some companies offer a furnishings package with bedding, towels, dishes, cooking pots, and utensils for a flat rate of about $85 per trip. Other companies offer add-on kits containing power cords and hoses, plastic trash bags, toilet chemicals, and a troubleshooting guide. Sometimes, purchasing these packages, or bringing items from home makes more sense than spending vacation time searching for them. Ask the rental company for a list of what's included in your rental so that you'll know what you need to bring or buy.

» **Connections for travel trailers:** When you find a company that rents travel trailers, you may be required to furnish your own tow vehicle and hitch, as well as electrical hookups on the tow vehicle.

» **Insurance:** Insurance on a rental RV normally isn't covered in your own automobile insurance, so ask your insurance agent for a binder that extends your coverage to the RV for the rental period. Many dealers require a binder before you rent a vehicle.

Most rental centers request a cleaning deposit, which isn't returned if you bring the vehicle back with the holding tanks full or the interior dirty or damaged. Some companies offer free airport pickup and return if you notify them of your flight number and estimated arrival time.

TIP

At the dealership, make sure that the dealer demonstrates all the components and systems of the RV you're renting. Take careful notes. As you would with a rental car, check for dents and damage from previous use, and document the damage with the dealer before leaving the lot. Also make sure that you're given a full set of instruction booklets and emergency phone numbers in case of a breakdown. Having a 24-hour toll-free number to call in case of a problem is best.

If you fall in love with your rental vehicle, you may be able to negotiate a purchase price that subtracts your rental fee from the total. You may get a good deal if the vehicle is a few model years old; most rental dealers get rid of vehicles after two or three years.

How to get the best rate

For the best rental rate, follow these tips:

» **Check prices with several companies before making a decision.** Establish exactly what the lowest-priced rental includes, such as free miles, the price per mile beyond the daily or weekly limit, amenities such as dishes and linens, and breakdown service.

» **Try to plan your trip during the off season or *shoulder season* (the period between the most popular and least popular travel times).** The times of year for these seasons vary, depending on the area where you're renting.

» **Find out whether your own automobile insurance covers rental insurance for an RV.** Your agent usually can provide a cheaper rate than the rental company.

» **Try to plan your trip in a loop so that you can avoid drop-off charges.** The rental agency serves as the starting and ending point.

» **Negotiate based on selection.** The more RVs a rental company has, the wider your range of choices. If you're flexible about what sort of rig you rent, you may be able to negotiate a better price when the selection is not limited.

Taking the Plunge: RV Purchases

Buying an RV is a big moment and certainly not a time to let a fast-talking salesman steer you into a hasty purchase.

TIP

For a first-time buyer, renting an RV of the type you're thinking about buying can be a big help in making up your mind. Just be sure to allow enough time to get comfortable with the RV — a week at minimum, preferably two weeks. To evaluate an RV properly, you need enough time to relax into the day-to-day logistics of handling it on the road and hooking it up in the campground.

A seal from the Recreation Vehicle Industry Association (RVIA), affixed near an RV's doorway, certifies that the vehicle complies with the current specifications of the American National Standards Institute (ANSI) for fire safety, plumbing and electrical systems, and liquid propane gas systems.

TECHNICAL STUFF

The RVIA represents the builders of most all RVs sold in the United States and most of the vehicles manufactured worldwide. RVIA makes periodic unannounced plant inspections to ensure that members maintain acceptable levels of compliance with the codes of the ANSI/NFPA 1192 standard for RVs. For more information, visit https://www.rvia.org.

Why you should visit an RV show

When the bug to buy an RV strikes, one of the best places to look is an annual national or regional RV show. These shows usually take place during the winter months and make especially safe hunting grounds for four types of people:

>> "Looky-loos" who have no idea what they want

>> Potential buyers who have done their research, know exactly what they want

>> RV owners who want to see the latest technical and design innovations and are happy with their RV

>> RV shoppers who want to make side-by-side comparisons of several RV brands and models before purchasing

What you get for the price of admission to an RV show is a chance to compare different types, brands, and models of RVs. On-site salespeople and factory representatives are happy to spend time answering your questions, handing out brochures with floor plans and operating statistics, and features that distinguish their vehicles.

BARGAIN ALERT

The action gets hot and heavy during the last day or two of a show, when prices may be reduced and stumbling across an offer that you can't refuse is possible. Show-only pricing is a common feature at these shows. On the other hand, if you're susceptible to sales talk, tread carefully; otherwise, you may be driving a brand-new RV home from the show. (Not that there's anything wrong with that!)

For a free list of RV shows, contact the RVIA or watch local newspaper and TV ads or RV magazines for a show in your area. (One of my favorites is the Florida RV Super Show in Tampa.)

How to deal with dealers

Check the phone book for local RV dealers, and spend an afternoon walking around the lot, looking at various types of vehicles, and mentally moving into them. Dealers usually can give you a take-home brochure that details all the features, floor plans, and specifications.

Every dealership has previously owned vehicles that it's taken as trade-ins or that it's selling for other owners. Generally, a used vehicle can be one third less to half the price of a new model. Purchasing from a reputable dealer improves the chance that the RV is in good condition and gives you a place to come back if you have a problem later.

Don't worry about taking up a salesperson's time if you're not yet ready to buy. Sooner or later, you will be, and dealers are accustomed to the allure of a new-yet-unfamiliar RV wannabe and veteran owners.

BARGAIN ALERT

Expect the best buys in the fall and early spring, when dealers want to get the previous year's still-new models off the lot to make room for next year's models. Ask to be put on dealers' mailing lists for any sales that they may have in the future.

Where not to shop for an RV

WARNING

Avoid parking-lot and campground "distress" sellers who give you a spiel about bad luck and desperate need for cash. Be extremely careful about buying from any private party unless you're familiar with the RV and can make a clear-eyed evaluation of it before signing the deal.

When you buy an RV, you're buying both a used car and a used house.

How to finance your purchase

Because RV buyers generally are considered to be more reliable for loans than car buyers are (only a few percent of all RV loans go delinquent), loans are easier to get. Check with banks, savings-and-loan associations, finance companies, credit unions, or the RV dealer. Loans for big new RVs typically range from 10 to 15 (or even 20) years, and many lenders ask for a 20 percent down payment or less. A few lenders may require a 25 percent down payment. Financing packages for used RVs can run up to 10 to 15 years. Use the Good Sam Finance Center (https://www.goodsamrvloans.com/rates) as your benchmark for financing expectations).

BUYER BEWARE: USED RVS

Before buying a used RV, take the following precautions:

- **Take a long test drive.** Watch the gauges closely, and personally check out all systems, from the toilet flush to the water pump and heater. Look for dry rot in any areas with wood or water stains, which may be signs of leaks.

- **Ask questions.** Ask the owner direct, specific questions about all systems in the vehicle.

- **Have the RV inspected.** Ask a knowledgeable friend or, better still, hire a certified RV mechanic to look at the vehicle.

  Check the book value of the unit. You can look up the current value at Kelley Blue Book (www.kbb.com) or NADA Appraisal Guide (www.nadaguides.com).

- **Shop around.** Visit at least one other dealer's lot to check comparable models and prices.

IN THIS CHAPTER

» **Maneuvering a big rig through bad weather and more**

» **Finding out which extra items can come in handy**

» **Dealing with electrical hookups**

» **Turning that RV into home sweet home**

» **Securing your RV when you're not using it**

Chapter **4**

Enjoying Your RV

An RV can seem like a great new toy for grownups, but as a vehicle and substitute house, a rig brings new responsibilities both on the road and in the campground. Check out the cautions, tips, and handling hints in this chapter to make your maiden voyage safe and comfy.

Driving Your RV

Driving an RV isn't difficult, but the experience is different from handling the family car. No special license or driver training is required in most states, depending on the size of the rig. Before hitting the road, you'll want to know a few basics and brush up on your road etiquette.

Focusing on the basics

TIP

Wherever you rent or buy your RV, someone will go over all the details with you, from driving the rig to hooking it up at the campground. Don't nod along, pretending that you know what he or she is talking about. If something isn't clear, ask questions until you understand.

If you're a novice RV driver (or even an experienced one), getting accustomed to a different model or type may mean having a round of practice at driving in a large, empty parking lot. After you get into the driver's seat and adjust your mirrors, ask someone to walk around the vehicle so you can identify blind spots. Most new motor homes have a rearview camera fixed on the rear of the rig with a monitor on the dash; these cameras help when the time comes to back up. In addition, many have side-view cameras that turn on with your left and right turn signal lights — a feature that's very useful in high-volume-traffic areas.

The increased length and width of an RV makes turning more awkward. Making adjustment is easy: You have to make wider turns. When turning right, keep your vehicle closer to the left of your lane than you would with your car, and drive farther into the intersection before turning the steering wheel to the right. When turning left, make comparable adjustments: Keep your vehicle closer to the right, and turn when you get farther than usual into the intersection.

WARNING

Always signal your intention to turn or change lanes well ahead of time. Your vehicle isn't as agile as the ones around you.

When you're backing into a campsite or getting out of a tight situation at a gas station, you want someone outside and behind you giving you hand signals or, better, giving you directions via a walkie-talkie.

On the road, or in lots or parking lots, check your position often in the rearview, side, and center mirrors or the rearview camera. Always be aware of the relationship of your vehicle to the painted lines marking traffic lanes and the edges of the roadway.

WARNING

Wind is a special consideration to bear in mind when you're driving an RV. The large, flat surfaces of a trailer or motor home will rock or sway when a heavy wind blows broadside. Be aware that you'll feel gusts of wind when large trucks pass you at high speeds. You'll also be buffeted by wind when you pass another vehicle or when one passes you, so expect a little push, and carefully compensate for it. Maintain awareness of passing vehicles by frequently checking the side mirrors.

ROAD ETIQUETTE

Only the most self-centered RVer is bad-mannered on the road. But like you, I've been in the position of following a big, tall, slow-moving RV that doesn't pull over to let me pass when the opportunity arises. To maintain harmony on the road, I offer these tips:

- **Don't hog the highway.** Pull over at turnouts or into slow-moving lanes so that vehicles behind you have a chance to pass. (In some states, laws stipulate that a slower-moving vehicle must allow following vehicles to pass at the first opportunity when five or more of them are trailing.) Allowing cars to pass not only makes the drivers behind you happy, but also makes you more relaxed.

- **Stay in the right lane except when passing another vehicle.** When you do pass, make sure that you have the speed and space to do so quickly and easily. Some motor homes don't have the necessary power to overtake vehicles on an incline (uphill), especially if the other driver happens to speed up as you attempt to pass. The possible exception to the rule to stay in the right lane applies to expressway/interstate driving. Constantly being in the merge-off or merge-on lane can be problematic for a large, heavy motor home. You're required to brake or speed up to integrate the cars that are coming up on your right side from the expressway on ramps. This isn't so easy when you're driving a 28,000-pound motor home that's 38 feet long plus 20 extra feet when it has a car in tow. It's much easier and safer to be in the lane to the left of the far-right lane, which can often mitigate the merging-traffic issue.

- **Turn off your high beams.** As you do when driving any other vehicle, turning off your high beams for an approaching car is a must. Doing so when you're driving into a campground after dark is also a good idea.

- **Make a friendly wave to oncoming RVs.** This customary practice is especially important when the other vehicle is similar to your own.

The biggest chore is mental. Take it easy on the road, slow down, and allow more room to change lanes or stop. Be aware of how much bigger, longer, and heavier your RV is than the average car or pickup on the road, and drive with that awareness in all actions you take.

Going beyond the basics: My tips

Having logged many miles in RVs and towing trailers, I consider myself to be an expert on the subject. I went beyond the basics years ago. What follows are just a few of the driving tips I've picked up along the way to share with you:

» **Buckle your seat belt.** When the vehicle is in motion, everyone inside needs to be seated with seat belts fastened. Wait until the RV is safely parked before getting up and walking around, fetching a cold drink from the refrigerator, going to the bathroom, or cooking something on the stove.

» **Drive with headlights on in the daytime.** If your motor home isn't equipped with daytime running lights, turn on your headlights. This safety measure makes your vehicle more visible in marginal light and from a greater distance, especially on long, straight expanses of highway. Many states require the use of headlights during the daytime, and I favor making this practice mandatory. When visibility is hampered in any way by natural conditions, fog, overcast skies, pollen clouds, or smoke from brush fires, I always turn on the headlights and taillights so that my RV is easier for other motorists to see.

» **Memorize your RV's height, weight, and width.** You need to know quickly whether your vehicle fits the parameters when you see a sign ahead, warning about a bridge with a 5-ton limit or a tunnel with 10 feet of clearance. See Chapter 25 for information about RV-specific GPS devices and apps that help you avoid that kind of surprise.

» **Watch for cautionary road signs.** Everyone in the RV, not just the driver, needs to keep a lookout, especially for signs denoting a tunnel ahead and listing maximum clearance. Signs that warn about narrow clearances in construction zones require slower speed and very alert driving. I've had to drive my motor home, which is more than 8 feet wide, down many miles of 9-foot roadways in construction zones sided with concrete barriers. You can do this with calm, caution, slower speeds, and ample references to the rearview and side mirrors.

WARNING

» **Take precautionary actions even if you don't see cautionary road signs.** Sometimes on streets in a town or city, you don't get ample warning of low-clearance tunnels or bridges. When a road dips to go under a railroad trestle, you may have to stop and have the co-pilot get out to make an assessment.

» **Slip on a pair of yellow sunglasses (sold in ski shops as ski goggles).** These sunglasses combat glare, fog, snow, and headlights when you're driving after dark. Some of these glasses are clip-ons that fit over your regular glasses.

» **Scan the road ahead with binoculars.** Before you change lanes in heavy traffic, the co-pilot can use binoculars to check out the road signs ahead. Binoculars are useful for trying to determine whether interstate entry/exit ramps require you to be in the right or left lane; they also help the co-pilot read signs at intersections.

» **Try to avoid driving at night.** I prefer starting early in the morning and stopping for the day by midafternoon. This schedule enables me to hit the road before most vehicles do and see what there is to see. After all, why drive along the spectacular California coast if you can't see it?

» **Drive defensively.** Other drivers don't seem to realize that motor homes are like big tractor-trailer rigs; they can't stop on a dime. Drive a safe distance from the vehicle in front of you in case you need to slow or stop unexpectedly. Many other drivers also make the erroneous assumption that RV drivers are elderly slowpokes when most of us drive at or just below the prevailing speed limit with the rest of the traffic. We're always half-expecting a driver to pull out of a side road in front of us, and we're rarely disappointed on that account.

One rule to follow: If you see a pickup truck waiting at a side road to pull into traffic, you can count on it pulling out in front of your RV.

Controlling your speed

WARNING

Although exceeding the speed limit is never a good idea, doing so can be especially inconvenient in Massachusetts, Michigan, Nevada, Tennessee, and Wisconsin. These states aren't signatories to multistate agreements that provide some level of mutual information-sharing and enforcement when you're traveling out of your home state. What that means is that drivers with license plates from these five states are subject to having their licenses confiscated and being required to go to the nearest office of a judge, sheriff, or justice of the peace to post bond and/or pay a fine. If an official isn't available, drivers may be jailed until a court appearance can be arranged, which may take several hours.

Saving Money on Fuel

BARGAIN
ALERT

Fuel conservation is important for all RVers. Cutting down on the amount of fuel you use helps not only your budget, but also the environment. What follows are tips for conserving and finding the best fuel prices:

» **Consider staying longer in one location.** Because I'm so happy and comfortable in my newer, larger motor home, I find myself staying longer in each place than I used to. This practice cuts fuel costs by reducing the average number of miles I drive per day. I get almost the same gas mileage in my 36-foot motor home as I did in my old 24-footer.

» **Contemplate not taking the tow-along, and walk or bike.** Enjoy a walk of a mile or two to the market, a museum, or a restaurant. Some RVers carry bicycles for making short trips from and around the campground.

» **Mind and maintain the speed limit.** Experts say that observing the speed limit saves fuel because the fuel economy of your vehicle decreases at higher speeds. Cruise control (for those vehicles that have this feature) also contributes to fuel savings because it helps you maintain a constant speed. Being light-footed on the gas pedal rather than applying too much throttle also saves gas.

» **Keep your air filter clean.** Make sure that your air filter is checked and replaced often. U.S. Department of Energy studies say that a dirty air filter can raise fuel consumption by as much as 10 percent. Keeping your engine tuned and not carrying any extraneous weight also helps.

» **Take advantage of gas competition.** I carry binoculars to check out posted gas prices along an interstate exit or on the outskirts of a town. Always go for the cheaper price, even when doing so requires turning around. Even in the same area, prices can vary a lot. A helpful website for finding the lowest prices in any area is GasBuddy (https://www.gasbuddy.com/GasPriceMap).

» **Pay cash when you can.** Sometimes, the cash price for gas is lower than the price if you pay by credit card. If you prefer using a credit card, watch for stations where prices are the same. If nothing is posted, ask before filling your tank.

Detecting Gas and Smoke

WARNING

Remember that you're most likely driving a vehicle that contains a propane tank. The propane tank simplifies your daily life by enabling heating and refrigeration to take place while your RV isn't hooked up to a campsite's power source. This tank also complicates your life because it's flammable. Some experts recommend driving with the propane tank turned off, and posted signs may require that you turn the tank off before entering many long highway tunnels. You must always turn off the propane refrigerator and furnace before pulling into a service station to fill up, and when you're done and have exited the gas-pumps area, be sure to turn them back on. Newer motor homes have AC-powered refrigerators and don't use propane.

Propane gas-leak detectors are now mandatory in RVs, and most new RVs come equipped with them. If you hear the warning signal, leave the RV, turn off the propane valve at the tank (reached from an outside access door), and leave the RV open to let the gas escape.

TIP

Occasionally, your gas-leak detector may go off when you're cooking garlic; the odor is like that of the odorant that's added to propane to make leak detection easier. If that happens, turn off the burner and remove the pan to make sure that it's the source of the alarm. If the alarm stops, open a window and a vent, turn the burner back on, and finish cooking.

Install a couple of smoke detector in your RV if it doesn't already have then. (A smoke detector is mandatory.) Always check the gas-leak and smoke detectors installed in your RV to make sure that their batteries are fresh.

Carbon-monoxide detectors are also mandatory in RVs. You want to inspect your RV regularly to make sure that the floor, sidewalls, doors, and windows have no holes or openings through which toxic fumes can enter the vehicle while you're driving. If you find any, seal them with silicone adhesive or make repairs before driving again. Carbon-monoxide detectors need to be replaced about every five years.

WARNING

Never run the generator while you're sleeping, and always open one of the roof vents when you're using the generator. In roadside rest areas, don't park for long periods in the vicinity of any tractor-trailers that are running their motors (to keep their refrigeration operating); the carbon monoxide from the big rigs can seep into your RV. *Note:* A generator won't operate when the gas level falls below three eighths to one quarter of a tank.

Equipping Your RV

Although an RV usually comes fully furnished and ready to go from the manufacturer, you'll probably want to pick up a few practical tools and gadgets. You can usually find these items at camping-supply stores or sometimes at the small convenience stores at campgrounds.

Marching into a specialty store and buying only what's on the shopping list can be difficult. As you look around, murmuring "Gee, look at that!" or "I didn't know there was an item like this," you start dropping objects into your shopping cart — thinking you must have them.

Picking up a basic hand-tools kit and an inexpensive auto-tool kit is a practical way to start. Small jobs can be done easily with the right tools.

TIP

Most RVs arrive with a short sewer hose and sometimes (but not always) a water hose. The first time you hook up, you'll notice that both are too short to be useful in many campgrounds, so the next items on your shopping list are new, *longer* sewer and water hoses. Look for a 15- to 20-foot sewer hose made up of smaller sections that twist-lock together and a threaded coupling device that enables you to secure the hose to the campground's sewer connection. You want a 25- to 50-foot labeled for potable-water hose, that is approved for drinking water use. Don't use a hose that's intended for watering the garden or washing the car. Consider using a water-pressure regulator to protect interior pipes.

WARNING

If you have a big, new motor home with plenty of air conditioning, your ideal electrical hookup is 50 amps, but many older campgrounds offer nothing higher than 30 amps, and some state parks only have a maximum of 20 amps. You'll have a clue right away at the campsite if your plug doesn't fit the receptacle in the electrical box. What you want are adapters that convert 50-amp to 30-amp service and 30-amp to 20-amp service. To use a 20-amp outlet with your 50-amp system, plug the 50-to-30-amp connector into your main electric shore line, plug the 30-to-20-amp connector into the 50-to-30-amp connector, and then plug everything into the 20-amp outlet — or just look for a 50-amp to 20-amp connector. When you use an adapter, you can no longer run all your electrical appliances, so load management is a must. Many modern motor homes are equipped with an automatic energy management system that dumps loads for you when you're running on 20- or 30-amp service. (For issues to keep in mind when dealing with amperages, see the next section, "Monitoring Electrical Hookups.")

At the campsite, you want your RV to be level for sleeping comfort and for keeping the refrigerator level — a *must*. Although many new motor homes come equipped with automatic hydraulic levelers installed under the body, older RVs may require the use of manual levelers, which can be anything from a couple of pieces of board for each tire to a commercially produced wood or plastic device. Make sure to evaluate a leveler carefully before buying it. Some of the plastic ones may not hold the weight of your RV; some stack-up versions are hard to maneuver the vehicle across. A *spirit level* (one of those little things with moving bubbles inside) laid on a countertop inside the RV lets you see how level the RV is at the campsite.

For TV lovers, a 50-foot length of antenna cable with male connectors on each end keeps everyone happy when the campground offers cable TV hookup. Also bring a female/male adapter because some campgrounds are so equipped.

In your cabinets, shelf liner in a ridged pattern helps keep items from sliding while the vehicle is moving; match the color to your countertop or wood tone, if you want. Tension rods of various lengths are useful for installing across your refrigerator or cabinet shelves to keep the items contained within from shifting. I find bubble packaging (an item that I usually get free in shipping boxes) to be a godsend for packing glassware and dishes.

Finally, two all-purpose items are a heavy-duty extension cord for outdoor use and duct tape, the wide silver-backed tape (called *gaffer's tape* in the film industry) that can hold just about anything together until you can get to a repair shop. On my first RV trip, I carelessly left a roof vent open while picnicking near a Colorado lake during a heavy wind. I even wondered about a white plastic object that I saw cartwheeling down the hill . . . until a rain shower came up and rain started coming in. A hasty retrieval of the plastic vent cover, a trip up the back ladder to the roof of the RV, and most of a roll of duct tape repaired the damage and kept out the rain.

Monitoring Electrical Hookups

Many older campgrounds, especially in state parks, may have 20- or 30- amp electrical hookups when your ideal electrical hookup is 50 amps. Also, modern RVs have three-prong plugs that require adapters for older two-prong sockets. (See the preceding section, "Equipping Your RV," for info on adapters.) You can use the lower amperage if you remember not to run the air conditioner, microwave, and TV set at the same time. As larger RVs with more electrical appliances and conveniences come on the market, the requirement for additional amperage raises the limits to 50 amps. Many campgrounds have modified some of their sites to handle this greater need.

WARNING

The total amperage of all electrical units that you're using in your RV shouldn't exceed the amperage limitation of your campground hookup. Amperage limitations vary from one campground to another and are offered at 15, 20, 30, or 50 amps. Manufacturers note the amperages used by their appliances, such as TVs, refrigerators, microwaves, and air conditioners. Make a list of these amperages, and refer to the list when you're in doubt.

If you exceed the hookup amperage limitation, the power goes off, which usually isn't a huge problem if you're in a campground that's equipped with circuit breakers. But some older campgrounds still use fuses, and resetting them is difficult for the campground staff.

TIP

To avoid tripping the campground's circuit breaker, make it your routine to turn off one appliance before you turn on another. I find that simply turning off the electric water heater often solves the problem because the water heater uses an abundance of power. Small appliances such as toaster ovens also draw much more power than you'd expect.

Preparing for Winter Camping

My first winter camping trip was strictly an accident. The trip included a 30-day visit to Colonial Williamsburg in Virginia, which experienced unusual snowfall on Christmas Day. My site had water connections and sewer. By morning, the water hose had turned into a 25-foot-long ice pop. This experience explains the first rule in the following list:

» **Avoid the big freeze.** Don't connect your water hose to an outdoor faucet overnight when temperatures are expected to fall below freezing. Instead, use water from the RV's supply, and refill when necessary. Don't forget to set your furnace thermostat inside to a low temperature (usually around 60°F) to keep onboard water pipes from freezing, and add a generous amount of RV antifreeze to keep drains from freezing.

» **Don't get buried.** Avoid parking under trees, branches can give way under the weight of ice or snow overnight. Don't let snow accumulate on the refrigerator's exhaust. Some exhaust units are located on the side of the RV or on the roof with a vent cover that may be blocked by heavy snow.

» **Heat things up a bit.** If you're spending time in a very cold climate, you may want to add thermostat-controlled heater mats to the on-board tanks; RV supply companies sell them.

» **Handle snow with care.** If you're going into snowy or icy terrain, carry chains or have snow tires for your tow car and RV. Also, drive with extreme care. Even an experienced RVer finds handling a motor home or towing a trailer to be much trickier in snow and on ice covered roads. *Note:* A heavy motor home can be very difficult to stop on an icy surface.

Furnishing Your RV

Manufacturers furnish the typical Type A or Type C motor home at the factory with these built-in features: a kitchen counter and cabinets; a cooktop (with or without gas oven); a refrigerator/freezer; a dinette or free-standing table and chairs; a sofa or easy chair; a double or queen-size bed or short king; wardrobe and drawer storage; a bathroom with toilet, sink, and shower; air conditioning; a furnace; a TV set; and a microwave or combination convection/microwave oven.

Some new motor homes are all electric on the appliances. The driver and front passenger seats (pilot and co-pilot seats) often swivel to face the living area, adding two more comfortable seats to the arrangement.

Depending on the vehicle size and the manufacturer, if you order a new RV it may be optioned to include swivel and/or reclining chairs, an oven, a microwave or convection oven, a second TV set in the bedroom, a shallow tub with showerhead above, a washer/dryer combination, an icemaker, a pullout pantry with wire or wooden shelving, a desk/dressing table combination in the bedroom, and a pull-up table adjacent to the sofa or swivel chair, adding uses to the living space. Travel trailers and fifth-wheels contain all these items except the driver and navigator chairs. RV floor plans vary regarding the arrangement of living spaces and the amount of storage available.

The clever design of RV interiors incorporates more furnishings than you'd expect, though you may want to add decorations. I like to add flowers and pots of herbs for color, small rugs on top of carpeting or wood floors, colored baskets for decoration and storage in the kitchen/dining area, and additional cushions for color and comfort on the sofa and the bed. In built-in niches around the cabinets, I added handmade wooden carvings to decorate the wood cupboards I picked up on my travels and used glue to affix them permanently; they look factory installed. Books and magazines brighten a tabletop and offer a diversion to occasional bad weather, but you will want to stow them (and any plants or cut flowers) safely before hitting the road.

Cleaning Your RV

Keeping the RV as clean as possible day by day while on the road is easier than going through the equivalent of spring cleaning every week or two. A rechargeable vacuum is very helpful for cleaning as you go.

Outside the vehicle

Although car owners are accustomed to wielding a hose in the driveway or in one of the little wash-it-yourself bays at a car wash, cleaning the outside of a motor home by yourself is akin to bathing an elephant; you can't do it in a short driveway or the average car wash even if you want to. Even using a coin-operated car wash with an extra-large bay is difficult but doable if the facility has enough height clearance. It's easy to run out of quarters and patience long before the job is done. Most campgrounds don't allow you to wash the vehicle at the campsite. Always check and comply with the rules.

Washing

For a big-time RV wash, which you want to do after the vehicle has been in storage or slogged through some dusty terrain, look for a truck wash. You're going to find these on interstate highways adjacent to popular truck stops. Simply get in line behind the trucks; check for enough overhead clearance; and ease your way into the wash bay, where an energetic team armed with hoses cleans your RV, soaping, rinsing, wiping, and (optionally) waxing until your home on wheels is sparkling. For this service, which takes 30 minutes after you get into the bay, expect to pay $30 to $100, depending on the services you select. Be sure that all the windows and roof vents are closed tightly before you pull into the wash bay. While the truck wash crew cleans the outside, you can do some cleaning inside: washing windows and mirrors, and polishing the woodwork and cabinetry.

Dusting and debugging

TIP

To cut down on costly full-vehicle wash jobs, you can use a dry mop from the supermarket. Each evening, after settling in, do a quick once-over on the exterior with the dry mop to get the day's dust and grime off. Include the windshield and the vehicle's front end, scrubbing with a wet brush or windshield scrubber to remove the bugs that accumulated during the day's drive. Putting the job off until morning lets the bugs solidify into something like cement and doubles your job of cleaning.

Waxing

Before waxing your RV, check the manufacturer's recommendations for exterior care. Modern motor homes with painted surfaces don't require waxing at all. My now-9-year-old Fleetwood has full body paint and looks as marvelous today as when I bought it; I've washed it using only cold water, a soft brush, and a mild biodegradable auto-wash detergent.

Whether you own a motor home, travel trailer, or fifth-wheel, waxing an RV is a big expensive job if done professionally. Many camp-grounds and RV-supply stores offer waxes and protective materials. The work is up to you. To spread the joy around: Wax the front of the vehicle one day, half the driver's side a few days later, the rest of the driver's side more days later, and so on. After a week, you'll have cleaned the whole vehicle. You need to do it regularly if waxing is required to save the finish of your exterior. Waxing is *much* cheaper than a new paint job.

Inside the vehicle

Keeping the interior clean is a matter of tidying up daily. Regular tasks, such as cleaning the windows and mirrors, can be done when you stop to fill up with gas. A tank that takes 50 gallons or more of gas takes 10 or 15 minutes to fill, giving the navigator enough time to clean some of the following:

» **Woodwork:** Spray polish wood cleaner repels dust and keeps wood surfaces looking clean.

» **Upholstery:** RV upholstery is usually tough and hard to stain. I find that spot-cleaning with a spray upholstery cleaner (one that comes with a brush attachment) does the job well.

» **Glass:** For windows and mirrors use a spray-and-wipe glass cleaner and a paper towel to make them spotless and shiny again in no time.

- » **Floors:** A portable vacuum cleaner that can run on rechargeable batteries is handy for quick cleaning or even heavy-duty cleaning in an RV.

  Spot-cleaning spills on the carpet is not a problem because carpets in motor homes are stain-resistant. I put a washable rug over high-traffic areas including the residential entrance, front of the sink, beside the bed, and between the sofa and easy chair.

- » **Kitchen:** Wiping up kitchen spills when they happen helps keep the galley clean. I clean out the refrigerator when I bring the RV back home from a trip, and wipe it clean it once a week on the road. I always give the sink a quick wipe-over daily.

Holding tanks

RVs have two holding tanks — one for *gray water* (the water from the kitchen and bathroom sinks and shower) and one for *black water* (the waste from the toilet). Maintenance of these tanks requires using a liquid or powder made for RV tanks that deodorizes and dissolves solids. RV manufacturers recommend using biodegradable toilet paper, which breaks up more readily in the tank. Look for *RV-approved toilet paper*, *septic-tank-approved*, and *septic-safe* when you choose a brand.

TIP

If you're not on an extended stay, keep the black-water outlet closed when you're hooked up to the sewage drain in a campground. The gray-water outlet can remain open. When the gauge informs you that it's time to empty the tanks, close the gray-water outlet to allow water to build up in the tank, and empty the black-water tank first. Flush out the tank at the end by pouring three gallons of water in the toilet. When finished, close the black-water valve. Next, run about a gallon of fresh water into the gray-water tank from the kitchen faucets; then open the gray-water valve. This flushes the hose as the gray-water tank empties. Close the valve, unhook the hose, and flush the hose again before storing. Wear disposable rubber gloves when handling sewage hoses and fittings.

Storing Your RV

When you live in a city condo or a homeowner-association development, needing an RV storage area is often a fact of life. Many people in suburbs and cities face parking limits for their RVs as well. Smaller units, like a folding camping trailer or truck camper, can be stored in garages, and a van camper may be kept in the driveway as it resembles a family car. But motor homes and trailers often need to be stored somewhere away from the residence. Outdoor-storage fees average $75 to $100 a month for a 36-foot motor home. Covered or indoor storage can cost twice as much.

When storing the vehicle, do the following:

>> Clean and defrost the refrigerator, leave the door open, and put an open box of baking soda inside.

>> Disconnect the coach and vehicle battery.

>> Empty the holding tanks, leaving a bit of water and deodorizer in the tanks to keep the seals moist. Add 2 gallons of RV antifreeze when you're storing the vehicle where temperatures fall below 40°F; one surprise hard freeze can do a lot of damage.

>> Close the propane-tank valve.

>> Draw all the shades and close the windshield curtain to keep the shaded and interior cooler.

>> Lock all doors and outside compartments.

>> Fill the lead-acid batteries to the top of the split ring with distilled water.

When you store an RV in a cold climate, drain all the freshwater supply tanks, add some nontoxic RV antifreeze to the black-and gray-water holding tanks after they've been emptied and cleaned, empty the water heater, and pump antifreeze into the supply lines to each faucet. If you're not well versed in doing these jobs, I recommend using the services of a licensed plumber, camping-supply store's service department, or an RV dealer that offers this winterization service. If the work is done properly, the annual cost of about $200 can save you many costly repairs in the spring.

Chapter **5**

Settling In for the Night

Okay, take a deep breath. Get ready to check into a campground and spend your first night on the road. If you're worried about whether you can handle it, don't fret. Review choosing destinations in Chapter 2 for those features important to you. Then plow ahead in this chapter, which tells you everything you need to know.

For translations of campground lingo, see the appendix.

Understanding Campground Recommendations

In each driving chapter of this book, I provide campground lists: lists that include relaxing campgrounds and active campgrounds. The relaxing campgrounds that are among my favorites tend to be ones with quieter ambience and more natural surroundings, which I often prefer to campgrounds that offer organized activities such as square dancing as well as pancake breakfasts, swimming pools, and whirlpool spas.

Every camper has different priorities. Sometimes, location is the most important aspect (such as when you want to be first in line the next morning for a popular museum or attraction and prefer it to be as close as possible to that place). At times, you may want to get away for a few days and hear nothing but birdsong and critters passing, and you couldn't care less whether the proprietors are fixing a pancake breakfast the next morning. At other times, you may want an 18-hole golf course, a heated spa, a pool, and some square dancing with barbeque on Saturday nights.

The campsites are considered relaxing may be long on scenery and space but short on amenities or even campsite connections for electricity, water, and sewage. Some of the active campgrounds may be more elegant and highly rated. You find each type of campground in the driving chapters later in this book, as well as those that offer a balance.

To help you narrow your campground choices, use the worksheet "Sweet Dreams: Choosing Your Campground" at the back of this book.

Using Campground Directories

Although I don't always consider their ratings, I find the published campground directories to be invaluable when traveling, particularly when I'm making one-night stops and need to stay at a place just long enough to eat dinner and sleep. Being able to call ahead for last-minute reservations is helpful, so having a cellphone comes in handy. Careful reading of a campground's information entry can tell you the site's width (important if you have an awning or slide-outs), what electrical power you can expect, whether pull-throughs are available, whether you can cool off under shade trees, whether the campground is open year-round or seasonally, has full hookup, or has a dump station on the premises. For tips on using directories to select a site, see the nearby sidebar "Choosing a site unseen."

Directories can also tell you whether a campground is privately or publicly owned. Calling ahead for reservations and specific information at private campgrounds is easy, because charts and computer records of empty and occupied sites are kept up to date. In public campgrounds, rangers may be too busy to tell you anything beyond whether the campground is full. Most states' parks now use a centralized reservation system that requires you to use a toll-free number or make your reservation online. State parks often keep a few sites free for last-minute visitors. Even if the campground isn't full, don't expect it to hold a site until you arrive, because most public campgrounds don't accept reservations at the local camp office. Campers obtain the few nonreserved sites on a first-come, first-served basis.

For a list of recommended campground directories, see the appendix.

CHOOSING A SITE UNSEEN

If you're picking a campsite sight unseen from one of the voluminous park directories, here are some tips that I've found useful:

- **Ratings reflect the extras that a campground offers, from playgrounds to clubhouses to cafes on the premises.** If these amenities aren't important to you, pay more attention to the sizes of the sites — especially the widths — and whether grass and trees are mentioned. New ratings reflect access to Internet and phone jacks at the campsite.

- **Campgrounds with playgrounds, swimming pools, lakes, fishing, and game rooms attract families with children.** If you want to avoid families, look for simpler surroundings.

- **If you're a light sleeper, carefully study the directions to the park from the interstate.** "Convenient" and "EZ-on-and-off" can be code words for "beside the interstate." Some RV parks are what I call *three-point campgrounds* — near enough to the highway that you can hear trucks on the interstate, planes taking off and landing at a nearby airport, and post-midnight freight trains that sound loud whistles at rail crossings right down the road from the camp.

- **Read between the lines.** If a park has a large number of sites, but only a few are available, it may mean that plenty of year-round residents commute from the campgrounds to daily jobs, reducing some of the vacation atmosphere.

Comparing Private and Public Campgrounds

Privately owned campgrounds are convenient, usually offer full hookups, take advance reservations, and have staff on duty during business hours. On the downside, they sometimes offer narrow sites as close as 15 to 20 feet apart and often are set up in a parking-lot configuration, which usually gives you a level setup and well-located hookups but may not offer grass or shade.

I prefer finding private campgrounds that are members of a large national group, such as KOA or Good Sam, because they're required to meet certain minimum standards of upkeep to retain their membership and because they focus on traveling vacationers rather than full-time residents. (See Chapter 1 for information about becoming a member of these associations to take advantage of discount offers.)

Another kind of privately owned campground offers sites that are individually owned, but like timeshare condos, they can be rented out when owners don't need them. These campgrounds may ban certain types of motor homes or trailers, as appearance is important to them. Often, they insist that RVs be less than 10 years old or meet "pride of ownership standards." All of them ban tents.

WARNING

When you buy a membership in a timeshare campground, you join a network of campgrounds where you can stay for a couple of dollars per night. Although this deal may sound like a good one, the membership fees or dues usually range from $475 to $5,000 (plus an annual maintenance fee), so you need to compute how many nights you plan to spend in campgrounds during the next few years at an average of $20 to $60 or so a night. The fee may cover more nights than you think you can use. Also consider whether the membership chain has enough campgrounds to keep you happy on those nights you'll travel that year and whether they're located where you want to stay.

Some private campground owners go to plenty of trouble to create attractive campsites with terraces, privacy plantings, and extras ranging from level concrete pads to small personal storage sheds on each site. An outstanding example of lavish camping is the super-deluxe site at Twin Creeks Campground in Buffalo, Wyoming (see Chapter 18). Campers who opt for the $110-per-night price get a fenced site with gazebo, patio table, built-in propane barbecue grill, glass and wrought-iron patio table with chairs, planters full of bright petunias, and an abundance of trees and shrubs.

In general terms, though, if you're looking for scenery and privacy, you often find much prettier and larger campsites at the public camp-grounds in national forests or state parks and even in some (but not all) national parks. What you won't always find are hookups or the ability to make advance reservations or sites long enough for your RV.

One favorite public campgrounds is City of Rocks State Park in south-ern New Mexico (Chapter 19), where gigantic boulders surround sites that are far apart and provide privacy. In Arkansas's Jacksonport State Park (Chapter 17), the sites are near a river and are wide and grassy, with mature shade trees. Oregon's Sunset Bay State Park is on the ocean, with beachcombing, hiking trails, and a colorful light-house nearby (Chapter 20). All three of these state parks also provide hookups.

TIP

Some of the most crowded campgrounds in the United States are in national parks such as Yellowstone. During peak season, you may want to stay in a private campground near a popular national park rather than in the park itself if you find the crowds to be too distracting.

Choosing a Site

When I started RVing, I wanted only model sites, secluded from other campers, surrounded by shade trees, preferably at the end of a row facing a view. The site had to be level — you'd be surprised how few sites outside paved parking-lot campgrounds are really level — with a nice picnic table and fire pit or barbecue. These characteristics still are ideals to aspire to, but I had to get real. If mine was the last RV to pull into the only campground with a vacancy sign at Mount

Rushmore National Memorial at twilight on Fourth of July weekend, I took what was left and appreciated the fact that I found a spot.

TIP

When site selection is abundant, I have a long list of preferences:

» **Large:** The site must be big enough to park (and drive through or back in) my 36-foot motor home and still have space for *slideouts* (portions of the living and/or bedroom walls that open to expand the interior), chairs, table, and charcoal grill, as well as the 16 feet needed for my towed car.

» **Room:** The width of a site becomes more important now that so many RVs of all types offer one or more slideouts. Some older campgrounds can't handle slideouts and say so in their directory listings; others have room for slideouts but no leftover space for you to use as a recreational area.

TIP

Any campsite less than 15 feet wide limits comfortable use of the site for durations longer than overnight.

» **Length:** The umbilical cords from the vehicle to the electric, water, and sewer connections must reach comfortably. Consider carrying extensions on board to alleviate this issue.

» **Level:** Whenever you don't have a big new RV with hydraulic/electric jacks that level automatically, you have to do plenty of running back and forth inside and outside the vehicle to check *spirit levels* (those little things with moving bubbles inside). Sometimes, you have to wedge wooden blocks under the tires until that pesky little bubble hits the center. Sometimes, close is close enough if you do not want to buy or use leveling jacks.

» **Location:** I want to be away from the highway and campground entrance, and not too near the swimming pool, bathing facilities, office, laundry, dumpster, playground, or dog-walking area.

» **Lookout:** Watch for potentially noisy neighbors, any low-hanging branches or wires that can damage roof air conditioners or TV antennas, and wet or marshy ground that can mire you down if it rains all night. In addition, always check the location of trees that can block opening slideouts or awnings, or interfere with reception if you have a satellite TV.

A campsite may or may not contain a picnic table, grill, or *fire ring* (a fire pit encircled by rocks) — critical amenities for tent campers but luxuries for RVers, who already have tables, chairs, and cooktops inside their vehicles.

TIP

If you're going to stay in one campground for a while, look for an end site with hookups on the left side of the site so that your door, folding chairs, and picnic table can face open space and perhaps even a view rather than the RV next door and its hookups.

If you have no choice but to make your rig the filling in an RV sandwich, consider this: Unlike tent camping, in which campers spend all their waking hours outdoors, RVs (especially motor homes and trailers) enable you to go indoors for privacy. Even when you're parked only a foot or two away from the neighboring RV, you can close your curtains, draw the shades around your windshield, and turn on some soft music, and you're totally alone.

Parking Your Rig

Choosing the spot to park your RV overnight requires looking for the most level area and lining up the hookups in your RV with the connections on the site. If you have a back-in site, ask your co-pilot (if you have one) to get out and help back you in. If you have a pull-through, pull into the center of the site. In either case, make sure to leave room for the opening of slideouts and awnings. Your exact position, however, depends on your hookups, which are accessible from the left rear of the RV. The electrical connection usually is a metal box mounted on a small post, with the water connection on the same post or nearby and the sewer connection somewhere in the general vicinity. You may have to get out of the vehicle to pinpoint the sewer connection, because it's usually a small hole in the ground covered with a white plastic cap that may or may not have a cemented collar around it.

Occasionally, in older campgrounds, you may find side-by-side connections that allow two campsites to share basic connections, with two water faucets, two electrical connections, and two sewer holes in the same area. Because most RVs hook up from their left rear, you and the neighboring RV would park facing in opposite directions.

After you're in the position you want, level the vehicle by using your built-in leveling system or drive up on blocks under the tires to achieve a level state. This practice is essential not only for your comfort and convenience, but also for the proper functioning of equipment such as the refrigerator.

Hooking Up

First-time RVers and sometimes old hands may have some fears about the process of hooking up in a campground, but after a few times, you settle into a routine like this: Park and level your vehicle (see the preceding section, "Parking Your Rig"), and hook up.

REMEMBER

You want a pair of work gloves and, for the sewer connections, disposable gloves.

Here's a blow-by-blow account of what to do:

1. **With clean hands or sterile gloves, connect your RV's water hose (which is connected to your water intake) to the campground faucet.**

   Using a water-pressure regulator attached to one end of the hose is wise, because many campgrounds have strong water pressure. I carry a small pair of channel lock pliers just large enough to tighten the hose connections, as well as a supply of hose gaskets, which collapse with use and can cause leaks at the faucet or the street connection on the RV.

2. **Plug your electrical shore cord into the campground outlet, which is in a metal box affixed to a post and usually located at the left rear of the site.**

Your RV's *shore power cord* is the external electrical cord that connects the vehicle to a campground electrical hookup. Inside the box, you may have several connector choices, which can be 20, 30, or 50 amps. Each amp rating has a unique connection.

WARNING

Most outlets have an on/off switch or circuit breaker that you need to turn to the off position before plugging or unplugging your line. Turning the switch off prevents a surge that can knock out a circuit breaker in the vehicle.

If your shore power cord fits into one of the outlets, you won't need to use an adapter. You'll soon learn to recognize the amperage of each rated outlet by sight.

3. **After you're plugged in properly, turn on the switch or circuit breaker on the pedestal that powers the campground's outlet.**

A good check of electrical service is the timer light on your microwave, which lights up and perhaps starts blinking if you have electricity.

4. **If you have an automatic switchover from propane to electric on your refrigerator (as most RVs do), check the indicator lights on the refrigerator control panel to make sure that the refrigerator has been set to AC electric.**

Some models have a toggle button labeled Auto that handles this task for you when it's switched on.

At this point, your electricity is connected and should be working properly. Next comes the part that most novice RVers dread, although it's as simple as the other two connections.

5. **Connect your sewer hose to your RV drain outlet and to the campground sewer pipe.**

Connect the sewer hose to the drain first; then bring up to the RV. Many campgrounds have threaded connection for an elbow that's part of your sewer-hose assembly. Insert the elbow and turn it into the drain at least one full turn. Check for a secure connection before hooking up to the RV. The hose connections to the RV and extension hoses are twist-lock connectors.

CAMPGROUND ETIQUETTE

In the RVing magazines, a proportion of the letters deal with other campers who failed to show proper etiquette in a campground. Inconsiderate behavior ranges from failing to clean up after your pet to running your generator after hours. To avoid becoming the subject of one of these letters, here are some good rules to follow:

- **Avoid claim-jumping.** Anything that marks a campsite, from a jug of water on a table to a folding chair set out in the parking space, means that the site is occupied and that the campers are away in their car or RV. You may not set the marker aside and move into the site.

- **Mind your fellow campers' personal space.** Teach your kids never to take a shortcut across an occupied campsite; they should use the road or established pathways to get where they're going. No one wants to watch a parade of kids and dogs troop through his or her site.

- **Keep your pets from roaming.** Do not let your dog roam free in a campground. Pets should always be on a leash outside the RV and exercised in a designated pet area.

- **Avoid using your generator whenever possible, even within designated generator-use hours, to keep the noise and fumes from disturbing other campers.** If using electrical appliances such as microwaves and TVs is that important, you should consider staying in a private campground with hookups, where you won't need a generator.

- **Avoid loud, prolonged engine revving in the early morning and late evening.** Fumes from your engine drift into the open windows of a nearby RV, and the noise can wake someone who wanted to sleep in.

- **Don't play radios or TVs loudly at any time in a campground.** Many of your fellow campers are there to enjoy the peace and quiet.

- **Never, *ever* dump wastewater from holding tanks — even gray water—on the ground.** Although some people claim that it's good for the grass, wastewater may contain fecal matter from diapers or salmonella bacteria if raw meat has been rinsed in the sink. This material can be transferred to anyone who touches or steps on contaminated ground. Gray or black water belongs only in a dump station or sanitary-sewer system.

- **Don't cut trees for firewood.** Most campgrounds sell firewood at stands or the camp store. Even picking up or chopping deadwood is forbidden in many parks.

- **Watch what you throw in the fire.** Never leave aluminum foil, aluminum cans, bottles, or filter-tipped cigarette butts in a campground fire ring or grill to make litter. Also, never crush out cigarettes on the ground without picking up the butts and putting them in the garbage.

- **Don't leave porch or entry lights on all night in camp.** The lights may shine in someone else's bedroom window.

TIP

I suggest that you drain any fluid stored in the tanks when you hook up, rather than the next morning, when you're in a hurry to get rolling. (If you stay for several days, drain the sewer tank when you hook up and again when you unhook.) Drain the black-water tank first, close that valve (it's labeled), and then open the gray-water valve. This procedure helps you flush the hose while emptying the tank. You can leave the gray-water valve open while camping, but you shouldn't leave the black-water valve open unless you're on a level site and the RV is level, because solids that settle in the tank are hard to clean out.

You're finished: Wash your hands, and relax with a cold drink.

Sleeping by the Side of the Road: A Good Idea?

A majority of states permit some overnight parking in highway rest areas except where posted. Carefully consider your personal safety if you plan to park your RV overnight in a rest area, a mall parking lot, a truck stop, or by the side of the road, because violent incidents can occur in these areas. Some of my friends do, often overnighting in a 24-hour retail store parking lot, and they consider me to be a money-wasting wimp for insisting on a stay at a secure campground.

At my last count, only 13 states allowed overnight stays or more than three-hour stops at a highway rest stop. The Ohio Turnpike offers overnight parking at service plazas, some with electricity, limited to one night. I found this to be convenient (if a bit noisy) and appreciated the fact that on a time-limited trip, I didn't have to get off my planned route. I've also stayed in RV-designated rest areas along US-10 in Louisiana overnight.

TIP

Consider campground fees to be a modest investment in security and peace of mind.

Chapter **6**

Meeting Special Travel Needs and Interests

When I say that RVing is for everybody, I mean it. No other form of travel adjusts so readily to any sort of special need.

RVing with Kids

KID FRIENDLY

RV vacations are family-friendly in the extreme. I can start with the usual reason: RVing is a cheap and convenient way to take the whole family on vacation. In most cases, having the kitchen and bathroom with you makes the "I'm hungry" and "I have to go potty" requests easy to deal with, and traveling together as a family can foster closeness and communication. The simple truth is that kids love RVing and camping. In fact, you can help your children grow into teens and adults who appreciate travel by allowing them to use a paper map, a book like this one, and a time and money budget to plan their own "mystery trip," with their parents as chauffeurs, over a long weekend. They pick the destination and route, and plan and arrange all aspects of the trip.

Veterans of family RV travel suggest involving children in the planning stages, rotating seats in the car or RV en route to the campsite, and assigning duties at the campsite. Older children can be responsible for packing items and handling last-minute duties at home, like locking the doors and windows and removing perishable food from the refrigerator.

Even infants can go camping happily. Experts recommend carrying a toddler in a backpack carrier and an infant in a front-pack carrier, both of which are made specifically for hiking. Bring along a folding stroller and playpen, mosquito netting, and a baby guardrail for the bed to use while in camp. A baby seat that clamps to a picnic table also enables a small child to join the rest of the family at meals.

Packing sunscreen to protect children's delicate skin is essential. So is bringing along a gentle insect repellant.

For more tips on traveling with kids, check out these websites:

» **Family Travel Network** (www.familytravelnetwork.com) offers travel tips and reviews of family-friendly destinations, vacation deals, and campgrounds.

» **Family Travel Files** (www.thefamilytravelfiles.com) provides an online magazine and advice on camping, cruising, and journeying domestically or abroad with kids.

For information on traveling with other families, see "Joining an RV Club" later in this chapter.

RVing with Pets

As you travel, you meet many RV owners who favor their particular brand of travel because they can take their pets along with them. The Travel Industry Association of America says that 6 percent of all traveling dog owners take their pets with them on vacation, whereas only 1 percent of cat owners do. I'm willing to bet that some 50 percent of all traveling dog owners (and probably 25 percent or more of cat owners) take their pets along on their RV vacations.

WARNING

Check campground information in advance to make sure pets are permitted. Some campgrounds assess a surcharge; a few impose pet restrictions, which means that they determine to allow pets on an individual basis, based breed or size. Always call ahead to ask.

Although a few campgrounds have fenced dog runs where pets can frolic off the leash, almost all require dogs to be on leashes in the campground at all times. Owners also are required to clean up after their pets. Some campgrounds provide dispensers of plastic bags at the dog runs and receptacles for the used bags. Otherwise, carry your own cleanup bags, and dispose of them properly.

WARNING

Dogs should *not* be left alone in an RV at the campground or tied up outside the RV while you're away. Never leave your pet in the RV for more than 10 or 20 minutes in mild weather when you're running an errand, and don't leave your pet alone in the RV at all when temperatures are hot.

The following tips can help you and Fido have an enjoyable RV trip:

> » **Feed pets at night.** Feed them after you're finished driving for the day, especially if they're susceptible to motion sickness.
>
> » **Give pets water only during the day.** Give your pets bottled water, without any additives for taste, which you need to introduce at home before the trip. As you would for humans, use bottled water, because the mineral content in water changes from one campground to the next. A contented tummy is something that you want a traveling pet to have.
>
> » **Bring familiar toys and bedding for the pet.** Like security blankets, objects from home can comfort your pet on the road.
>
> » **Help your pet become accustomed to the RV.** If you have access to the RV before the trip, spend some time in it with your pet.

» **Keep your cat's litter box in the shower or tub.** Encase the litter box in a 30-gallon plastic trash bag, put the box in the trash bag bottom down, dump a 10-pound bag of cat litter into the box, and snap on the litter-box cover.

» **Carry a couple of small washable throw rugs.** Putting a small rug over the RV carpeting can protect it from muddy little cat or dog feet.

Debate continues as to whether pets are safer while kept in or out of a kennel crate in a moving RV. Defenders of crates (many of them professional dog handlers who travel to and from shows in RVs) say that occupants are safer when the animal is confined while the vehicle is in motion. People who favor freeing pets during the ride claim that it enables animals to protect themselves from injury. A challenge for a single traveler with free pets is keeping them off the dashboard and out of the windshield, as well as preventing them from blocking the mirrors and clear views of the road.

TIP

A good online resource for information about traveling with your pet is `https://www.petswelcome.com`, which also dispenses medical tips and lists the names of animal-friendly lodgings and campgrounds, kennels, and veterinarians.

RVing for People with Disabilities

Recreational vehicles can be made as accessible and comfortable for the physically challenged — especially those in wheelchairs — as any home. Mechanical seat lifts, either installed at the factory or retrofitted into existing units, can be added to motor homes for people who have trouble climbing steps. Wider doors, raised toilets, roll-in showers, roll-under sinks, lower kitchen counters and cabinets, and a permanent place to lock in the wheelchair while the RV is in motion are options that can be installed at the factory or by aftermarket custom shops.

More campgrounds offer handicap-accessible campsites with wide, level paved sites to accommodate wheelchairs, walkers, and electric scooters. Many provide improved access to public toilets and showers by installing ramps and handrails.

Wheelchair travelers aren't the only ones who adjust well to RVs. Many other handicapped travelers — from those on dialysis to those requiring a supply of oxygen — find much more comfort and security in a well-equipped motor home than they do in an automobile, plane, or train.

The Recreation Vehicle Industry Association (RVIA; ☎ 703-620-6003) publishes a directory with information about RV accessibility for travelers with disabilities. Another valuable resource is the Society for Accessible Travel and Hospitality (☎ 212-447-7284; www.sath.org), which offers a wealth of travel resources for people with all types of disabilities and informed recommendations on destinations, access guides, and companion services. Annual membership fees are $49 for adults and $29 for seniors and students.

For information on RVing with other travelers who have disabilities, see the listings for Good Sam Club and Handicapped Travel Club in "Joining an RV Club" later in this chapter.

RVing for Seniors

For anybody who has ever been in a campground, "RVing for seniors" is redundant, because seniors make up at least half of the RVing public. But for anyone nearing retirement age who's thinking about taking up RVing for the first time, I say, "Go for it!"

I've heard stories about couples who worked for years saving for their retirement, planning to buy an RV and travel full-time, only to have one of the pair die. In surprising numbers the surviving spouse went ahead with the plans — often against advice of family — and thrived.

Some small, residential-style RV parks advertise as being "for seniors only" or "for over 55." Seniors who want to avoid children (except visiting grandchildren) for a long stay can count on peace and quiet in these places. But as a transient RVer, moving every few days, I enjoy staying in campgrounds with mixed ages, couples, and families.

BARGAIN ALERT

Senior discounts on attractions and activities are becoming more common all the time; always ask about senior discounts. I've even found supermarkets that offer senior discounts on designated days.

The U.S. National Park Service offers the America the Beautiful National Parks Pass–The National Parks and Federal Recreational Lands Annual Pass–Senior Pass, which gives seniors 62 and older lifetime entrance to national parks for a one-time processing fee of $80. You can purchase these passes at any NPS facility that charges an entrance fee. Besides free entry, the pass provides a 50 percent discount on some federal use fees for camping, swimming, parking, boat launching, and tours. For more information, go to https://www.nps.gov/fees_passes.htm or call ☎ 888-467-2757.

AARP (☎ 888-687-2277; www.aarp.org) provides travel information, a magazine, and a wide range of discounts and benefits, and a monthly newsletter. People age 50 or older can join; membership is $42.

Joining an RV Club

Although every campground is a place to make new friends when you stay more than a day or two, many travelers want to find and stay in touch with others who have the same interests. Joining an RV travel club enables travelers to do just that. The sociability of this type of travel attracts singles who may otherwise feel like wallflowers in a campground full of couples. Others find comfort in traveling to new places in groups, particularly if the destination is a foreign country, such as Mexico, where the language, customs, and risks may be unfamiliar.

Caravan tours and rallies

RVers who prefer to travel or camp with a group can join any number of like-minded people for a paid vacation tour in their own rigs rather than a tour bus. These caravans are the RV equivalents of group tours, with structured itineraries, sightseeing, communal meals, a level of support services, and social functions. RVers also can attend rallies, which are friendly get-togethers with other owners of the same brand of RV.

Popular caravan destinations include Mexico, Alaska, and New England at autumn-foliage time. To find out about caravan and club tours, read general monthly RV publications such as *Trailer Life* and *Motor Home Magazine, Highways* (for Good Sam Club members), or other club or RV manufacturer publications. For details about these publications, see the appendix. Popular caravan groups include the following:

» Fantasy RV Tours (☎ **800-952-8496**; https://www.fantasyrvtours. com)

» Adventure Caravans (☎ **936-327-3428**; https://adventurecaravans. com)

RV clubs

Many RV clubs offer membership to everyone from people who drive certain brand-name RVs (you get mail about these clubs if you buy a new RV that has a club or association) to associations such as Good Sam that also sell RV services and promote membership campgrounds. Within Good Sam, you find subdivision clubs for families with children, retired military veterans, singles, ham-radio operators, and so on. To find Sam Club chapters, visit https://www.goodsam.com/club/ chapters.

Following is a sample of specialized RV clubs and associations that aren't affiliated with manufacturers:

- » Baby Boomer RV Club (https://groups.yahoo.com/group/BabyBoomerRV_club): For RVers born between 1940 and 1960.

- » Family Motor Coach Association (☎ **800-543-3622** or 513-474-3622; https://www.fmca.com): Members get their ID numbers handsomely displayed on their RVs. The group provides a monthly magazine and benefits, including insurance. The cost is $60 for a family, including initiation fee and first-year dues.

- » Good Sam Club (☎ **800-234-3450;** https://www.goodsamclub.com): A broad-range club with insurance, campground affiliates, financing, and other services. The club has about a million members and special-interest chapters for hobbyists, singles, the deaf, and others.

- » Handicapped Travel Club (☎ **305-230-0687** or 305-987-5329; www.handicappedtravelclub.com): For people with disabilities who enjoy traveling and camping. The club also welcomes non-disabled people. To become a member, go to the URL (http://www.handicappedtravelclub.com/register/me) to register and become a new member.

- » Loners on Wheels (☎ **866-569-2582** or 575-544-7303): Loners on Wheels is a club for single RVers, numbering around 3,000 widowed, divorced, or never-married members. Call for a sample newsletter.

- » Road Scholar (formerly known as Elderhostel; ☎ **800-454-5768;** https://www.roadscholar.org): Offers study groups for RV owners at universities or on the road in caravans along historic routes.

IN THIS CHAPTER

» Finding the best maps

» Making connections — cable TV, computers, and more

» Insuring your RV

» Taking necessary precautions

» Packing a lethal weapon

Chapter 7

Odds and Ends

So you're ready to hit the road in your RV. But before you lock the door behind you, wait a minute: Do you need to know anything else? You definitely need maps and RV insurance. You may or may not opt to carry a cellphone, GPS, cable connections or satellite TV equipment, a firearm, or a computer. Details on all these things follow.

Mapping the Way

I love maps. I pore over them the way fashionistas devour every page of *Vogue* or bikers glue themselves to the latest *Cycle World.* Every U.S. map I own shows somewhere I've been or plan to visit someday.

When I was young, back in the days before drivers filled their own gas tanks and washed their own windshields, friendly service-station owners not only filled the tank, checked the oil, and cleaned the windshield, but also provided a state map for free. You still can find maps in service stations today, but now you must pay for them.

BARGAIN ALERT

The best places to get free road maps these days are tourist-information and welcome centers near state lines. The offices usually are located on major state highways or interstates. If state maps aren't prominently displayed on the counter or in racks, ask someone behind the desk for one. Besides official state road maps, these centers display rack after rack of local, regional, and city maps, some of them pinpointing landmarks and other major attractions.

I always carry at least one road atlas containing maps of all 50 U.S. states. Although most maps look the same at a glance, each has certain features that are useful to RV travelers:

» *Good Sam Club Road Atlas* (☎ **800-234-3450;** https://www.goodsamclub.com) has icons on state maps that designate the locations of Good Sam campgrounds and repair facilities.

» *National Geographic Road Atlas 2019: Adventure Edition with United States, Canada, Mexico included* (*National Geographic Recreation Atlas*) Spiral-bound – March 1, 2019 (☎ **888-225-5647;** https://www.nationalgeographic.com) highlights scenic attractions with spiral binding so that the pages lie flat when you're using them.

» *Rand McNally Road Atlas* (☎ **800-333-0136;** https://www.randmcnally.com) is updated annually, with each issue containing some 4,500 changes, so I buy the new edition every year. Rand McNally also issues a large-scale road atlas that I particularly like because larger print is easier to read in a moving vehicle.

Real road techies may want to invest in a global positioning system (GPS) receiver and high-tech navigation software, which promises that you won't get lost — at least not most of the time. To me, these tech toys take some of the fun out of reading a map, but gadget fans may enjoy them. A few good manufacturers that have units designated for RVs include the following:

» Garmin International (☎ **800-800-1020** or 913-397-8200; https://www.garmin.com)

» Magellan Corporation (☎ **800-669-4477;** https://www.magellangps.com)

» Rand McNally (☎ **877-446-4863**; GPS sales support, https://www.randmcnally.com/electronics/rv)

Staying Connected on the Road

If you're one of those people who likes to know what's happening all the time, you don't have to lose touch on the road. With cable and satellite TV, cellphones, and Internet connections, you can continue to watch your favorite shows, call your friends, and even conduct business.

Cable TV

Many private RV parks offer cable TV connections as an option, sometimes with a dollar or two added to the nightly fee. If you don't have a built-in exterior cable connection, you can use a length of coaxial cable hooked to the campground connection at one end and route it through a window to your RV's TV set. Carrying your own cable is best, though, because campgrounds rarely provide cables. Don't forget to turn off the switch to your roof antenna. (Look for a little red light by the switch that tells you when it's on.) Having cable with male and female connectors is wise because campground cable connections often vary.

Satellite TV

Many newer RVs have satellite dishes mounted to the roofs of the vehicles, with internal wiring leading to a control box installed (usually) near the TV set. Software for the program system you use usually is included with the package. The two major systems are DISH (https://www.dish.com) and DIRECTV (https://www.directv.com). One disadvantage of having a mounted dish is that in many campgrounds, trees always seem to be in the path of the satellite signal, requiring you to move the vehicle to make a connection. Mention whether you have such a system when you check in so that the registrar can assign you a tree-free site, if one is available.

I carry a portable dish on a tripod, using a secondary control box from home, so I don't have to have a separate account for the RV. The dish can be set almost anywhere — on the ground; on a picnic table; or in front of, beside, or behind the RV — making it much more versatile than a fixed dish atop the RV.

Fixed to the motor home or portable, manual aim or automated, satellite dishes are particularly advantageous when you travel in rural areas with little or no local TV reception or when you plan to stay in such an area for several days.

Your dish programming is set to your home time, so as you move to other time zones, programs air according to your television schedule at home. West Coast travelers who are RVing on the East Coast, for example, find that they can't see their 8 p.m. programs until 11 p.m. When you use your home satellite receiver, the local (home) stations won't always be available. You can call your provider and request local stations for your current location.

Cellphones

I always carry a cellphone with me and consider having one to be a must for travel more than 50 miles from home. Sometimes, due to extreme geography, some places where I like to drive and camp frequently, if not always, are in borderline or no-service areas. I find cellphones to be helpful for dialing ahead for campground reservations and returning business calls, and I'm certainly happy to have one in case of an emergency.

If you're happy with your current cellphone service, stay with it. Otherwise, if you plan an RV vacation, find out what kind of service you can expect on the road and at your destination. Some plans include long-distance and roaming charges throughout the United States for a flat fee. Go over your plan with your provider before you hit the road. Check out all available systems and prices before deciding on a plan for your RV vacation.

If you don't have a phone or happen to be in a dead zone, some private campgrounds and public ones may have a pay phone on the premises.

It's a rare treat indeed to trade quarters for talk time. Using a rotary-dial phone is even more fun, bringing back fond memories of days gone by.

If you're venturing deep into national parks, you may want to consider buying or renting a satellite phone (*satphone*), which is different from a cellphone in that it connects to satellites rather than ground-based towers. Check out prepaid satellite phones if you think you may need one. These phones work only where you can see the southern horizon. In North America, you can rent Iridium satellite phones from Roadpost (☎ **888-290-1616** or 416-253-4539; https://www.roadpost.com).

Online services

Online RV bulletin boards and chat groups enable RV enthusiasts and wannabe RVers to exchange dialogue, offer helpful hints, and discuss the pros and cons of various vehicle brands. Logging onto one of the RV sites before a trip is fun and helpful. You can find a list of forums at www.rv-info.net/rvforums.html. Or visit the popular RV Talk forums at https://forum.rvusa.com.

While you're on the road, you may want to access your email. Some campgrounds offer email access, sometimes free, through a kiosk or public terminal in the main office, store, laundry room, or recreation room. Many campgrounds have wireless Internet connections (Wi-Fi), allowing you to get on the Internet from your own computer in the motor home. (In this book, campgrounds listed with Internet access are designated as having data ports; those with wireless connectivity are designated as Wi-Fi.)

Buying RV Insurance

I was pleasantly surprised to find that RV insurance was very affordable even in costly Southern California. A safe driving record, a shorter use period during the year, and slightly older drivers (on average) mean less risk for the insurer. Before buying, check with your own automobile insurance carrier and the following specialized RV insurance carriers:

» AARP Insurance (☎ **800-541-3717**; https://www.aarp.com)

» AON Recreation Insurance (☎ **800-449-8943**; www.aonrecreation.com)

» Foremost Insurance Co. (☎ **800-237-2060**; https://www.foremost.com)

» Good Sam Club's National General (☎ **800-234-3450**; https://www.goodsamclub.com)

» Progressive Insurance (☎ **855-347-3939**; https://www.progressive.com)

Securing towing insurance in case of a breakdown is a good idea. In many cases, AAA members can extend that company's towing coverage to their RVs by paying an extra fee. Good Sams Club and Coach-Net also offer roadside assistance coverage.

If you're renting an RV, the rental company usually carries basic insurance on the vehicle, covering bodily injury, property damage, uninsured motorist, no-fault, and fire and theft. You may be liable for a deductible on collision and comprehensive. Check out this insurance before taking out the vehicle. You may want to pay an additional sum for vacation-interruption protection in the event of a vehicle breakdown; rental agencies usually can provide this coverage.

Staying Safe and Secure on the Road

Staying overnight in a parking lot or truck stop instead of a legitimate campground or public park just to save a few dollars presents additional risks. Your RV, especially if it's big and shiny, advertises your net worth to anyone who has thievery on the brain. If you're stranded, it's dark, and all the campgrounds are full, you may have to take what you can get, but I often see RVers who choose to stay for free in parking lots with their folding chairs and even charcoal grills out on a patch of asphalt instead of heading for a real campground where the ambience is much more pleasant and worthwhile even if it costs a few dollars more.

WARNING

Campgrounds generally are safe, but not the way they used to be. Back when I was a tent campers, I departed on hikes and left all my worldly goods protected only by the tent zipper. These days, I tend to lock the RV even when I'm just going to the campground store or laundry.

Privately owned RV parks probably are safer in the long run than public campgrounds that aren't sufficiently staffed. Reports of stolen folding chairs and bicycles happen from time to time.

In the long run, I recommend that you use the same security precautions in a campground that you would at home.

Carrying a Gun

If you want to start a lively argument around a campground, open with a question about RVers carrying guns. With many states passing open-carry laws and making it easier to obtain concealed-carry permits, and with neighboring states offering reciprocity on these permits, carrying a gun becomes a matter of choice. Choosing to carry a gun in an RV requires you to do your homework on the laws of all states you'll enter and to obey those laws. If children are present in the RV, you should take the same safety precautions that you'd take at home, such as gun safes, trigger locks, and separate locked storage for ammunition. It is definitely in your best interest to find out what the law is in your destination and in all the states you'll pass through along the way. Forewarned is forearmed (so to speak).

WARNING

Entering Mexico with a firearm of any sort can land an RV owner in jail — and has done that in several documented cases. Canada also prohibits you from entering the country with guns of any sort. Don't take a chance: The days of RVs simply being waved through border crossings are gone.

Another thing to keep in mind is that laws in many states consider RVs to be motor vehicles when moving and homes only when parked. Therefore, when your RV is in transit, any firearms you're carrying must be unloaded and locked in a container, with the bullets stored separately from the weapon.

REMEMBER

Firearms are prohibited in many state parks, and private ones also have restrictions. Many camp operators don't ask in open-carry states like Arizona, however.

3

Exploring the East

IN THIS PART . . .

Getting to Lobster Land

Finding your way to Niagara Falls

Traveling the picturesque parkways of the Appalachian Mountains

Cruising along the Gulf Coast highways and by-ways

Exploring the historic Natchez Trace

Chapter 8

The Coast of Maine: Lobster Land

The rocky coast of Maine evolved through the centuries from a now-submerged mountain range. A sheet of ice scoured, melted, and then flooded the mountains, leaving only the peaks remaining. Somes Sound, which bisects the lower half of Mount Desert Island in Acadia National Park, is the only true *fjord* (narrow sea inlet bordered by steep cliffs) on the East Coast.

The mystique of the craggy shore and pounding waves, the sharp peeps of shorebirds and the clanging of bell buoys, stalwart lighthouses puncturing lingering fog, the crisp saltwater scent, weathered buildings, and peeling lobster pots lend color, sound, taste, touch, and smell to the experience that is Maine.

Maine offers the traveler a blend of scenic beauty and culinary sensations: the vivid orange-red hue of a freshly boiled lobster; the creamy white-on-white blend of Maine potatoes, cream, clams, and fatty bacon in a chowder; and the natural sweet taste of a handful of fresh-picked wild blueberries.

Choosing Your Route

Kittery, on the Maine/New Hampshire border at I-95, is one hour north of Boston. The drive follows US 1 parallel to I-95 72 miles to Brunswick, and turns east away from I-95 to follow the Maine coastline through Bath, Rockland, Camden, Belfast, Bucksport, and Ellsworth. Then you drop south to Bar Harbor and Mount Desert Island by following SR 3 for 10 miles, taking the bridge across Mount Desert Narrows to the junction with SR 102, and turning east on SR 3 for another 6 miles into Bar Harbor. The distance is approximately 225 miles.

TIP

If you encounter traffic snarls on US 1, you can use the parallel I-95, a much faster interstate route. Note, however, that between York Village at Exit 1 and Portland at Exit 15, I-95 is also called the Maine Turnpike, and a $7 toll is charged. Tolls vary, depending on the number of axles on the vehicle.

Roads around popular beach resorts such as Scarborough, Old Orchard Beach, and Saco often are jammed with slow-moving traffic, but you'll find the going a bit easier as you get farther north.

Planning Ahead

The best time to visit Maine is also the most crowded, because everyone enjoys the warm summer months and colorful fall season. May, which is too early for the summer folk and the blackflies, can be a good alternative, as can late August and September, which see fewer tourists and a modest reduction in insect life. Unfortunately, after schools and colleges open in September, many small-town New England establishments close for the long winter because the minimum-wage crowd goes back to school and only a few other workers remain.

You need to make campground reservations well in advance (think March or April, if you're visiting in summer) for the most popular RV parks, especially those in national or state parks. Reservations are particularly necessary if you're driving a large motor home (some New England campgrounds are short on long sites) or planning a lengthy stay in any campground. Many of the campgrounds along this drive were built back in the 1940s and 1950s, the days of tents and tiny trailers (the two-wheel tow-alongs called Minnie Mouse trailers). Big, wide-body motor homes with two or more slideouts fit with little to no room to spare, but I found out early that parking one is worth the effort. Just make reservations as far ahead as possible and emphasize your vehicle's needs so that you can guarantee a workable space. If you ask for a pull-through, plus a 30- or 50-amp hookup, you'll be able to reserve a campsite that fits your RV like a glove. (If you don't know what *pull-through* and *hookup* mean, see the Quick Concierge in the back of this book.)

When packing, it's a good idea to take along an umbrella and raincoat, hiking boots, hot-weather gear (such as shorts and T-shirts), and cool-weather gear (such as slacks and sweaters or sweatshirts). Maine coastal weather changes quickly and frequently, sometimes several times a day. Fortunately, with an RV, you're carrying your own closet and dressing room with you, so you can easily change outfits when the weather demands it.

Although the distance covered isn't great, you need to allow 10 to 14 days for a leisurely visit, with time to enjoy camping and to seek out lobster pounds (casual live-lobster markets with on-site cooking, takeout service, and/or picnic tables) and little antiques shops. If you want to spend more time in New England, you can add Cape Cod or a venture north to the Canadian maritime provinces of New Brunswick, Nova Scotia, and Prince Edward Island.

TIP

Urban residents of the Northeast seeking a getaway can squeeze the highlights of this tour into a three-day weekend, but round-trip, the journey totals 450 miles from the Maine–New Hampshire border to Bar Harbor and back. The drive between Portland and Bar Harbor takes 3½ to 4 hours with no stops.

For a weekend trip, you can spend the first night at a campground on Maine's southern coast around Saco or Biddeford, drive through Portland to Freeport early Saturday morning (allowing a couple of hours of shopping at L.L. Bean and the factory outlets), and then drive on to Rockland for a quick afternoon tour of the Farnsworth Art Museum. If you're an Andrew Wyeth fan, give priority to the renovated church that houses the Wyeth Center; if you want to see a variety of artists, go first to the museum itself; and if you adore furnished Victorian houses, make your major stop the Farnsworth Homestead.

Get to Bar Harbor in the late afternoon and stay in a campground that provides shuttle service into town so that you can take a leisurely stroll through the shops and enjoy a lobster dinner before returning to your RV for the night. Check out early, and as long as your RV can clear an underpass that's 11 feet, 8 inches high, spend the morning driving the Park Loop Drive in Acadia National Park. If the day is clear, drive to the summit of Cadillac Mountain; if it's foggy, you won't find a view, so don't bother tackling the very curvy road in inclement weather. Return to US 1 from Bar Harbor, take Alternate US 1 to Bangor, and return south via I-95.

TIP

Here are some tips to keep in mind as you plan your trip:

» Rockport and Camden, where the mountains meet the water, are picturesque enough to fill your camera's memory card, but you need to find a parking spot big enough for your RV before you settle down to shoot. Several public parking lots are adjacent to the Rockland Harbor Trail, a 4-mile footpath that winds along the historic waterfront. In Camden, look for street parking along Elm Street (US 1) on the hill above the waterfront area.

» On your way into Bar Harbor, you may want to stop at the Acadia Information Center (☎ 800-358-8550), on SR 3 just after you cross the bridge, to pick up armloads of maps and brochures, as well as information about Acadia National Park. The center is open from mid-May through mid-October from 10 a.m. to 6 p.m. daily (and from 8 a.m. to 6 p.m. in summer).

» I suggest lingering several days in Bar Harbor to browse the colorful, whimsical shops along Main, Cottage, and Mount Desert streets around the Village Green and to spend some time exploring nearby Acadia National Park. If time is short, spend most of the day in the park and hit the shops after dinner; most shops are open until 9 p.m. in summer. Seasonal shops open in early to mid-May and close by the end of October.

WARNING

» Don't count on being able to park a trailer or large motor home anywhere in downtown Bar Harbor. A designated lot is on the edge of town at the south end of Main Street, but if you have a large RV or are towing an RV, your wisest choice is to leave the unit at the campground and take a car or the free shuttle-bus service offered in the summer months.

Must-See Attractions

Acadia National Park

Although you can cram the scenic wonders of Acadia National Park into one day's drive, you'll be rewarded if you allow some extra time. The entrance fee is $30 per car and is good for seven days. An annual pas s costs $55. Seniors 62 and over can obtain an annual for $20 or a lifetime pass for $80.

For a one-day visit, drive scenic Park Loop Road (closed in winter), which makes a 27-mile circle out of Bar Harbor from SR 3 south of town, with all the attractions pointed out by signage. If you start by heading south on the loop toward the Wild Gardens and Sand Beach, you can cover the sometimes-traffic-clogged one-way stretch from Otter Cliffs to Seal Harbor early in the day. Take a lunch or tea break at Jordan Pond (see "Good Eats" later in this chapter), and end the day with a drive up Cadillac Mountain, which at 1,530 feet is the highest mountain on the Atlantic coast of North America.

If you have another day to spend in the park, consider taking a bike ride along some of the 45 miles of carriage roads between Hulls Cove Visitor Center and Jordan Pond, where motor traffic is forbidden. John D. Rockefeller, who hated automobiles, commissioned these gravel roads for horse-drawn vehicles, walkers, and bicyclists.

Or you may opt for a hike up Acadia Mountain. A moderate 2-mile, round-trip trail through pines and birch trees sets out from the Acadia Mountain parking area 3 miles south of Somesville on SR 102. (To get there from Bar Harbor, drive west on SR 233, which turns into SR 198 at Somesville.) Afterward, treat yourself to a lobster lunch at Beal's Lobster Pier in Southwest Harbor (see "Good Eats" later in this chapter).

TIP

Find the best detailed information and maps for Acadia at the Hull's Cove Visitor Center (☎ **207-288-3338;** https://www.nps.gov/acad/index.htm), on SR 3 north of Bar Harbor. From April 1 through October 31, the center is open daily from 8:30 a.m. to 4:30 p.m.; in July and August, it's open daily from 8 a.m. to 6 p.m.

WARNING

Although Park Loop Road — one of the park's most popular attractions — generally is accessible for RVs, I suggest leaving your RV in the campground, especially if you're driving a large motor home or towing a trailer, because parking space is limited in many park turnouts. Likewise, if you have an unusually tall RV, note that the SR 3 bridge underpass on Park Loop Road near Blackwoods doesn't clear vehicles higher than 11 feet, 8 inches. Also, the Stanley Brook park entrance from the southeast doesn't permit vehicles higher than 10 feet, 4 inches.

The park offers ranger-led group tours as well as bus and trolley tours.

You can avoid knocking off your TV antenna by traveling the route in a car or by bicycle. Rentals are available from Acadia Bike and Coastal Kayak Tours, 48 Cottage St. (☎ **800-526-8615** outside Maine, or 207-288-9605), and Bar Harbor Bicycle Shop, 141 Cottage St. (☎ **207-288-3886**). A local shuttle bus (Island Explorer; ☎ **207-667-5796**) makes frequent circuits among campgrounds, town, and designated points in the national park during the summer. The shuttle buses are equipped with bicycle racks.

Farnsworth Art Museum

Rockland

When the Farnsworth family's sole remaining member, an eccentric and reclusive maiden lady, died in 1935 at 96, executors were astonished to find that she left a sizable estate, along with directions to preserve the home and create an art museum. Today, the complex consists of the Farnsworth Homestead, the Farnsworth Art Museum, the Wyeth Center, and a teaching center in Rockland and Olson House in Cushing.

The Farnsworth Homestead is a well-preserved mid-19th-century home with many of its original furnishings. Informative displays tell visitors about the Farnsworth family, and volunteer docents relate the history of the house and the town.

The seven galleries of the Farnsworth Art Museum (most of the floors in this contemporary building are underground) showcase not only the Wyeths — grandfather N. C., son Andrew, and grandson Jamie — but also American artists including Gilbert Stuart, Thomas Eakins, Winslow Homer, Childe Hassam, and Rockland-born sculptor Louise Nevelson.

The Wyeth Center is housed in a converted church stripped down to bare-wood floors and movable sailcloth dividers framed in mahogany. The ground floor displays book illustrations by patriarch N. C. Wyeth, who lamented for much of his life that his work wasn't appreciated as fine art. The top gallery is dedicated to Jamie Wyeth, a strikingly original artist in his own right, who is best known for his portraits of John F. Kennedy and Andy Warhol.

Allow at least a half-day for the complex.

16 Museum St. (US 1). ☎ ***207-596-6457.*** *https://www.farnsworthmuseum.org. RV parking: Museum parking lots (some enclosed and too low for large vehicles) and street parking in the area. Admission: $15 adults, $13 seniors, $10 students 18 and older with valid ID, free* *kids 17 and under; includes a visit to Olson House (see listing later in this section). Open: Farnsworth Homestead guided or self-guided tours Memorial Day–Columbus Day daily 10 a.m.–5 p.m.; closed Mondays. Farnsworth Art Museum and Wyeth Center Memorial Day–Columbus Day daily 10 a.m.–5 p.m., rest of the year Tues–Sun 10 a.m.–5 p.m.*

L.L. Bean and Freeport's Factory Outlets
Freeport

BARGAIN ALERT

The L.L. Bean dynasty has been around since 1911, when Leon Leonwood Bean sold 100 pairs of leather-and-rubber hunting boots and had 90 pairs returned because the boot fell apart due to faulty stitching. He returned the money to the buyers, corrected the problems in construction, and went into the mail-order sporting-goods business backed by a retail store that was kept open 24 hours a day, 365 days a year. Today, the company he founded stocks more than 12,000 items, and the main retail flagship store at 95 Main St. (☎ **800-441-5713**) is still open for business 24/7.

But L.L. Bean no longer is alone in the pretty little town of Freeport. Now other name brands vie with Bean in an easy-to-stroll village atmosphere. My favorite bargain spot is L.L. Bean's Factory Outlet Store (☎ **800-341-4341** or 207-552-7772), across Main Street from the parent store and around the corner on Depot Street. Allow half a day to a full day, depending on your stamina and your pocketbook.

The L.L. Bean Factory Outlet store is next to the special free RV parking area. Although you aren't permitted to stay overnight in the parking lot, the town has several campgrounds (see "Our Favorite Campgrounds" later in this chapter).

For a free visitor guide, call ☎ **800-865-1994** or 207-865-1212, or go to https://www.visitfreeport.com.

On US 1, 16 miles north of Portland. RV parking: Free lot located 1 block south of Main Street at Depot Street; overnight parking not permitted.

Olson House
Hathorne Point near Cushing

In 1948, Andrew Wyeth painted *Christina's World* in tempera, depicting a young Christina Olson wearing her favorite pink dress and dragging her crippled body up the hill to the family home, where she lived with her brother Alvaro. Wyeth, who spent his summers in Cushing, continued to devote many hours to the Olson farm, painting images of the house and the views from its windows, even after Christina and Alvaro died — he on Christmas Eve 1967 and she a month later. Both are buried in the small family graveyard by the sea, a short distance behind the spot where Christina is depicted in the painting.

Today, the house and farm are preserved and tended by the Farnsworth Art Museum. Allow at least an hour.

Hathorne Point Road. (Take Wadsworth River Road from the center of Thomaston, turning east by the Maine Prison Showroom — which sells crafts turned out by inmates of the state system — and follow the road 6 miles to Pleasant Point Road; turn left and follow it 1½ miles to Hathorne Point Road, which you then follow 2 miles to its end. The Olson House is located on the left. The signage is good all along the route after you make the turn in Thomaston.) ☎ **207-354-0102.** *https://www.farnsworthmuseum.org. RV parking: Park along the shoulder of the roadway rather than in the small lot behind the house, if you're driving a large motor home or towing a trailer. Admission (Olson House only, self-guided tours): Included in Farnworth Art Museum admission. Open: Memorial Day–Columbus Day daily 11 a.m.–4 p.m.*

Portland Head Light
Cape Elizabeth

The historic Portland Head Light, commissioned by George Washington in 1790, built of "rubblestone set in lime" and finished in 1791, is the oldest of Maine's lighthouses. Still in service and virtually unchanged from its beginning, the lighthouse is part of Fort Williams, a military outpost for coastal defense. In the former lighthouse keeper's quarters, a small museum chronicles the history of the lighthouse and provides anecdotal details. Allow one to two hours.

1000 Shore Rd., Fort Williams. (From I-295 in downtown Portland, take SR 77 south and, shortly after crossing the bridge, turn east on Cottage Road, which becomes Shore Road. Follow the signs.) ☎ *207-799-2661. RV parking: Designated parking area. Fee charged for parking based on time. Open: Early Apr–May 30 Sat–Sun 10 a.m.–4 p.m., May 31–Labor Day daily 10 a.m.–4 p.m.*

More Cool Things to See and Do

The family-friendly coast of Maine offers many things to see and do. During your drive, you'll run across many examples, particularly commercial attractions that may not be included in the list that follows:

» **Have a clambake.** In the summer, **Cabbage Island Clambakes** (☎ **207-633-7200;** https://www.cabbageislandclambake.com), on Cabbage Island, offers traditional lobster-and-clam lunches and dinners. Board the *Argo* at Pier 6 in Boothbay Harbor (12 miles south of Wiscasset on SR 27); cruise to the island; and feast on local lobster, clams, corn on the cob, and boiled potatoes.

RV parking is available on the street. Admission is $69.50 (cash) per person for the cruise and clambake. Children younger than 18 months ride free. A children's meal is offered for $30.50 but doesn't include the clambake meal. The clambake runs daily from June 15 through Labor Day. Reservations are required, and credit cards are not accepted. Cruises leave Monday through Saturday at 12:30 p.m. and Sunday at 11:30 a.m.

» **Ride a Stanley Steamer.** At this museum, you won't just walk past the exhibits; these exhibits are way too interesting for RV folks. At **Owls Head Transportation Museum** (☎ **207-594-4418;** http://owlshead.org), you get to see machines in action and maybe even ride one if you visit on a summer weekend. From the Red Baron's World War I Fokker triplane to Clara Bow's Rolls-Royce and a hissing Stanley Steamer automobile, the exhibits still are in working order. Call ahead to see what's going to be cranked up when you're in the vicinity. Allow one to two hours, depending on your interest and available activities.

The museum is located 2 miles south of Rockland on SR 73 at the Knox County Airport; signage is plentiful. RV parking is available in a large lot. Admission is $14 for adults, $10 for seniors, and free for kids 18 and under. It's open year-round daily from 10 a.m. to 5 p.m. and closed on major holidays.

» **Take a walk on the wild side.** Environmentalists and birders will want to visit the **Rachel Carson National Wildlife Refuge** (☎ **207-646-9226;** https://www.fws.gov/refuge/rachel_carson/) to walk a self-guided 1-mile nature trail through a pine forest and along the Little River to a salt marsh. Pick up the map at the resident manager's office near the entrance. You'll find the trailhead by the refuge headquarters north of Wells. Allow one hour.

The refuge is on SR 9 north of Wells, 7 miles east of US 1. RV parking is available in designated parking areas, but those areas may be crowded in summer and fall. Admission is free. The refuge is open year-round daily from sunrise to sunset. Bring your camera and binoculars.

» **Hop a trolley.** The **Seashore Trolley Museum,** 195 Log Cabin Rd., north of Kennebunkport (☎ **207-967-2712;** https://trolleymuseum.org), was founded in 1939 with a single $150 acquisition: a red open-sided car from Maine's Biddeford-Saco Line. Today, the museum houses the world's largest collection of rolling cars, some 250 of them, in an exhibit hall or spread around an old railroad right-of-way with overhead wires that power the still-working relics. Visitors ride one of the trolleys to the exhibit barn, where they can admire a San Francisco cable car from 1910; an ornate 1906 Manchester and Nashua Street Railway car from New Hampshire; and trolleys from Glasgow, Rome, Montreal, and Budapest. Allow one to two hours.

To get to the museum, drive 3½ miles north of Kennebunkport via North Street, which becomes Log Cabin Road. RV parking is adjacent to the museum. Admission is $12 for adults, $10 for seniors, $9.50 for kids 6 to 16, $5 for children 3 to 5, and free for kids 5 and under. It's open from May through mid-October daily from noon to 5 p.m. The last trolley departs at 4:15 p.m.

Our Favorite Campgrounds

Along US 1 between Kittery and Bar Harbor, you find no scarcity of campgrounds (nearly three dozen) and plenty of casual eating spots; Maine virtually invented the roadside diner. You can make reservations at most private campgrounds and at some, but not all, public ones in state and national parks. Having reservations in July and August is a very good idea. If you're visiting in May, June, or September, you can sometimes rely on serendipity to find a place.

All campgrounds listed below are open year-round and have public flush toilets, showers, and sanitary dump stations unless designated otherwise. Toll-free numbers, where listed, are for reservations only.

Bar Harbor Campground
$$$$ Bar Harbor

Contrary to its peers, this privately owned RV park accepts no reservations and lets campers select their own sites instead of assigning them. This policy gives all procrastinators and serendipity fans a chance to find campsites in midsummer without planning ahead. The campground has both pull-through and back-in sites, some with grass and shade.

RFD 1, Box 1125. Off f SR 3. (From the junction of SR 3 and SR 102, follow SR 3 for 5 miles south; the campground is on the left.) ☎ **207-288-5185.** http://www.thebarharborcampground.com. *Total 300 sites; 175 with water and 20-, 30-, and 50-amp electric; 70 full hookups, 75 pull-throughs. Data port, laundry, pay showers, Wi-Fi. Rates: Call for seasonal rates. No credit cards. No reservations. Open: Late May–early Oct.*

Blackwoods Campground
$$ Acadia National Park

Located in the scenic heart of Acadia National Park, Blackwoods prefers reservations for its 45 RV sites (no hookups) and stipulates no slideouts, a 35-foot maximum vehicle length, and a maximum height of 11 feet, 8 inches. The reservations office begins accepting requests the first week of February for the summer months. Most of the heavily wooded sites in the campground are for tents, and the hardier backwoods aficionados may snub RVers as softies.

But if you're willing to forgo your TV, microwave, and A/C (which you don't often need in Maine anyway), you can enjoy a genuine camping experience by day and sleep in a comfortable bed by night. Your refrigerator, heater, and water heater can run off your propane supply, and if you want to stay for the maximum 14-day limit, you can fill your freshwater tanks and empty your holding tanks when necessary without leaving the campground. The 20-foot-wide sites are back-ins only.

Off SR 3. (From Bar Harbor at the junction of SR 3 and SR 233, follow SR 3 south 5 miles to the campground.) ☎ **207-288-3338 or 807-444-6777**. www.acadiamagic.com/Blackwoods.html. *Total 45 RV sites with water (seasonally); no hookups and no slideouts. Rates: $20–$30 per site per night. DISC, MC, V. Open: Year-round, but water turned off Dec to May.*

Desert Dunes of Maine Campground

$$$$ **Freeport**

Beside the commercial tourist attraction Desert of Maine, 40 acres of unlikely sand dunes operated as a billboard-type roadside phenomenon, Desert Dunes provides shuttle service to downtown Freeport, freeing RVers from having to unhook or move their rigs during a stay. Both wooded and open sites are available. Kids like exploring the dunes and looking for "precious stones" sprinkled in the sand for them to find.

95 Desert Rd. (Exit 19 from I-95 on Desert Road and then go west 2 miles.) ☎ ***207-850-3025.*** *https://www.desertofmaine.com. Total 18 sites with water and 20- and 30-amp electric, data port, laundry, pool. Rates: Call for rates. DISC, MC, V. Open: June 21 to mid-Oct.*

Saco/Old Orchard Beach KOA

$$$$–$$$$$ **Saco**

Comfortable and centrally located, this campground offers big wooded sites and many pull-throughs. It's a short drive from several excellent lobster pounds (see "Good Eats" later in this chapter) and offers plenty of food opportunities when you don't feel like cooking. A snack bar serves nightly desserts (including blueberry pie) and pancake and waffle breakfasts. A lobster cruise and other New England tours leave from the campground. The management is friendly and efficient.

814 A Portland Rd. (Exit 5 from the Maine Turnpike, go east on I-95 to Exit 2B for US 1, and drive north 1½ miles; the campground is on the left.) ☎ ***800-562-1886*** *or 207-282-0502. https://koa. com. Total 83 sites with water and 20- and 30-amp electric, 50 full hookups, 55 pull-throughs. Laundry, pool. Rates: Call for latest rates. MC, V. Open: Early May–Oct.*

Shore Hills Campground

$$$–$$$$$ Boothbay

Only 3½ miles from Boothbay Harbor, this Good Sam resort has swimming, saltwater fishing, and canoeing on Cross River, picnic tables, and fireplaces. You can rent tackle if you did not bring your own. You can leave your rig at the campsite and take the campground shuttle to Boothbay Harbor. Both pull-throughs and back-ins are a good 24 feet wide and 60 to 70 feet long.

553 T Wiscasset Rd., SR 27. (From the junction of US 1 and SR 27, go south 7½ miles on SR 27 to the campground, on right.) ☎ 207-633-4782. www.shorehills.com. Total 135 sites with water and 30- and 50-amp electric, 91 full hookups, 24 pull-throughs. Laundry, Rates: $49–$70 per site. No credit cards. Open: May–Oct.

Good Eats

When you carry your own kitchen, you can elect to visit casual eateries rather than fancy restaurants or to order takeout.

Lobster central

A big reason to travel through Maine in an RV is the fact that you can buy fresh lobster every day to eat in, take out, or cook later, even on a budget, because of an establishment called the lobster pound. Every town has at least one of these simple spots. The owners usually send their own fishing boats out to haul the lobsters home every day and then dump them into a huge vat of seawater — not one of those wimpy lobster tanks that you see in fancy urban restaurants. A lobster pound is a repository of spunky, fighting specimens that a lobster wrangler must wrestle to get on the scales and into a pot of boiling water.

You pay by the pound (around $10 to $14) to get your whole lobster cooked to order; a 1¼- or 1½-pounder makes a generous portion for one average eater and takes about 20 minutes to cook. (If you want to buy a live lobster and cook it later yourself, ask the lobster wrangler for his or her recipe.) The server usually includes a dish of hot melted butter and sometimes a package of crackers or potato chips. Everything else on the menu — fried potatoes, onion rings, chowder, steamed clams, and corn on the cob — is extra.

If an entire lobster seems to be too much to handle, order a lobster roll, which is hot or cold chunks of lobster mixed with melted butter (hot) or mayonnaise and chopped celery (cold) and heaped into a buttered, toasted hot-dog bun sliced open across the top rather than the side. Plan to pay around $20 for a roll, based on the market price of lobster during your visit.

What follows are some of my favorite spots for whole lobsters and lobster rolls. Many are open seasonally only (May to September) and may not follow regular schedules, so definitely call ahead (if a phone number is listed).

» **Bayley's Lobster Pound,** Pine Point, Scarborough (☎ **800-932-6456** outside Maine or 207-883-4571), off US 1 at the end of SR 9: Bayley's is the place to go if you want to ship live Maine lobsters to a dear friend. (The friend has to be dear, because the prices are high — not for the lobster but for the air freight.) Open daily from 10 a.m. to 6 p.m. in summer.

» **Beal's Lobster Pier,** Clark Point Road, Southwest Harbor (☎ **207-244-3202;** https://www.bealslobster.com): One of the greats, Beal's serves soft-shell lobster and steamer clams at picnic tables at the end of a pier. You can purchase sides of steamed corn, onion rings, and even jug wine at a subsidiary establishment next door to the picnic tables. Be prepared to shoo away the local gulls, who'll land near your table, eyeing your lobster. Open daily from Memorial Day through October from 11 a.m. to 8 p.m.

» **Harraseeket Lunch & Lobster Company,** South Freeport Harbor (☎ **207-865-3535**): Swing by here for a quick picker-upper. Just don't try to go down the narrow road that leads to the pier in a large RV; the locals have passed an ordinance against doing so. Park on the main road (South Freeport Road), and walk the quarter mile down to the restaurant. If you don't want to order lobster from the pound in back, you can line up at the lunch counter (which opens daily at 11 a.m.) and order anything from lobster rolls to clamburgers and homemade whoopie pies (two patties of devil's-food cake sandwiched with marshmallow cream and dipped in chocolate). Open May 1 through October 15 daily from 11 a.m. to 8 p.m.

» **The Lobster Shack at Two Lights,** 225 Two Lights Rd., Cape Elizabeth (☎ **207-799-1677**): Located at Two Lights lighthouse since the 1920s, the Lobster Shack sits atop a rocky plateau with plenty of picnic tables and a view. The venerable family-run eatery serves homemade clam chowder, boiled lobster dinners, lobster rolls, fried clams, and even burgers and hot dogs. Open April through mid-October daily from 11 a.m. to 8 p.m.

» **Lobsterman's Co-op,** 97 Atlantic Ave. (near the aquarium), Boothbay Harbor (☎ **207-633-4900**): Here, you find a wooden pier with outdoor picnic tables and a choice of hard-shell or soft-shell lobster (defined on a hand-printed sign as SOFT SHELL = LESS MEAT, SWEETER TASTE). Open from Memorial Day to Columbus Day from 11:30 a.m. to 9 p.m.

» **Mabel's Lobster Claw,** 124 Ocean Ave., Kennebunkport (☎ **207-967-2562**): Mabel's won the endorsement of George H. W. and Barbara Bush. You can order a whole boiled lobster, a baked stuffed lobster, a lobster roll dressed with mayonnaise and garnished with lettuce, and (as if you needed a few more calories) peanut butter ice-cream pie with hot-fudge topping. Open April through November daily from 11:30 a.m. to 9 p.m.

BARGAIN ALERT

» **Maine Diner,** on US 1 at 2265 Post Rd., Wells (☎ **207-646-4441**): The diner serves the absolutely best hot lobster roll slathered in melted butter. Its famous lobster pie also is memorable. Open 11 months (closed in January) daily from 7 a.m. to 8 p.m.; closed on major holidays.

» **Nunan's Lobster Hut,** 9 Mills Rd., Cape Porpoise (☎ **207-967-4362**), 3 miles northeast of Kennebunkport on SR 9: The hut is famous for steaming its lobsters in a small amount of water rather than tossing them into a tank of boiling water, as most places do. The restaurant throws in a bag of potato chips and a hard roll with butter, and also sells homemade apple and blueberry pie. It takes no reservations or credit cards. Open Thursday through Sunday from 5 to 9 p.m.

More than lobster: Markets and meals

Although Maine is mainly about lobster and (for some visitors) lobster rolls for lunch every day, you can find other goodies, such as chowders (clam and fish) and popovers.

» **Bar Harbor Inn,** Newport Drive, Bar Harbor (☎ **207-288-3351;** https://barharborinn.com: At this classic inn, adjacent to the municipal pier, you can get a great breakfast 7 a.m. to 10:30 a.m. in the Reading Room from 7 to 10:30 a.m.; have dinner from 5:30 to 9 p.m.; and dine on Gatsby's Terrace, which has a front-row waterfront view and is open from 11:30 a.m. to dusk.

» **Jordan Pond House,** Acadia National Park, Park Loop Road, north of Seal Harbor (☎ **207-276-3316**): Despite the lines during peak season, you'll want to queue up for a teatime feast of hot popovers, homemade jams and ice creams, cookies, and pastries. The restaurant also serves lunch and dinner, but teatime on the lawn (weather permitting) is tops. Open from mid-May through late October daily from 11:30 a.m. to dusk.

» **Moody's Diner,** US 1, Waldoboro (☎ **207-832-7785**): Breakfasts are the big attractions. Open Monday through Thursday from 5 a.m. to 9 p.m., Friday and Saturday from 5 a.m. to 11:30 p.m., and Sunday from 6 a.m. to 9 p.m.

Fast Facts

Area Code
The area code in Maine is **207**.

Driving Laws
All RV passengers must wear seat belts. The speed limit on interstate highways is 75 mph. Speed limits in urban areas are lower.

Emergency
Call ☎ **911**.

Hospitals
Hospitals along the route include Rockport (☎ 207-596-8000), and Bar Harbor (☎ 207-288-5081).

Information
Helpful sources include the Maine Office of Tourism (☎ **888-624-6345;** https://visitmaine. com or https://www.maine.com) and Acadia Information Center (☎ **207-667-8550;** https:// www.visitbarharbor.com/).

Pharmacies
Most towns have a drugstore.

Post Office
The US Post Office in Bar Harbor is located at 55 Cottage St. (☎ **207-288-3122**).

Road and Weather Conditions
For weather and construction information in Maine, New Hampshire, and Vermont, call ☎ **511**.

Taxes
Maine charges a 5.5 percent sales tax. Meals are taxed at 8 percent. The gasoline tax is 37 cents per gallon, including local taxes.

Time Zone
Maine is on Eastern time.

IN THIS CHAPTER

» Pointing out the Finger Lakes

» Misting up at Niagara Falls

» Batting 1.000 at Cooperstown

» Laughing with Lucy and Desi

» Jiggling at the Jell-O Gallery
museum

Chapter **9**

Western New York: Cooperstown to Niagara Falls

From the thundering cascade of Niagara Falls, the popular honeymoon destination for the first half of the 20th century, to the serene Finger Lakes, flanked by vineyard-covered slopes, western New York has some awesome scenery to lure the RVing vacationer.

Here, you can visit original aspects of the area: the Lucy and Desi Museum in Jamestown, the squeaky cheese curds for sale at the cheese factories around Cuba and Dewittville, and the Jell-O Gallery museum in LeRoy.

The roads are decent, the campgrounds are spacious and appealing, the food is tasty, and the natives are friendly. So visit western New York for a unique journey through this historic slice of Americana.

Choosing Your Route

You can start this drive in Cooperstown, 225 miles northwest of New York City, and zigzag north, south, and west from there, ending up some 500-plus miles later at Niagara Falls on the Canadian border. From Cooperstown, head north via SR 80 to Ilion and Herkimer; west to Utica and Rome for the historic Erie Canal Village; and then west to Syracuse via I-90 or the slower, more scenic back road, SR 5.

From Syracuse, you can follow SR 175 to Skaneateles; take US 20 to the junction with SR 89, which follows the western shore of Cayuga Lake to Ithaca; and continue southwest on SR 13 to Elmira. From there, the jog to Corning on I-86 is a short one. Back up into the Finger Lakes, follow the western shore of Seneca Lake on SR 14 north to Geneva, and head west to Rochester on I-90.

From Rochester, you can swing south to I-86, following I-490 to SR 19, and then take SR 19A from Letchworth State Park, take SR 305 from Belfast to Cuba. Follow I-86 west to Jamestown and then drive along Lake Chautauqua to the town of Chautauqua. Follow SR 58 to Cassadaga; jog to I-90; go northeast to Exit 57; take US 62 to US 20A; and drive east to East Aurora. From there, follow SR 400 to Buffalo then north to Niagara Falls on I-190. The drive is 725 miles.

TIP

This zigzag drive through western New York can be simplified and stripped down to basic components if you start in Cooperstown and spend half a day at the National Baseball Hall of Fame. Then follow SR 28 to I-90, head west to Rome, and pause at the Erie Canal Village for a couple of hours before going on to Syracuse. Pause for a tip of the hat to the feminist cause at West Seneca; take a quick photo of Seneca Lake; and shuffle off to Buffalo, allowing a half-day to see Niagara Falls.

TIP

Chapter 25 recommends getting a GPS navigation device. On the routes in this chapter, or any of the traveling chapters, it is suggested to first know where you are going by using a paper map and then to also load into your GPS all your way points and destinations for the day. Having them preloaded in the GPS daily makes it easier and saves time as your travel each leg of the route.

Planning Ahead

Any time of year when it isn't snowing or freezing is a good time to visit western New York, so cross out the winter months for a visit unless you have winter tires, four-wheel drive, and nerves of steel. The best times are spring and autumn, with summer a close second.

You should make campground reservations whenever possible during the peak season, Memorial Day through Labor Day. Niagara Falls KOA and others nearby are busy with visitors from both sides of the border.

When packing, take along a range of clothing, because you may encounter warm, humid summer temperatures to a sudden cool, rainy day when you'll want a jacket or sweater. Clean T-shirts and shorts with sneakers are acceptable summer tourist garb throughout western New York. I suggest dressing up one notch if you're in a city.

REMEMBER

If you're planning to cross into Canada at Niagara Falls, you'll need your passport to get in and back into the United States. If you plan to cross with your RV refrigerator full, check food rules on both sides of the border. The rules are different in each country and often change.

Allow a week to ten days for this drive, especially if you want to spend time at the National Baseball Hall of Fame in Cooperstown (baseball fans can spend days there) or sightsee at Niagara Falls.

TIP

Here are some driving tips to keep in mind:

» Pretty, tree-shaded Cooperstown has limited parking even for cars, not to mention RVs and trailers, so I recommend parking in one of the free lots on the edge of town (signs are posted) and use the trolley to shuttle among the attractions.

» Ithaca, the home of Cornell University and Ithaca College, is one of many New York towns named for classical cities. Built on steep hills, the city is a challenge for drivers of large RVs. If you want to look around, park in one of the large lots downtown near the river around Buffalo Street, and explore on foot.

SENECA FALLS: FEMINIST TOUR STOP

In the same way that Memorial Day was initiated in nearby Waterloo as a holiday honoring the dead from the Civil War, the town of Seneca Falls is noted for its role in highlighting the rights and achievements of women. Elizabeth Cady Stanton, a housewife and mother of seven, organized and led the first women's-rights convention there in 1848.

Many powerful women are associated with this area. In Seneca Falls, Stanton and Amelia Jenks Bloomer invented and paraded in the full skirt named for the latter. In Auburn, Harriet Tubman was a major force in the Underground Railroad. And in Rochester, serious feminists must pause for a look at the National Historic Park tribute to suffragist Susan B. Anthony.

Highlights in Seneca Falls include **Stanton's birthplace,** 32 Washington St. (☎ **315-568-2991;** open daily except holidays 9 a.m.–5 p.m.); the **National Women's Hall of Fame,** 76 Fall St. (☎ **315-568-8060;** https://www.womenof thehall.org/; open daily 10 a.m.– 4 p.m. except major holidays; $5 adults, $4 seniors, $8 families), honoring outstanding women from the arts, athletics, science, government, and philanthropy; and **Women's Rights National Historical Park,** 136 Fall St. (☎ **315-568-2991;** https://www.nps.gov/wori; open daily except Thanksgiving, Christmas, and New Year's 9 a.m.–5 p.m.; free); see the restored Stanton home and first convention site.

SALAMANCA SECRETS

Salamanca is believed to be the largest American city on an Indian reservation — in this case, the Allegany Indian Reservation. The town has two interesting museums. The fine **Seneca-Iroquois National Museum,** 82 West Hetzel (☎ **716-945-1760;** https://www.senecamuseum.org; open Monday 11 a.m.–5 p.m., Tues and Thurs 9 a.m.–8 p.m., Wed 10 a.m.–8 p.m., Fri and Sat 9 a.m.–5 p.m., Sun 10 a.m.–5 p.m., $9.50 adults, $6 seniors, vets, and students, $5.25 children 7–17) combines history with contemporary arts and crafts. The **Salamanca Rail Museum,** 170 Main St. (☎ **716-945-3133;** open Tues, Thurs, and Sat 10am–4 p.m.), has a 1912 passenger depot (now used for exhibition space) that marks the spot where three major railroad lines once converged.

Must-See Attractions

Corning Glass Museum
Corning

The striking exhibit hall displays fine contemporary glass art, including several examples by Dale Chihuly. The Glass Sculpture Gallery, the Hot Glass Show, the Corning Museum of Glass, the Studio, the Steuben Factory, the Windows Gallery, the Glass Innovation Center, and the Glass Shops offer a primer on everything you ever wanted to know about art glass, from glassblowing to the 3,500 years of glass history. Allow two hours or more if you want to browse the shops.

1 Museum Way. ☎ 800-732-6845 or 607-937-5371. Parking: Designated lot. Admission: $20 adults; $17 seniors, military, and college students; free for ages 17 and under. Open: daily 9 a.m.–5 p.m. Closed New Year's Day, Thanksgiving, Christmas Eve, and Christmas Day.

KID FRIENDLY

George Eastman House and International Museum of Photography and Film
Rochester

Bank clerk George Eastman worked for years to turn photography into a more portable art, and by 1888, he had his first Kodak on the market. Soon afterward, he gained control of the celluloid-coating process that made film. His elegant mansion has been restored as it was in his day, with many original furnishings, and modern galleries showcase masterworks of photography and motion pictures. A collection of some 6,000 still cameras and a library of 42,000 books and manuscripts about film and photography are open by appointment. Allow two to three hours.

900 East Ave. (SR 96). ☎ 585-271-3361. https://www.eastman. org. RV parking: Designated lot. Admission: $15 adults, $13 seniors, $5 students, $5 ages 4–17, under 4 free. Open: Tues–Sat 10 a.m.–5 p.m. (until 8 p.m. Thurs), Sun 1–5 p.m. Closed major holidays.

Herschell Carrousel Factory Museum

North Tonawanda

KID FRIENDLY

This grand old factory-turned-museum focuses on carousels, including how they were made and who made them. A self-guiding brochure takes you through the various work areas in the factory and describes what went on in each area. A beautiful collection of carousel horses plus a working 1916 Allan Herschell carousel are on the premises. You and the kids get a free ride with each admission. Allow two to three hours.

180 Thompson St. (off Oliver Street/SR 429). ☎ **716-693-1885.** *https://www.carrouselmuseum.net. RV parking: Some parking in lot behind museum; otherwise, street parking in residential neighborhood. Admission, including carousel ride: $7 adults, $5 seniors, $3.50 ages 2–16. Open: July–Aug Mon–Sat 10 a.m.–4 p.m.; Apr–June Sun noon–4 p.m.; and Sept–Dec Wed–Sun noon–p.m. Closed Jan–Mar.*

Lucy Desi Museum

Jamestown

Lucille Ball, of *I Love Lucy* fame, was born in Jamestown in 1911, and this museum was dedicated to her and her husband and straight man, Desi Arnaz, in the summer of 1996. TV and movie clips, interactive displays, collections of artifacts and clothing, and even a replica of Lucy's bedroom/study with its original furniture. A gift shop sells souvenirs. Allow two hours.

10 W. Third St. ☎ **877-582-9326** *or 716-484-0800. www.lucy-desi.com. RV parking: Street parking. Admission: $16 adults, $15 seniors, $11 ages 6-17, and 5 and under free. Open: Mon–Sat 10 a.m.–4 p.m., Sun 1–4 p.m.*

Mark Twain's Study

Elmira

BARGAIN ALERT

A glass-windowed octagon built in 1874 to resemble a riverboat pilot house was created for Twain's use as a study when he visited his sister-in-law's Quarry Farm outside Elmira. Inside, he wrote some of his most famous works, including *The Adventures of Tom Sawyer* and *The Adventures of Huckleberry Finn*. In 1952, the study was moved to Elmira College. (Previously, the Langdon family resisted all efforts by Henry Ford to buy the study for his Dearborn, Michigan, museum.) Memorabilia, period furniture, and photographs are on display. Allow one hour.

1 Park Place, Elmira College. ☎ **607-735-1941.** `https://www. elmira.edu/academics/distinctive_programs/twain_ center.` *RV parking: Street or designated lot. Free admission. Open: Mid-June to Labor Day daily 10 a.m.–5 p.m.; the rest of the year by appointment only.*

National Baseball Hall of Fame
Cooperstown

KID FRIENDLY

This is one of America's favorite family summer destinations. Many visitors stay in the area several days to cover everything. The legendary Doubleday baseball on display is believed to have been the ball used in 1839 when Abner Doubleday invented baseball in Elihu Phinney's cow pasture one afternoon — if, in fact, that ever happened, which some experts doubt. Additional artifacts are on hand, from Jackie Robinson's warm-up jacket to Joe DiMaggio's locker; Ty Cobb's sliding pads to Yogi Berra's glove; and bats used for record-breaking home runs by Babe Ruth, Roger Maris, Mickey Mantle, Hank Aaron, and Mark McGwire. The original game, called "town ball," involved anywhere from 20 to 40 people and is reenacted occasionally at the **Farmers' Museum** (see "More Cool Things to See and Do" later in this chapter). Allow three hours to three days.

25 Main St. ☎ **888-425-5633** *or 607-547-7200.* `https://base ballhall.org.` *RV parking: Very limited in town; leave large RVs in designated parking areas on the edges of town, and take shuttle transportation to the museum. Admission: $25 adults, $20 seniors, $15 ages 7–12. Combination ticket with Fenimore Art Museum and Farmers' Museum: $42 adults, $18.50 ages 5–12. Open: May–Sept daily 9 a.m.–9 p.m., Oct–Apr daily 9 a.m.–5 p.m. Closed New Year's Day, Thanksgiving, and Christmas. Day.*

Niagara Falls

Niagara Falls, New York and Canada

You can view the awesome trio of waterfalls — American Falls and Bridal Veil Falls on the American side, and Horseshoe Falls on the Canadian side — on foot, in a boat, from an observation deck, and from vantage points in two countries. A first-time visitor should take consider a guided tour and put up with being herded along instead of standing in long lines, especially during peak season, when many of the 12 million annual visitors are milling about. You also need to consider just how wet you're willing to get in pursuit of a great photo. Although virtually all the tours provide plastic raincoats, you're still likely going to get splashed.

If you're staying in one of the nearby campgrounds, such as the Niagara Falls KOA, you can book a bus sightseeing tour that picks you up at the campground. The most-praised vantage point (and one of the wettest) is the deck of one of the *Maid of the Mist* **boats** that cruise directly in front of the three falls. (*Maid of the Mist* has its own parking lot, accessed by Prospect Street.) If you're on foot, the **Cave of the Winds tour** begins with an elevator ride from Goat Island down to the base of Bridal Veil Falls and a stroll across a wooden walkway to within 25 feet of the falls.

If you want to tour the site on your own, allow even more time, and try to leave your RV at the campground. Niagara Reservation State Park, south of town off the Robert Moses Parkway, provides a close-up of American Falls. Goat Island, with two big parking lots, is accessed from First Street, by the Niagara Rapids Bridge (also called Goat Island Bridge).

From Table Rock House on the Canadian side, reached by Niagara Parkway, 1 mile south of Rainbow Bridge, three tunnels open to good vistas of the falls. To cross the border into Canada, you need a passport and to get back into the United States, you also need a passport.

More Cool Things to See and Do

Deciding whether an attraction belongs in the "must-see" or "more cool things" category is often a toss-up. Following are some mainstream and offbeat places to go in western New York. You may find that some of these qualify as "must-sees" on your trip:

» **Live in style.** East Aurora is the home of the Roycroft design style, strongly influenced and represented by designer Gustaf Stickley and his Mission furniture. Perhaps the most stunning display of this design is the elegant **Roycroft Inn,** 40 S. Grove St. (where you can stay overnight if you feel inclined to leave your vehicle), (☎ **716 652-5552** and the **Elbert Hubbard Roycroft Museum,** 363 Oakwood Ave., East Aurora (☎ **716-652-4735;** www.roycrofter.com/museum.htm), which displays examples from the American wing of the Arts and Crafts movement from the early 20th century. Allow one to two hours or more if you're a fan of the style.

RV parking is available on the street. Admission is free, or by a donation. The museum is open June 1 through October 31, Wednesday, Saturday, and Sunday from 1 to 4 p.m.; call for exact hours.

» **Sing "Oh, the Ear-eye-eee was a'risin'."** A National Historic Landmark, the **Erie Canal Museum,** 318 Erie Blvd., East Syracuse (☎ **315-471-0593;** https://eriecanalmuseum.org), is in the last of the weigh-lock buildings that once served as weigh stations along the canal. You can see crew quarters inside a replica canal boat and find out about immigration along the canal during the 19th century. Allow two hours. A guided tour costs $3.

RV parking is available in a designated lot or on the street. Admission is free, but a donation of $4 is requested. It's open Monday through Saturday from 10 a.m. to 5 p.m. and Sunday from 10 a.m.–3 p.m.

» **The Farmers' Museum** is 1 mile north of town on SR 80, Lake Road, Cooperstown (☎ 607-547-1450; https://www.farmersmuseum.org). Parking is available in a designated off-road lot. Admission is $12 adults, $11 seniors, and $6 ages 7 to 12. A combination ticket with the Fenimore Art Museum is $18 adults and $8 children. A combination ticket with the Fenimore Art Museum and the Baseball Hall of Fame is $42 adults and $18.50 ages 7 to 12.

TIP

If you want to visit the Farmers' Museum and/or the Fenimore Art Museum along with the Baseball Hall of Fame, note that the latter two are closed from January through March. The Farmers' Museum is open April 1 through May 12 Tuesday to Sunday from 10 a.m. to 4 p.m. Limited buildings are open and staffed, and a reduced admission rate applies. From May 13 through Columbus Day, the museum is open daily from 10 a.m. to 5 p.m. and fully staffed, and all buildings are open. From Columbus Day through October 31, it's open Tuesday through Sunday from 10 a.m. to 4 p.m., with limited buildings. The museum is closed the rest of the year except for Thanksgiving weekend and a Candlelight Evening in December.

» **Follow Leatherstocking trails.** A fine collection of American art and examples of folk art from the permanent collection of the **Fenimore Art Museum,** SR 80, Lake Road, Cooperstown (☎ 607-547-1400; www.fenimoreartmuseum.org), fill the former home of author James Fenimore Cooper. Allow two hours.

RV parking is available in a designated lot. Admission is $12 adults and $11 seniors. A combination ticket with the Farmers' Museum is $18 adults and $8 children. A combination ticket with the Farmers' Museum and Baseball Hall of Fame is $42 adults and $18.50 ages 7 to 12, but as mentioned, the Farmers' Museum and Fenimore Art Museum are closed from January through March. The Fenimore museum opens April 1 each year. Until May 12, it's open Tuesday through Sunday from 10 a.m. to 4 p.m. From May 13 through Columbus Day, it's open daily from 10 a.m. to 5 p.m. From Columbus Day through December 31, it's open Tuesday through Sunday from 10 a.m. to 4 p.m. It's closed Thanksgiving and Christmas.

» **Glitter, New York style.** All that glitters around the **Herkimer Diamond Mines,** 4601 SR 28, Herkimer (☎ **800-562-0897** or 315-891-7355; `https://www.herkimerdiamond.com`), is more likely to be doubly-terminated quartz crystals than diamonds, but beginners can keep what they dig, and you can buy samples from a gift shop. Digging equipment is available. Allow two to three hours.

The mines are at the Herkimer Diamond KOA. There's plenty of space for RV parking. Admission is $14 adults and $12 kids 7 to 12; there's a $1 discount for campground residents. The site is open April through November 1 daily from 9 a.m. to 5 p.m., weather permitting.

» **Follow the Jell-O brick road.** The brick walkway leads to the **Jell-O Gallery,** 23 E. Main St., LeRoy (☎ **585-768-7433;** `http://www.jellomuseum.com`), where a carpenter named Pearle Wait invented this amazing dessert. His wife, May, named it Jell-O, taking her inspiration from a coffee substitute named Grain-O. The pair couldn't market it successfully so they sold the rights to Grain-O mogul Orator F. Woodward for $450. This museum re-creates the product's history, including advertising art, Jell-O jokes, and interactive displays. Allow one to two hours.

The parking lot in this residential area is small, but RV parking is available on the street. Admission is $5 adults and $1.50 kids 6 to 11. It's open Monday through Saturday from 10 a.m. to 4 p.m. and Sunday from 1 to 4 p.m.

Our Favorite Campgrounds

Western New York has plenty of private and public campgrounds, plus New York's popular state parks, so no need to worry about where to sleep. Campground reservations are needed in July and August around Cooperstown, Niagara Falls, and state parks that accept reservations. If you're traveling in spring or fall, you shouldn't have a problem finding a space without reservations except during major events, such as an auto race at Watkins Glen or the New York State Fair in Syracuse.

All campgrounds in this section are open year-round and have public flush toilets, showers, and sanitary dump stations unless designated otherwise. Toll-free numbers, where listed, are for reservations.

Allegany State Park

$$–$$$ **Salamanca**

This sprawling, wooded, 65,000-acre site is the largest state park in New York, with two RV camping areas that provide 20-amp electric hookups but no water hookups; fill your freshwater tank before arriving. Hiking, boating, swimming, and mountain biking are available activities. Reserving space during the peak summer season is a good idea.

2373 ASP, Route 1, Ste. 3. (From I-86, Southern Tier Expressway, take Exit 19 or 20 to Red House or Exit 18 to Quaker.) ☎ 716-354-9121. Red House campground: Total 68 sites with 20-amp electric; no water. Quaker campground: Total 95 sites with 20-amp electric; no water. Handicap access, laundry. Rates: $18–$30 per site. Credit cards OK. 14-day maximum stay. Reservations can be made at https://www.reserveamerica.com for both campgrounds. Closed in winter.

Herkimer Diamond KOA

KID FRIENDLY

$$$$–$$$$$ **Herkimer**

Making this park appealing are big grass campsites in a large open meadow and the adjacent West Canada Creek, which offers fishing and boating. But the big draw is the "diamond" mines, designated dig sites where you and the kids can shovel up sparkling quartz crystals to keep. Digging tools are available at the site.

4626 SR 28. (From junction of I-90 and SR 28, Exit 30, go north 8 miles on SR 28 to campground, on the right.) ☎ 800-562-0897 or 315-891-7355. https://koa.com. Total 95 sites with water and 30- and 50-amp electric, 50 full hookups, 23 pull-throughs. CATV, data port, laundry, pool. Rates: $73–$95 per site. AE, DISC, MC, V. Open: Apr 15–Nov 1.

Letchworth State Park

$$ Castile

"The Grand Canyon of the East" is a scenic state park with whitewater rafting, hiking, swimming, and hunting and fishing (licenses required). Horseback riding can be arranged. Sites are large, with 20-amp electrical hookups but no water hookups. Plan to arrive with freshwater tanks filled.

1 Letchworth State Park. (From SR 36 and SR 39 junction, go south 2 miles on SR 36 to park entrance, and follow signs to campground 5½ miles, on the left.) ☎ **585-493-3600.** *https://parks.ny.gov/ parks/. Total 270 sites with 20-amp electric, no water. Handicap access, laundry, 2 pools. Rates: $19 per site. Open: Camping area mid-May to mid-Oct.*

Niagara Falls KOA

$$$$–$$$$$ Grand Island

On an island in the Niagara River near Niagara Falls, this campground is very popular in July and August, so be sure to make reservations. The park is well-kept, with pavement, grass, and a fishing pond. Car rentals and tours can be booked at the camp office.

2570 Grand Island Blvd. (From Buffalo, go north on I-190 to Exit 18A, and go north 2 miles on Grand Island Boulevard to campground, on the left.) ☎ **800-562-0787** *or 716-773-7583. https://koa.com. Total 208 sites with water and 30- and 50-amp electric, 128 full hookups, 172 pull-throughs. Data port, laundry, pool. Rates: Call for latest rates and reservations. DISC, MC, V. Open: Apr 1–Oct 31.*

Spruce Row Campsite and RV Resort

$$$–$$$$ Ithaca

Mature spruce trees that add privacy and shade fill Spruce Row, a pleasant, family-run campground on a quiet country road outside Ithaca. Sites are a good size. A fishing pond and large swimming pool with a sand/concrete beach are on the premises.

2271 Kraft Rd. (From SR 13 and SR 96 junction, go north 7 miles on SR 96 to Jacksonville Road, north ½ mile to Kraft Road, and east 1 mile to campground, on the right.) ☎ **607-387-9225.** *www.sprucerow.com. Total 90 sites with water and 20- and 30-amp electric, 23 full hookups, 45 pull-throughs. Data port, laundry, pool, Wi-Fi. Rates: $32–$405 per site. DISC, MC, V. Open: May 1–Oct 11. If you plan to stay for a while, this park offers a season rate of $2,280 for a full-hookup site.*

Yogi Bear's Jellystone Park

$$$$–$$$$$ Cooperstown

KID FRIENDLY

This highly rated Good Sam park provides a 35-acre lake for fishing (no license required) and offers rowboats, paddle boats, miniature golf, and plenty of themed family activities.

111 E. Turtle Lake Rd. (From SR 51 and CR 16 junction, go north ¾ mile on SR 51 to CR 17 and west 1 mile to East Turtle Road to the campground, on the left.) ☎ **800-231-1907** *or 607-965-8265. https://www.campjellystone.com. Total 190 sites with water and 30-amp electric, 27 full hookups, 5 pull-throughs. Data port, laundry, pool. Rates: $49–$59 per site. MC, V. Open: May 1 to mid-Oct.*

Good Eats

Whether you're in the mood for dining or snacking, western New York has a spot for you to quench your appetite.

The full-meal deal

Around western New York, almost anything can be breaded or batter-dipped and deep-fried as a meal or snack. Local favorites include such treats as grape pie (you'll find it around Naples in the

Finger Lakes); white hots (mild) and red hots (spicy) in the frank-furter category; and Buffalo's beef on weck, and Buffalo wings.

» **Anchor Bar and Restaurant,** 1047 Main St., Buffalo (☎ **716-886-8920;** https://www.anchorbar.com): According to a duly notarized proclamation by the city's mayor in 1977, this restaurant is the birthplace of spicy buffalo wings in 1964. The late Teressa and Frank Bellissimo, proprietors, are credited to have created them as a snack for friends of their son who dropped by the restaurant one busy Friday night. Other claimants say the wings were a local staple but that Teressa added the celery stalks and blue cheese dressing. Sauce choices are plain or mild, medium, medium-hot, hot, or suicidal. Open Sunday through Thursday 11 a.m. to 11 p.m. and Friday and Saturday 11 a.m. to 12 p.m.

» **Charlie the Butcher's Kitchen,** 1065 Wehrle Dr. at Cayuga, Williamsville (☎ **716-633-8330;** https://www.charliethebutcher.com): This small, casual lunch counter near the Buffalo airport specializes in beef on weck, a sandwich with thinly sliced roast beef stacked in a *kummelweck,* a Kaiser roll topped with coarse salt and caraway seeds. Open Monday through Saturday from 10 a.m. to 10 p.m. and Sunday from 11 a.m. to 9 p.m.

» **Eckl's Restaurant,** 4936 Ellicott Rd., Orchard Park (☎ **716-662-2262**): Another classic eatery featuring the beef on weck (*kummelweck* roll) sandwich, Eckl's garnishes its version with hot, freshly ground horseradish. Open daily from 4:30 to 11:30 p.m.

» **Schwabl's,** 789 Center Rd., West Seneca (☎ **716-675-2333;** www.schwabls.com): This place makes a great. roast beef sandwich. The unmatched beef on weck boasts tender slices of rare round roast on a *kummelweck* moistened with pan juices and a dab of horseradish. An old-fashioned bar at the entrance serves classic Manhattans and martinis. Open Monday through Saturday from 11 a.m. to 9 p.m. and Sunday from noon to 8:30 p.m.

» **Ted's Red Hots,** 2312 Sheridan Dr., Tonawanda (☎ **716-834-6287;** https://www.tedshotdogs.com): Order a foot-long hot dog cooked before your eyes on a charcoal grill until it is dark brown, sizzling, and smoky. Add your choice of toppings; try the hot sauce at least once. Don't walk out without a side of Ted's crisp onion rings; crunchy outside, chewy and sweet inside. Open daily from 10:30 a.m. to 11 p.m. *Note:* Ted's Red Hots has eight other locations.

Nibbles along the way

Western New York produces plenty of cheese, mostly cheddar types, and does a lively business in fresh cheese curds, which around Salamanca may also be batter–dipped and deep–fried as snacks.

» **Cooperstown Brewing Company,** River Street, Milford (☎ **877-346-3253** or 607-286-9330; https://www.cooperstown brewing.com): This English-style microbrewery produced Old Slugger, among other popular varieties. Self-guided tours are still available daily year-round, beginning Thursday through Sunday 12 p.m. to 5 p.m.

» **Cuba Cheese Shop,** 53 Genesee St., Cuba (☎ **800-543-4938** or 585-968-3949; www.cubacheese.com): The shop carries a hundred varieties of imported and domestic cheeses, including some made on the premises. Fresh cheese curds are big sellers; taste a free sample. Open Monday through Friday from 8:30 a.m. to 6 p.m., and Saturday and Sunday from 8:30 a.m. to 5 p.m.

» **DiCamillo's Bakery,** 811 Linwood Ave., Niagara Falls (☎ **800-634-4363** or 716-282-2341; https://www.dicamillo bakery.com): DiCamillo's has been turning out Italian breads, including flatbread and biscotti, for more than 80 years. The retail outlets pride themselves on displays and packaging in addition to the goodies inside. Open Monday through Saturday from 6 a.m. to 7 p.m. and Sunday from 6 a.m. to 6 p.m.

Fast Facts

Area Code
The following area codes are in effect in this part of New York state: **315, 585, 607,** and **716.**

Driving Laws
In New York state, seat belts must be worn. The speed limit on interstates and controlled-access roads is 65 mph, or lesser posted speeds. New York state highways have a speed limit of 55 mph. Speed limits in urban areas are lower.

Emergency
Call ☎ **911.**

Hospitals
Along the route, major hospitals are located in Syracuse, Rochester, and Buffalo, among other places.

Information
For tourism information, call ☎ **800-225-5697,** or go to https://www.iloveny.com. Call **511** for traffic or transportation information.

Road and Weather Conditions
For road and weather advisories, call New York State Thruway (☎ **800-847-8929**), or go to https://www.dot.ny.gov/index.

Taxes
Sales tax is 4 percent; local taxes can add another 4.75 percent. The state gas tax is 45.6 cents per gallon, including local taxes.

Time Zone
New York state is on Eastern Standard Time.

Chapter **10**

The Blue Ridge Mountains: Skyline Drive and Blue Ridge Parkway

The Blue Ridge Mountains once considered to be America's western frontier, and the resilient Scotch-Irish settlers who built homesteads with logs and chinking were pioneers in the same mold as those who later set out in covered wagons to cross the plains to Oregon. The men split chestnut trees into rails, calling the zigzag fence patterns snake, buck, or post and rail. The women made quilts from cloth scraps and named them Double Wedding Ring, Flower Garden, and Crazy Quilt.

Skyline Drive and Blue Ridge Parkway are the essence of the Southern mountains. They meander to touch a mountainside homestead or a stretch of wilderness unchanged since the days of Daniel Boone. Back roads and byways seem to beckon around every curve.

Skyline Drive mileposts are numbered from north to south, beginning with 0.6 at Front Royal's toll entrance station and ending with

105 at Rockfish Gap and the entrance to Blue Ridge Parkway, which begins numbering its own mileposts north to south at 0 again, ending with mile 469, where the parkway intersects US 441 in Cherokee at the entrance to Great Smoky Mountains National Park. Although frequent turnouts are found along the way, few are long or wide enough for a motor home or a vehicle towing a trailer.

Expect to find long and slow-moving lines of traffic during spring blossom, late summer, and autumn foliage seasons. Often facilities along the route are closed in winter. Plan early-morning starts, when the air is clearest, and stop in early afternoon to set up camp or hike. Check the morning weather report for fog potential before heading out.

Choosing Your Route

The best way to enjoy a drive through this region is to begin a north-to-south journey just south of the Washington/Baltimore urban area in Front Royal, Virginia, at the beginning of Skyline Drive in Shenandoah National Park. Follow Skyline Drive south to the place where it merges with Blue Ridge Parkway. Then continue along the parkway through Virginia and North Carolina all the way to Great Smoky Mountains National Park. For convenience — in case you want to fly in and rent an RV for the drive — you can make the southern terminus Knoxville, Tennessee. The distance of the drive, without detours, is 643 miles.

TIP

The smooth, two-lane roads of Skyline Drive, Blue Ridge Parkway, and Newfound Gap Road across Great Smoky Mountains National Park are closed to commercial vehicles. *Note:* Posted speed limits are *strictly* enforced. The maximum speed limit on Blue Ridge Parkway is 45 mph.

For the shortest version of this route, choose one drive, depending on where you want to be based. You can travel Skyline Drive and see Shenandoah National Park easily over a weekend from the Washington area. Anywhere in western Virginia and western North Carolina allows access to Blue Ridge Parkway for a weekend of touring. One thing that makes Great Smoky Mountains National Park the most-visited national park is its location; it is within a day's drive or so of more than half the population of the United States.

Chapter 25 recommends getting a GPS navigation device. On the routes in this chapter, or any of the traveling chapters, it is suggested to first know where you are going by using a paper map and then to also load into your GPS all your way points and destinations for the day. Having them preloaded in the GPS daily makes it easier and saves time as your travel each leg of the route.

Planning Ahead

All seasons are beautiful on these drives, but winter can bring heavy fogs, even light snow, or a glaze of black ice on the roadway, so you should plan to travel in spring, fall, or summer.

Beginning in March, azalea, pink rhododendron, and mountain laurel decorate the roadsides, with some color lingering through summer.

In summer, shade trees that follow the roadway provide a cool escape from the lowlands heat.

Autumn is magnificent. The route becomes a spectacle of crimson-leafed black gums and sourwoods, maples and dogwoods, birch and buckeye, orange sassafras, and purple sumac.

Fog can occur during any season in the mountains. When you encounter fog on Skyline Drive or Blue Ridge Parkway, try to exit and drive to a lower elevation out of the fog. When you're on lower ground, take a break and do some shopping or sightseeing, or drive in your intended direction parallel to the parkway. The narrow two-lane roads have no guardrails, so maneuvering an RV, especially one that's towing a trailer, can be tricky. If you're driving slowly, you may become a hazard to others, who may not see you until they're on your rear bumper.

Because this region, especially Great Smoky Mountains, is one of the most visited in the United States, you need to make campground reservations wherever possible between Memorial Day and Labor Day. Even spring and autumn weekend can be busy in Shenandoah and Great Smoky Mountains national parks.

You should pack a variety of clothing weights, even in summer. The mountains can be cool and rainy, and you'll want a jacket or sweater. Always take rain gear. Hiking boots are preferable to jogging shoes on mountain trails, but take along both. Plan to spend at least a week or two weeks, if time permits, and try to get in some hiking, biking, golfing, or fishing.

TIP

Stop at the first visitor center on Skyline Drive and on Blue Ridge Parkway for free mile-by-mile folders that list the highlights and facilities along the routes.

Must-See Attractions

Biltmore Estate
Asheville, North Carolina

As splendid as any Loire Valley chateau, the massive, 250-room Biltmore mansion and its gardens, crafts shops, and winery paint a picture of how the other half once lived. The Vanderbilts were considered American royalty, and in the late 1800s, with the help of architect Richard Morris Hunt and landscape designer Frederick Law Olmstead, they created a kingdom in the mountains. Today, for the price of a ticket, anyone can tour this splendid estate. Allow a half-day to a full day. Check the schedule for concerts. Many places deserve a visit, and this attraction is near the top of the list.

1 Approach Rd. (Exit Blue Ridge Parkway at the US 25 North exit and follow the signs 4 miles to the estate.) ☎ 800-411-3812 or 828-225-1333. https://www.biltmore.com. RV parking: Designated lots. Admission: For self-guided tour of house and grounds, depending on the season, $65 ages 16 and older, $30 ages 6–15, free for ages 5 and under; rooftop and backstage tour extra. Open: Daily 9:30 a.m.–5 p.m. Estate grounds open at 8 a.m.

Cades Cove

Great Smoky Mountains National Park, North Carolina and Tennessee

KID FRIENDLY

An auto or bicycle tour to Cades Cove (an isolated mid-19th-century community) down an 11-mile, one-way road off Newfound Gap Road is a must for any visitor to the Great Smokies. The road is flat and easy for older kids to bicycle; it's closed to auto traffic Wednesday and Saturday mornings until 10 to allow bikers full use of the roadway. You can rent bicycles at the Cades Cove Campground store for riding around the valley. The road is closed from sundown to sunrise. Passing isn't allowed, so if you're an impatient driver, plan an early-morning start for your trip. You can make a leisurely drive through the park in an hour; or take time to do some hiking.

25 miles west of Newfound Gap Road via Little River Road and Laurel Creek Road. ☎ **865-436-1200.** RV parking: Some turn-outs are large enough for RVs. Admission: Free. $20 camping fee. Open: Cades Cove Road, sunrise to sunset; closed to cars, Wed and Sat mornings until 10 a.m.

Manassas National Battlefield Park

Manassas, Virginia

Known as Bull Run to the Union forces and Manassas to Confederates, this famous Civil War battlefield was the scene of two Southern victories in the early days of the war, cementing the reputation of General Stonewall Jackson as a strategist and hero. A visit to the 4,500-acre park includes an audiovisual presentation of the battles, an electric map tracing the fighting, and guides for auto tours through the battle sites. Allow three hours or longer.

6511 Sudley Rd. ☎ *703-361-1339.* https://www.nps.gov/mana. *RV parking: Designated area at the visitor center. Admission: Free for all ages. Open: Daily 8:30 a.m.–5 p.m. Closed Thanksgiving and Christmas.*

Mast General Store
Valle Crucis, North Carolina

A genuine piece of Americana, this country store has been in operation since 1883, and some of the stock looks as though it's been there since then. Once known for selling everything "from cradles to coffins," the store sells over 500 candies, some from giant candy barrels; (amazingly) 5-cent cups of coffee from a potbellied stove; and denim, bandannas, and tractor caps. Allow two hours.

SR 194. ☎ *828-963-6511. https://www.mastgeneralstore.com. RV parking: Street parking. Admission: Free. Open: Summer Mon– Sat 7 a.m.–6:30 p.m., Sun 12–6 p.m.*

Monticello
Charlottesville, Virginia

This gracious home of our third president, Thomas Jefferson, along with its original furnishings, his gardens, and his grave, tells a great deal about the man and the statesman. The house is elegant but on a human scale, designed by Jefferson himself, who hated the 18th-century brick buildings of Williamsburg. Lewis and Clark brought back the moose and deer antlers in the entry hall from their expedition. Always a generous host, at his death Jefferson was $100,000 in debt — a sum equivalent to more than $2 million today. Allow three hours.

3 miles southeast of town on US 53. ☎ *434-984-9822. https:// www.monticello.org. RV parking: Designated lot. Admission: $29.95 adults, $10 ages 5–11. Open: Mar–Oct daily 8 a.m.–5 p.m., Nov 1–Feb 28, 9 a.m.–4:30 p.m. Tickets reduced to $26 during win- ter season. Closed Christmas.*

Museum of American Frontier Culture

KID FRIENDLY

Staunton, Virginia

Scenic Skyline Drive and Blue Ridge Parkway take you past typical mountain farmhouses, but where did the settlers of this region come from? The Museum of American Frontier Culture has exhibits of old-world farmsteads inspired from their beginnings in England, Ireland, and Germany — the origins of many of the area's early settlers — to show their influence on American farms. Heirloom plants and rare breeds of farm animals are on display alongside costumed inhabitants who work the farms and talk with today's visitors. Kids enjoy the hands-on experience with farm animals. Allow two and one-half hours for a guided visit and three hours for a self-guided visit.

From intersection of I-81 and I-64, take Exit 222 from I-81, following SR 250 west ½ mile to the museum entrance. ☎ **540-332-7850.** *www.frontiermuseum.org. RV parking: Designated lot. Admission: $12 adults, $11.50 seniors, $11 students 13–18 with ID, $7 ages 6–12. Open: Late Mar–Nov 30 daily 9 a.m.–5 p.m.; Dec 1–early Mar daily 10 a.m.–4 p.m. Closed Thanksgiving, Christmas Day, and New Year's Day.*

More Cool Things to See and Do

The Blue Ridge Mountains offer many other activities, from walking through the Oconaluftee Indian Village to the rides at Dollywood.

» **Go home again.** Novelist Thomas Wolfe wrote about his childhood in **Asheville** in *Look Homeward, Angel,* not troubling to disguise the details much. For many years, he was snubbed or ignored by his hometown. Today, the family home (his mother's boardinghouse) is open as a memorial at 52 N. Market St. (☎ **828-253-8304;** http://wolfememorial.com). A destructive fire resulted in a lengthy restoration period (1998–2004), but it's now complete and better than ever. Allow two hours.

RV parking is on the street. Admission is $5 for adults and $2 for students 7 to 17. Open November through March, Tuesday through Saturday from 10 a.m. to 4 p.m. and Sunday from 1 to 4 p.m.; April through October, Tuesday through Saturday from 9 a.m. to 5 p.m. and Sunday from 1 to 5 p.m.

KID FRIENDLY

WARNING

» **Hooray for Dollywood!** Pigeon Forge, Tennessee, once a tiny village of farmers and potters, has been turned into Disneyland Southeast by native daughter Dolly Parton. Despite its humble beginnings, **Dollywood,** 1020 Dollywood Lane (☎ **800-365-5996;** https://www.dollywood.com), offers some appealing features, including an 1885 Dentzel carousel with hand-carved animals, a train pulled by an old steam locomotive, and fun rides for the kids. Allow a half-day to a full day.

Don't plan on driving by for a look-see; the road funnels the traffic into the parking lot, and getting back out the entrance in an RV can be tricky.

RV parking is available in a designated lot. Admission prices change, so call ahead to get prices and to make reservations for your visit. The park is closed January through March and on certain days of the week, depending on the season.

» **Visit the first Americans.** The **Museum of the Cherokee Indian,** US 441 and Drama Road, Cherokee, North Carolina (☎ **800-438-1601** or 828-497-3481; https://www.cherokeemuseum.org), uses everything from "hear phones" to holographic images to tell the story of this civilized tribe that occupied these hills for 10,000 years until it was forced out on the Trail of Tears march to Oklahoma. Allow two hours.

RV parking is available in a designated area. Admission is $12 for adults, $7 for kids 6 to 13, and free for those under 6. It's open daily September to May from 9 a.m. to 5 p.m. and June to August from 9 a.m. to 7 p.m.

» **Splash toward victory.** The **National D-Day Memorial,** off I-81 and Blue Ridge Parkway at the intersection of SR 460 Bypass and SR 122, Bedford, Virginia (☎ **800-351-3329** or 540-586-3329; https://www.dday.org), commemorates the Allied troops who landed on the Normandy beaches on June 6, 1944, in an unequaled military action under the command of General Dwight D. Eisenhower. Allow 30 minutes.

RV parking is available on the street. Admission is $10 for adults, $8 for veterans, $6 for students, and free for children under 6. It's open daily from 10 a.m. to 5 p.m. Ticket sales close at 4 p.m.

> » **Travel to the 1750s.** The **Oconaluftee Indian Village,** US 441 and Drama Road, Cherokee, North Carolina (☎ **800-438-1601**), re-creates community life in the 18th century in this authentic village, populated by craftspeople who demonstrate the basket and beadwork typical of the Cherokees. Allow two to three hours.
>
> RV parking is available in a designated area. Admission is $20 for adults and $11 for kids 6 to 12. It's open April 16 through November 9 Tuesday through Sunday from 9 a.m. to 4:30 p.m. Also, open on Mondays from October 22 to November 9.

Our Favorite Campgrounds

As you can see in the following sections, plenty of campsites are close to the mountain drives in this chapter. Almost every exit from Blue Ridge Parkway and Skyline Drive leads to a private RV parks where, even in peak season, you may be able to find an overnight campsite.

A few lodges and restaurants are spaced along Skyline Drive and Blue Ridge Parkway, but again, most exits lead some miles into small towns where you can often find a fast-food outlet, restaurant, or grocery store.

All campgrounds listed in this section are open year-round and have public flush toilets, showers, and sanitary dump stations unless designated otherwise. Toll-free numbers, where listed, are for reservations only.

KID FRIENDLY

Front Royal Campground
$$$$–$$$$$ Front Royal, Virginia

This scenic mountain resort is a good starting point for the drive and a handy base camp for Washington, D.C., and the Shenandoah Valley. Numerous activities are available for kids, as well as a playground area, a pond with freshwater fishing and rental tackle, and a basketball court. You can also take tours to Washington and get discount tickets to the nearby Skyline Caverns.

Off US 340. (From I-66, Exit 6 or 13, go 2 miles south of Front Royal on US 340; entrance is 1 mile past Skyline Caverns.) ☎ **540-635-2741.** https://www.frontroyalcamp.com/. *Total 96 sites with water and 20- and 30-amp electric, 42 full hookups, 34 pull-throughs. Data port, handicap access, laundry, pool, and spa. Rates: $31–$62 per site. DISC, MC, V. Open: Apr 1–Nov 1.*

Yogi Bear's Jellystone Park

$$$$–$$$$$ Luray, Virginia

KID FRIENDLY

This Good Sam park is the answer to a kid's query, "What'll we do?" Activities include a 400-foot water slide, fishing pond (and tackle), paddleboats, miniature golf, and a pool and playground. And it's five minutes from Shenandoah National Park and Luray Caverns. Sites are suitable for big rigs.

Off US 211. (At junction of I-81 and US 211, Exit 264, go west 5 miles on US 211 to the campground, on the left.) ☎ **540-300-1697.** https://campluray.com. *Total of 176 sites; water and 30- and 50-amp electric, 125 full hookups, 35 pull-throughs. Laundry, pool. Rates: Call for rates and reservations. AE, DISC, MC, V. Open: Apr 1–Nov 15.*

Blue Ridge Parkway campgrounds

The nine campgrounds along Blue Ridge Parkway, open May through October, offer facilities such as gift, book, and crafts shops; gas stations; hiking trails; and ranger talks. Not all campgrounds have all facilities. Camping sites can handle RVs up to 30 feet long. Each campground has a dump station but no hookups for water or electricity. Restroom facilities and drinking water are provided, but showers and laundry facilities are nonexistent. Each campsite has a table, fireplace, and handicap access. Rates are $20 per site per night. You can stay at these campgrounds for a maximum 21 days between June 1 and Labor Day. Online reservations are accepted at https://www.recreation.gov/ for some campgrounds and at ☎ 877-444-6777; others are first-come, first-served. For more information, check out https://www.nps.gov.blri. Bad weather leads to early closings.

- » **Crabtree Meadows Campground** (milepost 339.5; ☎ 828-675-4236): Total 22 sites, 10 pull-throughs. Paved, mostly shaded.

- » **Doughton Park Campground** (milepost 231.5; ☎ 336-372-8568): Total 25 sites. Narrow back-ins. No slideouts, gasoline, or food.

- » **Julian Price Memorial Park** (milepost 296.9; ☎ 828-963-5911): Total 68 sites, 30 pull-throughs. Paved, mostly shaded, narrow sites, handicap access; fishing and boat rentals on Price Lake. No store, gasoline, or food.

- » **Linville Falls Campground** (milepost 316.5; ☎ 828-765-7818): Total 20 sites, 5 pull-throughs. Paved, some shaded; fishing access on Linville River. No gasoline or food.

- » **Mount Pisgah Campground** (milepost 408.6; ☎ 828-456-8829): Total 67 sites, 13 pull-throughs. Paved, patios, mostly shaded.

- » **Otter Creek Campground** (milepost 60.9; ☎ 434-299-5125): Total 24 sites. Paved, narrow back-ins, some shaded. No gasoline.

- » **Peaks of Otter Campground** (milepost 86.0; ☎ 540-586-4357): Total 53 sites, 25 pull-throughs. Paved and shaded sites; fresh-water fishing in Abbott Lake.

- » **Roanoke Mountain Campground** (milepost 120.4; ☎ 540-982-9242): Total 30 sites, 6 pull-throughs. Paved, some shaded. No gasoline or food.

- » **Rocky Knob Campground** (milepost 167.0; ☎ 540-593-3503): Total 28 sites. Paved, some shaded, fishing. No slideouts or gasoline.

Great Smoky Mountains National Park campgrounds

Ten developed campgrounds are in Great Smoky Mountains National Park, but not all are suitable for big RVs because of the access roads. Those listed here are the most suitable for RVs. Campers with smaller vehicles can check out the other campgrounds listed on the map that you receive as you enter the park. Park campgrounds have no hookups, but they do provide fireplaces, tables, restrooms, and water. Some sites are suitable only for tent camping. Between May 15 and October 31, stays are limited to 7 days; the rest of the year, stays can be 14 days. During the summer period, it's wise to make reservations at the **Cades Cove, Elkmont,** and **Smokemont** campgrounds; call ☎ 877-444-6777 for reservations or ☎ 865-436-1200 for information. For more information, check out https://www.nps.gov/grsm.

» **Balsam Mountain Campground:** Total 46 sites, 30-foot length limit. Rates: $17.50 per site. No reservations. Open: Late May–Oct.

» **Cades Cove Campground:** Total 159 sites. Paved, some shaded; back-ins can handle up to 35-foot RVs. Dump station. Rates: $21–$25 per site. Open: Year-round.

» **Cataloochee Campground:** Total 27 sites. Dirt. Back-ins can handle up to 31-foot RVs. No slideouts. Stream nearby. Rates: $25 per site. No reservations. Open: Mar 15–Nov 15.

» **Cosby Campground:** Total 165 sites. Some shaded, back-ins only, 25-foot maximum length. No slideouts. Rates: $17.5 per site. No reservations. Open: Mid-March through early November.

» **Deep Creek Campground:** Total 92 sites, 26 feet maximum. Paved, mostly shaded, narrow, back-ins, dump station, stream. Rates: $21 per site. No reservations. Open: Early Apr–Oct.

» **Elkmont Campground:** Total 220 sites. Gravel, some shaded; back-ins can handle up to 35-foot RVs. No slideouts. Rates: $21–$27 per site. Open: Mid-Mar through late Nov.

» **Smokemont Campground:** Total 142 sites, 45 pull-throughs. Paved, shaded, narrow, handicap access, dump station; fishing and swimming in Oconaluftee River. Up to 40-foot RVs. Rates: $21–$25 per site. Open: Year-round.

Shenandoah National Park campgrounds

These three campgrounds along Skyline Drive in Shenandoah National Park operate May through October, with facilities such as gift, book, and crafts shops; restaurants; gas stations; and hiking trails. Sites are available for RVs, but there are no hookups. Drinking water, rest-rooms with flush toilets, pay showers, and a laundry are available. Dump stations exist for RVs. Some sites are paved and have handicap access. The maximum stay is 14 days. You can reserve a site online through https://www.recreation.gov/ or call ☎ 877-444-6777.

> » **Big Meadows Campground** (milepost 51.3; ☎ **540-999-3500**): Total 227 sites, 32 pull-throughs, some paved, some gravel; stream for fishing. Rates: $20–$45 per night. Reservations required during peak season. DISC, MC, V.
>
> » **Lewis Mountain Campground** (milepost 57.5; ☎ **540-999-3500**): Total 31 sites, 3 pull-throughs. Paved, mostly shaded. Rates: $15 per night. No reservations.
>
> » **Loft Mountain Campground** (milepost 79.5; ☎ **540-999-3500**): Total 221 sites, 140 pull-throughs. Paved. Rates: $15 per night. No reservations.

Good Eats

Although all the classic Southern dishes — from fried chicken to collard greens and black-eyed peas — abound throughout the region, the culinary theme that ties together the mountains of Virginia, North Carolina, and Tennessee is country ham. If your previous acquaintance with ham is the supermarket kind or spiral-cut, honey-baked ham on a Super Bowl Sunday or at a buffet, this mahogany-colored, chewy, salty meat may surprise you. Pioneers preserved meats without refrigeration, by rubbing the fresh meat with a salt, sugar, and perhaps saltpeter, and then covering them in salt for four to six weeks. Then they would hang the hams in a smokehouse to be infused with hickory smoke.

In addition to other specialties, many of the home-style restaurants in the following list offer country ham.

» **Apple Barn,** 230 Apple Valley Rd., off US 441, Sevierville, Tennessee (☎ **800-421-4606** or 865-453-9319; `https://www.applebarncidermill.com`): What began as a barn where cider was made from the orchard's apples is now a food-production complex that's open to visitors. Apples are mashed into cider, butter, pies, dumplings, doughnuts, wines, and candies. A restaurant and grill are on the premises and a crafts shop selling baskets and birdhouses. The restaurant is open daily from 8 a.m. to 9 p.m. Store hours are 9 a.m. to 5:30 p.m.

» **Jarrett House,** 100 Haywood St., Dillsboro, North Carolina (☎ **828-477-4948;** `www.jarretthouse.com`): One of my all-time favorite restaurants is this family-style dining room in a small-town inn, with a front porch lined with rocking chairs. Budget-priced family-style meals may include country ham, fried chicken, hot biscuits, fried apple slices, and the specialty dessert: a rich, creamy vinegar pie. Open Tuesday through Saturday from 4:30 to 9 p.m.

» **Mabry Mill Coffee Shop,** Blue Ridge Parkway milepost 176, near Meadows of Dan, Virginia (☎ **276-952-2947**): Cornmeal and buckwheat pancakes cooked from stone-ground grains from the mill next door accompany rainbow trout, country ham, eggs, and homemade biscuits, and are served all day long. You can buy grains at the mill or in the coffee shop. The coffee shop is open late April through November 3, Monday through Friday from 7:30 a.m. to 5 p.m. and Saturday and Sunday 7:30 a.m. to 6 p.m.

» **Michie Tavern,** 683 Thomas Jefferson Pkwy., SR 53, Charlottesville, Virginia (☎ **434-977-1234;** `https://www.michietavern.com`): This historic tavern (pronounced *mik*-ee) serves traditional Southern lunches at moderate prices, and bus tours sometimes fill the place. Offerings include fried chicken, black-eyed peas, stewed tomatoes, and Virginia wines. Open daily from 11:15 a.m. to 3:30 p.m.

» **Mrs. Rowe's Family Restaurant,** I-81 at Exit 222, 74 Rowe's Road, Staunton, Virginia (☎ **540-886-1833;** www.mrsrowes.com): A favorite country kitchen, Mrs. Rowe's is conveniently located just off I-81 (easy on, easy off) and is a good place to satisfy a generous appetite. Hearty breakfasts star country ham, pancakes, muffins, and sticky buns. Lunches and dinners offer hot biscuits, homemade applesauce, mashed potatoes, skillet-fried chicken, ham, corn pudding, and the Southern favorite banana pudding. Open daily from 7 a.m. to 7 p.m.

» **Snappy Lunch,** 125 N. Main St., Mount Airy, North Carolina (☎ **336-786-4931;** www.thesnappylunch.com): Stop here for breakfast or lunch. Andy suggested to Barney on the Andy Griffith Show that they go down to the Snappy Lunch to get a bite to eat. The recommended order is the fried pork-chop sandwich — a crunchy, tender, juicy pork chop dipped in batter and grilled. Try it with lettuce, tomato, and mayonnaise. Open Monday, Tuesday, Wednesday, and Friday from 5:45 a.m. to 1:45 p.m., and Thursday and Saturday from 5:45 a.m. to 1:15 p.m.

Shopping along the Way

One pleasure of touring the Southern mountains is finding high-quality crafts made in the age-old ways, elegantly crafted, but not inexpensive.

» **Folk Art Center,** milepost 382, Blue Ridge Parkway near Asheville, North Carolina (☎ **828-298-7928;** https://www.southernhighlandguild.org): The Southern Highland Craft Guild has promoted the crafts of this region for over 70 years. Craft demonstrations are presented at the center from April through October, and juried shows are scheduled throughout the year. Pottery, quilts, rocking chairs, baskets, handcrafted toys, weavings, and other works of skilled craftsmen are on display; most are for sale. Open daily from 9 a.m. to 6 p.m.

» **Parkway Craft Center,** at Moses Cone Manor, milepost 294, Blue Ridge Parkway near Blowing Rock, North Carolina (☎ **828-295-7938;** https://www.southernhighlandguild.org/folk-art-center/): Like the Folk Art Center, this facility sells premium examples of genuine mountain crafts. Open daily April through November from 9 a.m. to 5 p.m.; closed on major holidays. The center closes for the season on November 30.

Fast Facts

Area Code
You'll find the following area codes in the Blue Ridge Mountains: **828** in North Carolina; **423** and **865** in Tennessee; and **434, 504,** and **804** in Virginia.

Driving Laws
All occupants must wear seat belts in North Carolina and Tennessee; front-seat passengers must wear them in Virginia. The maximum speed limit on interstate highways in North Carolina, Tennessee, and Virginia is 70 mph; the speed limits on all roads are as posted. Speed limits in urban areas are lower in all three states.

Emergency
Call ☎ **911** in all states. Cellphone users can touch ☎ *47 in North Carolina and ☎ *847 in Tennessee.

Hospitals
Major hospitals along the route are located in Roanoke, Virginia, and Asheville, North Carolina.

Information
For North Carolina, go online to https://www.nc.gov or https://www.visitnc.com, or call for information on Blue Ridge Parkway (☎ **828-298-0398**) or Great Smoky Mountains National Park (☎ **865-436-1200**). For Tennessee, contact the Department of Tourist Development (☎ **615-741-8299;** https://www.tn.gov). For Virginia, visit https://www.virginia.gov or https://www.virginia.org, or call for information on Travel Guide (☎ **800-742-3935**) or Blue Ridge Parkway (☎ **704-271-4779**).

Road and Weather Conditions
For North Carolina, sources include ☎ **919-733-2520** and https://www.ncdot.org; for Tennessee, ☎ **800-342-3258** (weather conditions) or https://www.tn.gov/tdot; and for Virginia, ☎ **800-367-7623** (roadway assistance) or www.virginiadot.org.

Taxes
North Carolina state sales tax is 4.5 percent; local taxes can raise rates to 7.5 percent. Tennessee state sales tax is 7 percent; local taxes can raise rates to 9.750 percent. Virginia state sales tax is 4.3 percent; local taxes can raise rates to 5.3 percent.

State gas taxes are 36.2 cents per gallon in North Carolina, 26.4 cents per gallon in Tennessee, and 16.2 cents per gallon in Virginia.

Time Zone
North Carolina, eastern Tennessee, and Virginia are on Eastern Standard Time.

Chapter 11

The Gulf Coast: Tallahassee to New Orleans

Sugary white-sand beaches, scrumptious shrimp, antebellum gardens, scarlet and pink with azaleas, and oak trees dripping Spanish moss are sights that mark the Gulf Coast. Much of this scenic byway is periodically changed by hurricanes. Reconstruction is often slow, and much of the Mississippi and Louisiana coasts take years to recover. Unkind as the weather may be some years, tourists still love to visit this area, and some like to visit a casino or two along with the beaches and seafood delights. When you just want to enjoy good value for your vacation dollar head on down to this lovely area. This nearly-always-sunny strip of vacation land runs from Tallahassee across Florida's Panhandle, along the Gulf shores of Alabama and Mississippi, and straight into the nonstop party town of New Orleans.

In the Florida Panhandle, where Mickey Mouse never paraded and Cuban coffee is hard to find, you can meet old-timers that relish smoked mullet and swamp cabbage; they mix, sometimes reluctantly, with the hotshot jet pilots at Pensacola Naval Air Station and the chic residents of Seaside, the Panhandle equivalent of the Hamptons. Florida writer Marjorie Kinnan Rawlings (author of *The Yearling*) described her neighbors as people who made do, lived off the land, never put on airs, and wore their Southern heritage with pride.

The fashionable coast between Apalachicola and Pensacola boasts some of the top-ranked beaches in America, according to Dr. Stephen Leatherman (a.k.a. Dr. Beach), a coastal geologist who puts out a listing of the nation's best. After a few years of his listings, the area's tourist offices began to call it the Emerald Coast. An older, less tourist-conscious nickname for the region is the Redneck Riviera.

Alabama and Mississippi serve up all the lush romance of their Gulf Coasts in an economical 150 miles or so, with oceanside golf courses, Vegas-style casinos, and RV parks and campgrounds so close to the beach that you're lulled to sleep by the sound of the waves. A few more minutes on the road, and you're in New Orleans, the Big Easy, where you can let the good times roll.

Choosing Your Route

Tallahassee, in the center of northern Florida on I-10, is a good starting point for a drive through the Gulf Coast region. You can drive south on US 319 for a few miles, turn off on SR 363 to the historic town of St. Mark's, and continue west on US 98 and 319 to Panacea and Carrabelle on the Gulf of Mexico. St. George Island and St. Joseph's Peninsula, each with state-park campgrounds, are available to take you on a detour off onto US 98 around Apalachicola and continue along the Gulf Coast past Mexico Beach into Panama City.

Between Panama City and Pensacola lie the most fashionable stretches of Florida's Emerald Coast. From Pensacola, you can make another detour to Gulf Islands National Seashore; follow SR 292 (Gulf Beach Highway) into Alabama, where it becomes SR 182, to Gulf Shores. A circle around Mobile Bay highlights Alabama's Gulf Coast attractions. Then follow US 90 (or the faster I-10, which runs parallel) past Pascagoula, Biloxi, and Gulfport, and continue on I-10 into New Orleans. The full distance of the drive is approximately 610 miles.

TIP

If you want to take a shorter version of this drive, go from Tallahassee southwest to Apalachicola, and continue west along the Emerald Coast to Pensacola, pausing at whatever beaches and campgrounds strike your fancy. The distance between Tallahassee and Pensacola on the route outlined earlier in this section is 310 miles. To return from Pensacola to Tallahassee quickly (with a refrigerator stocked with fresh seafood), take I-10 east back to Tallahassee. This loop drive is 505 miles.

Planning Ahead

This Gulf of Mexico coastal drive can be made any time of year, but be aware of weather reports. Beach lovers should opt for summer, when the water is bathtub-warm (85°F) for swimming but the air temperatures are too high for taking long hikes and exploring. Flower fanciers love the route in early to late spring, when the azaleas and camellias are blooming everywhere and the days are mild and sunny. In early fall, the weather is warm enough for sunning and swimming (Gulf of Mexico water averages 75°F in March and November). In winter, the weather is mild, encouraging beachcombing, birdwatching, and exploring small towns for antiques and local color.

Making reservations for RV camping is a very good idea during summer, spring break, and around holidays, although you should be able to find a spot without reservations in winter and during weekdays in early spring and late fall. Along the route between Tallahassee and New Orleans are some 36 communities with RV camping availability.

Pack swimming apparel and light cotton clothes for spring, summer, and fall, and add a light jacket or sweater for most winter days. Dress is casual everywhere along the coast, so don't plan on bringing jackets and ties or fancy dresses and high heels unless you're taking some time off from the RV to stay in one of the expensive coastal resort hotels. Always carry sunglasses, a sun hat, and sunscreen. Having insect repellent is a good idea; plant-based essential oils such as citronella, cedar, eucalyptus, and soybean can work for short periods if you're not allergic to them and want to shy away from DEET-based repellents. Always follow the safety precautions.

TIP

Here are some tips to keep in mind as you traverse Florida and the Gulf Coast:

» Bring rain gear, because this coast gets wind and rain periodically throughout the year, especially during hurricane season. Stay tuned to weather forecasts from June through November, and if a big wind is forecast, it's smart to consider heading inland with your RV.

» If you happen to be driving south of Panama Beach at any time during college spring break, the area is bound to be busy, and the beaches will seem to belong to the college-age visitors. When you're north of Panama City Beach, however, you can expect more-sedate populations.

» When you're enjoying the beaches of the Gulf Coast, especially during hurricane season (June to November), always look at the flags that denote water conditions. Blue flag means calm water that's safe for swimming, yellow tells us to take care, and red means don't go in the water or get out of it now.

EATIN' AND ANTIQUIN', MOBILE STYLE

Mobile, 305 years old in 2007, was the French capital of America before there was a New Orleans, and the city logo proudly shows off a historic home, the battleship *USS Alabama*, an azalea in full bloom, and a shrimp. What does it all mean? The historic home is to remind you that Mobile offers tours of antebellum houses. The battleship, open daily for tours in Battleship *USS Alabama* Memorial Park, is a World War II veteran. The azalea stands for world-famous Bellingrath Gardens and Home, a glorious splash of seasonal flowers year-round. And if the shrimp makes you think of Forrest Gump, you won't be surprised to discover that its author, Winston Groom, has a home just outside Mobile.

RVers who are seeking other gratification in the area need to make the scenic drive on US 98 and 98A along the eastern shore of Mobile Bay. En route, you can visit the Bloody Mary capital of the Eastern Shore, as **Manci's Antique Club,** 1715 Main St. (☎ **251-375-0543;** www.mancisantiqueclub.com), in downtown Daphne, calls itself. This club displays the largest collection of Jim Beam decanters outside the distillery's own. Open daily from 11 a.m. to 2 p.m. and from 5:30 to 10 p.m.

Fairhope is lined with antiques shops and art galleries, and punctuated with a long pier jutting out into the bay.

Point Clear is home to the Grand Hotel, now a Marriott and the latest in a line of classic Southern resorts built on this spot, and to the Punta Clara Kitchen, where homemade candies abound.

On the western side of the bay, SR 193 leads to Bellingrath Gardens and Home and beyond to Dauphin Island and Fort Gaines, where you can look across to Fort Morgan, the Civil War fortress barricaded with a string of underwater mines across the channel that inspired Admiral David Farragut's famous command, "Damn the torpedoes — full speed ahead!"

In Mobile, on the city's northwestern edge on Old Shell Road, a snack-time stop, the Dew Drop Inn has been serving up great hot dogs since 1927.

NEW ORLEANS: EASING INTO THE BIG EASY

New Orleans is one of the friendliest cities on Earth — to everybody except RVers, that is. It's not that the good folks of Louisiana don't welcome us; they do. But their roads, even the interstates, are bumpy and rough, causing our pots and pans to rattle as we bounce through.

Equally troubling are the confusing roadway markings for the interstate, expressway, and surface-street system, which can catapult an innocent RVer into the traffic-clogged French Quarter or the Superdome before you can say *"Laissez les bon temps roulez"* ("Let the good times roll," a traditional Cajun partying cry).

So instead of driving into the heart of New Orleans in your RV, select an RV park in an outlying area, preferably one that has frequent shuttle service to and from downtown if you don't have your own car; park and secure your living quarters; and then set out to have fun in a city that never sleeps.

Must-See Attractions

Battleship *USS Alabama* Memorial Park
Mobile, Alabama

KID FRIENDLY

The decommissioned World War II battleship that carried a crew of 2,500 is on display, along with the submarine *USS Drum,* a B-52 aircraft, cannons, tanks, armored personnel carriers, and helicopters. Kids love to climb all over the military hardware and explore the hidden corners of the ship, which is Alabama's most popular tourist attraction. Allow two to three hours.

Battleship Parkway, Mobile Bay. (Exit from I-10.) ☎ **251-433-2703.** *www.ussalabama.com. RV parking: Large area. Parking: $4. Admission: $15 adults, $6 children 6–11. Open: Oct–Mar 8 a.m.–4 p.m., Apr–Sept 8 a.m.–6 p.m.*

Bellingrath Gardens and Home
Theodore, Alabama (south of Mobile)

TIP

Six themed formal gardens are strung together with a series of bridges, walkways, pools, and streams to create one of the most appealing floral displays in the world. In spring, 250,000 azaleas blaze with color; in summer, everything comes up roses; in autumn, chrysanthemums bloom by the thousands; and winter's poinsettias and camellias glow in the semitropical landscape. The 15-room Bellingrath family home (he was the first Coca-Cola bottler in the Mobile area) houses collections of antique china and glass, including 200 pieces of Edward Marshall Boehm porcelain. A cafe is also on the estate. Allow two hours for the gardens only and three hours for gardens and house.

12401 Bellingrath Gardens Rd. (From Mobile, take Exit 22 off I-10 and travel south on SR 163, Dauphin Island Parkway, to SR 193, which continues to the gardens; signage is frequent.) ☎ **800-247-8420** *or 251-973-2217.* https://bellingrath.org. *RV parking: Large designated parking areas. Admission: Gardens only, $14 adults, $8 ages 5–12, free for children 4 and under; gardens and house, $22 adults, $14 ages 5–12, free for children 4 and under. Open: Daily 8 a.m.–5 p.m. Closed Thanksgiving, Christmas Day, and New Year's Day.*

Gulf Islands National Seashore
Florida and Mississippi

Extending 150 miles from Destin, Florida, to Gulfport, Mississippi, Gulf Islands National Seashore is divided into 11 sections, 6 of them in Florida and 5 of them in Mississippi. Miles of uncrowded beaches famous for acres of soft white sand and sea oats attract day visitors and overnight campers in modest numbers. Two campgrounds, Florida's Fort Pickens and Mississippi's Davis Bayou (see "Our Favorite Campgrounds" later in this chapter), are usually available on a first-come, first-served basis. Much of the parkland consists of offshore islands reachable only by boat. Areas accessible by motor vehicles offer hiking trails, bike paths, and nature trails.

Headquarters: 1801 Gulf Breeze Pkwy., Gulf Breeze, Florida 32561, or 3500 Park Rd., Ocean Springs, Mississippi 39564. ☎ **850-934-2600** *(Florida) or* ☎ **228-875-9057** *(Mississippi).* `https://www.nps.gov/guis`. *RV parking: Designated off-road areas. Admission: $3 per person, $8 per vehicle; $16 RV campground. Open: Year-round.*

National Museum of Naval Aviation
Pensacola, Florida

Climb into a cockpit trainer, observe a flight simulator in action, see A-4 Skyhawks like those flown by the Blue Angels, learn the history of flying from wooden planes to the Skylab module, and see big-screen aviation films with a pilot's point of view in the adjoining IMAX theater. Allow three hours; real buffs spend a whole day. If you are interested in seeing the Blue Angels practice, be sure and call to check on admission and parking procedures ahead of time.

1750 Radford Blvd., Naval Air Station. ☎ **850-452-3604.** `https://www.navalaviationmuseum.org`. *RV parking: Designated lot. Admission: Free. Open: Daily 9 a.m.–5 p.m. Closed Thanksgiving, Christmas Day, and New Year's Day. Check website for special-events calendar.*

Walter Anderson Museum of Art
Ocean Springs, Mississippi

This museum displays the astonishing works of an eccentric loner named Walter Anderson. A master artist who painted plants, animals, and people of the Gulf Coast, he sometimes isolated himself in primitive conditions on an uninhabited barrier island for months at a time. After his death in 1965, his family went into the small cottage he used as a studio to find the "little room," every inch of its floor, walls, and ceilings covered with paintings of plants, animals, and an allegorical figure thought to represent the Mississippi River. The little room, his paintings and murals, and ceramic pieces from the family's Shearwater Pottery collection are on display here. Allow two hours.

510 Washington Ave. ☎ 228-872-3164. `https://www.walter` `andersonmuseum.org.` *RV parking: Use street parking because the museum lot is small. Admission: $10 adults, $8 seniors and students, $5 ages 5–15, free for children 4 and under. Open: Mon–Sat 10. a.m.–5 p.m. Closed Sun.*

More Cool Things to See and Do

Fascinating attractions line the Gulf Coast. A few more of my favorites follow, although you'll no doubt make your own discoveries.

KID FRIENDLY

» **Explore black history.** With 5,000 items and 500,000 documents, one of the most extensive collections of African-American artifacts in the United States, the **Meek Eason Black Archives, Research Center and Museum,** Carnegie Center, Gamble Street (☎ 850-599-3020; `http://famu.edu/index.cfm?MEBA`), at Florida A&M University in Tallahassee, displays everything from slave-era implements and old, non-PC Aunt Jemima pancake-mix packages to the first ironing board, built in 1872, by a servant named Sarah Boone, who got tired of ironing on the floor and propped a board up on legs. A hands-on Underground Railroad exhibit fascinates the kids. Allow two hours.

RV parking is available in a designated guest parking area or on the street. Admission is free. The museum is open Monday through Friday from 10 a.m. to 4 p.m. Closed holidays.

» **Meet the mad potter of Biloxi. Ohr-O'Keefe Museum of Art,** 386 Beach Blvd., Biloxi (☎ 228-374-5547; `https://georgeohr.` `org`), honor the mad potter of Biloxi, George E. Ohr, who had a genius for self-promotion. The museum has 130 pots of his creation. Admission is $10 for adults, $8 for seniors and students, $5 for children 5 and up, and free for children under 5. The museum is open Tuesday through Saturday from 10 a.m. to 5 p.m.

» **See where ice cubes were invented.** In 1851, Dr. John Gorrie invented a machine to cool the rooms of malaria patients, but when it kept clogging its pipes with ice cubes, he realized that he was on to something and invented ice cubes, ice making, and air conditioning. The machine in the **John Gorrie State Museum,** 46 Sixth St., Apalachicola (☎ **850-653-9347;** https://www. floridastateparks.org/johngorriemuseum), is a replica; the original is in the Smithsonian. Allow one hour.

RV parking is available on the street. Admission is $2 for adults and free for children 6 and under. The museum is open Thursday through Monday from 9 a.m. to 5 p.m. The museum is closed Tuesday and Wednesday, as well as Thanksgiving, Christmas Day, and New Year's Day.

» **Look out for alligators!** Bike, hike, and canoe numerous trails and streams in **St. Mark's National Wildlife Refuge,** 1255 Lighthouse Rd. (☎ **850-925-6121:** https://www.fws.gov/ refuge/st_marks), bordering Florida's Apalachee Bay. An excellent visitor center has maps and advice.

The refuge entrance is south of Newport on SR 59. RV parking is available in designated lots at the visitor center and on trail-heads. Admission is $5 per vehicle and free with a National Park Card or Florida State Park Card. It's open during daylight hours; the gates are open from 6 a.m. to 9 p.m. If you want more infor-mation, contact the US Fish & Wildlife Service, Box 68, St. Mark's, FL 32355.

KID
FRIENDLY

» **Trail Tarzan.** Many of the early Tarzan movies with Johnny Weissmuller and Maureen O'Sullivan were filmed at Florida's **Wakulla Springs State Park,** 550 Wakulla Park Dr., Wakulla Springs Lodge (☎ **850-421-2000;** https://www. floridastateparks.org/parks-and-trails/edward-ball- wakulla-springs-state-park) and so was the 1954 horror classic *The Creature from the Black Lagoon.* The clear, almost bot-tomless springs and lush jungle foliage make this area a popular family vacation area. Take a glass-bottom boat ride across the springs.

RV parking is available in designated areas in the park and at the lodge. Admission is $6 per vehicle and $2 per pedestrian and bicyclists. The park is open daily year-round; the lodge is open for overnight guests.

Our Favorite Campgrounds

The Gulf of Mexico is a favorite destination for RVers, whether they're family vacationers, snowbirds, or full-timers, and plenty of RV parks, state parks, and recreation areas with camping line the way. Supermarkets, country stores, restaurants, cafes, and national fast-food outlets also generously dot the route.

All campgrounds listed here are open year-round and have public flush toilets, showers, and sanitary dump stations unless designated otherwise. Toll-free numbers, where listed, are for reservations only.

KID FRIENDLY

Audubon RV Resort

$$$$ Slidell, Louisiana

If you take my advice in the "New Orleans: Easing into the Big Easy" sidebar earlier in this chapter, you'll settle in here or at the New Orleans West KOA, because at both parks, you can happily leave your RV behind while you take a shuttle to the French Quarter. This park, 30 minutes from New Orleans, offers new facilities and a shady rural setting. Amenities include freshwater fishing, car rentals, and swamp tours — a kid favorite.

56009 SR 433. (Off I-10, Exit 263, go southeast 1 mile on SR 433 to campground, on the right.) ☎ **985-402-5891.** *https://audubonrvresort.com. Total 95 full hookups with 30- and 50-amp electric, 69 pull-throughs. Data port, handicap access, laundry, pool, shuttle to French Quarter. Rates: $40 and up per site. DISC, MC, V.*

BARGAIN ALERT

Gulf Islands National Seashore/Davis Bayou

$$ Ocean Springs, Mississippi

Davis Bayou, the Mississippi campground inside Gulf Islands National Seashore, is much smaller than its Florida equivalent at Fort Pickens, and the paved back-in sites are narrower, though they can accommodate RVs up to 45 feet. Sites are open on a first-come, first-served basis. It's on the ocean side of US 90 near a golf course and a shopping mall.

*3500 Park Rd. (From Biloxi, go east 5 miles on US 90 to the campground, on the right.) ☎ **228-875-3962** or 228-630-4100 then dial 0. Total 51 sites with water and 30-amp electric, no full hookups, no pull-throughs. Rates: $22 per site. DISC, MC, V.*

Gulf Shores/Pensacola West KOA

$$$–$$$$$ Lillian, Alabama

Just across Perdido Bay from Pensacola, Florida, this quiet rural campground is a short walk uphill from a swimming beach with a fishing pier. If you want to, stay a while; long, shady sites are appealing, and so are the Saturday-night ice-cream socials.

*33951 Spinnaker Dr. (From junction of US 98 and CR 99, go south 1½ miles to campground, on the left.) ☎ **800-562-3471** or 251-961-1717; https://koa.com. Total 111 sites with water and 30- and 50-amp electric, 100 full hookups, 94 pull-throughs. CATV, data port, laundry, pool, spa. Rates: Call for current rates and discounts. DISC, MC, V.*

Gulf State Park Campground

$$$–$$$$ Gulf Shores, Alabama

Despite its large size, this state park is one of the best in the country for RVers, with big pull-through and back-in sites, plenty of grass, some shade, and some side-by-side hookups. There's a 2½-mile beach of powdery white sand, a long fishing pier, boating, a nature trail to hike, and a resort hotel with all-you-can-eat buffets if you don't feel like cooking. Reservations are a good idea in spring and summer.

*22050 Campground Rd. (From junction of SR 59 and SR 182, go east 2 miles on SR 182 to CR 2, north ½ mile to park, on the right.) ☎ **800-252-7275**. Total 496 full hookups with water and 30- and 50-amp electric, 65 pull-throughs. Handicap access, laundry. Rates: $25–$70 per site; vary by season and site type. DISC, MC, V.*

New Orleans West KOA

$$$–$$$$$ River Ridge, Louisiana

I've stayed here numerous times and always enjoyed the well-kept surroundings and friendly management. Besides the daily shuttle bus, a city bus that goes into downtown New Orleans stops at the campground entrance. Car rentals are available at the campground. Sites are large, mostly shady back-ins. The location is about 15 minutes from the casino and the French Quarter.

11129 Jefferson Hwy. (From the junction of I-10 and SR 49, Exit 223A, go south 3 miles on SR 49, and then ¾ mile east on SR 48 to campground, on the left.) ☎ **800-562-5110** *or 504-467-1792.* https://koa.com. *Total 106 sites with 30- and 50-amp electric, 95 full hookups, no pull-throughs. CATV, handicap access, laundry, pool, Wi-Fi. Rates: $45–$60 per site. AE, DISC, MC, V.*

Good Eats

Southern cooking has a well-deserved reputation worldwide, and the Gulf Coast provides the best examples anywhere. In this section, you can find out more than you ever wanted to know about fresh shrimp, and great home-style, all-you-can-eat dining. And the prices are great!

Seafood markets

Delectable fresh shrimp in big, bigger, and biggest sizes are for sale all along the Gulf Coast at prices that are unbelievably cheap to urbanites from the Northeast and the West Coast. The finest local shrimp are called Royal Red; ask for them by name. For tips on preparing them, see the nearby "Put another shrimp on the barbie" sidebar. Although several good seafood sellers are along the route, here are two of my favorites:

» **Joe Patti Seafoods,** 524 S. B St., Pensacola, Florida (☎ **850-432-3315;** https://www.joepattis.com): Open Monday to Saturday from 7:30 a.m. to 6 p.m. and Sunday from 7:30 a.m. to 6:30 p.m.

PUT ANOTHER SHRIMP ON THE BARBIE

Although you can buy boiled, fried, or grilled shrimp in every little restaurant and takeout along the route, the most delicious are those that you buy fresh and cook yourself. In only a few minutes, they turn red and are ready. What follows are favorite ways to serve 'em up.

- Steam them in their shells in boiling salted water or beer with a little bit of shrimp-boil seasoning (bay leaves and dried herbs).

- Grill them in the shell on your barbecue grill.

- Peel them and stack them on skewers to lie over the coals.

- To turn out instant shrimp scampi, peel them and cook them quickly in a frying pan with a little butter or olive oil and chopped garlic and herbs.

- Peel them, leaving the tail part of the shell for a handle. Dip shrimp in flour that's been salted and peppered, then dip them in beaten egg with a little water, and dip them in dry breadcrumbs. (Japanese panko crumbs are best; you can find them in the Asian-food sections of supermarkets.) Finally, deep-fry them in a half-inch of hot oil for a few minutes on each side. Yummy!

- Put ¼ cup Cajun spice and ¼ cup white flour in a bag, and shake. Add six to eight peeled shrimp, and shake the bag some more. Take shrimp from the bag add to the deep fryer one at a time, and cook about 2 to 3 minutes after the last shrimp is in the fryer.

» **Pier 77 Seafood Restaurant and Market,** 3016 Thomas Dr., Panama City, Florida (☎ **850-235-3080;** http://pier77pcb.com): Stop here for super-jumbo shrimp and frozen clam strips. Open daily from 9 a.m. to 6 p.m. You'll sometimes find live music on Friday and Saturday nights.

More markets

Two favorite markets specialize in produce, bread, and cheese:

» **Burris Farm Market,** SR 59, Loxley, Alabama (☎ **251-964-6464**): Stock up on fruits, vegetables, and breads. Open daily 8 a.m. to 6 p.m.

» **Loxley Farm Market,** 5201 S. Hickory Lane, Loxley, AL (☎ **251-964-4602**): The market features fresh fruits and vegetables, including vine-ripened tomatoes. Open Monday to Saturday from 8 a.m. to 6 p.m. and Sunday from 9 a.m. to 5 p.m.

Snacks and full-meal deals

Along the Gulf of Mexico, you find great seafood and other tasty treats:

» **Aunt Jenny's Catfish Restaurant,** 1217 Washington Ave., Ocean Springs, Mississippi (☎ **228-875-9201**; www.coastseafood.com/jennys.html): Obviously, fried catfish filets — all you can eat — are the main meal here, along with fried okra, fried green tomatoes, and turnip greens. Open Monday to Wednesday from 4 to 9 p.m., Thursday from 11 a.m. to 9 p.m., Friday and Saturday from 11 a.m. to 9:30 p.m., and Sunday from 11 a.m. to 8 p.m.

» **Bradley's Country Store,** 10655 Centerville Rd., Tallahassee, Florida (☎ **850-893-1647**; www.bradleyscountrystore.com): Homemade smoked sausages and special sausage biscuits hot off the griddle are the attractions at this store's lunch counter. Open Monday through Friday from 8:30 a.m. to 6 p.m., Saturday from 8 a.m. to 5 p.m., and Sunday from 11 a.m. to 4 p.m.

» **Dew Drop Inn,** 1808 Old Shell Rd., Mobile, Alabama (☎ **251-473-7872**): Stop here for hot dogs with chili, sauerkraut, mustard, ketchup, and pickles. Or order the cheeseburgers that singer Jimmy Buffett, a Mobile native, raves about. Open Tuesday through Friday from 10 a.m. to 8 p.m., and Monday and Saturday from 10 a.m. to 3 p.m.

» **Owl Cafe,** 15 Avenue D, Apalachicola, Florida (☎ **850-653-9888**; www.owlcafeflorida.com): A favorite with the locals, the Owl serves excellent clam chowder, real crab cakes, and fried grouper. Open Monday through Saturday from 11 a.m. to 3 p.m. and Sunday from 10 a.m. to 3 p.m.

KID FRIENDLY

» **Punta Clara Kitchen,** 17111 US Hwy. 98, Point Clear, Alabama (☎ **251-928-8477;** https://www.puntaclara.com): A candy and gift shop in an 1897 gingerbread house delights visitors and sells pecan butter crunch, bourbon balls, and buckeyes (peanut butter balls dipped in chocolate). Open Monday through Saturday from 9 a.m. to 5 p.m. and Sunday from 12:30 to 5 p.m.

» **Three Georges Candy & The Nuthouse,** 226 Dauphin St., Mobile, Alabama (☎ **251-433-6725;** http://3georges-com. 3dcartstores.com): Three Greek friends, all named George, established this confectionary in 1917, and their descendants turn out hand-dipped chocolates and tasty handmade Southern sweets such as divinity, pralines, and heavenly hash. Open Monday through Thursday from 9 a.m. to 6 p.m., Friday and Saturday from 9 a.m. to 8 p.m., and Sunday from 11 a.m. to 6 p.m.

Fast Facts

Area Code
Area codes along this drive include **251** for Alabama, **850** for Florida, **504** for Louisiana, and **228** for Mississippi.

Driving Laws
In Alabama, Florida, Louisiana, and Mississippi, riders in the front seats must wear seat belts. The maximum speed limit on interstate highways in Alabama, Florida, Louisiana, and Mississippi is 70 mph. Speed limits in urban areas are lower.

Emergency
Call ☎ **911** in all states.

Hospitals
Major hospitals along the route are in Tallahassee, Mobile, Biloxi, and New Orleans.

Information
Helpful sources in the individual states include the Alabama Tourism Department (☎ **800-252-2262;** https://tourism.alabama.gov/group-and-international-travel/), Visit Florida (☎ **888-735-2872;** https://www.visitflorida.com), Louisiana Office of Tourism (☎ **800-227-4386;** https://www.louisianatravel.com), and Mississippi Division of Tourism (☎ **800-927-6378;** https://visitmississippi.org).

Road and Weather Conditions
Call the following for road and weather advisories. For Alabama: ☎ **334-242-4128;** https://www.dot.state.al.us. For Florida: ☎ **888-558-1518;** https://www.fdot.gov. For Mississippi: ☎ **601-987-1211;** https://www.dps.ms.gov. In Louisiana, cellphone users can dial ☎ ***577** for state police assistance.

Taxes
Alabama state sales tax is 4 percent; local taxes can raise it to 11 percent. Florida state sales tax is 6 percent; local taxes can raise it to 8.5 percent. Louisiana state sales tax is 4.45 percent; local taxes can raise it to 11.45 percent. Mississippi state sales tax is a flat 7 percent; local rates can add 1 percent.

State gasoline taxes are as follows: Alabama, 18 cents per gallon; Florida, 32 cents per gallon; Louisiana, 20 cents per gallon; and Mississippi, 18.4 cents per gallon.

Time Zone
Eastern Florida is on Eastern time. Western Florida from Apalachicola, as well as Alabama, Mississippi, and Louisiana, are on Central time.

Chapter **12**

The Natchez Trace: Natchez to Nashville

Consider leaving the clogged arteries of crowded interstates behind to enter a shaded, curved, rural highway that doesn't allow commercial traffic or speeding; 50 mph is the limit. Along the way, you find campgrounds, crafts shops, picnic areas, and nature trails to explore, including a boardwalk through an eerie swamp with lime-green water and sunken trees.

In spring and summer, this route is green with thick, lush grass and plenty of hardwood trees, with occasional glimpses of small farms and villages through the roadside foliage. The highway is easy and undulating but not wide. Most, but not all, overlook turnoffs are spacious enough for large motor homes or vehicles pulling trailers.

The Natchez Trace meanders over 444 miles from a point northeast of Natchez, Mississippi, to a point southwest of Nashville, Tennessee, passing the places where TV megastar Oprah Winfrey, rock idol Elvis Presley, and blues musician W. C. Handy were born, and where Meriwether Lewis (of Lewis and Clark fame) died under mysterious circumstances.

An 8,000-plus-year-old Indian trail, the *trace* — an old-fashioned term for a path or roadway — was turned into a scenic highway drive in the 1930s. The route preserves some 300 segments of the old trace that was commissioned in 1806 by Thomas Jefferson. And don't worry about the speed limit; it's so peaceful and scenic along the way that you won't even be tempted to rev up the RV.

Choosing Your Route

The best way to approach the Natchez Trace drive is to begin in Natchez and go north to Nashville, although it's just as simple to begin in Nashville and drive south to Natchez. If you're driving from Nashville to Natchez and have extra time, check out the Gulf Coast drive between New Orleans and Tallahassee in Chapter 11.

The trace is unfinished in a couple of spots. It begins 8 miles northeast of Natchez, so you travel on US 60 from Natchez to the marked beginning. Near Jackson, you need to bypass the parkway at the junction of I-20; follow I-20 to I-220 North; and continue on I-55 to Exit 105, which reconnects you to the parkway.

Similar to the Skyline Drive and Blue Ridge Parkway drive described in Chapter 10, the Natchez Trace has well-marked entrances and exits that take you onto commercial highways and in and out of towns and villages. Along the trace route there are numbered mileposts that double as addresses for sites along the route. The route begins at milepost 8 near Natchez and finishes past milepost 440 near Nashville.

At the end of the parkway, you exit via a dramatic bridge (past milepost 440) that swoops you down onto Route 100 about 10 miles west of Nashville. The total drive is close to 500 miles.

The easiest way to make a shorter version of this drive is to follow the 444-mile trace closely, overnighting at one of the campgrounds along the way, without turning off to see the attractions in Port Gibson, Vicksburg, Jackson, and Nashville or in the state of Alabama.

Planning Ahead

Although the parkway is comfortable to drive year-round, the best times are early spring and fall, when the weather is mild, the flowers are in bloom, and the pilgrimage tours through antebellum homes are on the agenda (see "More Cool Things to See and Do" later in this chapter). Winter usually is mild but can be rainy and sometimes chilly; summers are hot.

JEFFERSON'S ROAD: A 19TH-CENTURY ROUTE

In 1806, Thomas Jefferson ordered a roadway "12 feet in width and passable for a wagon" to be built along the trade routes originally used by flatboat men returning upriver from delivering their furs, tobacco, pork, and farm products in Natchez and New Orleans. This route was used for trade, mail, and military traffic.

Although traveling downriver was easy, the Kaintucks, as they were called, were unable to row or pole upstream against the current. After selling their goods (and maybe their rafts too), they had to walk or ride horseback to return home. The traders had little enough remaining from their profits after the gamblers, cutthroats, and prostitutes of Natchez-Under-the-Hill had finished with them, but the toughest part of the trip was yet to come — protecting themselves and their money from the highwaymen who often lurked along the trace. Jefferson was thinking about not only the traders, but also the postal-service riders who would use the roadway to deliver mail, as well as the military troops who might need the wide, clear pathway for wagons and cannons.

Ladies and gentlemen of fashion, circuit-riding preachers, frontier prostitutes, pioneer families, medicine peddlers, and flatboat men — everybody used the Natchez Trace. A despondent Meriwether Lewis died mysteriously along the trail in 1809, and in 1815, a triumphant Major General Andrew Jackson, better known as Old Hickory, marched his Tennessee militia along the trace back from the Battle of New Orleans.

In 1812, the first steamboat arrived in Natchez, and by 1820, the boats dominated the rivers. Eventually, except for a brief period during the Civil War, the little-used Natchez Trace reverted to woods again. Only in the 1930s, under the administration of Franklin D. Roosevelt, did clearing and restoration of the trace begin. Today's road closely follows the original.

LOUISIANA PURCHASE: THE DEAL OF THE CENTURY

In the annals of real estate coups, few can match the 1803 Louisiana Purchase, ordered by Thomas Jefferson and negotiated by future president James Monroe. Three years earlier, Napoleon had traded with Spain, swapping the Italian kingdom of Parma (home of Parmesan cheese) for the Louisiana Territory. In those days, the territory stretched from the west banks of the Mississippi River to the Rocky Mountains and from Canada to the Gulf of Mexico.

Monroe paid Napoleon around $15 million, or 4 cents an acre. Interestingly enough to mention is that all that Jefferson wanted was to regain control of the port of New Orleans and the land along the Mississippi so that Americans could continue to use the river for trade.

You don't always need campground reservations for the places in this chapter. You will need reservations for the Opryland KOA in Nashville, in June, when Fan Fair, a gathering of country-music fans from around the world, takes place.

For a full tour, allow five to seven days for the drive.

TIP

Although the trace route is well marked, consider keeping your GPS loaded with the destination for that day. That way if you take exits or detours off to an interesting destination, the GPS will aid in returning you to the route.

Must-See Attractions

Alabama Music Hall of Fame

KID FRIENDLY

Tuscumbia, Alabama

From the first touring motor home used by the band Alabama to artifacts of jazz innovator Sun Ra, this modern, interactive museum salutes the great musicians who were born or lived in Alabama. The list includes Hank Williams, Nat King Cole, Jimmie Rodgers, Jimmy Buffett, Tammy Wynette, Emmylou Harris,

Big Mama Willie Mae Thornton, Odetta, Martha Reeves, Bobby Goldsboro, Dinah Washington, Lionel Richie, Toni Tennille, and Wilson Pickett.

The museum was built here instead of in a major Alabama city because in the 1960s and 1970s, nearby Muscle Shoals housed popular recording studios. In those studios, Percy Sledge recorded the rhythm-and-blues classic "When a Man Loves a Woman," Aretha Franklin cut early soul records, and a young Duane Allman was a studio guitarist. Listening on individual earphones, kids of all ages groove to original music tracks performed by artists spanning decades. Allow two to three hours.

617 US 72 West. ☎ **800-239-2643** *or 256-381-4417.* https://www. alamhof.org. *RV parking: Large parking lot. Admission: $10 adults, $8 seniors and students, $6 children 12 and under. Open: Tues–Sat 9 a.m.–5 p.m. Closed Sun, Monday, and major holidays.*

Elvis Presley Birthplace and Museum
Tupelo, Mississippi

This two-room cottage was built by Elvis's father, Vernon, who borrowed $180 to have the house finished in time for the birth of Elvis Aron and his stillborn twin brother, Jesse Garon. The family was evicted two years later for failure to repay the loan. Besides the birthplace, you can see a small memorial chapel and pick up the map for a local driving tour that takes you past other Elvis shrines, such as Tupelo Hardware, where his mother bought him his first guitar for $12.98. Some Tupelo relatives say that Elvis really wanted a BB rifle instead. Allow one to two hours.

306 Elvis Presley Dr. (Exit US 78 at Elvis Presley Drive, and follow the signs.) ☎ **662-841-1245.** https://elvispresleybirthplace.com. *RV parking: Small parking lot; adequate street parking. Admission: Combination house and museum ticket $18 adults, $8 children 7–17, free 6 and under. Open: Mon–Sat 9 a.m.–5 p.m., Sun 1–5 p.m. Closed Thanksgiving and Christmas Day.*

Mississippi Agriculture and Forestry Museum
Jackson, Mississippi

Far more fun than it sounds, this sprawling complex includes a 1920s rural Mississippi town, complete with craftsmen and shopkeepers, and a working farm (moved here in its entirety from southern Mississippi) that includes several Mississippi mules, a breed famous for stubbornness. Kids enjoy wandering about the area, experiencing "the olden days," and ending up at a general store that sells cold soft drinks and a staple of Southern snack fare: the Moon Pie.

Inside the main building is a well-arranged historical museum, and in separate buildings around the complex are the Mississippi Crafts Guild display area and shop; the museum café; and the National Agricultural Aviation Museum and Hall of Fame, saluting crop dusters. All these facilities can be entered on the same ticket. The adjacent Mississippi Sports Hall of Fame and Museum (see the next listing) requires a separate admission ticket. Allow three hours.

1150 Lakeland Dr. (Take Exit 98B from I-55.) ☎ **800-844-8687** *or 601-432-4500.* www.mdac.state.ms.us/n_library/departments/ ag_museum/index_agmuseum.htm. *RV parking: Large parking lot. Admission: $5 adults, $4 seniors and military, $4 children 3–18, ages 2 and under free. Open: Memorial Day–Labor Day Mon–Sat 9 a.m.–5 p.m. Closed major holidays.*

Mississippi Sports Hall of Fame and Museum
Jackson, Mississippi

This museum salutes sports heroes of Mississippi and automatically makes every fan, young and old, who enters a hero too. With interactive machines, visitors can play golf, check the speed and impact of their baseball pitch, or take penalty kicks against a soccer goalie. A mockup press box lets wannabe sports announcers call the play-by-play for a game, and the locker room displays uniforms and equipment that famous players have used. A special second-floor museum salutes Mississippi baseball great Dizzy Dean, and touchscreen kiosks let visitors look up archival sports information and interviews. Allow three hours.

1152 Lakeland Dr. (Take Exit 98B or 98C off I-55 to Cool Papa Bell Drive.) ☎ ***800-280-3263*** *or 601-982-8264.* `https://msfame.com`*. RV parking: Large parking lot adjacent. Admission: $5 adults, $3.50 seniors, $3 students 6–17, free 5 and under. Open: Mon–Sat 10 a.m.–4 p.m.*

Vicksburg National Military Park
Vicksburg, Mississippi

The battlefield commemorates one of the most decisive battles of the Civil War. General Ulysses S. Grant and 50,000 men held the city under siege for 47 days. The national cemetery contains the graves of some 17,000 Union soldiers. A 16-mile auto tour around the park passes markers, monuments, and re-created breastworks. In the museum, you can see the gunboat *Cairo,* which was pulled up from the Yazoo River 100 years after it sank in 1862.

3201 Clay St. ☎ ***601-636-0583.*** `https://www.nps.gov/vick`*. RV parking: Visitor lot at center; turnouts along Park Road. Admission: $15 per motor vehicle. Open: Park daily dawn–dusk, visitor center daily 8 a.m.–5 p.m.*

More Cool Things to See and Do

Culturally rich and sometimes quirky attractions line the Natchez Trace from antebellum ruins to a coon-dog cemetery and the hometown of a well-known TV diva.

BARGAIN ALERT

» **Swig down a cheap Coca-Cola.** You can see the original bottling machinery from the world's first Coca-Cola bottling plant, used from 1894 to 1924 in Vicksburg at **Biedenharn Coca-Cola Company Museum,** 1107 Washington St. (☎ 601-638-6514; `www.biedenharncoca-colamuseum.com`). Allow one hour.

RV parking is available on the street. Admission is $3.50 for adults, $2 for kids 6 to 12, and free for kids 5 and under. The museum is open Monday through Saturday from 9 a.m. to 5 p.m. and Sunday 1:30 to 4:30 p.m.

» **Meet Helen Keller. Ivy Green,** 300 W. North Commons, Tuscumbia, Alabama (☎ **256-383-4066;** www.helenkellerbirthplace.org), the birthplace and childhood home of Helen Keller, a lecturer and essayist who lost her sight and hearing at 19 months of age, has been restored to the way it looked during her childhood. A production of *The Miracle Worker,* depicting how she overcame her handicaps, is presented here every summer. In the backyard is the famous water pump where the child first made the connection with language. Allow two hours.

To get there from US 72, follow Woodmount Drive to North Commons street West. RV parking is available in a large parking lot and on the street. Admission is $6 for adults, $5 for seniors, and $2 for kids 5 to 18. It's open Monday through Saturday from 8:30 a.m. to 4 p.m., and closed Sunday and major holidays.

TIP

» **Howl with the hounds. Key Underwood Coon Dog Memorial Graveyard** (☎ **800-344-0783** or 256-383-0783; https://www.colbertcountytourism.org) is the only cemetery in the world dedicated to the raccoon-hunting hound. More than 160 champions are buried here, some with elaborately carved granite tombstones such as that of Doctor Doom, listing his awards. Others have simple wooden markers with handwritten sentiments such as "He wasn't the best coon dog there ever was, but he was the best I ever had." Allow at least 30 minutes.

To get there from Tuscumbia, Alabama, take US 72 west for 7 miles, go left on CR 247 for about 12 miles, turn right at the sign, and follow the signs to park. For information, call Tuscumbia Tourism Bureau. RV parking is plentiful. Admission is free. The graveyard is open 24 hours.

» **Tune into a TV network diva.** The little town named **Kosciusko,** named for a Polish general in the American Revolutionary War, was the birthplace and early-childhood home of **Oprah Winfrey.** A road named for her goes past her first church, her family cemetery, and her birthplace. Allow one hour.

For information, contact the Kosciusko Altala Development Corp., 124 N. Jackson St. (☎ 662-289-2981; www.kadcorp.org). RV parking is available on the street. Admission is free. The roadway is always open.

» **Sing the blues and all that jazz.** Florence, Alabama, is home of the **W. C. Handy Birthplace, Museum and Library,** 620 W. College St. (☎ 256-760-6434; www.alabamamuseums.org). The blues genius, a trained musician with his own brass band, wrote a campaign song for Memphis political boss Edward R. Crump that introduced jazz breaks into a composed piece for the first time. Retitled "Memphis Blues," it's the first composition recognized as jazz. Allow two hours.

The facility in downtown Florence is just off US 72. RV parking is available on the street. Admission is $5 for adults and $4 for children under 17. Open Tuesday through Saturday from 10 a.m. to 4 p.m.

» **Revisit *Gone with the Wind*.** The 23 Corinthian columns are all that's left of a formerly grand Greek Revival mansion, now the **Windsor ruins,** on Rodney Road in Port Gibson, Mississippi. The mansion still evokes the ghost of the antebellum South. It survived the Civil War but succumbed to a fire in 1890 caused by a cigarette, a newly fashionable way to use tobacco at that time. Allow 30 minutes; photographers may want more time.

To get there, take US 61 south from Port Gibson, turn right on SR 552, and follow the signs. There's plenty of open area at the site for RV parking, but a short, narrow dirt road with bushes leads to it. Admission is free. It's open from dawn to dusk.

Our Favorite Campgrounds

The Natchez Trace provides plentiful overnight camping all along the route, either directly on the parkway or a few miles off on a side road. Few public campgrounds accept reservations, so if you're making the trip during a busy season, such as spring, plan to stop earlier in the day than usual to be sure that you'll have an overnight spot, or reserve a day or two in advance at privately owned campgrounds near the parkway.

The same convenience isn't true for eating on the road, so you'll be happy to have a stocked refrigerator and your own kitchen. Even where a town is near the parkway, special treats may not await; in some small communities in Mississippi, even fast-food places are hard to find. A grocery store or small-town drugstore may be the only place to find something already prepared for lunch. To help you find tasty food to eat in or take out, I guide you to some simple, homey places in the "Good Eats" section later in this chapter.

All campgrounds in this section are open year-round and have public flush toilets, showers, and sanitary dump stations unless designated otherwise. Toll-free numbers, where listed, are for reservations only.

David Crockett State Park

$$ Lawrenceburg, Tennessee

Davy Crockett lived in this area, and his cabin and a museum are open free of charge in town. At the 987-acre park, you find a water-powered gristmill and an interpretive center that reveals Crockett's interest in water-powered machinery. Sites are paved but fairly narrow, and some hookups are side by side.

Off US 64. At 1400 West Gaines Lawrenceburg, TN 38464. (From junction of US 45 and US 64, go west 1½ miles on 64 to the campground, on the right.) ☎ **931-762-9408.** https://www.tn.gov/environment/parks/DavidCrockettSP. *Total 107 sites with water and 30-amp electric, no full hookups, no pull-throughs. Handicap access, pool. Rates: $11–$35 per site plus $5 rec. fee. DISC, MC, V. No reservations.*

Nashville/Opryland KOA

KID FRIENDLY

$$$–$$$$$ Nashville, Tennessee

This well-run, conveniently located park is popular with Nashville visitors. A concierge arranges tickets and transportation for shows and events, and a coordinator offers daily tours. Another bonus is free live entertainment in the park's own theater from May through October. A branch of the Cock of the Walk catfish restaurant (see "Good Eats" later in this chapter) is next door, and within walking distance are other eateries, the Opryland

Hotel, and Opryland-area attractions. Playgrounds, pool, and entertainment give kids plenty to do.

2626 Music Valley Dr. (From junction of I-65 and Briley Parkway, take Exit 90B south or Exit 90 north, go south 4½ miles on Briley to McGavock Park, west ¼ mile to Music Valley Drive, and north 2 miles to the campground, on the left.) ☎ **800-562-7789** *or 615-889-0286.* https://koa.com. *Total 198 sites with water and 30- and 50-amp electric, 158 full hookups, 108 pull-throughs. Data port, handicap access, laundry, pool. Rates: Call ahead for seasonal site rates. AE, DISC, MC, V.*

Tishomingo State Park
$$ Tishomingo, Mississippi

The Civilian Conservation Corps (CCC) built this park in the 1930s, using rock quarried on-site. Over Bear Creek, note the swinging bridge, which dates from those days. Sites are paved and mostly shaded. Haynes Lake provides freshwater fishing and boating; a ramp, dock, and boat rentals are available. A fishing license is required; the state tourism board can tell you how to get one. (See "Fast Facts" at the end of this chapter, for the board's contact info.)

Off CR 90. (From junction of Natchez Trace Parkway and SR 25, go north ½ mile on 25 to park road [CR 90] and then east 1¾ miles to the campground.) ☎ **662-438-6914.** https://mississippi stateparks.reserveamerica.com. *Total 62 sites with water and 30- and 50-amp electric, no full hookups, no pull-throughs. Rates: $28–$45 per site. MC, V, checks, cash. 14-day maximum stay.*

Tombigbee State Park
$$ Tupelo, Mississippi

At this state park, you're near the Elvis birthplace and the famous battlefield, if you want to go sightseeing. The campground provides medium-size paved sites with patios, some with shade, as well as freshwater fishing, boating, a ramp, a dock, and boat rentals on Lake Lee.

Off Veterans Boulevard. (From the Natchez Trace, take SR 6 to Veterans Boulevard, drive southeast 3½ miles to park access road, and follow signs east 3 miles to the campground, on the right.) ☎ **662-842-7669.** `https://mississippistateparks.reserveamerica.com`. *Total 20 sites with water and 20- and 30-amp electric, 18 full hookups, no pull-throughs. Rates: Call for current rates and availability. MC, V.*

Trace State Park

$$–$$$ Pontotoc, Mississippi

BARGAIN ALERT

Large sites, most of them shaded and paved, are conveniently located near Tupelo and the Natchez Trace. Freshwater fishing, boating, boat ramp, dock, and boat rentals are available for would-be sailors. Elvis fans can drive into Tupelo instead to look at The Birthplace.

Off Faulkner Road. (From the Natchez Trace, take SR 6 west of Tupelo, drive 8 miles southwest to Faulkner Road, and go northwest 2¼ miles to the campground, on the left.) ☎ **662-489-2958.** `https://mississippistateparks.reserveamerica.com`. *Total 76 sites with full hookups with water and 30- and 50-amp electric, 3 pull-throughs. Reservations are recommended and can be made 24 months in advance. Rates: Call for seasonal site rates. MC, V.*

Good Eats

You find plenty of vegetables in this part of the world, but don't expect them to be cooked al dente. Southern vegetables are cooked until very well done as a rule and made tastier by the addition of seasonings such as butter, bacon fat, pot juices, and even sugar. Don't expect to find fresh herbs and olive oil or a judicious sprinkle of balsamic vinegar, but if you're willing to be open-minded, you may find some unfamiliar side dishes that please you. Particularly if you've never had them before, take a walk on the wild side and order fried green tomatoes, corn pudding, collard or turnip greens, yams, hominy, black–eyed peas or field peas, okra, squash, lima beans, or green beans (often called snap beans) cooked in water with a little chopped bacon or bacon fat until tender and succulent.

TIP

You always can find a wedge of lemon to squeeze over everything because lemon is an essential accessory in this land of sweetened iced tea. In the south sweet tea is the default here; if you don't want sugar, ask for unsweetened tea. When ordering tea at breakfast, be sure to specify *hot* tea! Don't ask for a soda; carbonated drinks are commonly called pop or soda pop in the Southern states.

SOUTHERN COOKING, STATE BY STATE

In northwestern Alabama, breakfasts can be feasts of grits, ham, biscuits, sausage, eggs, and gravy. Fried chicken stars at lunch and dinner (the former sometimes called dinner and the latter supper in the rural South), and you may run across dessert curiosities very much worth trying, such as Coca-Cola cake and mile-high meringue pies.

Mississippi cuisine is high on fried catfish — hardly unusual, as the state turns out 70 percent of all the catfish farmed in the United States. In fact, the catfish capital of the world is Belzoni, a few miles west of the Natchez Trace. Fried fish of all sorts usually is served with hush puppies (deep-fried balls of cornbread seasoned with onions) and sometimes hot tamales. The hot tamales are a mystery; nobody is sure where they originated, but most Mississippi restaurants, especially in the Delta, serve them as appetizers or side dishes. Rolled in parchment paper rather than cornhusks and ordered by the half-dozen or dozen, Mississippi hot tamales are smaller and a bit spicier than the typical Mexican version.

Down-home Tennessee restaurants around Nashville serve *meat-and-three*, which is your choice of meat and three side dishes (usually, vegetables). Country ham on a Southern menu, especially in Tennessee, describes a smoked or dry-cured ham that spends weeks in a bed of salt and turns out as a salty, densely textured, and intensely flavored meat that can be sliced and fried for breakfast or boiled whole, baked, and served cold in paper-thin slices. Don't miss Nashville's famous Goo Goo Cluster candy bars: peanuts, chocolate, marshmallow, and caramel.

Hot breads, usually biscuits and/or cornbread, are the general rule as well. By the way, unlike the cornbread and corn muffins in other parts of the United States, Southern cornbread rarely has sugar added. You won't find hot breads at barbecue joints; there, multiple slices of soft white bread straight from the grocery–store package come as a side dish.

TIP

Servings are large in this part of the country; one takeout meal often is enough for two. If the meal looks skimpy when you open the takeout box, add a homemade green salad or a dessert.

The following restaurants and food suppliers are popular favorites for regional cooking at moderate prices. Many require cash rather than credit cards, and most don't serve beer or wine with meals. Even when dining out in fancy restaurants, many Southerners drink iced tea, cola, hot coffee, or even a cocktail with meals.

BARGAIN
ALERT

» **Carl's Perfect Pig,** 4972 US 70, White Bluff, Tennessee (☎ **615-797-4020**): A pretty pink barbecue joint by the side of the road serves pulled or chopped sandwiches from pork shoulders that have been slow-cooked on a bed of hickory coals for 24 hours and steeped in a vinegar sauce overnight. Open Wednesday and Thursday from 10:30 a.m. to 5:45 p.m., Friday and Saturday from 10:30 a.m. to 7 p.m., and from Sunday 10:30 a.m. to 2:30 p.m.

» **Cock of the Walk,** 2624 Music Valley Dr., Nashville, Tennessee (☎ **615-889-1930**): An easy stroll from the Opryland KOA campground, this popular casual eatery provides sit-down and take-out service, and the latter, with its own order window, is much quicker. The fried catfish is delectable, and so are the fried shrimp and a sampler dinner that adds fried chicken. Side dishes include fried dill pickles (don't laugh 'til you taste them), fried onions, and a cooking pot of beans or greens. Cocktails, beer, and wine also are served. Open Monday through Thursday from 4 p.m. to 8:30 p.m., Friday from 4 p.m. to 9 p.m., Saturday from 11 a.m. to 9 p.m., and Sunday from 11 a.m. to 8:30 p.m.

» **Loveless Motel and Cafe,** 8400 SR 100, Nashville, Tennessee, about 10 miles southwest of town (☎ **615-646-9700;** www. lovelesscafe.com): A motel by the side of the road with a neon sign that says LOVELESS in pink and green serves fantastic breakfasts: country ham, grits, gravy, eggs, homemade biscuits, and homemade jams and jellies. Lunches and dinners are great too, with meals built around country ham or fried chicken. (Get one of each and trade tastes.) The same generous servings of hot biscuits, butter, and homemade jams come with every meal, and the cafe sells jars of jam to go. Open daily from 7 a.m. to 9 p.m.

BARGAIN ALERT

» **Rocking Chair Restaurant,** 814 US 72 West, Tuscumbia, Alabama (☎ **256-381-6105**): The Sunday-lunch turkey special comes with mashed potatoes and green beans; a four-vegetable plate is crowded with black-eyed peas, candied yams, white beans with ham, fried okra, and hot biscuits and cornbread. The whole thing costs less than $10. Open Monday through Thursday from 9 a.m. to 9 p.m., and Friday through Sunday from 9 a.m. to 5 p.m.

» **Walnut Hills,** 1214 Adams St., Vicksburg, Mississippi (☎ **601-638-4910**): This restaurant is famous for its Southern fried chicken, ribs, smothered pork chops, stuffed peppers with Creole sauce, rice and gravy, green beans with potatoes, lima beans, fresh-field peas, yellow squash with onions, glazed carrots, coleslaw, corn muffins, iced tea, and blueberry cobbler. Open Monday, Wednesday, Thursday, and Friday from 11 a.m. to 8:30 p.m., Saturday from 11 a.m. to 8 p.m., and Sunday from 11 a.m. to 2 p.m. Closed Tuesday.

Shopping along the Way

Mississippi Crafts Center, 950 Rice Road, Ridgeland, Mississippi (☎ 601-856-7546; www.mscraftsmensguild.org), sells handicrafts created by local artists and craftsmen, including weavers from the local Choctaw and Chickasaw people. Items are attractively arranged in this unpainted mountain cottage. Standouts include quiltwork handbags, pottery, Choctaw baskets, and books about the region. Prices range from affordable to expensive. The center is open Monday through Saturday from 9 a.m. to 5 p.m. and Sunday from noon to 5 p.m. To get here, take exit 105A from Trace Road to Ridgeland.

Fast Facts

Area Code
The following area codes are in effect along the Natchez Trace: in Alabama, 251; in Tennessee, 931, 615, and 256; and in Mississippi, 601 and 662.

Driving Laws
In Alabama, Mississippi, and Tennessee, riders in the front seats must wear seat belts. The maximum speed limit on interstate highways in Alabama, Mississippi, and Tennessee is 70 mph. Speed limits in urban areas are lower.

Emergency
Call ☎ 911. Cellphone users can dial ☎ *847 in Tennessee.

Hospitals
Major hospitals along the route are in Vicksburg, Mississippi; Jackson, Mississippi; and Nashville, Tennessee.

Information
Helpful sources in the individual states include the Alabama Tourism Department (☎ 800-252-2262; https://tourism.alabama.gov/group-and-international-travel/); Mississippi Division of Tourism (☎ 800-927-6378; https://visitmississippi.org); and in Tennessee, the Department of Tourist Development (☎ 615-741-8299; https://www.tnvacation.com). For information on fishing licenses in Mississippi, call ☎ 800-546-4868 or 601-362-9212.

Road and Weather Conditions
Contact numbers include ☎ 601-987-1211 for the Highway Patrol in Mississippi; ☎ 800-858-6349 for road construction (https://www.fhwa.dot.gov/trafficinfo/ms.htm), and ☎ 800-342-3258 for weather conditions in Tennessee (https://www.fhwa.dot.gov/trafficinfo/tn.htm). In Alabama, dial 511 from your cellphone or visit (https://www.dot.state.al.us/).

Taxes
Alabama state sales tax is 4 percent; local taxes can raise it to 11 percent. Mississippi state sales tax is 7 percent but rises to 8 percent in some municipalities. Tennessee state sales tax is 7 percent; local taxes can raise it to 9.75 percent.

State gasoline taxes are as follows: Alabama, 21.91 cents per gallon; Mississippi, 18.4 cents per gallon; and Tennessee, 27 cents per gallon.

Time Zone
Alabama, Mississippi, and western Tennessee are on Central time.

4

Discovering Mid-America

IN THIS PART . . .

Checking out the Blooms and Briskets in Texas Hill Country

Seeing Ohio sports teams, rock and roll, country meals, and zoos

Finding the fabled Paul Bunyan in Minnesota

Taking a circle drive around the largest body of fresh water in North America.

Riding to discover mountains, down-home foods, and country music in the Ozarks

Chapter **13**
Texas Hill Country: Bluebonnets and Barbecue

The heart of Texas is hardscrabble country, pink and gray granite and white limestone, Longhorn cattle ranges, and flood-washed gullies. Yet the tough terrain has a soft heart. As the singing cowboy said, the stars at night are big and bright and the sage is like perfume. In springtime, the hills are blanketed with wildflowers: bluebonnets, scarlet Indian paintbrush, buttercups, and poppies as thick as those that put Judy Garland and her companions to sleep in *The Wizard of Oz.*

The Texas Hill Country is full of surprises, such as San Antonio, where every day brings an opportunity for a celebration and the barbecue is a billion times tastier than those chain-restaurant ribs coated with thick, sweet, red sauce from a bottle. Austin has rock-'n'-roll and country-music ties to Janis Joplin and Lyle Lovett. Luckenbach is where Willie Nelson would hang out. Find cool jazz spots along San Antonio's River Walk, and bratwurst and beer gardens in Fredericksburg.

Texas is also is one of the most RV-friendly states, with plenty of campgrounds parks, great bargain-priced takeout food, and well-paved roads. What are you waiting for? Yeehaw! Let's hit the road!

Choosing Your Route

San Antonio is an excellent starting point for a circle tour of Texas Hill Country. From here, you drive northeast 30 miles on I-35 to New Braunfels, a prominent community settled by Germans; strike out on back roads east to Luling and Lockhart, center of barbecue country; and head north to the colorful old town of Bastrop and the hot-sausage capital of Elgin. Then drive north to Taylor for more barbecue and roses, west to the Texas capital of Austin, and due west to Johnson City and Fredericksburg on US 290. Go north to Llano on SR 16, a scenic back road, and west to Mason through bluebonnet fields on SR 29. Turn southwest to Junction and make a loop back into San Antonio on I-10 through Kerrville. The route is 400 miles plus a few side-road detours.

TIP

If you're going to be in the area and want to make a quick trip around the Texas Hill Country in a couple of days, you can do so if you cut out a couple of small towns and many of the barbecue joints. Begin in San Antonio, as the main driving tour does; take a quick look at the Alamo and River Walk; and then head north to New Braunfels for a stop at the Smokehouse for some smoked meats. From there, strike out on CR 12 North to its junction with CR 697, go east to Driftwood, and stop at the Salt Lick for a barbecue lunch or dinner. Continue north to rejoin US 290 at Dripping Springs, and turn west for Johnson City, visit the Lyndon B. Johnson National and State Parks there and in Stonewall. Drive into Fredericksburg; look at the Admiral Nimitz Museum; have a German meal; and follow US 87 to rejoin I-35 at Comfort, for a little antiquing, if time allows. Then follow I-35 back into San Antonio.

BLUEBONNETS IN BLOOM

The first time you see a field of bluebonnets *(Lupinus texensis)*, you probably won't believe your eyes. This isn't a little cluster or a photogenic patch, but a blue carpet of countless bluebonnets in every direction.

In a good spring, you witness one floral spectacle after another, each more magnificent than the previous. Sometimes, splashy red Indian paintbrush kicks in; at other times, you see lavender verbena or what the Texans call yellow buttercups, that look a lot like black-eyed Susans. Herds of Texas Longhorns graze among the flowers.

You can see bluebonnets between West Texas and central Texas, around Sonora and Junction, in the Hill Country around Austin, and from there almost to the Louisiana border. Some good wildflower-spotting areas are US 377 from Junction on I-10 east to Mason and then east along SR 29 to Llano. In the same vicinity, the Highland Lakes Bluebonnet Trail meanders from Austin north along FM (farm-to-market road) 1431 past human-made lakes and small wineries, and through the little towns of Marble Falls, Burnet, Buchanan Dam, Kingsland, and Llano. Some stretches are narrow, so if you're driving or towing a large RV, check road conditions locally.

Planning Ahead

The best time to go is spring, when the wildflowers are at their peak — and from the end of March through April and into early May, depending on winter rainfall and spring weather. To get information on the best times and areas in Texas for maximum bloom visit https://www.facebook.com/texaswildflowerreport.

You can enjoy an RV vacation in the Texas Hill Country year-round. Winters are mild; summers are warm to hot but not sweltering; and fall is perfect, except that the wildflowers are no longer at their peak.

TIP

When bluebonnets are in bloom, any Texan with a motor vehicle heads for the Hill Country for a leisurely drive along the best wildflower routes, especially on Saturdays and Sundays. RVers often drive the scenic routes on weekdays and then spend weekends in and around San Antonio and Austin when urban dwellers have gone to the country.

Pack light, cotton clothes for summer, along with some safari pants and long-sleeved jackets for hikes. Spring brings showers, so prepare by bringing umbrellas and raincoats. Winter is chilly on overcast days; bring a jacket or sweater and pack so you can layer your clothing.

Allow a week for a leisurely drive around the Hill Country; add more time if you want to spend more than a day in San Antonio or Austin.

Must-See Attractions

Admiral Nimitz Museum & Historical Center and the National Museum of the Pacific War

Fredericksburg

This monument to this World War II admiral is more than military history; the Nimitz family was among the German settlers in the area, and the museum is housed in the restored Nimitz Steamboat Hotel, owned by the family and is the admiral's birthplace. Film clips, interactive exhibits, and displays indoors and out make this museum a trip through time. An expansion of the original museum added the Museum of the Pacific War. Allow three hours.

304 E. Main St. ☎ 830-997-4379. https://www.pacificwarmuseum.org/. RV parking: Park on side streets around the museum. Admission: $15 adults, $12 seniors, military $10, $7 students, free kids 5 and under. Open: Gardens daily 8 a.m.–4:45 p.m., museum daily 9 a.m.–5 p.m. Museum of the Pacific War, same admission prices as Nimitz.

The Alamo
San Antonio

If all you remember about the Alamo comes from movie of the same name, filmed on a special set constructed down on the Rio Grande near the border, you may be startled to see that the real thing is in the middle of San Antonio. A high-rise hotel and office buildings dwarf the Franciscan mission that was the site of that bloody battle between Mexicans and Texans in 1836. The museum relates the story. In front of the Alamo, note the cenotaph, that lists the men who died in the battle. The facade of the chapel is one of the most-photographed spots in the nation. Allow three hours.

300 Alamo Square. ☎ 210-225-1391. https://www.thealamo.org. *RV parking: Some nearby public parking lots can handle RVs. Admission: Free. Open: Mon–Sat 9 a.m.–5:30 p.m., Sun 10 a.m.–5:30 p.m. Closed Christmas Eve and Christmas Day; limited hours Mar 6 (the anniversary of the fall of the Alamo).*

KID FRIENDLY

Institute of Texas Cultures
San Antonio

This museum really comes to life on weekdays during the school year, when busloads of children listen to museum docents explaining the history and traditions of some 25 ethnic groups that settled Texas. Meanwhile, a fiddler plays "Irish Washerwoman" and talks about Irish settlers in one area; in another, a man near a chuckwagon discusses trail cuisine and cooking. Allow up to four hours.

Hemis Fair Park, 801 E. Durango Blvd. ☎ 210-458-2300. http://www.texancultures.com/. *RV parking: Large parking lots in the area; watch for RV- and bus-parking signs. Admission: $10 adults, $8 seniors, $8 military, $6 kids 6–17, free 5 and under. Open: Mon–Sat 9 a.m.–5 p.m., Sun noon to 5 p.m. Free for all every second Sun.*

Lyndon B. Johnson National Historical Park
Johnson City

The boyhood home of the 36th president reflects his early life and comfortable, if sometimes accident-prone, childhood. Gain insights at the visitor center and then walk down into the Johnson Settlement, where LBJ's grandparents and other relatives lived. Allow three hours.

On US 290 just outside Johnson City. ☎ 830-868-7128. https://www.nps.gov/lyjo/index.htm. *RV parking: Street parking in the area. Admission: Free. Open: Visitor center daily 8:45 a.m.–5 p.m., Johnson Settlement daily 9 a.m. to sunset. Closed New Year's Day, Thanksgiving, and Christmas Day.*

Lyndon B. Johnson National and State Historical Parks
Stonewall

The larger part of the divided national park is in Stonewall, 14 miles west of Johnson City and 16 miles east of Fredericksburg. Go first to the visitor center, where you can take an air-conditioned tour bus through the famous LBJ Ranch, the late president's pride and joy. (This tour is the only way visitors can enter the ranch itself.) Depending on the bus schedule (tours are 90 minutes), take a walk through the Sauer-Beckmann Living History Farm, next to the visitor center. You see a herd of Longhorns, and at the farm, women in long cotton dresses and sunbonnets boil wash in a big iron pot outdoors, clabber milk to make cottage cheese, churn butter, and preserve ham and bacon.

Located on US 290 just east of Stonewall. ☎ 830-868-7128. https://www.nps.gov/lyjo/index.htm. *RV parking: Large parking lot adjacent to visitor center. Admission: Parks free tours are $3 for all. Open: Visitor center daily 8 a.m.–5 p.m., Sauer-Beckmann Living History Farm daily 9 a.m.–4:30 p.m., LBJ Ranch bus tours daily 10 a.m.–4 p.m. Closed New Year's Day, Thanksgiving, and Christmas Day.*

El Mercado

San Antonio

A commercial Mexican-themed market, El Mercado is fun for strolling but better for eating a hearty, inexpensive Tex-Mex meal in one of the outdoor cafes, which make good spots for margarita-sipping and music-listening too. You can shop for typical Texan and Mexican souvenirs. Allow one hour for looking around; add more for a meal or margarita stop.

514 West Commerce St. ☎ 800-843-2526 or 210-207-8600. https://www.visitsanantonio.com. RV parking: In a parking lot located under the I-35 freeway overpass 1 block west of El Mercado on Dolorosa Street. Admission: Free. Open: June–Aug daily 10 a.m.–7 p.m.; Sept–May daily 10 a.m.–6 p.m. Closed New Year's Day, Easter, Thanksgiving, and Christmas Day, but some restaurants may be open during holidays.

River Walk

San Antonio

An already-delightful city multiplied the fun back in 1939 by creating River Walk, a meandering walkway one level below the downtown streets on the edge of the San Antonio River. River Walk is the city's beating heart and the pulse of its party mood. The sidewalk wends its sun-dappled way through downtown a few stairsteps below traffic in a pedestrian-scale world of sidewalk cafes, paddleboats, sightseeing barges, and morning-through-midnight street life. In one trip, you may walk by musicians playing Dixieland and Cajun music or by an Irish tenor singing "Danny Boy." Don't leave San Antonio without taking a stroll here day or night, or both!

Entrance access from city streets including South Alamo, Lojoya, Presa, Navarro, St. Mary's, Market, Commerce, and Crockett. ☎ 210-226-6256. https://www.thesanantonioriverwalk.com. RV parking: Parking lots are at Commerce Street near the Convention Center and at the Southwest Craft Center, 300 Augusta St., near Navarro; you can park your RV in the lot near El Mercado and walk the 6 blocks of Commerce or Dolorosa to River Walk. Admission: Free for strolling. Open: Walkway always open; restaurants and bars operate late morning until late evening; shop hours vary.

More Cool Things to See and Do

Attractions include Enchanted Rock to a collection of circus artifacts and miniatures fill the Texas Hill Country. The San Antonio Zoo is world-famous for its breeding-in-captivity program, and the Buckhorn Hall of Horns, Fins, and Feathers is good for a surprise or two.

» **Go batty in Austin.** In summer, sunset is the time to see the **bats of Congress Avenue Bridge,** the nation's largest urban colony. They fly from under the bridge in search of their evening meals — 20,000 pounds of insects. These bats are in residence from late March to the end of October. Watch from the bridge. Allow 5 to 15 minutes for the bats' exit after they start. Take pictures after a few minutes of flight. Find out more about the species at http://www.batcon.org/our-work/regions/usa-canada/protect-mega-populations/cab-intro?highlight=WyJhdXN0aW4iXQ==.

» **Fish got to swim, birds got to fly.** Located in a century-old saloon, the zany **Buckhorn Hall of Horns, Fins, and Feathers,** in the Texas Ranger Building, 318 E. Houston St., San Antonio (☎ **210-247-4000;** www.buckhornmuseum.com), has 4,000 exhibits, including Ol' Tex, a stuffed Longhorn with an 8-foot, 9-inch spread of horns. Allow one to two hours.

RV parking is available in a small parking lot adjacent to the museum, as well as on the street. Admission is $19.99 for adults and $14.99 for kids 17 and under. Open daily from 10 a.m. to 7 p.m.

» **Like a rock.** Rock-climbing, hiking, and picnicking are great at **Enchanted Rock State Natural Area,** 18 miles north of Fredericksburg, off FM 965 (☎ **830-685-3636;** https://tpwd.texas.gov/state-parks/enchanted-rock), but unfortunately, the rest of the world already has discovered it, so restrictions are plentiful. During heavy-use periods, the park closes for the day when the maximum number of visitors is reached. Local tribes venerated the rock, which is a National Natural Landmark. Allow a half-day to a full day if you're able to get in.

RV parking is available in a large lot below the office. Admission is $6 for adults and free for children 12 and under. It's open daily from 8 a.m. to 10 p.m.; the office closes at 9 p.m. No RV over-nighting is allowed.

TIP

» **Giddy up! Did you bring the champagne?** The most romantic way to see Austin is to book a horse-drawn carriage for a tour of downtown. Call **Austin Carriage Service** (☎ **512-243-0044**), which charges $50 per half-hour for up to six people.

» **This Bud's for Hondo.** The late Hondo Crouch, Texas writer and all-round character, purchased the tiny town of **Luckenbach** (https://www.luckenbachtexas.com), which was made famous in a song by Willie Nelson and Waylon Jennings. It's busiest on Sunday afternoons, when many people show up with guitars and drink longneck bottles of Shiner Bock beer to live out the song's lyric "in Luckenbach, Texas, ain't nobody feelin' no pain." You can hoist one at the Feed Lot (☎ **830-997-3224**) from 9 a.m. to 11:30 p.m.

From Fredericksburg, drive east on US 290 for 6 miles; turn south on FM 1376; continue another 4 miles; and then take the second left, where the sign (if it's there) says *Luckenbach Road.*

» **A Sunday kind of house.** The local historical society created the **Pioneer Museum Complex,** 325 W. Main St., Fredericksburg (☎ **830-990-8441;** www.pioneermuseum.com), a replica of old Fredericksburg, with an eight-room furnished home and store from 1849, a wine cellar and brewery, barn, blacksmith shop, Sunday house, log cabin, and fire museum with old equipment. Allow two hours.

RV parking is available on the street. Admission is $7.50 for adults, $3 for children 6 to 17, and free for children 5 and under. It's open Monday through Saturday from 10 a.m. to 5 p.m. and Thursdays in October and November from 10 a.m. to 4:30 p.m.

KID
FRIENDLY

» **It's a jungle out there.** One of the best zoos in America, the **San Antonio Zoo,** 3903 N. St. Mary's, at Brackenridge Park, San Antonio (☎ **210-734-7184;** www.sazoo-aq.org), is noted for its success with breeding in captivity and its sanctuaries for endangered species, such as snow leopards, cranes, and rhinos. The exhibits gives kids a chance to see exotic animals. Allow a half-day.

RV parking is available at the zoo under US 281. Admission is $18.99 for adults, $16.90 ages 12 to 17, $15.99 for ages 3 to 11, and free children 2 and under. Open daily from 9 a.m. to 5 p.m.

Our Favorite Campgrounds

Texas is an RV-friendly state, so you find plenty of privately owned and state-owned campgrounds, all with hookups. As for good eats, they're inescapable in this land of barbecue and Mexican restaurants. Because the Texans themselves are big-time RVers, you want to make campground reservations whenever possible, especially for spring weekends when the bluebonnets are blooming. During the heat of summer, campgrounds are less crowded than in the spring (spring break is very busy) or fall, when the summer weather cools down. In the middle of summer, Texas is hot, topping 100°F on occasion. In the winter, weather is mild, and campgrounds aren't crowded.

All campgrounds listed in this chapter are open year-round and have public toilets, showers, and sanitary dump stations unless designated otherwise. Toll-free numbers, where listed, are for reservations only.

Fredericksburg KOA

$$$–$$$$ Fredericksburg

At a junction in the road not far from Luckenbach, this comfortable campground is convenient to the attractions of Fredericksburg and to the LBJ Ranch and parks.

5681 US 290 E. (5 miles east of Fredericksburg at the junction of US 290 and FM 1376, on the right). ☎ **800-562-0796** *or 830-997-4796.* `https://koa.com`. *Total 84 sites, all full hookups with 30- and 50-amp electric, 65 pull-throughs. Data port, food service, handicap access, laundry, pool, SATV, Wi-Fi. Rates: $46–$59 per site. MC, V. D.*

Junction KOA
$$$$ Junction

Located on the Llano River, this quiet, rural campground offers good deer- and birdwatching, as well as freshwater fishing (with tackle for rent). A restaurant and golf course are nearby.

2145 N. Main St. (Take Exit 456 from I-10 and drive south half a mile to the campground, on right.) ☎ **800-562-7506** *or 325-446-3138.* `https://koa.com`. *Total 52 sites with water and 30- and 50-amp electric, 42 full hookups, 51 pull-throughs. CATV, data port, laundry, pool, Wi-Fi. Rates: $37 and up per site. DISC, MC, V.*

Lone Star RV Resort
$$$$–$$$$$ Austin

Conveniently close to Austin, this Sun RV Resorts park has back-in sites on terraced levels with shade trees and larger pull-through sites on top of the hill with less shade. Car rentals are available.

7009 S. I-35. (Take Exit 227 south or Exit 228 north from I-35; travel north on east frontage road to the campground, on right.) ☎ **800-284-0206** *or 512-444-6322.* `www.austinlonestar.com`. *Total 151 sites with water and 30- and 50-amp electric, 64 full hookups, 64 pull-throughs. CATV, data port, laundry, pool, spa, Wi-Fi. Rates: $133 per site for 4 guests. AE, DISC, MC, V.*

Oakwood RV Resort

$$$–$$$$ Fredericksburg

KID FRIENDLY

Sites in this campground are shaded but narrow. Many activities are available, including golf, shuffleboard, horseshoes, and croquet. Each site has a concrete patio, picnic table, and grill.

78 FM 2093. (From the junction of US 290 and SR 16S, drive 2 miles south on SR 16S, also known as Airport Road and as FM 2093; campground is on the right.) ☎ 800-366-9396 or 830-997-9817. https://oakwoodrvresort.com. *Total 127 sites with water and 30- and 50-amp electric, 125 full hookups, 30 pull-throughs. CATV, data port, laundry, phone jacks, pool, spa. Rates: $37–$57 per site. MC, D, V.*

Pedernales Falls State Park

$$$ Johnson City

Swimming, tubing, hiking, and freshwater fishing are available on the Pedernales River. Sites are wide, with some shaded back-ins.

Off FM 2766. (From US 281/290 in town, take FM 2766 east 9¼ miles; the park is on the left.) ☎ 830-868-7304. https://tpwd.texas.gov/state-parks/pedernales-falls. *Total 66 sites with water and 30-amp electric. No full hookups, no pull-throughs. Rates: Check state website for current rates. DISC, MC, V.*

Good Eats

Regional cooking, takeout, and family restaurants on a side road with long lines of patrons waiting for Sunday dinner in the midday — all these are signs of good-eats establishments. Because the Texas Hill Country is about barbecue, I begin there and then tell you about some equally ethnic places, from Tex-Mex to German.

Barbecue joints

Texans like beef, so the pride of a *pit boss* is slow-cooked cuts of beef brisket. Cooking fuel depends on local supply, with mesquite dominant in the Hill Country and pecan wood as you move east. It can seem that everybody in central Texas has a barbecue establishment. Some of these places don't keep regular hours, but if smoke is coming out of one and you can smell the meat, it's open. If you're going to try only one sample of Texas beef barbecue, make it a slice of dry-rub brisket. Brisket likely started the whole Texas barbecue craze, so give it a try.

The best barbecue joints in Texas are casual places where the clients line up to order their food and then eat it wherever convenient.

Here are a few iconic rules about barbecue places:

>> You may pay more by stopping at a barbecue joint that advertises with billboards on the freeway.

>> When BBQ proprietors sell their own bottled sauce, they may be putting more effort into the sauce.

>> Never try imposing your tastes in barbecue on the proprietor. The reasons he's does the selling and you the buying is that he makes barbecue *his* way.

>> Don't be overwhelmed by the number of side dishes; they take your attention away from the meats.

>> Don't add sauce or seasoning before tasting. The best barbecue stands up to a taste test on its own.

>> Always know what you want before you get in line. Do not stand and ask the server what's good.

TIP

Street and lot parking for RVs is generally easy to find near most barbecue vendors because they're in small towns or residential or industrial areas. Some have their own lots, with room for big RVs.

This list highlights favorite Texas Hill Country barbecue vendors:

» **Black's Barbecue,** 215 N. Main St., Lockhart (☎ **512-398-2712**): Despite a display of tacky roadside signs such as BLACK'S IS OPEN 8 DAYS A WEEK, this establishment turns out wonderful smoked pork loin, tasty enough when hot but delectable cold the next day on sandwiches spread with chipotle-flavored mayonnaise. Open Sunday through Thursday from 10 a.m. to 8 p.m. and Friday and Saturday from 10 a.m. to 8:30 p.m. Closed Thanksgiving and Christmas Day.

» **Dozier's Grocery,** 8222 FM 359, Fulshear (☎ **281-346-1411**): Take Exit 720 from I-10, drive 12 miles south on SR 36 to CR 1093, and then east 5 miles to Fulshear. This rural store dishes up pecan-smoked brisket and sausages, and offers a hearty barbecue sauce. Dozier's sells Bob's Texas-Style Potato Chips, made in Brookshire. Open Monday through Thursday from 9:30 a.m. to 6:30 p.m., Friday and Saturday from 9:30 a.m. to 7 p.m., and Sunday from 10 a.m. to 7 p.m.

» **Hinze's Barbeque & Catering,** 2101 SR 36 S., Sealy (☎ **979-885-7808**): Take Exit 720 from I-10, and drive 1 mile north to Sealy. Pecan wood cooks the barbecued beef brisket and exceptional side dishes of pinto beans, okra gumbo, and onion-bacon potatoes, served cafeteria-style. Open daily from 10:30 a.m. to 9 p.m.

» **Kreuz Market,** 619 N. Colorado St., Lockhart (☎ **512-398-2361;** https://kreuzmarket.com): The ambience is gone now that Kreuz (pronounced *kritz*) has left its older, no-frills location and reopened in a new building, but the flavor of the beef is still great. Sold by the pound. Open Monday through Saturday from 10:30 a.m. to 8 p.m. and Sunday from 10:30 a.m. to 6 p.m.

» **Louie Mueller,** 206 W. Second St., Taylor (☎ **512-352-6206;** https://www.louiemuellerbarbecue.com): This venerated establishment is the anchor business in an ancient block marked by recent newcomers, a café, brewery, and antique shops. Barbecued brisket doesn't get any better than it is here; order the thin add peppery, oniony sauce on the side. Open Monday through Saturday from 11 a.m. to 6 p.m. or until the day's barbecue is sold out — usually, early afternoon to midafternoon. Closed Sunday.

» **The Salt Lick,** 18300 FM 1826, Driftwood (☎ **512-858-4959;** https://saltlickbbq.com): Driftwood is 20 miles southwest of Austin on FM 1826 between FM 967 and FM 150. An old stone ranch house out in the boonies, open since 1969, The Salt Lick is an institution. Open-pit-barbecued brisket, ribs, and sausage — all served with potato salad, coleslaw, beans, pickles, onions, and bread — make up the family-style meal. BYOB in your RV refrigerator. Open daily from 11 a.m. to 10 p.m.

» **Smitty's,** 208 S. Commerce St., Lockhart (☎ **512-398-9344;** http://smittysmarket.com): In the place where Kreuz Market (in Lockhart, in a new location) used to be, the place exudes authenticity and produces perfected barbecued meats. The brisket and the shoulder roast are charred on the outside, and tender on the inside. Open Monday through Friday from 7 a.m. to 6 p.m., Saturday 7 a.m. to 6:30 p.m. Sunday from 7 a.m. to 3 p.m.

» **The Smokehouse,** 3306 Roland Ave., San Antonio (☎ **210-333-9548;** https://www.thesmokehousebbqsa.com/): This place, formerly known as Bob's Smokehouse, is still called that by some people. Take Exit 578 from I-10 and drive south on Roland Avenue (at Rigsby). An unpainted building in southeastern San Antonio is covered with slogans such as BOB KNOWS: BAR-B-Q MUST COME OFF A PIT, NOT FROM UNDER RED LIGHTS. Ribs (pork, beef, and lamb) and brisket top the takeout orders, with double sauce on the side. Open Tuesday through Thursday from 11 a.m. to 5 p.m., Friday and Saturday from 11 a.m. to 7 p.m., and Sunday from noon to 6 p.m. Closed Mondays.

» **Southside Market and Bar-B-Q,** 1212 SR 290, Elgin (☎ **512-285-3407**): The sausages, called Elgin Hot Guts served with saltine crackers, are fantastic, but the market also sells brisket, mutton ribs, and barbecue sandwiches. There's a stocked meat market on one side and an ice-cream-cone bar on the other side. Open daily from 9 a.m. to 9 p.m. Closed Thanksgiving, Christmas Day, and Easter.

Beyond barbecue: Old-timey good eats

Texas is full of good eats. Try these Hill Country places:

» **Altdorf's,** 301 W. Main St., Fredericksburg (☎ **830-997-7865**): This homey German *biergarten* serves German dinners, and Texas chow such as rib-eye steaks, tacos, and enchiladas. Try a sausage dinner (bratwurst, knockwurst, or bockwurst) or a meat specialty such as *Wiener schnitzel*, sauerbraten, or *rindsrouladen.* Open Wednesday and Thursday from 11 a.m. to 9 p.m., Friday and Saturday from 11 a.m. to 10 p.m., and Sunday from 11 a.m. to 3 p.m. Closed Monday and Tuesday.

» **El Mercado,** Market Square, 514 W. Commerce St., San Antonio (☎ **210-207-8600**): This historic Mexican market began in the days of the "chili queens" — local women who served a spicy meat-and-beans concoction called chili con carne at night, from stalls near Alamo and later from this marketplace. Today, you can sample ice-cream cones and pecan pralines while enjoy-ing mariachi bands shop the eclectic collection of Southwestern items. Open daily from 10 a.m. to 6 p.m. (and until 7 p.m. in the summer). Closed New Year's Day, Easter, Thanksgiving, and Christmas Day.

» **Mi Tierra Café y Panaderia,** 218 Produce Row in El Mercado (see the preceding item; ☎ **210-225-1262;** https://www. mitierracafe.com): If you're lucky, the menu will feature the world's best *carne machaca*, served for breakfast with eggs, refried beans, tortillas, and salsa. In the pastry shop, you can buy crisp hot *churros*, *bunuelos*, and *ricardos* (named for the chef who invented it). Open 24 hours a day year-round.

» **Po-Po Family Restaurant,** 435 NE I-10 Access Rd., Boerne (☎ **830-537-4194;** https://popo-restaurant.com): In Boerne, this rustic rock roadhouse with the neon EATS sign out front has been there since 1929, serving at various times as a dance hall, ice rink, machine shop, and hatchery. Today, it's known for fried; catfish, frog legs, shrimp. Fried chicken, made from Ma Burgon's, the founder's original recipe, is still a favorite. Open daily from 11 a.m. to 9 p.m.

Fast Facts

Area Code
The area codes are **325, 512,** and **830.**

Driving Laws
In Texas, all riders must wear seat belts; violators pay steep fines. The maximum speed limit on interstate highways is 80 mph. Speed limits in urban areas are lower.

Emergency
Call ☎ **911.** For emergency assistance on the road, call Texas Motorists (☎ **800-525-5555**).

Hospitals
Christus Santa Rosa Hospital is in New Braunfels; other major hospitals along the route are in Austin and San Antonio.

Information
To contact Texas's Department of Tourism, call ☎ **800-888-8839** or go to www.traveltex.com. For brochures, call ☎ **800-452-9292.**

Road and Weather Conditions
Call ☎ **800-452-9292** or go to https://www.txdot.gov.

Taxes
Texas has a 6.25 percent sales tax; some local taxes may raise it to 8.25 percent. The state gasoline tax is 20 cents per gallon.

Time Zone
Texas is on Central time.

Chapter **14**

The Heart of Ohio: A Circle around Circleville

The Buckeye state is the heart of America. "Why, oh why, oh why, oh why did I ever leave Ohio?" sang the unhappy-in–New York heroine of the Broadway musical *Wonderful Town*, written by Leonard Bernstein, Betty Comden, and Adolph Green. The roads of Ohio are lined with history (eight presidents lived there) and rife with calories (Skyline chili parlors in Cincinnati and pies from just about everywhere). And can you think of any place cooler than the Rock and Roll Hall of Fame and Museum in Cleveland, designed by architect I. M. Pei?

A blend of urban, industrial, and rural, Ohio gave birth to the Wright brothers, Thomas Edison, astronauts Neil Armstrong and John Glenn, and the tire industry, but on the back roads near Millersburg, the world's largest Amish community tend family farms without electricity or the internal combustion engine. Native Americans left their marks in the form of earthen mounds; the most famous is shaped like a serpent.

Choosing Your Route

Your circle drive around the heart of Ohio begins in Dayton, swings east to Springfield along I-70, and then south to Yellow Springs and Xenia on US 68. From Xenia, take US 42 through Waynesville and Lebanon south to Cincinnati. Follow the Ohio River along scenic US 52 to Aberdeen; then go north on SR 41 and SR 73 to see the Serpent Mound. Afterward, SR 73 takes you south to Portsmouth on the river.

From Portsmouth, travel east on US 52 to SR 93, and turn north to Jackson, where you make a short detour east into the scenic Hocking Hills via SR 93 to SR 56. Return on SR 56, driving northwest to Circleville. From there, take US 23 north to Columbus, the capital.

From Columbus, go east on I-70 to Zanesville and Norwich along parts of the old National Road. Return to go north on SR 79 near Hebron to Newark. Go east on SR 16 to SR 60 and south 3 miles to Dresden; then return to SR 16, turning east to Coshocton. From there, drive north on SR 83 to Millersburg at the beginning of the Amish country. Take US 62 east, detour south on SR 557 to Charm. Return to US 62 to continue through Berlin to Winesburg and Wilmot; turn southeast on US 250 for 3 miles to SR 212, and follow it eastward to Zoar.

From Zoar, take I-77, the fast route north to Cleveland, pausing at points of interest near Canton and Akron. About 725 miles.

WARNING

On back roads, use caution; you may make a turn and run up behind a tractor; a horse-drawn Amish carriage; or a herd of cattle crossing the road. Also, back roads are famous for making sudden right or left turns at a property boundary where owners didn't want their land bisected.

TIP

If you're pressed for time, you'll need to concentrate on what interests you most — you can't cover Ohio in a weekend.

>> For crafts collectors and folks with hearty appetites, the Amish country fills the bill nicely. Start and end your trip in Columbus, driving north to Millersburg and Berlin, and then overnighting in that area.

» Scenery, hiking, and camping fans need to drive along the Ohio River from Cincinnati and then go to Hocking Hills, where campgrounds abound.

» A favorite weekend combination for Ohio sightseeing starts in Dayton, with all the airplane history. Next, drive south through the antiques capitals of Waynesville and Lebanon for shopping, pausing for a meal at the famous old Golden Lamb Inn. Then drive into Cincinnati for the trio of great museums at the Museum Center at Union Terminal.

Planning Ahead

Summer months are the prime season in Ohio, but that's also when local families take their vacation trips, so consider late spring or early fall. A good time is May, when rain threatens some days but temperatures are mild. Late September and early October are perfect but it can be crowded in the Amish country, because the harvest season is the most popular time to visit; April through June is less crowded. Weather conditions called lake-effect snow can hit in fall and winter. True lake-effect snow is when you can look up at blue skies while it's snowing.

WARNING

Be cautious about Midwestern weather. During spring's tornado season, local TV stations usually run a tornado-alert information strip along the bottom of the screen by county name, so always find out the name of the county where you're camping and the names of those nearby or where you're headed next. While you're in the campground, if an alarm sounds, leave your RV and make your way to the designated shelter and remain there until the alert is over. You may run into heavy, driving rains; then pull over to the shoulder and wait for it to subside.

TIP

Campground reservations shouldn't always be necessary in some of the RV parks; however, you need to reserve ahead for big holiday weekends such as Memorial Day, Independence Day, and Labor Day.

Pack a variety of clothing, because weather can change suddenly. Out in the country in hot weather, anything clean and decent is acceptable — like lightweight cotton shorts, shirts, and T-shirts — but have a sweater or jacket in case it cools off. Take an umbrella and moderate rain gear. If you want to walk around a large town or city, visit a nice restaurant, or attend a church service, pack long pants for men and dressy cotton slacks, a skirt, or a dress for women.

Plan seven to ten days for this casual drive over the back roads of Ohio.

Must-See Attractions

Amish Country

Centered on Millersburg

Ohio's Amish country offers enough attractions to fill a week of sightseeing. Pick up one of the free Amish country maps (found in most shops and restaurants) that carry ads for shops, restaurants, and sightseeing. For the best part of the journey, however, strike out along the back roads to glimpse farm families at work: men plowing the fields, women hanging out washing, and children on the way to school. Be respectful of their space and lifestyle during your visit.

SR 77 between Berlin and Mount Hope is a back road lined with farms and horse-drawn buggies going to and from town.

Dayton Aviation Heritage National Historic Park

Dayton

This four-part museum complex spread around the city salutes the Wright brothers and their contemporary and friend, African-American poet Paul Laurence Dunbar. From 1895 to 1897, the brothers operated the Wright Cycle Co. shop, which has been restored and furnished with period bicycles and machinery. The Dunbar House State Memorial is the home that poet Dunbar bought for his mother when his work was published successfully. Exhibits include a bicycle that the

Wright brothers gave him. Carillon Historical Park houses the *Wright Flyer III*, the first craft capable of controlled flight. The Huffman Prairie Flying Field was where the Wright brothers tested their planes and home to the first permanent flying school.

The Wright Brothers Memorial is in northeastern Dayton on SR 444, overlooking Wright-Patterson Air Force Base.

Allow one hour for each of the museums and 15 minutes for the memorial.

Wright Cycle Co.: 22 S. Williams St. ☎ ***937-225-7705.*** *https://www.nps.gov/archive/daav/cul_wrightcycleco. Admission: Free. Open: Summer daily 8:30 a.m.–5 p.m.* **Dunbar House State Memorial:** *219 Paul Laurence Dunbar St.* ☎ ***937-224-7061.*** *Admission: $6 adults, $5 seniors, $3 children, under 3 free. Open: Beginning in June, open Thursday to Saturday 10 a.m.–4 p.m. (call for appointment at other times).* **Carillon Historical Park:** *2001 S. Patterson Blvd.* ☎ ***937-293-2841.*** *https://www.nps.gov/daav. Admission: $10 adults, $9 seniors, $7 ages 3–17. Open: Tues–Sat 9:30 a.m.–5 p.m., Sun noon–5 p.m.* **Huffman Prairie Flying Field.** ☎ ***937-425-0008.*** *Accessed through Gate 12A at Wright-Patterson AFB off SR 444. Admission: Free. Open: Dawn–dusk.*

Museum Center at Union Terminal
Cincinnati

KID FRIENDLY

In a magnificently restored 1933 Art Deco railway station, the city has built three excellent museums: the **Cincinnati History Museum,** the **Museum of Natural History,** and the hands-on **Children's Museum.** You can walk through the Ice Age, explore a limestone cavern inhabited by live bats, and step onto a vintage steamboat from the Cincinnati landing. Because sightseeing can make you hungry, you also find a food court that includes a Skyline Chili branch. Allow three to four hours.

1301 Western Ave. ☎ ***513-287-7000.*** *https://www.cincymuseum.org. RV parking: Parking garage with height limits; try street* *parking or take public transportation to the museums. Admission: All-museum pass $14.50 adults, $13.50 seniors, $10.50 ages 3–12. Open: Mon–Sat 10 a.m.–5 p.m., closed Thanksgiving and Christmas Day.*

National Road Museum/Zane Grey Museum
Zanesville

Three for the price of one, this museum contains the road museum, a salute to native son Zane Grey, and a display of art glass made in the area. Road warriors love the dioramas depicting the various stages of the National Road from 1811 to the present day. You can follow the progress of travelers from early inns to early campers with tents and tin lizzies and then a panorama with a trolley, a biplane, and Model Ts. Conestoga wagons are displayed, along with toll-road signs and other vintage vehicles. Another room houses a full-size replica of the studio used by Zanesville-born Western writer Zane Grey. Allow two hours.

8550 E. Pike. (From Zanesville, go east 9 miles on I-70 and take Exit 164; follow signs to museum.) ☎ 800-752-2602 or 740-872-3143. RV parking: Large open lot capable of handling big rigs. Admission: $7 adults, $6 seniors, $3 ages 6–12. Open: Memorial Day–Labor Day Wed–Sat 9:30 a.m.–5 p.m., Sun 1–5 p.m. Closed in winter.

Portsmouth Floodwall Murals
Portsmouth

The pretty little river town of Portsmouth is where cowboy star Roy Rogers grew up and cruise boats sailing the Ohio River frequently call. The waterfront is lined with huge murals depicting an awesome panorama of town history from the prehistoric days to the present. Yes, Roy Rogers and his horse, Trigger, are in one of the murals. But my favorite is an evening depiction of the town during World War II, with a movie house, vintage cars, and soldiers in uniform. Some evocative shops in the Boneyfiddle Historic District are also appealing. Allow one hour.

*The murals line Front Street in downtown **Portsmouth's Visitors Center**. ☎ 740-353-1116. RV parking: Street parking. Admission: Free. Open: Always.*

Rock and Roll Hall of Fame and Museum
Cleveland

Cleveland's great rock and roll museum, designed by I. M. Pei with a glass pyramid reminiscent of the same architect's entrance to the Louvre in Paris, is a great place to spend a day. Some of the most important exhibits are underground in the Ahmet M. Ertegun Exhibition Hall, a large, darkish area housing all sorts of displays and interactive exhibits such as "One-Hit Wonders," saluting now-forgotten artists who had one big hit and then vanished from view. On life-size mannequins are John Lennon's collarless Beatles jacket, Alice Cooper's bondage outfit, one of David Bowie's exaggerated 1970s fashions, Michael Jackson's sequined glove, Leadbelly's 12-string guitar, Jim Morrison's Cub Scout uniform — you get the idea.

BARGAIN ALERT

Original rock 'n' rollers are happy to discover that the museum has a discounted senior rate, because many of them are eligible for membership in AARP.

Allow a half-day to a full day.

WARNING

1100 Rock and Roll Blvd. (Follow the signage from I-90.) ☎ 888-764-7625. 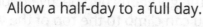 `https://www.rockhall.com.` *RV parking: This is a big problem, because the parking garage at the museum has a height limit that prohibits most RVs. Point your RV to the right, toward Burke Lakefront Municipal Airport, and when you reach the intersection facing the museum, look for a spot in the airport parking lot a block from the museum. Admission: $26 adults, $24 seniors, $16 ages 6–12, free for children 5 and under. Open: Daily 10 a.m.–5:30 p.m., Wed 10 a.m.–9 p.m. Some extra hours after Memorial Day. Nearby and worth a visit if you plan to stay another day is the Great Lakes Science Center at 601 Erieside Ave.*

Roscoe Village

Coshocton

A restored living-history 1850s village along the Ohio and Erie Canal, **Roscoe Village** is a sort of miniature Colonial Williamsburg. Craftsmen demonstrate weaving, pottery-making, and broom-making in the shops along the main street, and a horse-drawn canal boat takes visitors through a restored section of the historic canal. Seasonal celebrations are scheduled frequently, from May's Dulcimer Days to October's Apple Butter Stirrin' Festival. Allow three to four hours.

600 Whitewoman St. ☎ ***800-877-1830*** *or 740-622-9310.* https:// www.roscoevillage.com. *RV parking: Designated area. Admission: Free; tours $22 adults, $17 seniors, $13 ages 9–11, free 8 and under. Open: Daily 10 a.m.–4 p.m.*

Serpent Mound State Memorial

Peebles

Striking and unforgettable in photographs in magazines such as *National Geographic,* the sinuous, grass-covered **Serpent Mound** is a bit of a bust in person. Unless you're in a low-flying aircraft, you don't get the gorgeous perspective depicted in most photographs. You can climb to the top of the viewing tower, yet you still don't get a full overview. The Adena people constructed the 1,348-foot-long earthwork between 800 B.C. and A.D. 44. A pathway enables you to explore the perimeter of the mound, and a museum discusses theories on how and why the mound was built. Allow one hour.

3850 SR 73. ☎ ***937-587-2796.*** https://www.ohiohistory.org/ visit/museum–and–site–locator/serpent–mound. *RV parking: Plenty of space in designated lots, but a fee applies (cars $7, motor homes $9). Admission: Free. Open: Memorial Day–Labor Day Wed–Sun 10 a.m.–5 p.m., Apr–Memorial Day and Labor Day–Oct Sat–Sun only.*

US Air Force Museum

Dayton

Wear comfortable shoes if you plan to see all this museum; it's the largest of its kind in the world, filling 10 acres and displaying more than 300 aircraft inside and outside. From balloons to the B-1 bomber, from the plane that dropped the atomic bomb on Nagasaki in 1945 to the plane that took President Kennedy's body from Dallas to Washington, D.C., in 1963, air history is here. The museum also has an IMAX theater that offers two films, alternating hourly. Allow three hours.

Wright-Patterson Air Force Base, 5 miles northeast of Dayton off SR 4. ☎ **937-255-3284.** *https://www.nationalmuseum.af.mil/. RV parking: Huge parking lots with designated areas. Admission: Free. IMAX theater extra, $8 adults, $7 seniors, $4.50 students, $6 ages 3–7. Open: Daily 9 a.m.–5 p.m.; IMAX films on the hour beginning at 11 a.m. Closed major holidays.*

Zoar State Memorial

Zoar

In 1817, German separatists from the Kingdom of Wurttermburg founded the communal town of Zoar. Named for Lot's biblical town of refuge, Zoar flourished as one of America's most successful Christian communal societies until the society disbanded in 1898. Men *and* women had voting power on the town board; they produced their own food and operated blast furnaces, a blacksmith shop, a tin shop, a garden and greenhouse, and a wagon shop. They sold what they didn't need and had $1 million in assets by 1852. Today, except on Mondays and Tuesdays and from November through March, many of the town's buildings are staffed with costumed interpreters, and visitors are free to walk around the exteriors of all the public buildings at any time.

Zoar is off I-77, Exit 93, accessible by SR 212. ☎ *330-874-3011.*
https://historiczoarvillage.com. *RV parking: Street parking
or designated lots off the main route. Admission: $8 adults,
$4 ages 5–17. Open: Building interiors Memorial Day–Labor Day.
Closed November–March.*

More Cool Things to See and Do

Ohio's roadside attractions run the gamut from the world's largest
cuckoo clock to the birthplace of humorist James Thurber. You can
have fun and/or get informed at several spots along the way.

» *Sprechen-sie* **Ohioan?** The German village in Columbus is one
of Ohio's best-loved destinations. Saved from demolition in the
1950s, the 19th-century neighborhood is home to microbrewer-
ies, restaurants, shops, and galleries, and its brick streets are
inviting to walk. Stay as long as you like.

The **Visitors Information Center** is at 588 S. Third St.
(☎ **614-221-8888;** https://germanvillage.com). RV parking is
available on the street. Look for and observe the street signs.

**BARGAIN
ALERT**

» **Clean up your act.** Contrary to what you may think,
Hoover Historical Center, 1875 E. Maple St., North Canton
(☎ **330-490-7435;** https://www.visitcanton.com/directory/
hoover-historical-center), is not about a president, but about
the founder of the vacuum-cleaner company. At first, the vacuum was thought to be a miracle because "it beats as it sweeps
as it cleans." "To Hoover" came to mean the cleaner and the
cleaning action in many parts of the English-speaking world. This
museum contains 70 years of vacuum history plus a gift shop.
Allow one hour.

RV parking is available in a small lot or on the street. Admission
is free; donations are accepted. It's open Thursday through
Saturday from 1 to 4 p.m. Tours run hourly from 1 to 4 p.m.
Closed Sunday through Tuesday and major holidays.

» **Grind your own grist.** Lehman's Hardware (https://www.lehmans.com), a tradition in Ohio's Amish country, is a treasure trove of nonelectrical appliances, from hand-cranked wringer washing machines to wood-burning cookstoves, all new. Allow one hour or more.

Lehman's Hardware has two locations near each other: SR 77 in Mount Hope (☎ 330-674-7474) and 1 Lehman Circle in Kidron (☎ 330-857-5757). RV parking is available in lots large enough for Amish horses and buggies. Admission is free. It's open Monday through Saturday from 8 a.m. to 5:30 p.m.

» **Chat with a dead president.** The **McKinley Museum and National Memorial,** 800 McKinley Monument Dr., NW, Canton (☎ 330-455-7043; https://mckinleymuseum.org), honors the 25th president, who was assassinated in 1901. The animated figures of McKinley and his wife occupy the museum and talk about their life in the White House. Allow two hours.

RV parking is available in a designated lot. Admission is $10 adults, $9 seniors, and $8 ages 3 to 18. It's open Monday through Saturday from 9 a.m. to 4 p.m. and Sunday from noon to 4 p.m.

KID FRIENDLY

» **Meet woolly mammoths.** Ohio Village, 1982 Velma Ave. (at I-71 and 17th Avenue), Columbus (☎ 800-686-6124; https://www.ohiohistory.org/visit/ohio-village), re-creates an Ohio town in the 1860s with costumed interpreters and craftsmen, keeping kids and adults interested in the past. In the Historical Center, you can meet woolly mammoths and hear some hair-raising ghost stories. Allow two hours.

RV parking is available in a designated lot for a $4 fee. Admission is $12 adults, $10 seniors and students, and $6 ages 6 to 12. It's open Memorial Day through Labor Day from 9 a.m. to 5 p.m. and Sunday from noon to 5 p.m.

» **Is everybody happy?** A signature phrase of Jazz Age entertainer Ted Lewis from Circleville, remembered in his hometown with a museum showcasing his battered top hat and clarinet, and sheet music for his hits "Me and My Shadow" and "When My Baby Smiles at Me." Allow one hour.

The museum is located at 133 W. Main St. (☎ **740-477-3630** or 740-474-3231). RV parking is available on the street. Admission is free. It's open Saturday from 1 to 4 p.m.

» **Chuckle with a humorist.** A unicorn stands in the garden across from the **James Thurber House,** 77 Jefferson Ave., Columbus (☎ **614-464-1032;** www.thurberhouse.org), birthplace of the beloved humorist, whose short stories and drawings graced the pages of *The New Yorker* for many years. Thurber was also famous for his drawings A bookstore is on-site, and you also find literary events including readings by notable authors to literary picnics to a Birthday Gala for Thurber. Allow a half-hour to an hour.

RV parking is available on the street. Admission is free; tours on Sunday are $4 adults and $2 seniors and students. It's open daily from 1 to 4 p.m. and for author appearances. Call ahead.

» **Step into a painting.** Sundays in the park with George come alive in **Columbus's Topiary Garden** (☎ **614-645-0197;** www.topiarygarden.org), a replica in pruned shrubbery of Georges Seurat's painting *A Sunday Afternoon on the Island of La Grand Jatte* (which inspired the Stephen Sondheim musical *Sunday in the Park with George*), it has topiary people, boats, dogs, a monkey, and a pond to represent the Seine.

The garden is in the Old Deaf School Park, 480 E. Town St., in downtown Columbus. Admission is free, and it's open from dawn to dusk.

Our Favorite Campgrounds

Ohio has plenty of campgrounds, but make reservations for holiday weekends and during the summer season. Have reservations for festival dates because Buckeyes also enjoy RV camping during special events.

Campgrounds listed in this section have public flush toilets, showers, and sanitary dump stations unless designated otherwise. Toll-free numbers, where listed, are for reservations only.

Buckeye Lake KOA

$$$$–$$$$$ Buckeye Lake

Big Bands used to play at the lakeside pavilion on Buckeye Lake in the good old days. This KOA campground isn't far from the lakeshore but is convenient to all the attractions in Columbus. Big-rig sites offer 50-amp electrical connections, the management is friendly, and the swimming pool is heated.

Off SR 79. (From I-70, Exit 129A, go south on SR 79. 1½ miles to campground on the right.) ☎ **800-562-0792** *or 740-928-0706,* https://koa.com. *Total of 209 sites with water and 30- and 50-amp electric, 131 full hookups, 98 pull-throughs. cable TV, data port, laundry, heated pool, and Wi-Fi. Call for latest rates. MC, V, DISC. Open: April 2 through Oct 31.*

Dayton Tall Timbers Resort KOA

$$$$$ Brookville

Convenient to the Air Force Museum and the Wright Brothers memorials, this campground offers data ports at the campsites, a big swimming pool, and a pond; a golf course is nearby. Food service is available in this resort-style campground.

7796 Wellbaum Rd. (From junction of I-70 and SR 49, go north ½ mile on 49 to Pleasant Plan Road, then turn west ¾ mile to Wellbaum Road and south ¼ mile to campground, on the left.) ☎ **800-562-3317** *or 937-833-3888;* https://koa.com. *Total of 205 sites with water and 30- and 50-amp electric, 112 full hookups, 55 pull-throughs. Data port, laundry, 18-hole miniature golf, heated pool. Call for latest rates. MasterCard, Visa. Open: April 1 through Nov 1.*

Hocking Hills State Park

$$$ Logan

This scenic park is 12 miles south of town on SR 664, with paved sites, some shaded but all fairly narrow. Big rigs no longer must be stingy about using their electric appliances and air-conditioning because the hookups have been upgraded from a scant 20 amps to 30 and 50 amps. Scenery and hiking in the area, combined with a lake for swimming and fishing, make for a wonderful stay.

Off SR 664. (From Logan, go south 12 miles on SR 664 to the campground, on the left.) ☎ ***740-385-6842.*** *Total of 156 sites with 30- and 50-amp electric but no water, full hookups, or pull-throughs. Laundry, pool. Rates: $23–$27 per site. MC, V, DISC. 14-day maximum stay.*

Good Eats

Travelers in the Buckeye State can eat around the clock, finding snacks, solid meals with large portions, or sweets for between meals.

Meals of chili, sauerkraut, and Amish cooking

With modest prices, large portions, and hearty meals in these Ohioan restaurants — listed eateries win votes in *Ohio* magazine polls under headings like "Best Value" and "Favorite Neighborhood Restaurants."

» **Camp Washington Chili,** 3005 Colerain Ave. at Hopple, Exit 3 off I-75, Cincinnati (☎ **513-541-0061;** http://campwashingtonchili.com): This restaurant, a purveyor of Cincinnati's famous chili. Greek Americans created the Cincinnati version: a mild, chili spiced with cinnamon and allspice, poured over a plate of spaghetti, and sprinkled with cheese. That's "three-way" chili. Add chopped onions, for "four-way"; add a ladle of beans on top, it's "five-way." Open Monday through Saturday 24 hours; closed Sunday.

» **Der Dutchman,** 4967 Walnut St., Walnut Creek (☎ **330-893-2981;** https://www.dhgroup.com) and five other Ohio locations: Der Dutchman is an Amish eatery with its own bakery and family-style dinners. Find roasted chicken, roast beef, country ham, Swiss steak, and sides, a salad bar, and pies.

Open daily except Sunday from 7 a.m. to 8 p.m.

» **Golden Lamb Inn,** 27 S. Broadway, Lebanon (☎ **513-932-5065;** https://www.goldenlamb.com): This venerable inn is usually voted Ohio's favorite restaurant in *Ohio* magazine. Since 1803, the Golden Lamb has hosted Charles Dickens, Mark Twain, and ten American presidents, plus assorted ghosts. Although Dickens complained that the inn didn't serve spirits, now you can order a bottle of wine to enjoy with the tender lamb shanks, fried chicken, and fruit cobblers. Open Monday through Saturday 10 a.m. to 8 p.m. and Sunday 10 a.m. to 8 p.m.

BARGAIN
ALERT

» **Mrs. Yoder's Kitchen,** 8101 SR 241, Mount Hope (☎ **330-674-0922**): At this Amish restaurant, family-style dinners are priced by the number of main dishes ordered; up to three. "All you can eat here" is emphasized on the menu; carry-out from the meal isn't permitted. Instead, if you want takeout, order off the menu. Open daily except Sunday from 7 a.m. to 7 p.m. winter and 7 a.m. to 8 p.m. summer.

» **Ohio Sauerkraut Festival,** Old Main Street, Waynesville (☎ **513-897-8855;** https://sauerkrautfestival.waynesvilleohio.com): Held the second weekend in October, the festival draws over 200,000 visitors.

» **Schmidt's Restaurant and Sausage Haus,** 240 Kossuth St., Columbus (☎ **614-444-6808;** https://www.schmidthaus.com): At this restaurant in the unique German-village section of town, look for bratwurst; *Wiener schnitzel;* pork and sauerkraut; red cabbage; German potato salad; and the house dessert. Open

Sunday to Thursday from 11 a.m. to 10 p.m., and Friday and Saturday 11 a.m. to 11 p.m.

» **Skyline Chili** (https://www.skylinechili.com): This local chain has many locations around Cincinnati, including one in the food court in the Museum Center at Union Terminal. Skyline often wins for the best version of the chili, seasoned with cinnamon and allspice. Served with Oyster crackers on the side. Open weekdays from 9 a.m. to 10 p.m.

Snacks of chocolate, cheese, and ice cream

Ohio has its priorities straight. Along the drive are several havens for lovers of chocolate and dairy treats.

» **Coblentz Chocolate Co.,** 4917 SR 515 at SR 39 in Walnut Creek (☎ **800-338-9341** or 330-893-2995; https://coblentzchocolates.com): In a charming Victorian house in the heart of Amish country, Coblentz displays its homemade candies in wood-and-glass cases. Open in summer Monday through Saturday from 9 a.m. to 5 p.m. and to 6 p.m. starting in July.

» **Guggisberg Cheese Co.,** 5060 SR 557, Charm (☎ **330-893-2500;** https://www.babyswiss.com): You can't miss this in the tiny town of Charm; look for the big Swiss chalet with steel towers and a cuckoo-clock tower. Sample the cheeses and buy a whole Baby Swiss to go, along with other picnic-makings from the deli. Open Monday through Saturday from 8 a.m. to 5 p.m. and Sunday from 11 a.m. to 4 p.m.

» **Fanny May-North Canton (also known as Harry London Candies):** 5353 Lauby Rd. (right off I-77, Exit 113), North Canton (☎ **330-494-0833;** The factory offers tours from 10 a.m. to 2 p.m. ($3 adults, $2 ages 3–18) and chocolate for sale by the pound rate, even if you buy "one of those and two of these." Open Monday through Saturday from 9 a.m. to 6 p.m. and Sunday from noon to 5 p.m.

» **Young's Jersey Dairy,** SR 68, 2 miles north of Yellow Springs in Hustead (☎ **937-325-0629;** https://youngsdairy.com): Young's does quadruple duty as a bakery, soda fountain, sandwich shop, and ice-cream store. Shakes include the calf shake (two scoops of ice cream), the cow shake (four), and the bull shake (five). Hungry visitors order the King Kong sundae. Open daily from 7 a.m. to 9 p.m.

Shopping along the Way

Ohio, home to the world's largest Amish community, has potters, basket-makers, weavers, quilt-makers, and artists. Outside the Amish area, craftsmen staff historic villages and sell goods at special events.

BARGAIN ALERT

Basket Factory Outlet, 10959 Fisher Rd. NW, Bolivar (☎ **330-874-1388;** www.basketware.com/basketfactory), which is smaller than you might expect, is packed with baskets from around the world. Prices are modest. To get here from I-77, take Exit 93, go west on US 212, turn left onto Fort Laurens Road, and then turn right into the Lawrence Township Industrial Park. At the stop sign, turn left. The building is the second one on the left. Open Monday through Friday from 8:30 a.m. to 4:30 p.m.; closed Sunday and Monday.

Ohio boasts two antiques centers. Lebanon, on US 42 at the junction of SR 63 some 33 miles north of Cincinnati, has much history — Charles Dickens slept here — and is home to 70 antiques shops and boutiques in its downtown area, along with Ohio's oldest inn, the Golden Lamb Inn. Waynesville, at the junction of US 42 and SR 73 about halfway between Dayton and Cincinnati, has trademarked the title Antiques Capital of the Midwest for its 35-plus antiques shops.

Fast Facts

Area Codes
The following area codes are in Ohio: **216, 234, 330, 380, 419, 440, 513, 614, 740,** and **937.**

Driving Laws
In Ohio, seat belts must be worn in the front seats. The maximum speed limit on interstates and controlled-access roads is 70 mph in some areas. Speed limits in urban areas and lesser roads are lower.

Emergency
Call ☎ **911.**

Hospitals
Major hospitals along the route are located in Akron, Canton, Dayton, Cincinnati, Columbus, and Cleveland.

Information
Go online to https://ohio.gov/wps/portal/gov/site/tourism, or call ☎ **800-BUCKEYE (282-5393).**

Road and Weather Conditions
Sources include the Ohio Transportation Information System (www.dot.state.oh.us) and the Ohio Highway Patrol (☎ **877-7-PATROL [772-8765]**). In Ohio and adjacent states, call ☎ **888-264-7623** for road conditions.

Taxes
Sales tax is 5.75 percent to 7.75 percent, depending on the county. The state gasoline tax is 28 cents per gallon.

Time Zone
Ohio is on Eastern Standard Time.

Chapter **15**

Northern Minnesota: Paul Bunyan Country

Some unique American icons came out of Minnesota, including entertainer Judy Garland; folk/rock musician Bob Dylan; the Greyhound bus; the Mississippi River; and the giant fictional logger Paul Bunyan, who was so big when he was born that it took five storks to deliver him. According to legend, his footprints and those of his companion, Babe the Blue Ox, filled with water and became the state's 10,000 lakes.

I like Minnesota for its down-to-earth qualities, such as picture-perfect small towns in winter, with frozen lakes populated by characters like Jack Lemmon and Walter Matthau in the film *Grumpy Old Men.* For the less-hardy, Minnesota is best in spring, summer, and fall, when the weather is mild and the lakes have thawed. Fishing, canoeing, hiking, biking, and — lest we forget — shopping in the biggest mall in the United States, Bloomington's Mall of America, complete the experience.

MEETING PAUL BUNYAN

I fell in love with Minnesota at first because of the hilarious tales of St. Olaf that actress Betty White told on TV's *The Golden Girls*. I suspect that not too many travelers these days are drawn to Minnesota because of something as old as the Paul Bunyan yarns.

For those who don't know about Paul Bunyan (or the version that wasn't on *The Simpsons,* which was rather freely adapted), he was a giant logger with a pet blue ox named Babe, remembered in statues around north-central Minnesota. The unlikely stories of his strength and endurance originated in the logging camps of the North Woods. A public relations man named William Laughead, who worked for Red River Lumber Co., gave the tales a spin from 1914 to 1934 by issuing a series of illustrated booklets that glorified the Paul Bunyan myth. The folk hero got on the map in a big way in 1937 when the town of Bemidji erected one of the first bigger-than-life statues of the logger and his ox.

Some of the tales say that Bunyan was born in Maine, where the rocking of his cradle toppled 4 acres of timber. When he and Babe set out for the North Country, they left a trail of lake-size footprints behind them.

Choosing Your Route

Begin in Duluth, at the southwest edge of Lake Superior, and drive north via US 53 to the town of Virginia, the beginning of the great Mesabi Iron Range. Turn west on US 169 to Grand Rapids, continue west on US 2 to Bemidji, and drive south to the Mississippi headwaters at Itasca State Park by following US 2 West to Shevlin and turning south on SR 2 to Lake Itasca. From there, the route turns east through Paul Bunyan National Forest to the junction with SR 64, which you follow south to Akeley. At Akeley, turn west again, following SR 34 some 56 miles to the junction of US 10; then follow US 10 west to Moorhead, Minnesota. The distance is approximately 350 miles.

One optional detour takes you to the gigantic Mall of America in Bloomington, a suburb south of Minneapolis, adding 157 miles each way from Duluth. A second detour follows North Shore Drive (SR 61) along Lake Superior from Duluth to the Canadian border. The return, alas, is along the same route, but when you're halfway back to Duluth, you can cut off on SR 1 south of Little Marais and head northwest to Ely, and then follow SR 1/US 169 southwest to Virginia to join the longer drive. The North Shore Drive covers 264 miles.

TIP

Instead of traveling the entire Paul Bunyan route, you can opt for one of three short road trips in northern Minnesota. First, the North Shore Drive from Duluth along Lake Superior offers some great sightseeing, good camping, and easy driving (except for sometimes-bumper-to-bumper conditions in peak season). My second suggestion is a round-trip from Duluth up SR 53 to Virginia and the Iron Range, with a half-day at Minnesota Discovery Center; then head west across US 169 to Grand Rapids and return to Duluth on US 2. A third possibility is to take US 2 from Duluth west to Bemidji, visit Paul Bunyan and Babe the Blue Ox in Bemidji and Akeley, cover the Mississippi headwaters, and then return to Duluth on SR 200 and US 2.

Planning Ahead

Spring and fall temperatures are mild and comfortable, and summer temperatures, although humid because of all the surface water in this state adds up to 11,842 lakes, rarely rise above the 80s (°F). Fall foliage in the North Woods, a nickname for northern Minnesota, attracts sightseers, who take advantage of pick-your-own apples in orchards where the harvest coincides with the autumn-color season.

Northern Minnesota is rarely swamped with visitors, so campground reservations are needed only for the most popular parks on holiday weekends. Even in peak summer season, most RVers can find campground sites.

When packing, include layered clothing to cover weather extremes from a hot, sticky summer day on a lake to a sudden chill or early snowfall. Also bring along heavy-duty hiking boots, serious rain gear, and strong sunblock. Fishing gear, small boats, and whitewater rafting equipment can usually be rented on-site.

NORTH SHORE DRIVE

SR 61 strikes out north from Duluth along the shores of Lake Superior, traveling 168 miles to Grand Portage at the Canadian border, where you can catch ferries in season (May–Oct) to Isle Royale National Park. The drive is especially attractive in early autumn, when the leaves begin changing colors. Some half-dozen state parks with campgrounds are well spaced along the route.

Highlights along the way include Split Rock Lighthouse, the highest waterfall in Minnesota, in Tettegouche State Park near Little Marais; and Grand Portage National Monument, a re-created fur trading post 5 miles south of the Canadian border.

About 30 miles north of Duluth, right on the highway in the town of Two Harbors, is Betty's Pies, open only in summer but worth a stop. If the restaurant is too crowded for you to sit down, get a pie (or at least a couple of slices) to go (see "Good Eats" later in this chapter).

Rather than take the entire route north and then double back to Duluth, you can turn around at Grand Portage and continue south as far as Little Marais, where you can turn inland and drive northwest on SR 1 to Ely, home of the International Wolf Center in Ely (see "More Cool Things to See and Do" later in this chapter). Then continue southwest to pick up the longer drive in Virginia.

Allow a week for a leisurely drive. Add a day for the Mall of America, or more time if you want to linger there, and two days for North Shore Drive along Lake Superior.

Must-See Attractions

The Depot
Duluth

This renovated 1892 railway station is nicknamed "the Ellis Island of Minnesota" because of the numbers of immigrants who arrived here by train at the turn of the 20th century. Today, the bustling depot is a museum and entertainment complex.

Steam locomotives and wooden coaches fill the Lake Superior Railway Museum, framed by a life-size reproduction of downtown Duluth in 1910. You also find galleries operated by the Duluth Art Institute, the St. Louis County Historical Society, and the Duluth Children's Museum. One low-price ticket accesses the lot, and two museum stores sell collectibles and books. The Duluth Playhouse also is on the premises, and so are other performing-arts companies. Allow three hours.

506 W. Michigan St. ☎ 888-733-5833 (recorded info) or 218-727-8025. http://duluthdepot.org. RV parking: Designated area or street parking. Admission: $14 adults, $6 ages 3–12, free active military and vets. Open: Memorial Day–Labor Day daily 9 a.m.–6 p.m.; rest of the year Mon–Sat 9 a.m.–5 p.m. and Sun 1–5 p.m.

Great Lakes Aquarium
Duluth

The only all-freshwater aquarium in the United States gives visitors a look at what's in Lake Superior, including some 70 species of fish from the Great Lakes and a giant lake sturgeon in the Isle Royale tank. Thirty interactive exhibits, plus exhibits from other freshwater lakes and rivers of the world, are on display, including a current show of animals and fish from Africa's Lake Victoria. Allow two hours.

353 Harbor Dr. ☎ 218-740-FISH (3474). https://glaquarium.org. RV parking: Designated lot or street parking. Admission: $17.99 adults, $14.99 seniors, $13.99 youths 13-17, $11.99 ages 3-12, free under 3. Open: Daily 10 a.m.–6 p.m. Closed Christmas Day.

Headwaters of the Mississippi
Itasca State Park, Lake Itasca

In 1832, a scholarly geographer named Henry Schoolcraft, after trekking through the area with local Indians, decided that the headwaters of the great Mississippi River lay in this lake in northern Minnesota. Although both local Ojibwas and French trappers called it Elk Lake, he renamed it *Itasca* from syllables in the Latin term *veritas caput* (true head). It's fun for visitors to leap or tiptoe across the small trickling stream that eventually forms the Mississippi via a log footbridge or a footpath of slippery rocks. A museum at the site details the evidence. A quarter-mile walk along a wooded trail takes you to the headwaters. Allow one to two hours.

36750 Main Park Dr., Park Rapids. (Take US 2 west from Bemidji to its junction with SR 2 at Shevlin, turn south and follow SR 2 to Lake Itasca, and then follow signage to Itasca State Park's East Entrance off US 71.) Visitor center ☎ **218-699-7251.** https://www.dnr.state. mn.us/state_parks/park.html?id=spk00181#homepage. *RV parking: Large designated parking lot. Admission: Free. Open: Daily year-round.*

Minnesota Discovery Center
Chisholm

KID FRIENDLY

Here, you can also find plenty of snacks and dinners from the Ethnic Restaurant (see "Good Eats" later in this chapter), as well as a splendid museum on the history of the Iron Range and the various ethnic groups that arrived in the New World to work the mines. A small amusement park with a steam calliope, carousel, and Pellet Pete's miniature-golf course entertains kids. Other attractions include a gem and mineral display; the Polka Hall of Fame; a vintage-trolley ride to a reconstructed mining settlement called Glen Mine; early Scandinavian buildings; and a tribute museum to the Civilian Conservation Corps (CCC) camps of the 1930s, an organization that built many state and national park facilities. Allow a half-day to full day.

801 S.W. US 169 W. (Take I-35 north from the Twin Cities or Duluth to Cloquet, follow US 33 to US 53, take US 53 to Virginia, and follow US 169 west to Chisholm.) ☎ **800-372-6437** *or 218-254-7959.* https://www.mndiscoverycenter.comf. *RV parking: Large designated lots adjacent to the center. Admission: $9 adults, $8 seniors, $6 ages 3–17, free 2 and under; on special-event days, add $1. Open: June–Labor Day Tues–Sun 8 a.m.–9 p.m.; rest of year, Tues–Wed 9 a.m.–5 p.m., Thurs 9 a.m.– 8 p.m.*

Judy Garland Museum
Grand Rapids

Judy Garland was almost born in a trunk. In 1922, she arrived as Frances Gumm, the third daughter in a wannabe show-business family; her dad, Frank Gumm, managed the local movie house, and her mother, Ethel, played the piano to accompany the silent films. Garland started her career as Baby Gumm, tap-dancing on the theater stage between features, and graduated to the singing Gumm Sisters with her two older siblings. She changed her name to Judy Garland when she signed her first Hollywood contract. The Judy Garland Museum is next to her birthplace. You can tour the period home and visit the adjoining museum, which houses the *Wizard of Oz* carriage, Garland's test dress from the original movie, a Winkies sword, and an Emerald City bell-bottom coat. Allow three hours for the house and museum.

2727 US 169, Grand Rapids. ☎ 800-664-JUDY (5839). RV parking: Street parking. Admission: $10 per person ages 2 and up. Open: June–September daily 10 a.m.–5 p.m.; rest of year, Fri–Sat only 10 a.m.–5 p.m., closed Sun. Closed on major holidays.

Mall of America
Bloomington

KID FRIENDLY

Claiming to be the biggest shopping mall in the United States and the Midwest's largest entertainment complex, the Mall of America (MOA) offers the ultimate mall experience. Hundreds of brand-name shops, dozens of theme restaurants, a roller coaster, an aquarium, the LEGO center (a hit with kids), an aquarium, sports bars, dance clubs, and a simulated motor speedway do their part to separate you from your money — but offer plenty of bang for the buck. You can walk around and ogle the attractions without spending a cent. Or you can shop 'til you drop. There's no clothing tax at MOA.

I-494 and 24th Avenue. ☎ ***952-883-8800*** *(Mall of America),* ***952-854-7700*** *(NASCAR Silicon Motor Speedway),* ***952-854-LIVE*** *(5483; America Live! Entertainment complex),* ***888-DIVE-TIME*** *(888-348-3846; Underwater Adventures Aquarium).* https://www.mallofamerica.com. *RV parking: Extremely large lots surround the mall. Admission: Free. Open: Mon–Sat 10 a.m.–9:30 p.m., Sun 11 a.m.–7 p.m. Closed Thanksgiving and Christmas Day.*

More Cool Things to See and Do

Minnesota is a great state for lovers of the outdoors, with its countless lakes and forests. Animal fans can commune with wolves and bears in their natural habitats; fresh-food fanatics can pick their own fruits and vegetables in season for pennies; and trivia collectors find a treasure trove of oddities.

» **Like a rolling stone.** Singer **Bob Dylan's boyhood home** is in Hibbing, where he was born Robert Zimmerman in 1941. He attended the local high school, a fortress-like building erected by mine owners to entice workers to move to the area so that they could enlarge the mines in 1918. The home is at 2425 Seventh Ave. S. and is privately owned, so you can drive by for a look; don't attempt to visit.

» **Calling all loons.** A giant loon 20 feet long and 20 feet high floats on Silver Lake in the heart of Virginia. The big bird serves as the centerpiece to the Land of the Loon Festival, an arts-and-crafts festival that takes place over a weekend each June.

» **Leave the driving to them.** The **Greyhound Bus Origin Museum,** Hibbing Memorial Buildings, 23rd Street and Fifth Avenue East, Hibbing (☎ **218-263-5814;** www.greyhoundbusmuseum.org), displays some beautiful examples of vintage buses, beginning with the 1914 Hupmobile, the company's first vehicle, used to transport miners from Hibbing to nearby Alice. The 1956 Scenicruiser, with its big windows, and the first Bookmobile also are on display. Allow one hour.

RV parking is available on the street. Admission is $5 for adults, $4 for seniors, $2 students, and kids 6 to 12, $10 families. It's open mid-May through mid-September Monday through Saturday from 10 a.m. to 4 p.m. and Sunday from 1 to 4 p.m.

» **Howl at the moon.** The **International Wolf Center,** 1396 SR 169, Ely (☎ **218-365-4695;** https://www.wolf.org), not only tells the story of timber wolves through exhibits and displays, but also has a pack of wolves in residence in a natural-habitat area. A viewing theater enables visitors to watch wild wolves going about their daily routines, including feeding on roadkill deer (not a sight for the young or the squeamish). Scheduled night strolls near the center let you howl with the wolves. Intensive weekend programs are available. Allow a minimum of two hours.

RV parking is available in a designated lot. Admission is $14 for adults, $12 for seniors, $8 for ages 4 to 12, and free for 3 and under; prices vary for special weekend programs. Emotional-support animals are not permitted to enter. The center is open daily May through September weekdays 10 a.m. to 5 p.m. and Saturday 9 a.m. to 5 p.m., and weekends only October through May (Friday from 10 a.m. to 5 p.m., Saturday from 9 a.m. to 5 p.m., and Sunday from 10 a.m. to 2 p.m.).

» **Go for the goal.** The **US Hockey Hall of Fame**, US 53 at 801 Hat Trick Ave., Eveleth (☎ **800-443-7825** or 218-744-5167; https://www.ushockeyhall.com), salutes the stars, tells the history of the game, and even has a Zamboni display and a mini shooting rink with an electronic goalie for you to try to score against. The world's largest hockey stick, 107 feet long and weighing more than 3 tons, is on display along with a giant rubber puck. Allow one to three hours, depending on how much of a hockey fan you are.

RV parking is available in a designated lot or on the street. Admission is $8 for adults, $7 for seniors and ages 13 to 17, $6 for ages 6 to 12, and free for 5 and under. From May through November, the hall is open Monday through Saturday from 9 a.m. to 5 p.m. and Sunday from 10 a.m. to 3 p.m.; from December through April, it's open Friday through Sunday from 9 a.m. to 5 p.m. It's closed on major holidays.

» **Bear in mind.** The **Vince Shute Wildlife Sanctuary** (☎ **218-757-0172;** https://www.americanbear.org) shelters some 60 black bears (in addition to other native wildlife) on a 360-acre property. From a viewing platform, visitors can get close enough to photograph the bears without disturbing their habitat. Allow one hour.

To get to the sanctuary, take Highway 53 north to 1 mile south of Orr, turning left on County Road 23. Continue on CR 23 for 13 miles. Watch for the sign approximately 300 feet past CR 514 on the right. RV parking is available in a nearby lot, with a free shuttle to the sanctuary. Admission is $10 for adults, $8 for seniors, and $5 ages 6 to 17, free 5 and under. From May through early September, it's open Tuesday through Sunday from 11 a.m. to 7 p.m. Call the Orr Chamber of Commerce at ☎ **877-254-4691** or go to http://www.orrchamber.com/ for more information about the area.

Our Favorite Campgrounds

You'll have no trouble finding a place to camp, because northern Minnesota is chockablock with private campgrounds and state parks at a ratio of one or more per lake in some areas. Still, if areas seem to be crowded with campers as you travel through them, you can make a reservation for your next overnight stay.

All campgrounds in this chapter have public flush toilets, showers, and sanitary dump stations unless designated otherwise. Most campgrounds are closed in winter. Toll-free numbers, where listed, are for reservations only.

Bemidji KOA
$$$-$$$$$ Bemidji

The owners of this quiet, shaded rural campground love their trees and take good care of their park. You find plenty of level pull-throughs, although RVers with slideouts need to maneuver around trees at some sites. Activities on summer weekends include hot-dog roasts, movies, and bike rentals. The campground isn't far from the headwaters of the Mississippi, casinos, amusement parks, and shopping.

5707 US 2. (2 miles west of Bemidji, north side of US 2 between mileposts 109 and 110.) ☎ *800-562-1742 or 218-444-7562. https://koa.com. Total 62 sites with water and 30- and 50-amp electric, 32 full hookups, 39 pull-throughs. CATV, data port, laundry, heated pool. Call for current rates. MC, V. Open: May 10–Oct 15.*

Forest Hills RV & Golf Resort
$$$–$$$$ Detroit Lakes

As the name implies, campers get a resort atmosphere and two golf courses: an 18-hole championship golf course and an 18-hole miniature-golf course. Other bonuses include a large heated indoor pool and spa. Sites are large, measuring 42 feet wide by 60 feet long.

Off US 10. (From junction of US 59 and US 10, go west 3½ miles on US 10 to the campground, on left.) ☎ *800-482-3441. Total 107 sites with 30- and 50-amp electric, 49 full hookups, 10 pull-throughs. Data port, golf course, laundry, indoor heated pool and spa, Wi-Fi. Call for latest rates. MC, V. Open: May 1–Oct 1.*

Minneapolis SW KOA
$$$$ Jordan

Conveniently located near the Mall of America, this resort-style RV park has a heated indoor pool, miniature-golf course, volleyball court, and horseshoe pit. Golf and horseback riding are nearby. Also a member of Good Sam, the park provides wide sites, some with side-by-side hookups. Site surfaces are gravel and grass, with some patios and some shade. Big rigs are welcome.

3315 W. 166th St. (From junction of US 169 and SR 41, go south 4 miles on US 169 to the campground, on left.) ☎ **800-562-6317** *or 952-492-6440.* https://koa.com. *Total 95 sites with water and 30- and 50-amp electric, 33 full hookups, 53 pull-throughs. Data port, laundry, indoor heated pool, phone jacks, Wi-Fi. Rates: $38.49–$60.99 per site. DISC, MC, V. Open: Apr 1–Oct 6.*

Ogston's RV Park
$$$ Saginaw

Ten miles northwest of Duluth, this campground provides large sites, 40 feet wide by 100 feet long. The park has a pond with freshwater fishing, swimming, and boating.

(US 53) 5020 Ogston Dr, Saginaw MN 55779. (From junction of SR 194 and US 53, go north 4¾ miles on US 53 to CR 15, north ¼ mile on CR 15 to Miller Trund Road, and east ½ mile to the campground, on left.) ☎ **218-729-9528.** *Total 100 sites with water and 30- and 50-amp electric, all full hookups, 31 pull-throughs. Laundry. Rates: $40–$42 per site. No credit cards. Open: May 1–Oct 1.*

Vagabond Village Campground
$$$$ Park Rapids

The park sits beside Potato Lake and offers boating (aluminum boats, motorboats, pontoons, and canoes for rent), fishing, and swimming. The park also has a heated pool and a shuffleboard court. Make reservations if you plan to stay in July or August.

23801 Green Pines Rd. (From junction of SR 34 and CR 4, go north 6 miles on CR 4 to CR 40, west 1/3 mile to Green Pines Road, and south ½ mile to the campground, on right.) ☎ **218-732-5234.** https://www.vagabondvillage.com. *Total 55 full hookups with 30- and 50-amp electric, 10 pull-throughs. Rates: $47–$52 per site; $10 additional per adult. Open: May 15–Oct 1.*

Good Eats

Treats to look for in Minnesota include wild rice (especially the hand-picked wild version as opposed to paddy-grown wild rice), fresh walleye pike, the European nut pastry called *potica* (pronounced po-*teet*-sah), fresh-picked berries in season (see the nearby "Picking your own fresh berries" sidebar), Cornish pasties, Gouda and cheddar farm cheeses, Haralson apples, and smoked fish from Lake Superior.

» **Betty's Pies,** 215 SR 61 E., Two Harbors (☎ 218-834-3367): Betty's sells just what the name implies — plenty of homemade pies — plus sandwiches, salads, and soups, as well as the occasional slab of walleye pike. Pies range from custard to fresh blueberry (a dozen flavors a day), and Betty's also offers homemade cookies and cakes. Open daily from 7:30 a.m. to 9 p.m.

» **The Ethnic Restaurant,** Ironworld Discovery Center, US 169 W., Chisholm (☎ 800-372-6437 or 218-254-7959): On designated days and special-event weekends, the restaurant serves a $10 ethnic buffet that may include roast lamb, *sarmas* (stuffed cabbage), *porketta* (thinly sliced, highly seasoned roast pork), Swedish meatballs, and Slovenian *potica* (a dense, multilayered pastry filled with finely chopped walnuts in butter and cream). If the buffet isn't open during your visit, or if you want something simpler, look for the open-air snack bar, which offers porketta on a potato roll, gyros, sarmas, pasties, bratwurst with sauerkraut, Polish sausage, and pickle on a stick. From June 6 to August 29, the restaurant is open Thursday from 4 p.m. to 8 p.m. and Friday from 8 a.m. to 9 p.m.

» **Italian Bakery,** 205 S. First St., Virginia (☎ 218-741-3464; https://www.potica.com): This bakery is the home of potica, sold in 1- or 1½-pound loaves. Potica keeps wonderfully well in the refrigerator and freezes well. If you want a quick dessert, warm a slice in the microwave and top it with a scoop of ice cream. The biscotti also are delicious. Open Tuesday through Friday from 5 a.m. to 5 p.m.

PICKING YOUR OWN FRESH BERRIES

The whole family can have fun picking fresh berries in season. In northern Minnesota, strawberries peak in June and July; raspberries and blueberries, in July and August. Eat some, freeze some, or make jams and jellies in the RV kitchen to take home. Following are a few berry growers along the Paul Bunyan drive, although you may spot others. The berry growers ask that you call ahead, whether you're looking to pick your own berries or buy fresh-picked ones; they can give you their hours and directions to their farms. A handy website lists farms all over the country where you can pick your own produce by season. The page for Minnesota farms is www.pickyourown.org/MN.htm.

- **Blueberry Meadows,** Grand Rapids (☎ 218-326-0671), has four varieties of pick-your-own blueberries. Open from late July through Labor Day.

- **The Blueberry Patch,** Gilbert (☎ 218-865-4100), asks that visitors bring their own containers for blueberries; strawberry containers are provided. Supervised children are welcome. Open daily Monday through Saturday from 9 a.m. to 8 p.m. Hand-harvested wild rice also is for sale.

- **Lavalier's Berry Patch,** Grand Rapids (☎ 218-327-9199), has strawberries and blueberries to pick yourself or have picked for you.

- **Peterson's Berry Farm,** Eveleth (☎ 218-744-5759), offers strawberries, Saskatoons (Juneberries), raspberries, and blueberries; free picking containers are provided. Open from late June through August.

Shopping along the Way

If shopping is your passion, plan to detour your RV to the **Mall of America** in Bloomington (see "Must–See Attractions" earlier in this chapter).

The **Bemidji Woolen Mills Factory Store,** 301 Irvine Ave., Bemidji (☎ 888-751-5166; https://www.bemidjiwoolenmills.com), sells woolen goods produced on–site since 1920, along with sweaters, casual and dress wool slacks for men and women, and outerwear. Shop hours are Monday through Saturday from 8 a.m. to 5:30 p.m. and Sundays from 10 a.m. to 5 p.m.

Fast Facts

Area Code
The following area codes are in effect in Minnesota: **218, 320, 507, 612, 630, 651, and 952.**

Driving Laws
RV riders in the front seats and children 4 and under anywhere in the vehicle must wear seat belts. The speed limit on interstate highways is 70 mph. The limit in urban areas is lower.

Emergency
Call ☎ **911.** Call ☎ **651-282-6871** for the State Patrol.

Hospitals
Major hospitals along the route are in Duluth, Grand Rapids, and Minneapolis.

Information
Visit the Department of Tourism website at www.exploreminnesota.com, or call ☎ **888-868-7476** or 651-296-5029.

Road and Weather Conditions
Call ☎ **511,** or go to www.dot.state.mn.us.

Taxes
Minnesota sales tax is 6.875 percent; local taxes may raise this figure by 1 percent. The state gas tax is 28.6 cents per gallon.

Time Zone
Minnesota is on Central time.

IN THIS CHAPTER

» **Getting close to nature, nature, and more nature**

» **Circling the largest surface area of freshwater in the world**

» **Searching the beaches for the elusive agate stones**

» **Camping in unspoiled environments**

» **Dipping your toes in cool, clear water**

Chapter **16**

Lake Superior Circle Tour

Henry Wadsworth Longfellow wrote of the Great Lakes using the Ojibwe term *Gitche Gumee*, meaning *big water*. Lake Superior is exactly that: the largest surface area of freshwater in the world, totaling 31,820 square miles. With an average depth of 500 feet, the lake is estimated to contain close to 3,000 cubic miles of freshwater.

This trip is for you if you appreciate unspoiled stretches of green hardwoods and softwoods nuzzled next to unspoiled beaches and cliff-lined shorelines; if you're a hunter or fisher, pedal biker, or industrial-history buff; or if you're fascinated by boats and cargo ships. The shorelines are lined with pines; cedars; mighty oaks hundreds of years old; white and yellow birch trees; and a variety of grasses, wildflowers, and wild berries. Waterfalls, rivers, streams, and creeks weave their way under bridges to the lake. You can enjoy unparalleled sunsets and sunrises, and find picture-perfect lighthouses perched on rocky points. A seemingly endless supply of rock and sand beaches yield agates. In the fall, leaves turning colors will enchant both you and your camera.

CIRCLING THE BIG LAKE

I grew up 9 miles from this massive expanse of freshwater. I camped on its beaches; picnicked at public-access sites; fished from shores, docks, and tributaries; and rode pedal and motor bikes and motorcycles along its roadways. Perhaps seeing the iron-ore boats and fishing trawlers passing by heightened my desire to join the US Navy and travel by ship to new, equally picturesque, distant, and interesting places.

People who are seeing Lake Superior for the first time often say, "It's just like the ocean," and it is. I never tire of the beauty, tranquility, pleasure, and peace that come from being close to her waters. My hope is that taking this circle tour will also touch you in some positive way.

Along the way, you see waterfalls, the Pictured Rocks, classic lighthouses, the remains of mining and lumber facilities, and human-made wonders such as the Superior Dome. Every one of the beaches presents you with an opportunity to search the water's edge for agate, a stone of a silica combined with a specific quartz material called chalcedony, characterized by distinct grain and variety of colors.

One fantastic feature of this trip is the never-ending mesmerizing attraction of Lake Superior yielding nearby campsites, roadside trout fishing, and scenic surprises; it as good as it gets for an appreciatory nature trip in the 21st century.

On this trip you are crossing parts of Upper Michigan, Wisconsin, Minnesota, and Ontario. You should allow at least 11 to 14 days. The trip around the big lake is about 1,350 miles (2,100 km) without side trips.

Choosing Your Route

Begin this trip in Michigan by crossing the 5-mile-long Mackinaw bridge at Mackinaw City to St. Ignace and continuing north on Interstate 75 to Sault Ste. Marie. From the Soo (as the locals call it), the trip goes west to Paradise and then to Munising. From Munising, go west to Marquette and then northwest to the Copper Country of the Upper Peninsula, whose deep rock mines produced more than 4 billion pounds of copper from the Civil War years to the mid-1990s. After a short stay in Houghton County, go south and west, skirting the top of Wisconsin on the way to Duluth, Minnesota. From Duluth, go north to cross the US–Canada border (with your passport in hand). Make a short stop to resupply; then head northeast to Thunder Bay and Sleeping Giant Provincial Park. Finally, cross the border back to Sault Ste. Marie, Michigan. The total loop's distance is 1,350 miles if you don't take many side trips.

TIP

If you have only a long weekend to explore the area, driving any few hundred miles of this route would be rewarding. From either end of the lake, going east to Thunder Bay from Minnesota or west from Sault Ste. Marie, Michigan and back would make a nice trip covering roughly half of the route around the lake. From the west end of the lake, crossing from Canada, a trip going east to the Copper County of Michigan is possible. From the east end, crossing from Canada, and going to Pictured Rocks in Munising, Michigan would easily fill a weekend.

Planning Ahead

You need your international passport to do the whole tour. Enough campgrounds and fast-food and local restaurants line the way, but watch your gas gauge, because some stretches of road are long with few, if any gas stations.

The best times to go are late spring, summer, and early fall. Temperatures are mild and comfortable; summer temperatures can rise into the 80s (°F) but rarely do. Snow (often, lots of it) can be a spoiler any time beginning in mid-October.

WARNING

I don't recommend making this drive in winter; the freezing temperatures, winds off the lake, and lake-effect snow are a lot to deal with, and driving conditions may be unsafe. Also, no year-round RV parks are available.

There are no expressways east and west on this trip, so you'll encounter two-lane roads, passing through towns with 25 mph speed limits; keep watching for the speed limit signs. Also, you'll find long stretches of road without side passing lanes. Other RVs, logging trucks, tourists, and commercial truck traffic will ensure that you enjoy the scenery at an average speed of about 45 mph. Take your time, and enjoy the ride.

Must-See Attractions

Fort Wilkins State Park

Copper Harbor, Michigan

This historical park on the Keweenaw Peninsula is operated by the Michigan Department of Natural Resources. The park preserves a restored 1844 Army outpost, Fort Wilkins, which is on the National Register of Historic Places. The fort was established to maintain order among the early prospectors, miners, and native peoples. Costumed interpreters act out the history of the fort.

15223 US Highway 41, ☎ **906-289-4215.** *www.michigandnr.com/ parksandtrails/Details.aspx?type=SPRK&id=419. RV parking: In designated parking area. Admission: Park sticker, $11, or daily-use fee. Open: May 18–Oct 14 8:30 a.m.–dusk.*

Fort William Historical Park

Thunder Bay, Ontario

With 15,000 artifacts, Fort William Historical Park is a well-known heritage and cultural attraction that entices visitors from across North America. This site brings to life the reconstructed Fort William fur trading post as it existed in 1816. Allow two to four hours.

Wildlife abounds in the wilds of the Upper Peninsula and Ontario, including moose, which are not going to move as fast as the white-tailed deer or not at all. Early in the morning and evening and at night, exercise extra caution; be on the alert for animals, and keep your speed down. You don't want to be known as the RVer who hit a deer or moose on your previously relaxing trip.

1350 King Rd., Thunder Bay, CA ON P7K 1L7. ☎ 807-473-2344. http://fwhp.ca. RV parking is availabe. Admission: $14 adults, $12 seniors and students, $10 youths, free 5 and under. Open: Daily June 1 – Oct 14 Monday through Friday 9 a.m to 5 p.m. RV camping packages available mid-May to mid-Oct.

Great Lakes Shipwreck Museum
Paradise, Michigan

SS Edmund Fitzgerald and other notable shipwrecks, coupled with the state's maritime history, make this museum one of Michigan's most popular destinations.

18335 N. Whitefish Point Rd., Paradise, MI 49768. ☎ 906-492-3747. https://www.shipwreckmuseum.com. RV parking: Designated area. Admission: $12 adults, $8 children. Open: Daily May 1–Oct 31 10 a.m. – 6 p.m.

Locks Tour
Sault Ste. Marie, Michigan

This set of locks takes ships, ore boats, and pleasure craft through the lock to compensate for the differences in lake levels.

1157 E. Portage Ave., Sault Ste. Marie, MI 49783. ☎ 906-632-6301. http://www.soolocks.com/about_us-5/. RV parking: On street. Admission: $31 adults, $12 ages 5–16; dinner and themed cruises, $68 per person. Reservations required. Open: Most of the shipping season, mid-May to mid-October, when the ice takes over the lakes and St. Mary's River, nothing passes the locks. Schedule your tour for daylight hours, between 10 a.m. and 4 p.m. and make reservations at least a day ahead.

MTU Seaman Mineral Museum
Houghton, Michigan

A.E. Seaman Mineral Museum of Michigan Tech. This exhibit houses a mineral collection from all over the world and is the most extensive collection of minerals from the Great Lakes region. This display holds thousands of the building blocks of the world. The gift shop sells minerals as decorators, jewelry, bookends, and candleholders.

1404 Sharon Ave, Houghton, MI 49931. ☎ **906-487-2572.** https://www.museum.mtu.edu/visit/information. Open all year with these hours and days. Monday–Saturday 9 a.m. to 5 p.m. through October; Tuesday–Saturday 9 a.m. to 4:30 p.m. beginning November 1 Tuesday–Saturday 9 a.m. to 4:30 p.m. beginning November 1, closed Thanksgiving. Copper pavilion holding a large specimen of float copper is open during museum hours. Parking and RV Parking are free. Admission is good for two days; $6 for adults, $5 for seniors 65 and older, $3 for student (with college ID), $2 ages 9 to 17. Free for children 8 and under. Allow two to four hours.

Pictured Rocks National Lakeshore
Munising, Michigan

Colorful sandstone cliffs and the sandstone formations Miners Castle and Chapel Rock make this 32-mile boat tour very popular. Remains of shipwrecks are plentiful along the shoreline and shipwreck enthusiasts like the "glass bottom" boat tour to enjoy both the colored weathered cliffs and what is left of the sailing ships at the bottom. Cruises are just over two hours.

506 W. Michigan St. ☎ ***906-387-3700*** *(recorded info) or 218-727-8025.* https://www.nps.gov/piro/planyourvisit/pictured-rocks-boat-tours.htm. *RV parking: Designated area or street parking. Cruise admission: $38 adults, $10 ages 6–12, free ages 5 and under. Open: Daily mid-May–mid-Oct. Cruises begin at 10 a.m. and end at 6 p.m. Some sundown cruises start at 8 p.m. See full schedule at* https://www.picturedrocks.com/fares-schedule/.

Superior Dome
Marquette, Michigan

At 536 feet across, covering more than 5 acres, the Superior Dome is the largest-diameter wooden dome in the world. The dome is open and free for self-guided walking tours and viewing when no Northern Michigan University or hosted athletic events are scheduled. This building is a great example of civil engineering excellence and for use of wood, 781 Douglas fir beams, the ultimate renewable building material.

1401 Presque Isle Ave., Marquette, MI 49855. ☎ **906-227-2850.** *https://www.nmu.edu/SuperiorDome. RV parking: Street or some lots: Open: Year-round.*

More Cool Things to See and Do

The Lake Superior area is jam-packed with fascinating sights, activities, and outdoor pursuits — too many to list in this chapter. Whenever you're on a RV trip here, you'll struggle between staying on track and seeing where a sign leads. Be open to following at least one of those signs once on every trip.

Following are some of my favorite things to see and do; you'll find many more on your tour.

KID FRIENDLY

» **Canadian Bushplane Heritage Centre.** This hands-on museum preserves the history of bush planes and forest protection in Canada. The museum is at 50 Pim St. in Sault Ste. Marie, Ontario; ☎ **705-945-6242;** http://bushplane.com/index.php?id=exhibits.

Admission is $13.50 for adults, $12.50 for seniors, $8 for ages 13 to 21, $3 for ages 4 to 12, free ages 3 and under. The museum is open from mid-May to mid-October. Open daily: 9 a.m. to 6 p.m.

» **Delaware Mine Tour,** US 41 (12 miles south of Copper Harbor), 7804 Delaware Rd., Delaware, Michigan (☎ **906-289-4688**). Tour a copper mine dating back to 1846, when mules pulled the carloads of ore out of the mine. Allow two to three hours.

Admission is $11 for adults, $7 for ages 6 to 12, and free for 5 and under. The mine is open daily from May to October, starting at 10 a.m. to 8 p.m.

Our Favorite Campgrounds

RVing is quite popular in all states on this route and in Canada, so you'll meet many other rigs during the summer months. You'll find enough campgrounds along the route, some state or municipal and others privately owned. Few state parks and national-forest campgrounds offer full RV hookups with sewer connections, yet the scenery makes up for a few days without hookups.

On major-holiday weekends (Memorial Day, Fourth of July, and Labor Day) and during local events, local users fill the campgrounds, so making reservations is a good plan.

All campgrounds listed in this chapter have public flush toilets, showers, and sanitary dump stations unless designated otherwise. Toll-free numbers, where listed, are for reservations only.

Brimley State Park
$$$–$$$$ Brimley, Michigan

This park, one of the oldest in the state, located at Whitefish Bay, is right on the shoreline of Lake Superior and is only 9 miles from Sault Ste. Marie. Beautiful sandy beaches and you can see Canada across the water.

9200 W. 6 Mile Rd., Brimley, MI 49715. (From the intersection of M-28 and M-221, go right for 2 miles on 6 Mile Road, and then turn right on 6 miles road; campground is ¾ of a mile the on right.) ☎ **906 248-3422.** https://www.midnrreservations.com. Or call 1-800-447-2757 (1-800-44PARKS). This state campground has more than 200 sites with electric, some are 50 amp, and a dump station. Must use website or toll-free number for rates, reservations, and information. Open: Mid-May to mid-October. MC, V.

City of Houghton RV Park
$$$–$$$$ Houghton, Michigan

The unique park is located along the Portage Canal. For this park, reservations are almost a must during the whole season. Must be self-contained; no showers or restrooms. A kid-friendly waterfront park is next door, and historic downtown Houghton is a short walk down the waterfront, offering shops and restaurants.

1100 W. Lakeshore Dr. (From downtown Houghton on US 41 going west, stay left to merge onto M-26 going west, then merge to the right lane and watch for the park sign a slight way up the hill for Lakeshore Drive and the park. ☎ **906-482-8745.** *www.cityofhoughton.com/rec-rv.php. 25 full hookup sites. All sites overlook the canal and are well equipped. Rates: $45 per day. MC, V. Open: Mid-May–Oct.*

Indian Point Campground
$$$–$$$$ Duluth, Minnesota

Conveniently located close to town, the campsites are high above Spirit Bay. Tall maples, elms, and pines complete the setting.

7000 Pulaski St. (Exit 251 B from Intersate 35, Grand Avenue [M-23], south 6 miles to campground.) ☎ **218-628-4977** *or 855-777-0652. http://indian-point-campground.com/campsites. Total 191 sites with water and 30- and 50-amp electric, all full hookups, 97 pull-throughs. CATV, data port, handicap access, laundry, Wi-Fi. Rates: $39–$61 per night. MC, V. Open: May to Oct.*

Munising Tourist Park Campground

$$$–$$$$ Munising, Michigan

This campground is right on the lake and a great place to stay while visiting Pictured Rocks (see "Must-See Attractions" earlier in this chapter). Great views of the water from this park provide a great place to relax and stay a few extra days.

NE8518 M-28 West, Munising, Michigan. Head west on M-28 from downtown Munising for 3 miles; the park is on the right. ☎ **906-387-3145.** *Total 127 sites, 78 with water and electric hookups. Rates: $25–$41. Open: Mid-May–mid-October.*

Thunder Bay KOA

$$$–$$$$ Thunder Bay, Ontario

This highly rated campground lets you enjoy the natural beauty of nearby Lake Superior and the region's attractions.

162 Spruce River Rd., Shuniah, ON P7A 0N6. East of Thunder Bay off Thunder Bay Expressway CA 17, south on the Spruce River Road exit. ☎ **800-562-4162** *or 807-683-6221.* https://koa.com/campgrounds/ thunder-bay/. *Call for latest rates and reservations. MC, V. Open: Apr 15 to Oct 15.*

Van Riper State Park

$$$–$$$$ Champion, Michigan

This campground has fine scenery and provides a quiet retreat. An occasional moose walks through the campground and whitetail deer are frequent visitors. Great location to enjoy the fall colors starting in mid-September.

Travel west/north on US 41 from Marquestte for 35 miles. 851 Co Rd AKE, Champion, MI 49814. ☎ **906 339-4461.** *Make reservations through the online reservations at* https://midnrreservations. com. *Or call 1-800-447-2757 (1-800-44PARKS). Total 147 sites, some with water and 30- and 50-amp electric. Rates: $20–$29. MC, V. Open for camping mid-April to mid-October.*

Good Eats

Cafes and restaurants are plentiful in bigger cities and towns, but much of this trip includes very small towns. Don't expect to find too many fast-food joints along the way. Be thankful that you're carrying your own kitchen with a stocked refrigerator.

Cuisine found around Lake Superior includes fresh and smoked Lake Superior trout and whitefish, Cornish style pasties, saffron and cinnamon buns, ring bologna, natural casing hot dogs, Thimbleberry jam, blueberries, cudighi sandwiches, pannucakkua, also known as *kropsu* (Finnish baked pancakes), smoked fish, venison Jerky, Ternary Toast and wild rice — just a few of the tastes to experience on this trip.

REMEMBER

Be sure to stock up on groceries and gasoline whenever you see a suitable and convenient spot.

>> **Ambassador Bar,** 126 Shelden Ave., Houghton, Michigan 49931 (☎ **906-482-5054**): Get traditional pizza here, as good now as it was in 1966. Add whatever toppings you want, but be sure to use cheese and sausage as the base. Check out the murals on the walls and ceiling while you sip one of the regional micro-brewery beer offerings or some Bavarian wheat beer to go with the pizza. The bar offers other food; after you have tried the pizza on your first visit check out the Cudighi homemade Italian sausage with pizza sauce and white Colby cheese, or the Reuben sandwich — hot corned beef, creamy Swiss cheese, and spiced sauerkraut on crusty French bread (not rye).

The place fills up with college students most school-year weekends. The bar is open Monday to Thursday from 11 a.m. to 10:30 p.m., Friday and Saturday from 11 a.m. to midnight, and Sunday from 4:30 to 10:30 p.m.

» **Beaux Daddy's,** 1575 Hwy. 61, Thunder Bay, Ontario (☎ **807-622-1111**): Check out the battered walleye and deep-fried chocolate ice cream.

The restaurant is open Tuesday through Saturday starting at 4:30 p.m.; closes at 9 p.m. Tuesdays and 10 p.m. the rest of the week.

» **Peterson's Fish Market,** 4981 N. Highway 41, Hancock, Michigan (☎ **906-482-2343** market, **906-523-5744** fish fry): If you don't want to catch your own, this market is the place to buy fresh or smoked Lake Superior fish. Or have lunch here; you won't forget the fish and chips.

Parking is available on the street. The market is open Monday through Friday from 8 a.m. to 5:30 p.m., Saturday from 10 a.m. to 5 p.m., and Sunday from 11 a.m. to 2 p.m.

» **The Wicked Sister,** 716 Ashum St., Sault Ste. Marie (☎ **906-259-1086**; https://www.wickedsistersault.com): Try a burger, and don't miss the smoked-whitefish-spread appetizer.

The restaurant is open Monday to Saturday from 11 a.m. to 11 p.m. and Sunday from noon to 10 p.m.

Fast Facts

Area Code
The area codes are **906** in Upper Michigan, Ontario area codes are **226, 289, 343, 416, 519, 613, 647, 705, 807** and **905**, Minnesota: **218, 320, 507, 612, 630, 651,** and **952,** Northern Wisconsin **715.**

Driving Laws
All RV occupants must wear seat belts in Michigan, Wisconsin, Minnesota and all the Canadian provinces. Speed limit on highways in Ontario is 100 kph; in Michigan, the highway speed limit is 75 mph, Wisconsin 65 mph, Minnesota the maximum speed limit on interstate highways is 70 mph. The limit in urban areas is lower. Use ☎ **911** for emergency calls in Michigan, Minnesota, Wisconsin, and Ontario, Canada.

Hospitals
Major hospitals are in Marquette, Duluth, Thunder Bay, and Sault Ste. Marie, with smaller hospitals in other towns along the way.

Information
Sources include Ontario Travel (☎ **800-ONTARIO** (**800-668-2746**), https://www.ontariotravel.net/en/home, and Pure Michigan (**888**) **784-7328**), https://www.michigan.org. For Minnesota, visit the Department of Tourism website at www.exploreminnesota.com, or call ☎ **888-868-7476** or **651-296-5029.** In Wisconsin, visit https://www.travelwisconsin.com/.

Road and Weather Conditions

In Michigan, call **800-381-8477,** or visit https://www.michigan.gov/mdot. In Ontario, call **511** or 800-268-4686. When in Minnesota, call ☎ 511, or go to www.dot.state.mn.us. **Wisconsin:** Call 511 or visit: https://wisconsindot.gov/Pages/travel/511/511.aspx or call (☎ **800-432-8747).**

Taxes

Michigan sales tax is 6 percent; gasoline tax is 26.3 cents per gallon. In Ontario, sales tax is 7.25 to 10.5 percent; fuel tax is 13 percent.

Minnesota sales tax is 6.875 percent; local taxes may raise this figure by 1 percent. The state gas tax is 28.6 cents per gallon. In Wisconsin, the gas tax is 32.9 cents per gallon and the sales tax is 5 percent.

Time Zone

Michigan is on Eastern time; Wisconsin and Minnesota are on Central time; most of Ontario is on Eastern time; and Ontario west of 90° longitude is on Central time.

Chapter **17**

The Ozarks and Branson: Hot Springs to Springfield

For all their craggy remoteness, the Arkansas Ozarks, among America's oldest mountains, are only about 2,300 feet high. "Our mountains ain't high," goes the saying, "but our valleys sure are deep."

The Ozarks are the heart of American folk crafts and music, preserved primarily because the area has been remote and poor for almost a century. During the Depression of the 1930s, many of the people gravitated to the industrial cities of the North to make a living, leaving parts of the Ozarks to revert to wilderness. In the 1950s, when the South was tearing down Victorian buildings to put up modern facades, lovely but declining old towns such as Hot Springs and Eureka Springs made do because they couldn't afford modernization.

In the 1960s, a little-known lakeside Missouri town called Branson pioneered live country-music shows. By the 1980s, music stars flocked to Branson to build theaters, and the town grew into the second-most-visited tourist site in the USA, beat only by Orlando, Florida.

Choosing Your Route

A loop drive from Hot Springs, Arkansas, heads north on SR 7 to Harrison and then west via US 412. The route goes north via SR 23, west again via SR 12 to War Eagle and Rogers, and (via SR 112) north to Bentonville. From there, follow US 62 to the picturesque Victorian town of Eureka Springs and east to Bear Creek Springs; then drive north to Branson and Springfield, Missouri, on US 65.

Head back into Arkansas on US 65, turning east at Leslie on SR 66 to Mountain View, home of the Ozark Folk Center, and scenic Jacksonport State Park, with its spacious, appealing campground. A short jog south on US 67 takes you into Little Rock, which concludes the journey. The total distance is approximately 700 miles.

WARNING

Note that some of the most colorful roads through the Ozarks are narrow, steep, and winding. If you aren't comfortable maneuvering the back roads, you can stick to main routes, taking the less curvy SR 9 or I-30 to Little Rock, I-40 west to Fort Smith, and US 71 north to Bentonville. US 62 from Eureka Springs to US 65 at Bear Creek Springs also is easy to drive, and so is US 65 north to Branson and Springfield. Motor homes 27 to 36 feet long should be no problem if you drive carefully through the Ozarks on the routes suggested.

Traffic jams can occur on the streets of Branson, where you can spend extra time inching your way along SR 76 through the middle of town during the summer season. Locals tell stories about visitors who hop out of their RVs (leaving a driver behind, of course!), go shopping, and return to the vehicle a block or two farther along. One way to avoid the jam-ups is to leave your RV at the campground and take a local shuttle.

A more rugged stretch of mountains lies ahead in the Ozark National Forest. If you want a relaxing change of pace from the demanding road, take I-40 west from Russellville to Fort Smith, head north on I-540 to Bentonville, and pick up the original tour. The size of your rig and your comfort with challenging roads can help you decide the routes to take.

TIP

If you want to condense this scenic Ozarks drive and Branson entertainment holiday into a weekend, you can begin your drive in Hot Springs, Arkansas; follow SR 7 north through the Ozarks into Harrison; and go on to Branson, Missouri. The drive itself is slightly less than 200 miles but may take all day on the narrow, curvy roads.

An alternative route takes you from Little Rock north on I-40 to US 65; turn east at Clinton on SR 16 to Mountain View for a visit to the Ozark Folk Center. Follow scenic SR 14 northwest across the Buffalo National River Park at Buffalo Point. Then go on to Yellville, where you turn west on US 62/US 412 to join US 65 for the short trip north to Branson. This tour runs around 230 miles.

TIP

Downtown Hot Springs has limited parking space for RVs, so you're better off leaving the motor home or trailer at an RV campground and heading into town in a smaller vehicle. Town parking lots are across Central Avenue from Bathhouse Row along Bath and Exchange Streets and opposite the Arlington Hotel on Central Avenue, which is also SR 7. *Note:* Vehicles longer than 30 feet aren't permitted on Hot Springs Mountain Drive.

Planning Ahead

Branson bustles with events and shows between April and the end of October (some theaters put on Christmas shows). During the off season, many theaters and campgrounds close. The Ozarks are beautiful in spring — when the trees, redbuds, lilacs, and May apples are blossoming and the weather is mild — and in autumn, when fall temperatures color the leaves, and good weather is likely through October. In summer, days can be hot, and traffic is heaviest.

One you know when you want to go and where you want to stay, make campground reservations in Branson ahead of time. Making show reservations doesn't seem to be as important. Most RVers wait until they arrive and then make reservations and/or purchase tickets. Check https://www.explorebranson.com/shows to see who's playing when.

Branson has more than 100 shows to choose among, with 16,500 theater seats across an array of live-music theaters that offer daily matinee and evening shows; some even offer breakfast shows. Don't expect a late night, however; the last show usually starts at 8 p.m.

Dress is casual in this part of the world, so pack jeans, shorts, T-shirts, and lightweight cottons if you're coming in summer. For spring and fall, add a sweater or jacket, some lightweight rain gear, and hiking boots. You can easily arrange mountain biking, canoeing, whitewater rafting, hiking, fishing, and horseback riding when you're in the area, so bring along the gear for your favorite sport.

Allow about two weeks for your Ozarks vacation, depending on how many activities you schedule and the number of shows to take in.

Must-See Attractions

Bass Pro Shops Outdoor World
Springfield, Missouri

This vast sporting-goods store and museum offers everything you can imagine, from hunting and fishing licenses to fly-tying demonstrations and deer-processing books such as *Field Dressing and Skinning*. Four-story waterfalls flow inside the store, surrounded by craggy rock cliffs and mounted masterpieces of taxidermy. You can test your new rifle, too, at the indoor shooting range. A museum of the outdoors is part of the attraction, and a barbershop and a macho all-day eatery called Hemingway's, with a 30,000-gallon aquarium stocked with sharks. Allow two to three hours.

1935 S. Campbell Ave. at Sunshine (US 60 and SR 13). ☎ **800-227-7776**; *general information 417-887-7334; store 417-890-9453; museum* https://www.basspro.com/shop/en. *RV parking: Huge parking lot with plenty of room. Admission: Store free; museum $50 adults, $45 seniors, $30 ages 17 to 6, $5 5 and under. Open: Museum daily 9 a.m.–8 p.m.; store Mon–Sat 7 a.m.–10 p.m., Sun 9 a.m.–6 p.m.*

Branson Family Entertainment
Branson, Missouri

With numerous live-music theaters, the rapidly growing entertainment center of Branson claims more theater seats than Broadway, as much musical excitement as Nashville, and a wholesome atmosphere for the entire family. In past years, the various stars, some with their own theaters, have included the Lennon Sisters, Texas honky-tonk musician Mickey Gilley, violin virtuoso Shoji Tabuchi, occasionally Russian comic Yakov Smirnoff, Tony Orlando, and the Texas Tenors. Throw in a spectacle like Dolly Parton's Stampede show, which pleases crowds and kids. The star appearances tend to be seasonal (May–Oct), but the holidays bring some of the best Christmas shows, and some live shows are still performed from January through March.

Southwestern Missouri on US 65, 12 miles north of the Arkansas border. Branson Chamber of Commerce/Convention & Visitors Bureau ☎ 800-214-3661. https://www.explorebranson.com. *Most attractions closed mid-Jan to Feb. Show tickets: Vary by theater and performer but range from $15 to $50 or more for adults. Some breakfast shows and matinees; most evening shows at 8 p.m.*

Downtown Historic District
Eureka Springs, Arkansas

The downtown area of Eureka Springs is on the National Register of Historic Places, with colorful Victorian "painted ladies" lining the steep, narrow streets. Limestone walls built from native stone mark boundaries, and streets cross at angles, none making a perfect right angle. Some houses that appear to be single-story with an entrance on one street turn out to have four more floors below when you get to the next block downhill. You enter the Catholic church through its bell tower.

The town was founded to exploit its 63 healing hot springs, with boardinghouses springing up to feed and house health-seekers. The arrival of the railroad in 1883 spurred the building of more than 50 plush hotels in the next three decades. Today, crafts shops, art galleries, superb inns, and several outstanding restaurants make Eureka Springs a romantic getaway for urban honeymooners, with a generous and upscale collection of bed-and-breakfast inns.

WARNING

Don't attempt to drive your RV in Eureka Springs. Instead, leave the rig at the campground if you're staying in the area. Or park in one of the open-air lots at the base of the town (before the main roads climb uphill) and use the town's trolleys for sightseeing. Allow two to three hours.

Northwestern corner of Arkansas on US 62. Eureka Springs Tourist Center, ☎ 800-6-EUREKA (638-7352). www.eurekaspringschamber. com. RV parking: Scarce; use the Eureka Springs Trolley System (☎ 479-253-9572) for a 1-hour guided tour or transport around town; $15 adults and $7 children, plus tax. Tour includes free parking.

Fordyce Bathhouse
Hot Springs National Park, Arkansas

The Spanish Renaissance Fordyce Bathhouse, the most splendidly restored structure on the town's famous Bathhouse Row, doubles as the visitor center for the national park and a museum of thermal-bathing history. Go in, get park information from the rangers, and then look around. An 8,000-piece stained-glass skylight illuminates the De Soto Fountain, with its Art Deco statue of an Indian maiden offering a bowl of water to explorer Hernando De Soto. In the 1915 gymnasium, a fitness center displays punching bags, vaulting horses, and acrobatic rings. Allow one hour.

369 Central Ave., Hot Springs. ☎ 501-620-6715. https://www.nps. gov/hosp/index.htm. RV parking: On the street. Admission: Free. Open: Daily 9 a.m.–5 p.m.

Ozark Folk Center
Mountain View, Arkansas

The first folk cultural center in the United States was created in 1973 to preserve the music, dancing, handicrafts, and folkways of the Ozarks. Two dozen craftsmen work inside the center.

Cloggers (many of whom are elderly and who banter among themselves before, during, and after performances) dance to the tunes of musicians who play frequent sets throughout the day. All musical selections precede 1937; percussion and electronic amplification are not permitted. The center offers special gospel-music concerts on Sunday evenings. The center's restaurant serves honest Arkansas food (see "Good Eats" later in this chapter) and a snack bar vends barbecue sandwiches and fried peach and apple pies. Allow a half-day to a full day.

Folk Center Road, north of town off SRs 5, 9, and 14. ☎ ***870-269-3851.*** *https://www.arkansasstateparks.com/parks/ozark-folk-center-state-park. RV parking: Large lot at base of center; free tram uphill to center. Admission: Center $12 adults, $7 ages 6–12; music shows $12 adults, $7 ages 6–12; combination ticket $19.50 adults, $10.25 ages 6–12, $45 families. Open: Center April–Nov daily 10 a.m.–5 p.m.; music shows April–Nov Thurs, Fri, and Sat shows start at 7 p.m.*

More Cool Things to See and Do

The Ozarks is a haven of American innovations and creations that reflect earlier eras. Sometimes, you may think that you've entered not only another time zone, but also another century.

» **Paddle away the day.** During winter and spring, the Buffalo River reaches its peak flow for canoeists and rafters. **Buffalo National River Park,** the first designated national river, a natural stream that's unique in a state of multiple fishing streams and lakes created by the US Corps of Engineers.

At **Wild Bill's Outfitter,** Buffalo Point, junction of SR 14 and SR 268 No. 1, Yellville, Arkansas (☎ **800-554-8657** or 870-449-6235; https://www.wildbillsoutfitter.com/), you can rent canoes, rafts, and kayaks. You can find additional outfitters in Jasper where SR 7 crosses the park, in Ponca where SR 43 crosses the park, in Tyler Bend and Silver Hill where US 65 crosses the park, and in Buffalo Point where SR 14 crosses the park. RV parking is available on the road.

KID FRIENDLY

» In Hot Springs, Arkansas, check out **Ducks in the Park Tours,** 316 Central Ave. (☎ **501-624-3825**). RV parking is scarce in town; look for parking lots across from Bathhouse Row on Bath and Exchange Streets. Admission is $20 for adults, $19 for seniors, and $15 ages 3 to 12. Free for 2 and under. Tours run daily from 9 a.m. to 7 p.m.

» **Catch the Ozarks' own religious spectacle.** More than six million people have come to see the *Great Passion Play,* Statue Road off US 62 East, Eureka Springs, Arkansas (☎ **800-882-7529** or 479-253-9200; www.greatpassionplay.com), the story of the last week of the life of Jesus, with a large cast and many special effects. The popular Eureka Springs production has a cast of 250 actors, 40 sheep, 12 horses, 5 donkeys, and 3 camels.

RV parking is available in designated lots. Admission is $28 for adults, $18 for ages 12 to 16, and $14 for ages 4 to 11. Free for 3 and under. The play runs from late April through October on Tuesday and Thursday through Saturday at 8:30 p.m.; after Labor Day, it begins at 7:30 p.m.

» **Visit the little house in the Ozarks.** The **Laura Ingalls Wilder Historic Home,** 3068 Highway A, 1 mile east of the town square, Mansfield, Missouri (☎ **417-924-3626;** http://lauraingalls wilderhome.com), was the author's home from 1894 until her death in 1957. She wrote all nine of her *Little House* books here. The house is preserved as she left it, and handwritten manuscripts of the books are on display. Allow two hours.

RV parking is available in a large lot. Admission is $14 for adults, $7 for children 6 to 17, and free for children 5 and under. It's open March 1 through November 15 Monday through Saturday from 9 a.m. to 5 p.m. and Sunday from 12:30 to 5:30 p.m.

» **Flip for Missouri. Pea Ridge National Military Park,** on US 62 2 miles west of Garfield and 10 miles northeast of Rogers, Arkansas (☎ **479-451-8122;** https://www.nps.gov/peri/index.htm), commemorates the 1862 battle that decided whether Missouri would become a member of the Union or the Confederacy. The battle also was the first in the Civil War to involve Native Americans — two regiments of Cherokees on the Confederate side under the command of Brigadier General Albert Pike. Depending on which historian you read, on the second day, the Cherokee troops either stood aside and weren't sent into battle or went home after the first day, seeing little real reason to fight again. Allow two hours.

RV parking is available in a lot. Admission is $10 per person, $20 per vehicle, and $15 for a motorcycle. The park is open daily from 8 a.m. to 5 p.m. and closed on major holidays.

» **Count sheep.** *The Shepherd of the Hills,* 5586 SR 76, Branson, Missouri, 2 miles west of the strip (☎ **417-334-4191;** https:// theshepherdofthehills.com), is a rustic outdoor drama based on Harold Bell Wright's 1907 novel of the same name. (The book was made into a 1941 film starring John Wayne.) With a cast of 90 actors, a covey of animals, and a bit of a roaring bonfire, the play holds your attention, even in a 2,000-seat arena.

Toby Show, a lighthearted comedy, includes dinner, which features smoked turkey breast, pulled pork, corn on the cob, and cobbler.

RV parking is available in designated lots. The 4 p.m. show includes dinner. *Toby Show* costs $39.75 for adults and $26.50 for children ages 4 to 12. Free for 3 and under. *Shepherd of the Hills* costs $39.75 for adults and $26.50 for children 4 to 12. Open Tuesday, Thursday, and Saturday. Free for 3 and under.

KID FRIENDLY

» **Skip the cave, and hit the midway.** The original theme park, **Silver Dollar City,** on Indian Point Road in Branson, Missouri (☎ **800-475-9370** or 417-338-2611; https://www. silverdollarcity.com/theme-park), grew up around Marvel Cave in the 1960s, but today's visitors tend to skip the cave (the 500 steep steps leading down into it may be one reason) and visit the rides, shops, craftsmen venues, and country-music groups that perform daily throughout the park. Kids love the waterslide, the roller coaster, and rides on the paddlewheeler *Branson Belle.* Allow a half-day to a full day.

The park is 9 miles west of Branson on SR 76. RV parking is available in a large lot. Admission is $68 for adults, $55 for seniors, and $58 for children 4 to 11, free for 3 and under. It's open from mid-April to late December daily from 9:30 a.m. to 7 p.m.

» **Witness the dawn of Walmart.** In Bentonville, Arkansas, Sam and Mary Walton opened their first 5-and-10-cent store in 1945. Today, that store is the **Walmart Visitor Center,** 105 N. Main St., in Bentonville, Arkansas (☎ **479-273-1329;** https://www. walmartmuseum.com/visit/museum/), a museum filled with 1950s and 1960s merchandise, 35 electronic historical displays, and Sam's original desk. Allow one hour.

RV parking is available on the street. Admission is free. The visitor center is open from March through October Monday through Saturday from 9 a.m. to 5 p.m. and Sunday from 1 to 5 p.m.

Our Favorite Campgrounds

Arkansas state parks are RV-friendly. Most have hookups, and all are in scenic areas. With 9,700 miles of streams and rivers and 6,000 acres of surface water, the state promises plenty of fishing, boating, floating, and canoeing in public and private campgrounds. For July and August and spring weekends, I recommend that you make reservations, especially around Branson and Eureka Springs.

All campgrounds in this section are open year-round and have public flush toilets, showers, and sanitary dump stations unless designated otherwise. Toll-free numbers, where listed, are for reservations only.

KID FRIENDLY

Branson KOA
$$$–$$$$$ Branson, Missouri

Although you can't walk into town from here, free shuttle transportation to select shops and shows is provided in season. Sites are paved with picnic tables and barbecue grills. Kids will love the pool and playground. A free pancake breakfast is served daily.

397 Animal Safari Rd. (From US 65 and SR 76, go west 31/3 miles on SR 76 to SR 165, south ¾ mile to Animal Safari Road, and then west less than ¼ mile to the campground, on left.) ☎ ***800-562-4177*** *or 417-334-4414.* https://koa.com. *Total \. 160 full hookups with water and 30- and 50-amp electric, 120 pull-throughs. CATV, data port, laundry, pool. Rates: $57–$60 per site, deluxe sites $84. DISC, MC, V. Open: Mar 15–Dec 15.*

Crater of Diamonds State Park

$$ Murfreesboro, Arkansas

Few places allow you to camp and dig up diamonds that you can keep. A 35-acre field, the eroded surface of a diamond pipe and the only publicly accessible diamond mine in the United States is plowed to bring stones to the surface. Digging tools are for rent at the park, and the rangers help with identification. If diamonds aren't your passion, you can go fishing in the Little Missouri River.

Off SR 301. (From Murfreesboro, take SR 301 southeast 2 miles to the campground, on right.) ☎ ***870-285-3113.*** https://www. arkansasstateparks.com/parks/crater–diamonds–state– park. *Total 47 sites with water and 20- and 30-amp electric, and full hookups, no pull-throughs. Handicap access, laundry. Rates: $38.76 per site; higher weekends and holidays. AE, DISC, MC, V. 14-day maximum stay.*

Hot Springs KOA

$$$–$$$$$ Hot Springs, Arkansas

This campground has terraced sites with well-planned landscaping, so although individual spaces aren't large, they do offer a sense of privacy. Weekend pancake breakfasts are available.

838 McClendon Rd. (Drive east of city 4 miles on US 70, Exit 4, and follow signs to the campground, on left.) ☎ ***800-562-5903*** *or 501-624-5912.* https://koa.com. *Total 70 sites with water and 30- and 50-amp electric, all full hookups, 15 pull-throughs. CATV, data port, laundry, pool, Wi-Fi. Call for latest rates. AE, DISC, MC, V.*

Jacksonport State Park

$$ **Jacksonport, Arkansas**

This charming park, with a historic sternwheeler and 1872 courthouse, was a busy county seat and steamboat port until the arrival of the railroad. A quiet, peaceful campground today, the park offers big grassy sites on the White River with fishing and many mature shade trees.

205 Avenue St., off SR 69. (From Jacksonport, go north on SR 69 ¼ mile to the park, on left.) ☎ **870-523-2143.** *https://www. arkansasstateparks.com/parks/jacksonport-state-park. Total of sites with water and 20- and 30-amp electric, no full hookups, no pull-throughs. Handicap access. Rates: $27 per site. DISC, MC, V. 14-day maximum stay.*

Lake Dardanelle State Park

$$–$$$ **Russellville, Arkansas**

This handsome hilltop park by a lake with ducks and swans is divided into three campgrounds with shade trees and picnic tables. On Lake Dardanelle, you can boat, fish, or water-ski; the park's marina rents the necessary equipment.

Off SR 326. (From the junction of I-40 and SR 7, Exit 81, go south 1 block on SR 7 to SR 326 and then west 5 miles to the park, on right.) ☎ **479-967-5516.** *https://www.arkansasstateparks. com. Total 57 sites with water and 20- and 30-amp electric, 30 full hookups, 4 pull-throughs. Rates start at $34 per site. AE, DISC, MC, V. 14-day maximum stay.*

Springfield KOA

$$$$–$$$$$ **Springfield, Missouri**

This park, convenient to I-40 but far enough away that you don't hear the traffic noises, provides wide sites with many young trees and an adjacent 18-hole golf course with senior discounts.

5775 W. FM 140. (From I-40, Exit 70, go south ¼ mile on CR MM to FM 140 and then east 1¼ mile to the campground, on left.) ☎ ***800-562-1228*** *or 417-831-3645.* https://koa.com. *Total 78 sites with water and 30- and 50-amp electric, 42 full hookups, 71 pull-throughs. Data port, laundry, pool. Rates: Vary seasonally but average $52 per site. DISC, MC, V.*

Good Eats

Penny-pinchers are delighted with the Ozarks because prices, especially for restaurant meals, are generally lower than in many other areas of the country. Big, family-style, all-you-can-eat buffets are available in places such as Branson.

Here are some favorite places to pick up some down-home cooking. Most are open for lunch and early dinner, but don't arrive fashionably late, because they'll probably be closed.

» **B&B Bar-B-Q,** 230 S. East St., Fayetteville, Arkansas (☎ **479-521-3663**): The barbecue pit is fired with hickory, and the bread is homemade. You place your order from an orange phone in your booth, and when the phone lights up, your food is ready. Beef and pork barbecue, batter-dipped fries, fried dill pickles, and fried peach or apple pies dusted with sugar make a generous meal. Open daily from 10:30 a.m. to 8 p.m.

» **Catfish 'N',** 210 Dam Rd., on SR 7 near the Arkansas River Bridge in Dardanelle, Arkansas (☎ **479-229-3321**): Catfish 'N' serves up generous portions of fried catfish and hush puppies, fries, coleslaw, and pickled peppers. You can also get fried or boiled shrimp, fried chicken, and hot fruit cobbler for dessert. Open Thursday from 4 to 8 p.m., and Friday and Saturday from 4 to 9 p.m.

» **The Cliff House Inn,** SR 7, 6 miles south of Jasper, Arkansas (☎ **870-446-2292;** http://www.cliffhouseinnar.com/): This convenient spot, with a great view of Arkansas's Grand Canyon from its balcony, serves burgers, sandwiches, homemade pies, and main dishes (including catfish, fried chicken, and steak). Open Sunday to Thursday from 8 a.m. to 3 p.m., and Friday and Saturday from 8 a.m. to 8 p.m. The inn is closed from the middle of November to the middle of March.

KID FRIENDLY

» **Lambert's,** 1800 W. Highway J, off US 65, Ozark, Missouri (☎ **417-581-ROLL** [7655]; https://throwedrolls.com): Despite its nickname "the home of the throwed roll" Lambert's does-n't pelt you with your dinner — only certain parts of it. Dinners are all-you-can-eat, and the fluffy, slightly sweet dinner rolls are tossed at you as the servers make their rounds. Good main-dish selections include fried chicken, ham, white beans with a side of collard greens. The restaurant is open daily from 10:30 a.m. to 9 p.m. and closed on major holidays.

» **McClard's,** 530 Albert Pike, Hot Springs, Arkansas (☎ **501-624-623-9665;** www.mcclards.com): McClard's was a favorite hang-out for Bill Clinton when he was growing up in Hot Springs. He recalls the tamale spreads — one or two tamales topped with corn chips, beans, chopped beef, cheese, and onions. The restaurant is open Tuesday through Saturday from 11 a.m. to 8 p.m. No credit cards are accepted.

» **Serenity Farm Bread,** 1 block east of US 65, Leslie, Arkansas (☎ 870-447-2211): Baker David Lower bakes sourdough bread without yeast or sugar, using only freshly milled flour from organically grown wheat flour, sea salt, and filtered water. The tasty loaves include French, whole wheat, focaccia, and fruit-filled loaves. The bakery is open Monday, Tuesday, and Friday from 8 a.m. to 5 p.m.. The pastry shop is open Wednesday through Sunday from 9 a.m. to 3 p.m.

» **Skillet Restaurant and Ozark Folk Center Smokehouse,** Mountain View, Arkansas (☎ 870-269-3139; https://www.arkansasstateparks.com/parks/ozark-folk-center-state-park): The rustic restaurant at the Ozark Folk Center serves fresh trout and catfish, country ham, and fried chicken. If you want a small bite, the snack bar serves sandwiches and fried apple and peach pies throughout the day. The restaurant is open May through November, Monday through Saturday from 8 a.m. to 7 p.m. and Sunday from 8 a.m. to 2 p.m.

» **Springfield Brewing Company,** 305 S. Market Ave., Springfield, Missouri (☎ 417-832-TAPS [8277]); https://www.springfieldbrewingco.com): This nostalgic brewpub — with a rooftop beer garden, live music, and a Sunday brunch buffet — is a few blocks from Bass Outdoor World. It's open Monday through Friday from 11 a.m. to 11 p.m., and Saturday and Sunday from 9 a.m. to midnight.

» **Stubby's Bar-B-Q,** 310 Park Ave., Hot Springs, Arkansas (☎ 501-624-1552): Stubby's offers to-go or eat-in meals — smoky baked potatoes cooked in the barbecue pit; ribs coated with a rich, dark sauce; and coleslaw. The restaurant is open Sunday through Thursday from 11 a.m. to 8 p.m., and Friday and Saturday from 11 a.m. to 9 p.m.

» **War Eagle Bean Palace,** SR 98 south of SR 12E. 11045 Ware Eagle Road, between Eureka Springs and Rogers, Arkansas (☎ 866-492-7324; https://wareaglemill.com): From Eureka Springs, take SR 23 south to SR 12E, and turn south on SR 98 to the mill. A water-powered gristmill on the War Eagle River sells stone-ground grits, cornmeal, flour, waffle and pancake mix, hush-puppy mix, and a fish-fry coating, all in patterned cloth bags. The cafe is on the third floor, and there is no elevator; a first-floor table can be set up on request to seat up to six people. Breakfasts include buckwheat waffles with sorghum, stone-ground grits with sausage, and biscuits with sausage gravy. The restaurant is open March through December daily from 8:30 a.m. to 5 p.m. Lunch is served daily from 10:30 a.m. to 4 p.m.; breakfast is served Saturday and Sunday only from 8:30 a.m. to 10:30 a.m. The mill is open from 8:30 a.m. to 5 p.m.

Fast Facts

Area Code
The area codes are as follows: Arkansas **479, 501,** and **870**; Missouri **417** and **573**.

Driving Laws
In Arkansas and Missouri, all passengers must wear seat belts. The speed limit on interstate highways is 75 mph in Arkansas and 70 mph in Missouri. Speed limits in urban areas and secondary roads are lower.

Emergency
Call ☎ **911** in both states. Other sources include the Arkansas State Police (☎ **501-618-8100**) and the Missouri Highway Patrol (☎ **573-751-3313**).

Hospitals
Major hospitals along the route are in Hot Springs, Branson, and Little Rock.

Information
Contact the Arkansas Department of Tourism (☎ **501-682-7777** or 800-NATURAL [628-8725] for a vacation-planning kit; https://www.arkansas.com) or the Missouri Division of Tourism (☎ **573-751-4133**; https://www.visitmo.com).

Road and Weather Conditions
Contact the Arkansas State Highway and Transportation Department (☎ **800-245-1672** or 501-569-2374; www.arkansashighways.com) or the Missouri Department of Transportation (☎ **573-751-2551**; https://www.modot.org).

Taxes
Sales taxes are 6.5 percent (local taxes can add 2.125 percent) in Arkansas, and 4.225 percent (local taxes can add 3.888 percent) in Missouri. State gasoline taxes are 21.8 cents per gallon in Arkansas and 17 cents per gallon in Missouri.

Time Zone
Arkansas and Missouri are on Central time.

5

Seeing the West

IN THIS PART . . .

Discovering Buffalo Bill's fame and the lure of Yellowstone's wonders in Wyoming and Montana

Finding out that New Mexico's enchantments include a famous outlaw, UFO controversy, and History along with georgous sites and unequaled attractions

Visiting the Oregon Coast showcases Pacific Ocean shoreline walks, ocean bound critters, and fresh and salt water fishing opportunites

Driving the California Central Coast for beaches, butterflies, and barbecue

Seeing historical towns as if frozen in time on historic Route 66 from Oklahoma to Los Angeles

Witnessing nature and wildlife at its very best on the ALCAN trip from Seattle to Fairbanks

Chapter **18**

Montana and Wyoming: Tracking Buffalo Bill

A collection of stories about Montana called *The Last Best Place,* issued in 1988 to mark a century of statehood, pretty much sums up the state for outsiders who want to be insiders. Everyone from movie stars to tycoons is discovering Montana, but plenty of room still exists for the rest of us. Wait until you see the Beartooth Highway between Red Lodge and Yellowstone; no less an expert than TV's RV maven, the late Charles Kuralt, once called it the most beautiful roadway in America.

The same is true of Wyoming, which calls itself "high, wide, and handsome." Marked off in a near-square by some civil servants and disdained by pioneers in covered wagons heading for Oregon, the state began as big ranches, many of them owned by Europeans. Even today, cattle outnumber people by about three to one.

What's so fantastic about Montana and Wyoming — the Big Sky Country — is the emptiness, the openness, and the plenitude of land-scape. Driving an RV, knowing that everything you need for comfort is with you and that the road ahead waits with open campsites, road-side trout fishing, and scenic surprises, is as good as it gets in the 21st century.

Choosing Your Route

Setting out from Billings, Montana, and driving south on US 212 to Red Lodge, your tour follows the curves of spectacular Beartooth Highway (named for a rocky outcropping at the summit shaped like a bear's tooth) across a pass with a 10,940-foot summit that drops into Wyoming and Yellowstone National Park. Next, make a circle tour of Yellowstone highlights; after that, drive east along little-traveled Chief Joseph Highway into Cody. From Cody, go east on US 14 to Greybull; then travel south on US 16 to Worland and east on US 16 to Buffalo across the Powder River Pass. From Buffalo, return to Billings by driving north on I-90 back into Montana and pausing at Little Bighorn Battlefield National Monument. The distance traveled is 772 miles.

TIP

Buffalo Bill country is a little distant for a weekend stopover for most people, but if you're in the vicinity in summer and have a yen to see the best part in a couple of days, plan a driving tour from Billings to Red Lodge, Montana, over the Beartooth Highway to the Chief Joseph Highway and into Cody, Wyoming. In Cody, spend your spare time at the Buffalo Bill Center quintet of museums. Stay at the Cody KOA, and you can take a trail ride right from the campground.

Planning Ahead

The best times to take this drive are late spring, summer, and early fall. In winter, snow closes many of the scenic highways, sometimes with little warning, as well as most of the entrances into Yellowstone and most of the campgrounds. Early spring brings snowmelt and mud, and wildflowers don't bloom until June. July and August usually offer the most pleasant weather and always the biggest crowds, with sometimes-maddening traffic and no room to turn off at photo opportunities. Early fall, from Labor Day until early October, is probably the best time to visit because the weather is mild, although days may be rainy.

You can figure any time during late spring, summer, or early fall to be crowded in Yellowstone, so you need to make campground reservations months in advance for the immediate area of the park. Towns such as Billings, Buffalo, and even Red Lodge aren't as busy.

TIP

If you plan to drive the Yellowstone National Park loop (141 miles) on one long day of sightseeing, you probably don't need campground reservations. But if you want to spend more time in the park, make reservations at one of the five campgrounds in the park that accepts them (see the sidebar "Camping in Yellowstone National Park" in this chapter) or in a commercial campground just outside the park in West Yellowstone or Gardiner (see "Our Favorite Campgrounds" later in this chapter).

When you pack, keep in mind that Big Sky Country attire is casual and that you need to include garb for all kinds of weather. Rain gear is essential, as are hiking boots, jeans, jackets, and sweatshirts or sweaters. The days can get hot, with temperatures around Little Bighorn Battlefield sometimes topping 100°F in summer, but during that same week, you can drive to Beartooth Pass in below-freezing weather.

WARNING

Many of the roads in Yellowstone National Park are rough and bumpy because of winter freezes that buckle the pavement. Although roadwork goes on every summer, you may encounter gusts of dust (or mud, if it's been raining), traffic jams, and closed sections of roadway. You may run into frequent traffic jams from sightings of bear, buffalo, and elk. Allow twice as much time as you expect to negotiate Yellowstone's roads. You also find that many park turnoffs that work well for travelers in automobiles don't allow enough space for motor homes or towing long trailers. For maximum efficiency, consider leaving your RV in a campground and taking your car or a rental around the park.

TIP

In July and August, consider skipping Yellowstone and cutting 200 miles out of the drive. Doing so enables you to spend more time in the wide-open spaces and less on bumpy, traffic-clogged roads and in RV campgrounds that can resemble urban parking lots, only more crowded.

For the entire drive, including Yellowstone, allow two weeks.

BUFFALO BILL: AN AMERICAN LEGEND

William F. Cody was born in a log cabin in Iowa, signed on as a bullwhacker driving teams of oxen for 50 cents a day when he was 11, and by age 14 was the youngest Pony Express rider ever hired. During the Civil War, too young to be a soldier, he volunteered as a scout, ranger, and messenger with the 7th Kansas Cavalry on the Union side. He got the nickname "Buffalo Bill" in the late 1860s, when he was hired to kill buffalo to feed the workmen building the Kansas Pacific Railroad.

Buffalo Bill turned out to be bigger than life, thanks to dime novelist Ned Buntline, who told heroic stories about him in paperbacks during the 1870s and 1880s. Cody cashed in on the publicity and created a successful touring show about the Old West, with cowboys and Indians, roping and shooting, and stagecoach races around the ring.

The Buffalo Bill Wild West Show toured America and Europe for 30 years at the end of the 19th century and the beginning of the 20th. Queen Victoria wrote in her diary that she loved it. (She saw it twice.) The show starred such diverse Western characters as crack shot Annie Oakley; Buck Taylor ("King of the Cowboys"); and Chief Sitting Bull, who was paid $50 a week and all his favorite dish (oyster stew) that he could eat.

The city fathers of a newly developing town near Yellowstone in western Wyoming persuaded Cody to head their company because he was "the best-advertised man in the world." He agreed, but with the stipulation that the town be named after him. Cody built a luxury hotel in his namesake town and called it Hotel Irma, after his daughter. He moved to Cody after the Wild West show folded in 1913. He died during a visit to his sister in Denver, where he was buried in 1917.

Must-See Attractions

Beartooth Highway
Red Lodge, Montana

A drive over the 10,947-foot Beartooth Pass is one of America's great thrill rides, especially for an RVer. Even the curves have names like Mae West and Frozen Man. Have your cameras ready for once-in-a-lifetime views, and be prepared for some roadside snow play.

WARNING

In marginal weather and at the fringes of the late May–to–early October season, check the road conditions before setting out by calling the US Forest Service office in Red Lodge (☎ **406-446-2103**). After you hit the road, tackle the switchbacks with caution, especially when you're towing a vehicle. Most turnouts along the way are big enough for any RV, so if your courage fails, you can always turn around and go back. The alternate route to Yellowstone from Red Lodge is to return to I-90 and travel east to Livingston and south on US 89 to Gardiner and the north entrance to the park, near Mammoth Hot Springs.

US 212 between Red Lodge and the northeast entrance to Yellowstone National Park, 68 miles. ☎ 406-446-2103 for road conditions. http://beartoothhighway.com. Both roads are usually open from late May or early June until early to mid-Oct, depending on local snow conditions. Driving time is about 3 hours.

Buffalo Bill Center of the West
Cody, Wyoming

In the middle of Cody, six world-class museums are gathered in one sprawling complex that many call the Smithsonian of the West. The Buffalo Bill Museum is particularly lively, with posters from his shows, furniture, jewelry, and gifts that European royalty presented to him.

The Plains Indian Museum is magnificent, with life-size figures in various ceremonial dress. Filling the exhibit areas are cradle boards, painted buffalo robes, medicine blankets, pipe bags for carrying ceremonial pipes, grizzly-bear-claw necklaces, and ceremonial dresses used in the religious Ghost Dances of the 1890s.

The Whitney Gallery of Western Art, named for New York sculptor Gertrude Vanderbilt Whitney, displays a replica of artist Frederic Remington's studio and the original studio of Western illustrator W. H. D. Koerner, along with major Western works. The H. Peter and Jeannette Kriendler Gallery of Contemporary Western Art celebrates today's artists.

The Cody Firearms Museum, one of the world's largest and certainly the most detailed of its kind, includes an engraved gun that belonged to Annie Oakley, one of the stars of the Wild West show.

The Draper Museum of Natural History is an interactive walk-through of Yellowstone National Park's geology, including a path displaying slabs from different geologic ages and exhibits on current issues, such as the reintroduction of wolves into the environment.

The McCracken Research Library houses a collection of traditional cowboy songs and range ballads, as well as extensive archives of photographs, documents, films, books, and original manuscripts relating to the West.

Allow a half-day to a full day for the entire complex.

720 Sheridan Ave. ☎ ***307-587-4771***. *https://centerofthewest. org/. RV parking: Designated lots adjacent to the center. Admission to 6 museums good for 2 days: $19.50 adults, $18.50 seniors and students 18 and older with valid ID, ages 13–17 $13, 12 and under free. Open: Thurs–Sun Dec 1–Feb 28. Call ahead for summer hours. Closed on Christmas Day and New Year's Day.*

Chief Joseph Highway
Cody, Wyoming

The Chief Joseph Highway, SR 296, was a favorite of intrepid travelers who didn't mind the gravel roadway. Now this scenic route is completely paved, lightly traveled, and breathtakingly beautiful. Running 46 miles between the turnoff from Beartooth Highway (US 212) to SR 120, 17 miles northwest of Cody, the Chief Joseph is named for the Nez Perce chief who led his tribe through this area in 1877 while fleeing the US Army. The route follows William Clark's Fork of the Yellowstone River for the first part of the journey and then turns into a corkscrew of switchbacks as it climbs to Wyoming's highest bridge, 8,060 feet, at Dead Indian Summit. This construction, finished in 1995, completed Wyoming's goal to pave all its state highways. Allow two hours.

SR 296, between US 212 (Beartooth Highway) and SR 120 (17 miles northwest of Cody), a distance of 46 miles. Road open year-round.

Jim Gatchell Memorial Museum
Buffalo, Wyoming

With 15,000 artifacts arranged in two adjacent buildings, this museum offers the real story of the Wyoming range wars and the Indian wars set out in miniature dioramas. Gatchell was a druggist who collected historical artifacts from the day he opened his drugstore in 1900. Among the collections are dolls, firearms, Crow and Cheyenne beaded deerskin garments, buffalo and horsehide winter coats, and homemade knives confiscated from prisoners in the Johnson County Jail. Allow two hours.

100 Fort St. (at the corner of SR 16 and Main Street). ☎ 307-684-9331. https://www.jimgatchell.com. RV parking: Free city parking lot across from museum sometimes has space; otherwise, use street parking.

Admission: $7 adults, $5 seniors & retired military & veterans, Active Duty military free, $5 ages 12–18; $3 ages 6–11, free 5 and under, Open: May 26 to Sept 4 on Monday through Friday from 6 a.m. to 5 p.m., and Sundays 12 to 5 p.m., Sept 4 to May Monday to Friday 9 a.m. to 4 p.m. Closed on federal holidays though open July 4 and Veterans' Day.

Little Bighorn Battlefield National Monument
Crow Agency, Montana

The famous battle lasted less than an hour on June 25, 1876, when a force of some 5,000 Sioux and Cheyenne warriors, under the leadership of Sitting Bull and other chiefs, wiped out Custer's troops while two other battalions of the 7th Cavalry waited on a distant ridge for word to join Custer. The handsome, arrogant Custer, underestimating the Plains Indian forces, rashly decided to divide his 600 troops into thirds to create a pincers action and then attacked without waiting for the others.

From a visitors' center, you walk uphill to a fenced cemetery with tombstones that document the soldiers' names (insofar as they are known) and where the men were believed to have fallen. Although accounts vary, estimates put the number of Indian casualties at 150.

WARNING

Signs on the site caution visitors wandering around the battlefield to watch out for rattlesnakes.

Allow two hours.

Little Bighorn, 2 miles south of the town of Crow Agency, Montana, off I-90 at Exit 510, east on US 212 to battlefield turnoff (marked). ☎ *406-638-2621.* https://www.nps.gov/libi. *RV parking: Large lot at visitor center. Admission: $20 per passenger vehicle. Open: Call ahead for days, hours, and up-to date-information.*

Yellowstone National Park
Yellowstone National Park, Wyoming

Glorious, awe-inspiring, and sometimes infuriating, Yellowstone National Park has more attractions to offer a visitor than almost any other park in the country, but sometimes, finding them is difficult. In July and August, the roads can be bad and full of traffic. Yes, RVs can be among the worst culprits. You may be tempted to turn around and head out, back to less-crowded highways and friendlier campgrounds. The big burns — entire hillsides of dead trees for miles and miles — are depressing to look at and slow to return to life. Early autumn may bring drizzly days without diminishing the crowds; springtime often is muddy, making the already-bad roads worse. And more than 3 million visitors a year keep passing through.

Since an earthquake threw off its rhythm, Old Faithful has turned into Old Not-Quite-So-Predictable and you may have to wait anywhere from 35 to 120 minutes to catch the famous geyser act. You might do better, if time is limited, by driving through the geothermal areas, keeping your eyes open for eruptions. Steamboat, in the Norris Geyser Basin at Norris, is the tallest geyser but rarely shows off for visitors. Nearby Echinus is more reliable, spouting off about once an hour. (For the locations and routes of these other attractions, pick up the latest map at the park.)

Mammoth Hot Springs is the place to see Technicolor terraces of colored limestone boiling up from the earth and numerous animals on cold days; large elk congregate around Mammoth, where it's warm. Grand Canyon of the Yellowstone has plenty of RV parking at a large lot at the trailhead, a short walk from a dramatic viewpoint. Lamar Valley offers good, if distant, animal spotting for herds of buffalo. I've shot good close-ups during the fringe seasons at Sylvan Lake on the east entrance road and along the Firehole River at Lower Geyser Basin. Bears are a long shot; you may glimpse a bear along the highway, but sightings are much rarer than they used to be, because rangers now discourage the furry freeloaders and those who feed them.

WARNING

Never approach a wild animal on foot, and don't leave your vehicle when you see one; you could be maimed or killed. Be cautious in thermal areas. Never step off designated walkways or boardwalks onto the fragile crust.

Northwestern corner of Wyoming, with a few acres in the eastern edges of Idaho and Montana. ☎ 307-344-2117 for road information and general information; ☎ 307-344-7311 for lodging, dining, and camping reservations and up-to-date pricing information. https://www.yellowstonenationalparklodges.com. RV parking: Some designated RV parking in populated and commercial areas; 12 campgrounds with RV camping $20; some but not all *turnouts along the roadways large enough for RVs. Admission: $35 per car; $30 motorcycle or snowmobile, $20 for hikers, bicyclists, and skiers. Seniors with the America the Beautiful–National Parks and Federal Recreational Lands Pass–Senior Pass are free. Open: Year-round. Road access all year from the north entrance, US 89 at Gardiner, Montana; other park entrances open on seasonal basis but usually closed Nov–May.*

More Cool Things to See and Do

Montana and Wyoming are full of fascinating sights, activities, and outdoor pursuits. See the following list for some of my favorites; you'll find many more on your driving tour.

» **Ride the trail. Buffalo Bill's Trail Rides,** 5561 Greybull Hwy., Cody, Wyoming (☎ **307-587-2369**), set out from the Cody KOA Campground daily from June through September. Reservations are advised. Allow half a day.

» **Shoot the gunslingers.** Bring a camera, because the photogenic Cody Gunslingers congregate and shoot it out in and around the **Irma Hotel,** Sheridan and 12th Streets, Cody, Wyoming (☎ **307-587-4221**). Allow one hour.

Admission is free. The shootouts are held from Memorial Day through Labor Day Monday through Saturday at 6 p.m.

» **Greet a grizzly.** The closest you can safely get to a grizzly bear is at the **Grizzly Discovery Center,** Grizzly Park, near the west entrance to Yellowstone National Park in West Yellowstone, Montana (☎ **800-257-2570** or 406-646-7001; https://www.grizzlydiscoveryctr.org). Here, in a natural habitat, a not-for-profit center takes care of bad-boy bears from Canada and Alaska, such as Coram, Nakina, Sam, Sow 101, and Spirit, as well as a resident wolf pack. Allow two hours.

RV parking is available in a designated lot. Admission is $13 adults, $12.24 seniors, $8 ages 5 to 12, free for 4 and under. It's open daily from 8 a.m. to 4 p.m.

» **The Virginian Restaurant** (☎ **307-684-5976**) is open Monday through Saturday from 7 to 11 a.m. and noon to 9 p.m., Sunday from 9 a.m. to 2 p.m. The Saloon (☎ **307-684-8989**) is open from 11 a.m. to closing in the summer and 5 p.m. to closing in winter.

» **Do the touristy thing.** The big loopy handwriting still is clear behind the framed section of the sandstone pillar: *W Clark, July 25, 1806.* William Clark of Lewis and Clark fame couldn't resist leaving his name and the date of his visit carved on **Pompey's Pillar** (☎ **406-875-2400;** www.pompeyspillar.org), a 700-foot sandstone plug sticking up from the flats along the Yellowstone River east of Billings, Montana. A wooden staircase with hand-rails leads up 500 steps to the top of the pillar. Allow one hour.

Pompey's Pillar National Historic Landmark is 28 miles east of Billings, Montana, on I-90 at Exit 23; follow the signs. RV park-ing is available in a large lot by the visitors' center. Admission is free, but parking is $7. The site is open daily from Memorial Day through Labor Day 8 a.m. to 8 p.m. and Labor Day through September 30 from 9 a.m. to 4 p.m.

» **Set 'em up, Bill. . . .** Established in 1893 and a National Historic Landmark, **Sheridan Inn,** 856 N. Broadway, Sheridan, Wyoming (https://sheridaninn.com), was once owned and run by Buffalo Bill and boasted the Buffalo Bill Cody Saloon. Today, the inn is a fully functional hotel with 22 rooms and event space; ☎ **307-365-7861** for reservations and information.

RV parking is available on the street or in a designated lot. For more information on Sheridan, Wyoming, contact the Sheridan Convention and Visitors Bureau at ☎ **800-453-3650.**

KID FRIENDLY

» **Brave Butch Cassidy.** Historic buildings from all across Wyoming are set up in **Old Trail Town,** 1831 Demaris Dr., at the edge of Cody, Wyoming (☎ **307-587-5302;** www.nezperce.com/trltown.html), in a photogenic setting. Mountain man Jeremiah Johnson's grave is in the cemetery. See outlaw-hideout cabins such as Sundance Kid's Mud Spring Cabin and Butch Cassidy's Hole in the Wall Gang Cabin.

RV parking is available. Admission is $10 adults, $9 seniors, $5 kids 6 to 12, free for 5 and under. Active military is free. The site is open daily mid-May through mid-September from 8 a.m. to 8 p.m.

Our Favorite Campgrounds

Montana and Wyoming are RV-friendly states with plenty of public and privately owned campgrounds; good, lightly traveled roads (except those in Yellowstone National Park); and wide-open spaces. Although state parks and national-forest campgrounds usually don't offer full RV hookups, the scenery is so great and the vistas so wide that staying a day or two is worth the hassle of not having a hookup.

All campgrounds listed in this chapter have public flush toilets, showers, and sanitary dump stations unless designated otherwise. Toll-free numbers, where listed, are for reservations. For Yellowstone National Park campgrounds (except Fishing Bridge RV Park), see this chapter's sidebar "Camping in Yellowstone National Park."

Billings KOA

$$$$–$$$$$ Billings, Montana

The Billings KOA is the world's first KOA campground. This granddaddy of them all offers shady sites, some with gravel but most with grass. You can choose a spot on the Yellowstone River with freshwater fishing, trees, grass, or long pull-throughs with patios. When you don't feel like cooking, you can buy breakfast and evening barbecue dinners at the campground in summer.

547 Garden Ave. (From I-90 at 27th Street, Exit 450, go east 600 feet to Garden Avenue, turn right, and follow signs to second campground on the left.) ☎ ***800-562-8546*** *or 406-252-3104.* https:// koa.com/campgrounds/billings. *Total of 118 sites with water and 30- and 50-amp electric, 40 full hookups, 90 pull-throughs. CATV, data port, handicap access, laundry, pool, spa, Wi-Fi. Call for latest rates and information. AE, DISC, MC, V. Open: Apr 15–Oct 15.*

Buffalo Bill State Park

BARGAIN ALERT

$–$$ Cody, Wyoming

Two campgrounds belong to Buffalo Bill State Park: the North Shore Bay, 9 miles west of Cody on US 14/16/20, and North Fork, 14 miles west on the same highway. You find no hookups and narrow sites, but the areas are attractive, each offering fishing and boating, and you can't beat the price! Reservations are not accepted.

North Shore Bay, Buffalo Bill State Park. (9 miles west of Cody on US 14/16/20; campground is on the left.) ☎ ***307-587-9227.*** *Total of 35 sites, no hookups, 32 pull-throughs. Call for current rates. No credit cards. No reservations. Open: May–Sept. 14-day maximum stay.*

Twin Creeks Campground

KID FRIENDLY

$$$$–$$$$$ Buffalo, Wyoming

This campground has one deluxe campsite with a landscaped fenced patio, gazebo, propane barbecue, glass–and–wrought-iron picnic table with four chairs, and a planter filled with bright petunias. You can reserve the site. Other sites are much less elaborate and narrow. You can also enjoy freshwater fishing, a fenced dog walk, kid-pleasing miniature golf, and blueberry-pancake breakfasts with bacon and sausage in summer.

Off US 16. At 87 US 16 E, Buffalo, WY 82834. (From junction of I-90 and US 16, Exit 58, go west 1 mile on US 16 to campground, on the left.) 87 US 16 E, Buffalo, WY 82834. ☎ ***307-684-5423.*** https:// campnative.com/campgrounds/usa/wy/buffalo/twin–creeks– campgrounds. *Total of 58 sites with water and 30- and 50-amp electric, 45 full hookups, 37 pull-throughs. Data port, laundry, pool, spa. Call for latest rates and reservations. DISC, MC, V.*

Yellowstone Grizzly RV Park

$$$$–$$$$$ **West Yellowstone, Montana**

Conveniently located in town, Yellowstone Grizzly is a good choice for RVers who are towing or have rented a car and want to spend two or three days exploring Yellowstone National Park. Sites are wide, with patios and gravel, and pull-throughs are a comfortable 70 feet long. As many as six people pay the same rate as two, making this campground a good choice for families. Shops and restaurants are a short walk away.

*210 S. Electric St. (From junction of US 191 and Highway 20, go south ½ mile on 191/Canyon Street to Gray Wolf Avenue and west ¼ mile to entrance.) ☎ **406-646-4466**. https://www.grizzlyrv. com. Total of 191 sites with water and 30- and 50-amp electric, all full hookups, 97 pull-throughs. CATV, data port, handicap access, laundry, Wi-Fi. Call for latest rates and reservations. AE, DISC, MC, V. Open: May 1–Oct 21.*

Yellowstone National Park, West Entrance KOA

$$$$$ **West Yellowstone, Montana**

In a quiet location outside town, this campground offers large sites with patios. Daily breakfasts and barbecues are available in summer when you don't feel like cooking. You can rent bikes, arrange tours, book horseback riding nearby, and go fishing. Big, fancy motor homes can fit comfortably in the 64 pull-throughs.

*Off US 20. (The park is 6 miles west of west park entrance on US 20.) ☎ **800-562-7591** or 406-646-7606. https://koa.com/ campgrounds/yellowstone–park/. Total of 198 sites with water and 30- and 50-amp electric, 120 full hookups, 64 pull-throughs. Data port, handicap access, laundry, indoor pool and spa. Call for latest rates and reservations. DISC, MC, V. Open: May 22–Oct 1.*

CAMPING IN YELLOWSTONE NATIONAL PARK

Pay close attention if you want to book a campsite in Yellowstone National Park. Here's how it goes: Yellowstone has 12 campgrounds suitable for size appropriate RVs. Five campgrounds have sites that you can reserve by contacting Xanterra Parks and Resorts (☎ 307-344-7311; https://www.xanterra.com). Of those five, only one has hookups: Fishing Bridge RV Park, with 346 spaces, opens mid-May to early October. Rates change from season to season. If you've come to experience the great outdoors, with plenty of peace and quiet and birdsong, this campground may not be the place for you. If your RV is soft-sided, has any canvas on its body instead of metal, you won't be allowed to camp, because this is bear country. But if you want a convenient site in the park with a hookup, don't mind crowds, and know the dates you want to stay, you need to make a reservation ahead of time.

The other four campgrounds can be reserved, and are in heavily used. If you have a reservation date near the campgrounds' opening or closing dates, check before your arrival to make sure that the facilities are open; bad weather can cause late openings or early closings. These campgrounds are just as crowded as Fishing Bridge but without the benefit of hookups. Generator use is limited. All sites are back-ins.

The following campgrounds charge $20 plus tax per night per site, have a 14-day limit, and accept credit cards (Discovery, MasterCard, and Visa). For reservations, call ☎ 307-344-7311.

- **Bridge Bay:** On Yellowstone Lake not far from Fishing Bridge. 432 narrow, paved campsites; marina. Open late May to mid-September.

- **Canyon Village:** In Canyon Village, near the Grand Canyon of the Yellowstone. 272 narrow, grassy sites (no slideouts permitted). Open early June to mid-September.

- **Grant Village:** In Grant Village, on Yellowstone Lake. 425 narrow, grassy sites. Open mid-June to mid-September.

- **Madison:** On the Madison River, 14 miles from the west entrance. 277 paved, narrow (12 feet wide) campsites; no showers. Open early May to late October.

(continued)

(continued)

The park service operates seven campgrounds in Yellowstone National Park that accept no reservations (https://www.nps.gov/yell/pphtml/camping.html). Camping is on a first-come, first-served basis and limited to 14 days. Generator use is limited. Except for Mammoth Hot Springs, these campgrounds are in less-traveled areas of the park. *Note the vehicle size restrictions for each.*

- **Indian Creek:** On the Grand Loop Road, about halfway between Mammoth Hot Springs and Norris Geyser Basin. 75 narrow, paved sites (12 feet wide), maximum length of 28 feet. $14 a night per site, cash only. Open mid-June to mid-September.

- **Lewis Lake:** In a wooded area near a lake 12 miles north of the park's south entrance on US 89. 85 narrow, paved sites (12 feet wide), maximum length of 35 feet; no flush toilets or showers. $14 a night per site, cash only. Open mid-June to early November.

- **Mammoth Hot Springs:** At Mammoth Hot Springs, 5 miles south of the park's north entrance at Gardiner. 85 narrow, grassy sites (12 feet wide), maximum length of 35 feet; no showers. $16 a night per site, cash only. Open year-round.

- **Norris:** On Grand Loop, at Norris Geyser Basin, 25 miles south of the park's north entrance at Gardiner. 116 paved, narrow sites (12 feet wide) with some trees, maximum length of 28 feet; no showers. $16 a night per site, cash only. Open mid-May to mid-September.

- **Pebble Creek:** On the Lamar Valley Road 7 miles southwest of the park's northeast entrance at Cooke City. 36 narrow, paved sites (12 feet wide), maximum length of 30 feet; no flush toilets or showers. $14 a night per site, cash only. Open early June to mid-September.

- **Slough Creek:** Off Lamar Valley Road, near Tower Junction; access road is 2½ miles of gravel. 29 narrow, dirt sites (12 feet wide), maximum length of 30 feet; no showers. $14 a night per site, cash only. Open late May to late October.

- **Tower Fall:** 2½ miles south of Tower Junction, on Grand Loop Road. 32 narrow, dirt sites (12 feet wide), maximum length of 25 feet; no flush toilets or showers. $14 a night per site, cash only. Open mid-May to late September.

Good Eats

Restaurants in Montana and Wyoming are mainly in the plains and primarily in towns and cities. Don't expect to find fast food out on the scenic highways. Be thankful that you're carrying your own kitchen.

WARNING

Be sure to stock up on groceries and gasoline whenever you see a suitable and convenient spot.

» **Bogart's,** 11 S. Broadway, Red Lodge, Montana (☎ 406-446-1784): Pizza, hamburgers, and Mexican food, along with beer, bring a bigger-than-Bogart smile. A fan named the place after Humphrey Bogart, whose likeness adorns the place. RV parking is available on the street. Open Sunday to Friday from 11 a.m. to 8 p.m. and Friday and Saturday 11 a.m. to 9 p.m.

» **Hotel Irma,** 1192 Sheridan Ave., Cody, Wyoming (☎ 800-745-4762 or 307-587-4221; www.irmahotel.com): Try the prime rib, served daily, or lunch specials such as mountain trout and buffalo burgers. RV parking is available on the street or in designated city lots. Open daily from 6 a.m. to 8 p.m. winter, 6 a.m. to 10 p.m. summer.

» **Walker's Grill,** 2700 N. 1st Ave. N, Billings, Montana (☎ 406-245-9291): Open only for dinner, Walker's serves hot homemade bread, meatloaf with gravy and mashed potatoes, pizzas, burgers, and fries, and trendy salads. RV parking is available in a designated lot or on the street. Open daily from 5 p.m. to 10 p.m.

Fast Facts

Area Code
The area codes are **406** in Montana and **307** in Wyoming.

Driving Laws
All RV occupants must wear seat belts in Montana and Wyoming. The maximum speed limit on interstates in Montana and Wyoming is 75 mph. Speed limits are lower in urban areas and at night.

Emergency
Call ☎ **911** in both states.

Hospitals
Along the route, major hospitals are in Billings, Montana; Cody, Wyoming; and Sheridan, Wyoming.

Information
Sources include Travel Montana (☎ **800-847-4868**; https://www.visitmt.com) and the Wyoming Department of Tourism (☎ **800-225-5996** or **307-777-7777**; https://www.travelwyoming.com).

Road and Weather Conditions
In Montana, call ☎ **800-226-ROAD (7623)** or 511, or the Highway Patrol at ☎ **855-MHP-3777**. When in Wyoming, call ☎ **888-996-7623** or 307-772-0824, or dial **#ROAD (#7623)** on a cellphone. For conditions in Yellowstone Park, call ☎ **307-344-2117**.

Taxes
Montana doesn't have sales tax. In Wyoming, sales tax is 4 percent, but local taxes can raise it to 6 percent. State gasoline taxes are 27.8 cents per gallon in Montana and 14 cents per gallon in Wyoming.

Time Zone
Montana and Wyoming are on Mountain Standard Time.

Chapter **19**

New Mexico: Billy the Kid Meets E.T.

"**L**and of Enchantment" is the license-plate slogan for New Mexico, and the magic is everywhere. Red-rock canyons and mesas abut hazy blue hills, which in turn stand out against snowcapped peaks topping 10,000 feet. *Ristras* (strings of red chile peppers) hang from the eaves of adobe houses, and silver-and-turquoise jewelry winks at you from gas station counter cases. Ancient cliff dwellings rest within sheltered rocky overhangs, Native Americans invoke the spirits of the past with traditional dances, and aspen leaves quiver in the first cold winds.

The Sandia people arrived 25,000 years ago, the first of ten distinct groups to occupy the land. The Southwest is where, in the late 19th century, a slight, cocky Brooklyn-born boy nicknamed "the Kid" — later Billy the Kid — entered legend. Here too, some people believe that aliens crashed-landed a spaceship in the middle of the 20th century. A bear cub that survived a Lincoln County forest fire in 1950 entered America's annals as Smokey Bear, the animated animal on everybody's black-and-white TV sets who growled, "Only you can prevent forest fires." On July 16, 1945, at White Sands Proving Grounds, the world's first nuclear bomb test at Trinity Site broke windows 120 miles away in Silver City, the town where Billy the Kid grew up.

Choosing Your Route

El Paso, Texas, makes an ideal jumping-off point for entering southern New Mexico. The route follows the Rio Grande north, paralleling I-25 on rural roads that bisect pecan groves and chile fields to Hatch, some 65 miles away, and then turns west, following SR 26 and US 180 to Silver City (100 miles). Return south on US 180 to I-10, go east to Las Cruces, and then take I-70 past White Sands National Monument to Alamogordo (168 miles). Continue east to Roswell and north to Fort Sumner (200 miles). Drive east on US 60 to Clovis and south via I-70 back to Roswell (168 miles). Some 77 miles south is Carlsbad Caverns, and another 165 miles along US 62 returns you to El Paso. The total drive is 943 miles.

TIP

If time is short, you can eliminate some parts of this journey to make an accelerated dash to the main attractions. Get an early start from El Paso, and drive north on I-25 to Las Cruces, where US 70 (Exit 8) turns east to Alamogordo. Pause to take the Dunes Drive through White Sands National Monument, and continue along US 70 to Ruidoso Downs. The 69-mile Billy the Kid National Scenic Byway takes only an hour to cover; allow a second hour for a walking tour of Lincoln. If you have kids (or kids at heart) onboard, pause at Smokey Bear Historical State Park in Capitan. Roswell's International UFO Museum and Research Center is a must-stop. Then head south to Carlsbad Caverns National Park, allowing a minimum of an hour for a self-guided tour of the Big

Room. Return to El Paso via US 62/180. If you don't have reservations, your best bets for campground overnight lodging are around Alamogordo, Roswell, and Carlsbad.

Planning Ahead

Spring and fall are the best seasons to visit New Mexico. Winter brings snow to higher elevations, such as Silver City, although the deserts around Carlsbad usually are mild. Summer heat *sizzles* the terrain surrounding Carlsbad Caverns, but the temperature below ground stays at 56°F — a real treat. Even in winter, most days are sunny. The southern part of the state claims to get 300 days of sunshine a year. The mountains around Cloudcroft get 25 inches of rain a year, while the city of Las Cruces, less than 100 miles away, gets only 8 inches.

WARNING

Expect to see torrential late-afternoon thunderstorms in July and August, and *never* camp in a dry riverbed because of the potential danger of flash floods.

TIP

Although making campground reservations is a good idea, it's not essential in many parts of southern New Mexico, especially after summer. If you want to make reservations, you can do so at a commercial RV park near one of the major attractions. State parks, such as City of Rocks, don't accept reservations.

When packing, take along sweaters and jackets no matter when you visit because summer nights are cool — even in the desert — and Carlsbad Caverns is a constant 56°F. Winter days, even in ski resorts, are cold but usually dry and sunny. Bring plenty of sunscreen, because the sun's rays can reach your skin instantly through the cold clear air.

Allow 8 to 14 days to drive this itinerary, with time for hiking and exploring Carlsbad Caverns.

THE TRINITY SITE: TESTING THE FIRST ATOMIC BOMB

Due north of the White Sands National Monument, on the White Sands Missile Range — about 50 miles as the crow flies — is the Trinity Site. This guarded area is where the world's first nuclear bomb was tested on July 16, 1945. A stone memorial stands at Ground Zero, where the force of the blast melted the dirt into a strange glassy green substance called Trinitite.

The site is open to the public only two days a year: the first Saturdays of April and October, when tours are conducted from Alamogordo. Cars line up in single file with headlights on and proceed behind a military escort to Ground Zero. You also can visit the ranch house where the bomb was assembled. Some radiation remains at the site. For more information, call the chamber of commerce at ☎ 575-437-6120.

Must-See Attractions

Billy the Kid National Scenic Byway
Lincoln County, New Mexico

An official highway route proceeds along the Billy the Kid trail, starting from the new Billy the Kid Interpretive Center and adjacent museum, with a scaled-down walk-through version of the byway on US 70 in Ruidoso Downs. Nearby attractions commemorate the Western icon; Ruidoso Downs, for example, boasts a Billy the Kid Casino with 300 electronic slot machines. Allow one hour.

The 69-mile trail (90 minutes driving time, if you don't stop anywhere) goes west on US 70 and north on SR 48 to Ruidoso, where the Old Mill Gift and Book Shop on Suddarth Drive was destroyed by file in 2017 had claimed to be a Billy the Kid Hideout was a serious loss to the town. From Ruidoso, SR 48 continues north to US 380 and Capitan (Smokey Bear headquarters); dips south to Fort Stanton on SR 220; and continues east on US 380 to Lincoln, which is the key to the most historic part of the Kid's life, the Lincoln County War.

The whole town of Lincoln is a National Historic Landmark and a state monument. Kids of all ages enjoy the Old West atmosphere. A self-guided walking-tour map of the town is available at the Lincoln County Heritage Trust Historical Museum. Follow the trail from the museum to the Wortley Hotel, the old courthouse across the street, the Tunstall Store, the site of the Murphy-Dolan Store, and the site of the McSween House.

Billy the Kid Interpretive Center, US 70 East (☎ 575-378-5318; next to Hubbard Museum of the American West), Ruidoso Downs. ☎ 575-378-4142. www.billybyway.com. *RV parking: Large lot near the center. Admission: Center is free. Museum admission $7 adults, $5 seniors, $2 ages 6–16, free 5 and under. Open: Daily 9 a.m.–5 p.m. Closed major holidays.*

Carlsbad Caverns

Carlsbad Caverns National Park
Carlsbad, New Mexico

Even card-carrying claustrophobics won't mind going underground to the spacious caverns of Carlsbad, unless the elevator ride from the visitor center (down 75 floors) is too unnerving. The self-guided tour takes an hour (including the elevator ride down and back) and covers a lit circular trail around a gigantic cavern, big enough to contain 14 football fields. Highlights include Hall of Giants; Giant Dome; Lower Cave; and Top of the Cross, with its 255-foot ceiling. The Bottomless Pit (140 feet deep) is intimidating. Be prepared for a close encounter with a cluster of sleeping Mexican freetail bats. Most of the bats are far from the main tour routes, with one exception: Visitors gather every summer evening at bat-flight time in an amphitheater at the mouth of the cave to watch the 300,000-member colony speed out at the rate of up to 5,000 bats a minute. The bats are in search of their evening meal: 3 tons of insects. (Think of that fact this way: There'll be fewer mosquitoes and flies to pester you.)

TIP

Wear low-heeled, nonskid walking shoes, and anticipate a walk of approximately 1 mile inside the Big Room. Take a sweater; even when the outside temperature climbs to 97°F, the temperature inside the caverns is always near 56°F.

Although kids love the caves, they can't run about freely; because of the potential dangers, all visitors must stay on the pathways. The best tour for kids is the self-guided tour of the Big Room. Ranger-led tours are more informative, but kids may get anxious during the lectures. Allow a half-day.

3225 National Parks Hwy. (Drive southeast from Carlsbad 18 miles to Whites City, and take SR 7 west into the park for 7 miles to the visitor center.) ☎ 888-900-CAVE (2283), 575-785-2232 for information, or 877-444-6777 for reservations. https://www.nps.gov/cave/index.htm. *RV parking: Designated area in large lot at the visitor-center entrance. Admission: Cave tour $15 adults; free ages 15 and under. Additional fees for touring other areas of the caverns; bat-flight program free. Open: Visitor center daily year-round 8 a.m.–5 p.m.; Big Room opens at 9 a.m.; last tour at 2 p.m. for walking and last elevator at 3:30 p.m. Closed Christmas Day. No campgrounds in the park. No pets allowed in caverns; kennels available.*

Additional tours: Kings Palace Tour, ranger-led, 1½-hour tour of four caves, $8 adults, $4 ages 6–13, free 5 and under, reservations required; Slaughter Canyon Cave, ranger-led, slip-and-slide tour of cave without human-made walkways or added lighting, $15 adults, $7.50 ages 6–16, ages 5 and under not admitted, reservations required. ☎ 877-444-6777. Tours available daily in summer, Sat–Sun tours in winter only.

International UFO Museum and Research Center
Roswell, New Mexico

The city of Roswell has a tongue-in-cheek attitude about its flying-saucer fame. One city brochure is titled "Some of our most famous visitors . . . came from out of state."

The International UFO Museum and Research Center gets some 200,000 visitors a year from around the world, there to see displays on the Roswell incident in 1947 (see the sidebar "UFOs: The Roswell incident") and other claimed UFO sightings in New Mexico and elsewhere. A large gift shop does a brisk sale in UFO souvenirs and T-shirts. Allow two hours.

114 S. Main St. ☎ 800-822-3545 or 575-625-1907. https://www. roswellufomuseum.com. RV parking: Street parking; city streets are wide enough for RVs to park comfortably. Admission: $5 adults; $3 seniors, military, and first responders; $2 children 5–15, Free 4 and under. Open: Daily 9 a.m.–5 p.m. Closed Easter, Thanksgiving, Christmas Day, New Year's Day.

UFOs: THE ROSWELL INCIDENT

The International UFO Museum and Research Center, founded by key figures who were in Roswell and close to the events of July 1947, has been open since 1991. Lt. Walter G. Haut, public relations director for Roswell Army Air Field in 1947, wrote the first narrative of the events, which appeared in the *Roswell Daily Record* on July 8, 1947. Glenn Dennis, an ambulance driver for the Ballard Funeral Home in Roswell, was at the Army-base hospital on the night of the alleged crash and was told by medical staff that at least five bodies of aliens were recovered from the crash site and brought into the hospital. But within a week, all stories of the crash were denied; all informants and witnesses were hushed; and nothing else was heard about the incident until 1978 when UFO researchers began to interview people who claimed a connection to the event, then some writers published conspiracy books about Roswell in 1980. Haut and Dennis felt that a museum needed to be established in Roswell. Although Haut is convinced that aliens have visited Earth, the museum simply presents the known information.

Although details of the event often are confusing or conflicting, it seems to be irrefutable that *something* happened in Roswell in the summer of 1947. The truth is out there. . . .

Living Desert State Park
Carlsbad, New Mexico

KID FRIENDLY

The stars of the show at Living Desert are its birds and animals, all of them native to the Chihuahua Desert, most of them brought here because of injuries or illness and scheduled to be released back into the wild. Those that are too ill or too old to return stay on. The setting is a hilltop covered with native cacti and other plants. A well-manicured trail wends its way through the terrain and offers surprises at every turn. Kids have a chance to see animals in a natural environment. In the gift shop, you can buy small native cactus plants in pots. Plan to visit in the cooler early-morning hours when the animals are more active. Allow at least two hours.

Skyline Drive off US 285 north of Carlsbad; watch for signs.
☎ ***575-887-5516.*** www.emnrd.state.nm.us/PRD/LivingDesert.htm. *RV parking: Large paved lot in front of the museum. Admission: $5 adults. $3 ages 7–12, free 6 and under. Tours are self-guided. Open: Daily summer 8 a.m.–5 p.m.; winter 9 a.m.–5 p.m., with last tour at 3:30 p.m.*

New Mexico Museum of Space History
Alamogordo, New Mexico

KID FRIENDLY

You can't miss this gold-tinted, four-story glass tower as you drive south on US 54. The distinctive building houses the International Space Hall of Fame, which features a simulated walk on Mars, an IMAX dome theater and planetarium, an Astronaut Memorial Garden, and a Shuttle Camp program for kids. Allow two hours or more, depending on how far out you are.

At the end of SR 2001. (Turn east off SR 54 on Indian Wells Road, and follow the signs.) ☎ ***877-333-6589*** *or 575-437-2840.* www.nmspacemuseum.org. *RV parking lot. Admission: Museum $6 adults, $5.75 seniors and military, $4.50 ages 6–17; IMAX $6 adults, $5.50 seniors and military, $4.50 ages 4–12, free 3 and under. No credit cards. Open: Mon, Wed–Sat 10 a.m.–5 p.m., Sun noon to 5 p.m. Closed Tues, Thanksgiving, and Christmas.*

White Sands National Monument
Alamogordo, New Mexico

KID FRIENDLY

Imagine 60-foot pure-white gypsum sand dunes sparkling in the sunlight. For serious visitors, all sorts of discoveries await, from the bleached earless lizard whose species turns white for camouflage to the handful of plants tough enough to survive, surrounded by constantly shifting sands.

On nights during a full moon, park rangers and special guests present "howling at the moon" evenings.

The Dunes Drive goes 8 miles into the heart of the dunes, turns in a circle, and comes back out the same way. A picnic area, boardwalk, and two hiking trails are accessible from turnouts along the drive. Allow one hour for a visit to the dunes and boardwalk or more if you want to hike or picnic.

WARNING

No one is allowed to drive across the dunes, but hiking is permitted. Be aware that you can get lost easily, especially if a windstorm produces whiteout. The powdery white sand blows easily and can penetrate the seams of your RV even when doors and windows are closed.

TIP

Photographers need to visit at times other than midday, when the high sun flattens the terrain. Use a polarizer for best results.

15 miles southwest of Alamogordo on US 70/82. ☎ **575-679-2599.** `https://www.nps.gov/whsa/index.htm.` *RV parking: Parking lot at visitor center; frequent turnouts along Dunes Drive. Admission: $20 per vehicle, $10 per person 15 and up, free for children 14 and under. Dates and times for access change throughout the year, and there are periods of closure. Look for scheduled closes at* `https://www.nps.gov/whsa/planyourvisit/hours.htm.` *On typical open dates, you can enter at 7 a.m. Open: Visitor center daily Jan 2–Mar 9 9 a.m.–5 p.m., Mar 10–May 25 9 a.m.–6 p.m., May 25–Sept 1, 9 a.m.–7 p.m., Sept 2–Dec 24, 9 a.m.–5 p.m., Dec 26–31, 8 a.m.–5 p.m. Closed Christmas Day. No campground or camping in the park. (**Note:** Dunes Drive may be closed to private traffic when testing is taking place on the White Sands Missile Range.)*

More Cool Things to See and Do

New Mexico is full of fascinating sights, which include incredible mountain vistas free for the offering on various drives. Exercise caution; be sure to have your navigator be the one who takes pictures.

» **See the Kid's grave.** If you have the time and predisposition to make the long, arid drive up to **Billy the Kid's grave** in Fort Sumner (Chamber of Commerce ☎ 575-355-7705; http://www.fortsumnerchamber.net/), you may appreciate how long it took the outlaw to reach this destination on horseback. Take the time to poke around, although none of the local museums is world-class. The **Old Fort Sumner Museum** (☎ 575-355-2942) is adjacent to the gravesite and to **Fort Sumner State Monument** (☎ 575-355-2573); the **Billy the Kid Museum** (☎ 575-355-2380) is in Fort Sumner near the junction of US 60 and US 84. The Kid's tombstone has been securely set inside a fenced site after being stolen twice. Allow one hour for the gravesite and the museum, and one hour for the museum in town.

To get there, drive east on US 60/84 3 miles from Fort Sumner to SR 212; then turn south and drive 4 miles to Fort Sumner State Monument. RV parking is available in a large lot at the gravesite, adjacent to the Old Sumner Museum, and in a smaller lot at the Billy the Kid Museum; street parking is also available. Old Fort Sumner Museum is open daily from 9 a.m. to 5 p.m.; admission is free. The Billy the Kid Museum is open Monday through Saturday from 8:30 a.m. to 5 p.m. and Sunday from 11 a.m. to 5 p.m.; admission is free.

» **Take a walk in the clouds.** The town of **Cloudcroft** (Chamber of Commerce ☎ 505-682-2733; http://cloudcroft.net), at an elevation of 9,200 feet and surrounded by 500,000 acres of Lincoln National Forest, makes a cool, pretty spot for a morning or afternoon pause if you tire of the hot valley climate. The Lodge, built in 1899, still welcomes visitors to its restaurant, and a ski slope, golf course, and quaint Western-style boutiques provide distractions.

WARNING

Be aware that snow and ice in winter may require tire chains in this area; check conditions before leaving the Alamogordo area.

From I-70, 2 miles north of Alamogordo, take US 82 east 16 miles to Cloudcroft. RV parking is available on the street.

» **Appraise collectibles.** On the way to or from Silver City, pause at Deming's **Luna County Mimbres Museum,** 301 S. Silver St. (☎ **575-546-2382;** www.deminglunamimbresmuseum.com), housed in a 1917 brick armory, to see some good examples of some of the most elegant tribal collectibles: local black-and-white Mimbreno pottery. The museum is a starting point for a self-guided, historic walking tour of the town; pick up a map at the museum. Allow one hour; add an hour or more for the walking tour.

RV parking is plentiful on the street. Admission is by donation. The museum is open Monday through Saturday from 9 a.m. to 4 p.m. and Sunday from 1:30 to 4 p.m.

» **Horse around.** The nucleus of the **Hubbard Museum of the American West,** off US 70 East in Ruidoso Downs 1 mile east of the Ruidoso Downs Race Track (☎ **575-378-4142;** https://hubbardmuseum.org), is a much-loved 10,000-piece collection of horse artifacts collected by the late Anne C. Sterling, a New Jersey heiress and aficionado. But the best reason to go, even if you don't venture inside, is to see the magnificent sculptures of eight running horses in the outdoor monument. Allow one hour.

RV parking is available in a small lot or on the street. Admission is $7 for adults; $5 for seniors and military, $2 for ages 6 to 16, and free 5 and under. It's open daily in the summer from 9 a.m. to 5 p.m.

» **Drop the *the*.** Repeat after me: There is no *the* in Smokey Bear. If you didn't know that, you'll discover it right away at **Smokey Bear Historical State Park,** 118 Smokey Bear Blvd., Capitan (☎ **575-354-2748;** http://www.emnrd.state.nm.us/index.html). In May 1950, when firefighters found a badly singed bear cub clinging to a burned pine tree near the town of Capitan, a cartoon Smokey Bear in a ranger costume had already been informing campers about the dangers of forest fires for five years. The young black bear was named Smokey, and when his burns healed, he was sent to the National Zoo in Washington, D.C., where he was a favorite of visitors. After Smokey died in 1976, he was returned to Capitan for burial. Allow two hours.

RV parking is available in a designated lot. Admission is $2 for adults, $1 for ages 7 to 12, and free 6 and under. The park is open daily from 9 a.m. to 5 p.m. Closed Thanksgiving, Christmas Day, and New Year's Day.

» **Spy a petroglyph.** At **Three Rivers Petroglyph Site (☎ 575-525-4300;** https://www.blm.gov/new-mexico), you can see some 500 *petroglyphs* (images that have been scratched, carved, or chiseled into a rock face). The pictures of people, animals, fish, and reptiles were carved by the Mogollon people between A.D. 900 and A.D. 1400. A path wends for a mile through the hilltop site. Allow two hours or more to go hiking.

From US 54 about 30 miles north of Alamogordo, New Mexico, take SR 579 to the site; follow the signs. RV parking is available in a large lot at the site. Admission is $5 per vehicle, camping is $7 per site, and RV hookup is $18. The site is open daily from sunrise to sunset.

Our Favorite Campgrounds

More than 16 of the communities along the driving route have at least one RV campground, and most of them have several. You can eyeball the action early in the drive to figure out whether you need to make reservations for the remainder of the trip. If most campgrounds look full as you drive by in the afternoon, consider calling ahead to reserve a site. But usually, you'll have no problem finding lodging except perhaps in the Carlsbad Caverns area in tourist season (summer), over the Christmas holidays, and on Presidents' Day weekend.

REMEMBER

If you're traveling the route in summer, when temperatures can reach 90°F or more at lower elevations, look for an electrical hookup capable of running your RV's air-conditioning unit full blast.

WARNING

Never set up camp in dry streambed or riverbeds, because summer thunderstorms frequently cause flash floods.

All campgrounds listed in this chapter are open year-round and have public flush toilets, showers, and sanitary dump stations unless designated otherwise. Toll-free numbers, where listed, are for reservations only.

Alamogordo KOA Campground

$$$–$$$$ Alamogordo, New Mexico

Close to White Sands National Monument, the Space Center, and the Mescalero Apache Reservation, this tree-shaded campground, with grass and privacy walls, has narrow sites. The park is right on the edge of town, so if you don't want neighbors and urban surroundings, you may want to choose a different destination.

412 24th St. (1½ blocks east of US 54/70). ☎ *877-437-3003 or 575-437-3003.* https://koa.com/campgrounds/alamogordo/. *Total 38 full hookups with water and 20- and 30-amp electric. CATV, data port, laundry, pool, Wi-Fi. Rates: Visit the KOA website or call* ☎ *800-562-3452 for rates and reservations. Senior and Good Sam discounts available. DISC, MC, V.*

City of Rocks State Park

BARGAIN ALERT

$–$$ Deming, New Mexico

One of our favorite campgrounds in the world is this field of house-size boulders where rocks surround sites that sit far apart. Arrive early to get a good site, because reservations aren't accepted. Ten of the sites have electric hookups, so scope them out first. Even if you don't luck into a hookup, you'll still love this campground.

Off SR 61. (Follow US 180 north from Deming 28 miles to SR 61, and turn east for 5 miles.) ☎ *877-664-7787 reservations, 575-536-2800 information.* www.emnrd.state.nm.us. *Total 52 sites, 10 with water and 50-amp electric. Handicap access. No sanitary dump station. Rates: $8–$18 per site. No credit cards.*

Silver City KOA

$$$–$$$$$ Silver City, New Mexico

Cooler in summer than the other campgrounds in the area, this park also offers such bonuses as copper-mine tours, hiking trails, biking-trail access in the vicinity, and an outdoor cafe in summer. The park location, 5 miles east of town, is quiet.

11824 Hwy. 180 E. ☎ *800-562-7623 or 575-388-3351.* https:// koa.com/campgrounds/silver-city/. *Total 56 sites with water and 30- and 50-amp electric, 49 full hookups, 33 pull-throughs. Data port, laundry, pool, snack bar, Wi-Fi. Rates: Call for current rates and reservations. AE, DISC, MC, V.*

Town and Country RV Park

$$$–$$$$ Roswell, New Mexico

I headed straight for this campground, a Good Sam member, after visiting the International UFO Museum and Research Center because its brochure said "Crash Here; They Did!" The park is a big, modern RV park with everything a snowbird could want for the winter, including big-rig sites with 50-amp hookups, 90-foot-long pull-throughs, new bathrooms, and instant local-phone hookups.

331 W. Brasher Rd. (From Second and Main Streets, drive south on Main to Brasher Road, and go west 2 blocks.) ☎ *800-499-4364 or 575-624-1833.* www.townandcountryrvpark.com. *Total 64 full hookup sites, with water and 30- and 50-amp electric, 32 pull-throughs. CATV, data port, laundry, phone jacks, pool. Rates: Good Sam member rate $38 per site. DISC, MC, V.*

Good Eats

Restaurants and snack bars may be many miles apart in the wilds of southern New Mexico, so you'll be glad that you're carrying your own kitchen with a well-stocked refrigerator. Also, be aware that some of the small, scruffy-looking country kitchens that you encounter are word-of-mouth treasures passed from one chile-loving enthusiast to another.

Following are some good eating establishments in southern New Mexico and the area around El Paso, Texas:

» **Cattleman's Steakhouse,** 3045 S. Carlsbad Rd., Fabens, Texas (☎ **915-544-3200;** www.cattlemansranch.com): The restaurant isn't hard to find after you get to Fabens, about 25 miles south of El Paso on I-10. Just take Exit 10 from I-10 and head north, following the signs. This dude ranch and restaurant serves great steaks; a display case shows the raw steaks in each size so you can gauge your appetite. Reservations are suggested. A parking lot nearby can handle RVs. Cattleman's is open Monday through Friday from 5 p.m. to 10 p.m., Saturday from 12:30 to 10 p.m., and Sunday from 12:30 to 9 p.m.

» **Chope's,** SR 28, La Mesa, New Mexico (☎ **575-233-3420**): Chope's is where the chile growers eat chile rellenos, blue corn enchiladas, and green chile enchiladas. Park on the street. Open Tuesday through Friday 11 a.m. to 2 p.m. and 5 p.m. to 8:30 p.m. Closed Sunday and Monday.

» **Little Diner and Tortilla Factory,** 7209 Seventh St., Canutillo, Texas (☎ **915-877-2176**): Crowds always are standing in line at this popular place, which sells tortillas to go and a gamut of other New Mexico treats to eat in or take out. Dare to try the deep-fried masa patties called *gorditas* filled with spicy red chile sauce and chunks of pork. The large adjacent parking lot has plenty of space for RVs. It's open daily from 11 a.m. to 3 p.m.

» **Nellie's Café:** 1226 W. Hadley, Las Cruces, New Mexico (☎ **575-524-9982**): Servings are enormous, and the atmosphere is relaxed. Order anything with chiles, even the chile cheeseburger, and don't skip the refried beans. RV parking is available in lots nearby or on the street. The cafe is open Tuesday through Friday from 8 a.m. to 3 p.m. and closed Saturday, Sunday, and Monday.

» **La Posta Restaurant and Chile Shop,** 2410 Calle de San Albino, Mesilla, New Mexico (☎ **575-524-3524;** `https://www.laposta-de-mesilla.com/index.php?lang=en`): At the chile shop, look for hot sauces, salsas, recipe books, canned chiles, and items for your own cooking-with-chiles experience. In the restaurant — an American classic since 1939 — large portions of tacos, enchiladas, chile con queso, and tostados are served. RV parking is on the street. Both are open daily from 11 a.m. to 9 p.m.

THE HATCH CHILE

"You spell it *chili*, and I spell it *chile* . . ." but before we call the whole thing off, I'll explain. In New Mexico, the spicy *capiscum* pod always is spelled *chile*, as are many dishes made from it. Texans like the spelling *chili*, just as Anglo Indians often use *chilli*. Hatch is the state's center of chile-growing, and New Mexico leads the nation in production. The official state vegetables are chiles and *frijoles* (beans, usually the pinto variety).

Chiles come in two colors: red and green. The red chile is simply a riper version of the green chile. Most New Mexican restaurants give you the choice of red or green chile stews, soups, and sauces. Always ask which is hotter, because the heat varies considerably from pepper to pepper. The most commonly grown variety is the New Mexico long green, moderate on a heat scale that ranks jalapeños as moderately hot. Tiny serrano and habanero chiles rate much higher on the Scoville heat unit scale.

New Mexico chili is made primarily of fresh, frozen, roasted, or canned chile peppers; Texas *chili con carne* is meat only seasoned with dried chiles.

Shopping along the Way

BARGAIN ALERT

El Paso, Texas, is the place to buy cowboy boots because so many brands are available in the factory outlet stores lining I-10 east of town. When buying ready-made boots, make sure that the heel slips a little when you walk; when the sole gets more flexible, the slippage stops. If the heel doesn't slip when you try it on, the boot is too tight and will give you blisters. The instep should be snug; the shank should be long enough to cover your arch; and the ball of your foot should fit the widest part of the boot, not sit forward or back. Stores worth a peek are

» **Justin Outlet,** 7100 Gateway E., I-10 at Hawkins
(☎ **915-779-5465**)

» **Lucchese Factory Outlet,** 6601 Montana Ave. (☎ **915-778-8060**)

» **Tony Lama,** 7156 Gateway E., just off I-10 (☎ **915-772-4327**)

Fast Facts

Area Code
Area codes are **505** and **575** in New Mexico and **915** in El Paso, Texas.

Driving Laws
All RV occupants must wear seat belts in New Mexico. The speed limit on interstates is 75 mph. Speed limits are lower in urban areas.

Emergency
Call ☎ **911.**

Hospitals
Along the route, major hospitals are in El Paso, Roswell, and Carlsbad.

Information
Sources include New Mexico Tourism, 491 Old Santa Fe Trail, Santa Fe (☎ **800-733-6396**;

https://www.newmexico.org), and El Paso Convention and Visitors Bureau (☎ **800-351-6024**). For a New Mexico Vacation Guide, call ☎ **800-733-6396**, ext. 0175.

For reservations, contact New Mexico Campground Reservations (☎ **877-664-7787**).

Road and Weather Conditions
In New Mexico, call ☎ **800-432-4269.**

Taxes
New Mexico general sales tax is 5.125 percent; cities can add 8.938 percent in city sales tax. State gasoline taxes are 17 cents per gallon.

Time Zone
New Mexico and El Paso are on Mountain time.

Chapter **20**

The Oregon Coast: California to Washington

Oregon isn't like any other state. Oregonians are overwhelmingly, genuinely — there's no other word for it — *nice*. Even today, you can find reminders of those gentle eccentrics who 150 years ago packed up pianos and plows, cousins and cows, and set out along the Oregon Trail. And for anyone who remembers or read about the 1960s, the hippies at heart still live along the beaches or up in the hills above the Pacific.

If you look at a road map of Oregon — and you need to if you're making this drive — you can see that its major cities are lined up in a vertical row along I-5 an hour or two inland. But each of them — Portland, Salem, and Eugene — has a corridor road leading through the woods and over the hills to the closest beach. The heaviest tourist developments — restaurants, shops, motels, and jet-boat excursion companies — are found a mile or two on either side of the place where the corridor beaches. Get away from those access roads, and you find untrampled dunes, unspoiled beaches, and the wild surf of your dreams.

The coast is dotted lavishly with state parks that have RV hookups, overnight camping spots, and picnic tables. Although the water is often a bit cold for swimming for all but the hardiest, walking and beachcombing are world-class. Alert strollers may find Japanese fishing floats, bits of agate, and driftwood twisted into fantastic shapes. Kite flyers love the nearly constant sea breezes, sand-castle builders compete for the most grandiose constructions, and chowderheads can dig for Oregon razor clams and giant geoducks.

The area along the coast in large part revolves around the various runs and season for fishing. There are expensive homes along the coast occupied only in concert with the in-season fishing schedule. The many rivers emptying into the ocean are an angler's delight. If you're not up to catching your own, the local eateries offer delightful fish and chips, as well as fish sandwiches. Pass the tartar sauce, please.

Choosing Your Route

US 101 follows the Oregon coastline for almost all its 365 miles, dipping inland occasionally but always returning to the sea. When the main route leaves the water, minor side roads cling to the coast. This drive begins in the south, at the Oregon/California border, and continues north to Astoria, the spot where Lewis and Clark spent the winter of 1805–06. Or you can make the drive in the opposite direction simply by reversing the route directions. The entire route covers approximately 400 miles, or more if you take some of the side detours.

I added the Long Beach Peninsula in Washington State, just across the Columbia River from Astoria, because many Oregon-coast visitors consider the beach to be an extension of the coastal drive. Official mileposts along the way on US 101 begin with 0 at the Oregon/Washington border, in the middle of the Columbia River, and continue through mile 363 at the Oregon/California border. The Long Beach Peninsula extension adds another 40 or so miles.

TIP

At milepost 355.6 in Harris Beach State Park is an Oregon welcome center, where you can pick up maps and materials about the Oregon coast. Look particularly for the free *Oregon Coast Mile-by-Mile Guide to Highway 101*. The center is closed in the winter months.

TIP

Although driving the 360 or so miles of 101 along the Oregon coast in one day is possible, no one would prefer to do that much at a time. There's too much to miss if you drive at that pace. For a nice weekend along the northern coast, starting from Portland's main access route of US 26, drive over to Seaside and Cannon Beach, drive south through Tillamook to Lincoln City, and return to the Portland area by SR 18 through McMinnville and the Oregon wine country. To highlight the central coast for the weekend, start from Eugene, drive across SR 126 to Florence, drive north to Newport, and return to I-5 via US 20 to Corvallis. A short 45-mile drive down I-5 returns you to Eugene. For a weekend on the south Oregon coast, start from Brookings at the California border, drive north to Florence, and cross SR 126 to Eugene.

Planning Ahead

One can drive along the Oregon coast year-round, but summer is still the best time. Temperatures are warmer, and there's less rain. The winter weather in Oregon is a mixed bag. Here, I quote the Oregon Tourism Commission itself: "You've heard the old joke that people in Oregon don't tan. They rust. But lest you assume that it rains every day here in winter, let's set the record straight: Some days it snows."

Between December and February, the gray whales migrate south along the Oregon coast from Alaska to calving grounds in Baja, Mexico. They head north again in March through May, passing closer to the coast with their baby whales nearby. So winter and springtime are best for whale-watching. Fall offers dry, sunny days interspersed with days of drizzle.

WARNING

Whenever you go to the Oregon coast, be prepared for some rainy days. Always carry an umbrella when you venture out. On the worst days, you can try to settle in in your RV, reading, working puzzles, or baking cookies or muffins to munch on down the road. When the sun comes out, drop everything and head for the beach.

Expect crowds on summer weekends at the beaches, but during the rest of the week, long stretches of coastline can be amazingly empty. State parks are popular with Oregonians in the summer, so make campground reservations early whenever possible during that season. The rest of the year, you may well have a campground to yourself.

Obviously, you want to pack rain gear. Even those two-piece yellow slicker suits can come in handy if you enjoy walking along the beach in light rains when no danger of lightning is present. Although coastal temperatures are comfortable to cool, a short drive inland takes you into warmer weather, so take along lightweight cotton clothing. Sweaters, sweatshirts, and sweatpants make good Oregon RV travel clothes. Even in the best restaurants in Oregon, folks don't dress up much; I can't imagine a place where you'd need a tie unless you're combining your RV vacation with a business trip. Take sturdy walking shoes — preferably, hiking boots — with a spare pair in case one pair gets wet, and waterproof boots if you want to explore tidal pools.

Allow at least a week for a leisurely tour along the Oregon coast, although you can drive the route straight through in a couple of days (something I don't recommend, because you'd miss some wonderful experiences). With the natural beauty of the coast and the opportunity for sunset photos over the ocean, a month wouldn't be too long.

Must-See Attractions

Bandon Old Town
Bandon-by-the-Sea, Oregon

The Old Town of Bandon isn't *that* old. In 1936, a fire destroyed the original town, which was later rebuilt along the mouth of the Coquille River. Known as the Storm Watching Capital of the

World and the Cranberry Capital of Oregon, this town is a great place to look for agates on the beach, dig clams at Coquille Point, browse local art galleries, order fish and chips to go, and munch on a super-large cone of Umpqua Dairy ice cream. (The Umpqua ice cream alone makes the visit worthwhile.) The fun here is making your own special discovery while you stroll around. I suggest that you explore the area between First and Second Streets along Alabama, Baltimore, Chicago, Delaware, Elmira, and Fillmore Streets. Allow at least a half day.

Milepost 270 on US 101. Chamber of Commerce Visitor's Center ☎ **541-347-9616.** *https://bandon.com. RV parking: Designated lots; plenty of street parking. Open daily 10 a.m. to 4 p.m. Admission: Free. Shops typically open daily 8:30 a.m.–5:30 p.m.*

Columbia River Maritime Museum
Astoria, Oregon

The museum (renovated and expanded recently) has an indoor and outdoor collection that includes the conning tower of a submarine; the bridge of a US Navy destroyer; and displays of fishing boats, lighthouses, fishing, navigation, and naval history. You can tour a floating lighthouse and the lightship *Columbia,* ponder the personal effects of passengers who went down in ships hitting the reefs at the mouth of the Columbia River, and browse the museum store. Allow three hours.

1792 Marine Dr. ☎ **503-325-2323.** *www.crmm.org. RV parking: Two large parking lots adjacent to museum and street parking. Admission: $14 adults, $12 seniors, $5 ages 6–12. AAA discount. Open: Daily 9:30 a.m.–5 p.m. Closed Thanksgiving Day and Christmas Day.*

Fort Clatsop Lewis and Clark National Park
Astoria, Oregon

This replica of the old fort where the members of the Lewis and Clark expedition spent the winter of 1805–06 turned out to be more accurate than expected: In 1999, an anthropologist turned up a 148-year-old map showing that the site of the original was very close to where the copy was built. During the summer, buckskin-clad, fur-hatted expeditioners show visitors what day-to-day life was like for the Corps of Discovery. A gift shop has expedition books and videos. Allow three hours.

92343 Fort Clatsop Rd. ☎ *503-861-2471.* https://www.nps.gov/lewi. *RV parking: Large parking lot capable of handling tour buses. Admission: $7 adult, free ages 15 and under. Open: Daily 9 a.m.–5 p.m. year-round except Christmas Day.*

KID FRIENDLY

Oregon Coast Aquarium
Newport, Oregon

You can see tufted puffins in a walk-through aviary with windows that let you see them dive for fish underwater. A glass tunnel through the water puts you in the ocean with sharks, sea lions, seals, sea otters, and a giant Pacific octopus. Oregon Coast Aquarium is where Keiko, star of the film *Free Willy*, was rehabilitated before returning to the wild. Allow three to four hours.

2820 SE Ferry Slip Rd. ☎ *541-867-3474.* https://aquarium.org. *RV parking: Designated lots. Admission: Adult, $24.95; Seniors, $19.95; ages 13-17, $19.95; ages 3-12, $14.95; and 2 and under, free. Open: Memorial Day–Labor Day daily 9 a.m.–6 p.m., Labor Day and Memorial Day 10 a.m.–5 p.m. Closed Christmas Day. Rental wheelchairs available for $8 per day. Park RVs in north lot.*

KID FRIENDLY

Oregon Dunes National Recreation Area
Reedsport, Oregon

Stretching a whopping 45 miles along the coast between North Bend and Florence, with headquarters in Reedsport, the Oregon dunes have access areas with off-road parking, some large enough for RVs and some of it not quite. Eyeball entrances before entering to see if you can park and/or turn around. One good trail is the 2½-mile Umpqua Dunes route, accessed from the trailhead 10½ miles south of Reedsport near Lakeside. Or go to Oregon Dunes Overlook, 10 miles north of Reedsport on

US 101. Allow a generous amount of time. Have fresh batteries in the camera. A smaller class B or C with no tow car works best for trying to see everything.

855 US 101. ☎ ***541-271-3611.*** `https://www.fs.usda.gov/` `recarea/siuslaw/recreation/recarea/?recid=42465.` *Reedsport District office and Visitor Center open every day from 8 a.m.–4:30 p.m.*

Sea Lion Caves
Florence, Oregon

KID FRIENDLY

Wild Stellar sea lions, the largest of the sea lions, inhabit these caves or the rocks outside them year-round, spending fall and winter inside and spring and summer outside. Open since 1932, this attraction is fascinating for anyone who hasn't been to a sea-lion or seal rookery. An elevator descends 208 feet into the caves; you must negotiate some stairs and ramps to get to the elevator. Take a sweater or jacket, camera, and binoculars, and be prepared for plenty of noise and some very strong smells. Most kids get a kick out of the elevator ride and the novelty of being in a cave, although they may complain about the smell. Allow one hour.

91560 US 101. ☎ ***541-547-3111.*** `www.sealioncaves.com.` *RV parking: Designated RV lot. Admission: $14 adults, $13 seniors, $8 kids 5–12, 4 and under free. Open: Daily summer 9 a.m.–6 p.m., winter 9 a.m.–4 p.m.*

Tillamook Cheese Factory
Tillamook, Oregon

This factory tour, with its free samples, is Oregon's third-most-popular tourist attraction. The attraction draws many people who have no idea how milk from black-and-white cows turns into mild or sharp cheddar cheese. The Tillamook County Creamery Association was founded in 1918, and today's modern factory turns out 40 million pounds of cheese a year, plus excellent ice cream and other dairy products. Allow two hours.

4175 US 101. ☎ ***503-815-1300.*** *https://www.tillamook.com/. RV parking: Designated lots. Admission: Free. Open: Daily summer 8 a.m.–8 p.m., winter 8 a.m.–6 p.m. Closed on major holidays.*

More Cool Things to See and Do

Oregon seems as big as all outdoors, with so much to do along its beaches that you can never get bored. In addition to the suggestions in the following list, you may want to check out Cannon Beach (Chamber of Commerce ☎ 503-436-2623; https://www.cannonbeach.org/events); Chinook Winds Casino, on the beach in Lincoln City (☎ **888-CHINOOK [244-6665]**; https://www.chinookwindscasino.com); or whale-watching (☎ **541-765-3304**; https://oregonstate parks.org/index.cfm?do=parkPage.dsp_parkPage&parkId=183). Also ☎ **800-551-6949.**

KID FRIENDLY

» **Dig in.** Clam digging and crabbing don't require licenses in Yaquina, Alsea, Coos, Tillamook, and Netarts bays — just some basic skills and equipment. You can rent the equipment, and the vendor can clue you in to the technique. Get information booklets and locations from the **Oregon Department of Fish and Wildlife (☎ 503-947-6000;** https://www.dfw.state.or.us).

» **Rack up an elk.** At Dean Creek Elk Viewing Area near Reedsport, you can often get a good look at a Roosevelt elk or a whole herd. The best times are early morning and late afternoon. Bring a camera.

The viewing platform is 3½ miles east of Reedsport, Oregon, on SR 38. RV parking is available. Admission is free, and the viewing platform is always open. Visit at sunrise or sunset.

» **Follow the trail.** The Lewis and Clark Interpretive Center overlooks the often-foggy mouth of the Columbia River, where a lighthouse towers above Cape Disappointment. Walk along a series of ramps that traces the expedition and then look at the lighthouse from the grounds. If you climb quietly up the path from the parking lot, you may see deer that hang around the picnic area. Allow two hours.

Take the SR 100 loop from Ilwaco to **Cape Disappointment State Park** (formerly Fort Canby State Park), Ilwaco, Washington (☎ 360-642-3078). RV parking is limited to roadside parking at the foot of the stairs leading up to the center and lighthouse. Admission is free. The park is open daily from 10 a.m. to 5 p.m. A campground with hookups is located in the park.

» **Lighten up.** Cape Blanco, discovered in 1603 by a Spanish explorer. The lighthouse is open for summer tours, and is the westernmost point in Oregon. Allow one hour.

The lighthouse is located in **Cape Blanco State Park, ☎ 800-551-6949** (https://oregonstateparks.org/park_62.php), at milepost 296.6 on US 101, north of Port Orford, Oregon. RV parking is available. Admission is $2 adults, $1 ages 11 and under, and $5 families. The facility is open April through October Tuesday through Sunday from 10 a.m. to 3:30 p.m.

» **Hike the coast.** The scenery is dramatic, the waves thundering, and the trails exciting. RV roadside parking is limited at some lookouts and trailheads. Follow the trails; information is at each trailhead. Some hiking areas are Oregon Dunes National Recreation Area, Cape Perpetua Scenic Area, Samuel H. Boardman State Park, Humbug Mountain State Park, and Shore Acres State Park. Allow a half day, depending on how far you hike.

The Oregon Dunes Visitor Center is in Reedsport (☎ 541-271-3611; https://www.fs.fed.us/r6/siuslaw). The website has information about both the Oregon Dunes and Cape Perpetua visitor centers. You can also contact the **Cape Perpetua Visitor Center** at ☎ 541-547-3289. State parks information is available at ☎ 800-551-6949 or https://oregonstateparks.org.

KID
FRIENDLY

» **Cruise the bay.** Board the 49-passenger *Discovery* in Newport for tours of Yaquina Bay that may include visits to the Oregon Oyster Farm, an introduction to crabbing by onboard naturalists, whale-watching, and a close-up look at sea lions. Allow a half day.

Marine Discovery Tours is on Bay Boulevard in Newport, Oregon (☎ 800-903-2628; https://www.marinediscoverytours. com). Call for times, tour types, prices, and reservations.

» **Up a roguish river.** Rogue River Jet Boat Excursions start from Gold Beach, and goes upriver, making stops to see and photograph wildlife. Trips vary from 64 to 108 miles, and reservations are suggested. Allow at least one day.

Jerry's Rogue River Jets (☎ 800-451-3645; https://www. roguejets.com) and Rogue River Mail Boat Hydro-Jets have merged. The two-hour Sealife Cruise is $45 adults, $35 seniors, and $20 children. Daily departures run May 1 through October 30. Call for times, rates, and reservations.

» **String yourself along. The World Kite Museum and Hall of Fame**, 303 Sid Snyder Dr. SW, Long Beach, Washington (☎ 360-642-4020; www.worldkitemuseum.com), is the only American museum dedicated exclusively to kites. The stretch of sandy beach has good conditions for kite flying.

RV parking is available on the street. Admission is $5 adults, $4 seniors, and $3 children. The facility is open March through September daily from 11 a.m. to 5 p.m. and October through April from 11 a.m. to 5 p.m. Friday through Tuesday.

Our Favorite Campgrounds

The Oregon coast is dotted with campgrounds, both state parks (19 of with RV camping) and commercial parks (one or more in 26 coastal communities). Making reservations is a good idea for beachfront state parks in summer on the weekends; you should be able to find a spot almost anywhere during the rest of the year. An RV-friendly state, Oregon has 37 designated waste disposal or sanitary dump stations and a corresponding map showing access hours and locations. Call Oregon State Parks (☎ 800-551-6949; https://oregonstateparks. org) for a brochure, or pick one up at any state welcome center. Make reservations for state park campgrounds by calling ☎ 800-452-5687.

TIP

State park discovery season, from October through April, offers campers a savings of $4 a night for a full hookup site at any state park.

Nearly all the campgrounds in this chapter are open year-round and have flush toilets, showers, and sanitary dump stations unless stated otherwise. Toll-free numbers are for reservations only unless noted.

Astoria Warrenton/Seaside KOA
$$$$–$$$$$ Hammond, Oregon

Convenient to Astoria and Fort Clatsop National Memorial, this KOA is at the mouth of the Columbia River a mile from the beach and offers free shuttle service in summer. Free pancake breakfasts are served on weekday mornings, and weekends bring programs and activities. Fishing and clamming are nearby. Most sites are shaded.

1100 NW Ridge Rd. (From US 101, go 3 miles south of Astoria and follow signs to Fort Stevens State Park; the Seaside KOA campground is opposite the entrance of the park.) ☎ **800-562-8506** *or 503-861-2606.* https://koa.com/campgrounds/astoria. *Total of 231 sites with water and 30- and 50-amp electric, 142 full hookups, 96 pull-throughs. Bike rentals, CATV, data port, game room, grocery store, handicap access, laundry, indoor pool and spa, rec room, snack shack, outdoor sports facilities, Wi-Fi. Rates: $40–$60 per site. Call for latest prices. DISC, MC, V.*

Bullards Beach State Park
$$$ Bandon, Oregon

North of Bandon near the Coquille River, with freshwater fishing and boating available, 1,266-acre Bullards Beach offers access for RVers, horseback campers, hikers, and bicycle campers, with an assortment of hookup sites, *yurts*, and primitive and walk-in sites. The park's varied terrain includes a beach, forest, dunes, and a jetty and lighthouse.

Off MP-249. (From junction of US 101 and SR 42S [north end of Bandon], go north 2½ miles on US 101, turn on MP-249, and drive ¼ mile to the park, on the left.) ☎ **800-452-5687.** `https://oregonstateparks.org/park_71.php`. *Total of 186 sites with water and 20- and 30-amp electric, 104 full hookups, no pull-throughs. Some handicap access. Rate: $22 per site. MC, V. 10-day maximum stay.*

Fort Stevens State Park
$$–$$$ Warrenton, Oregon

The Union Army built a military installation on this site to protect the mouth of the Columbia River from Confederate attack. Although the Confederates never arrived, a Japanese submarine shelled the fort in 1942. The campground's 170 RV sites are wide, paved, well-spaced, some are shaded.

Off Fort Steven State Park Road. (From US 101 and Fort Stevens State Park Road, go northwest 4¾ miles to the park on the left.) ☎ **800-452-5687.** `https://oregonstateparks.org/par_179.php`. *Total of 477 sites with water with 20- and 50-amp electric, 174 full hookups, 30 pull-throughs. Handicap access. Rates: $18–$22 per site.*

Jessie M. Honeyman Memorial State Park
$$–$$$ Florence, Oregon

Dedicated to the memory of one of the early advocates for a state park system in Oregon, this park and campground, smack-dab against some of the most magnificent sand dunes in the Oregon Dunes State Recreation Area, offers hiking trails; dune-buggy activities (only in winter); and freshwater swimming, fishing, and boating. In May, rhododendrons burst out in splendid bloom. The sites are large enough for the biggest motor homes, sheltered from one another, and offer lush landscaping. In addition to RV hookup sites are tent sites and yurts for car campers.

US 101 (3 miles south of Florence). ☎ ***800-452-5687*** *or 541-997-3641.* `https://oregonstateparks.org/park_134.php`. *Total of 123 sites with water and 30- and 50-amp electric, 44 full hookups, no pull-throughs. Handicap access. Rates: $18–$22 per site. MC, V.*

Oregon Dunes KOA
$$$–$$$$$ North Bend, Oregon

Except for all-terrain vehicles on summer weekends, this park, close to the Oregon Dunes and just north of the town of North Bend, is pleasant. It rents ATVs and is one of the few RV parks with access to the Oregon Dunes National Recreation Area. You can book a dune tour in an antique military vehicle. The beach, a lighthouse, a casino, and fishing are nearby.

68632 US 101. (Head 9 miles north of Coos Bay, and 19 miles south of Reedsport on US 101.) ☎ ***800-562-4236*** *or 541-756-4851.* `https://koa.com/campgrounds/oregon-dunes/`. *Total of 55 sites with 30- and 50-amp electric, all full hookups, 41 pull-throughs. Data port, game room, grocery store, handicap access, laundry, SATV, Wi-Fi. Rates: $26–$54 per site. Call to verify latest prices. AE, DISC, MC, V.*

Sunset Bay State Park
$$–$$$ Charleston, Oregon

Enjoy walking the beach and exploring tidal pools. Sunset Bay is connected to Shore Acres and Cape Arago State Parks by a 4-mile trail as part of the Oregon Coast Trail. Options include fishing, swimming, boating, and horseback riding. Sites are wide and paved, with some full hookups.

10965 Cape Arago Hwy. (From junction of US 101 and Charleston Harbor exit in Coos Bay, drive west 11¾ miles on Cape Arago Highway to the west end of the Charleston Bridge, MP-12; park is on the left.) ☎ ***800-452-5687***. `https://oregonstateparks.org/park_100.php`. *Total of 63 sites with water and 30-amp electric, 29 full hookups, no pull-throughs. Handicap access. Rates: $18–$22 per site. MC, V. 10-day maximum stay.*

Winchester Bay RV Resort

$$$–$$$$ Winchester Bay, Oregon

This public marina and RV resort has large sites; a bike path and hiking trail; and saltwater fishing. It is located near the Oregon Dunes National Recreation Area and the Umpqua Lighthouse. Sites are pull-ins that face the water.

Off Salmon Harbor Drive. (From US 101 and Salmon Harbor Drive, go southwest on Salmon Harbor Drive to campground, on the right.) ☎ 541-271-0287. www.marinarvresort.com. Total of 138 sites with 30- and 50-amp electric, all full hookups, 60 pull-throughs. CATV, data port, handicap access, laundry. Rates: Regular sites $22–$27 per site mid-Oct to mid-May, $29–$36 mid-May to mid-Oct. MC, V.

Good Eats

Coastal Oregon towns have small diners and cafes, seafood sellers, cheese and candy makers, chowder houses, bakeries, and pie makers.

Full-meal deal

The Oregon coast is lined with good places to eat, from mom–and-pop diners to fish markets with real fishing boats tied up out back.

» **Lighthouse Deli and Fish Co.,** 3640 US 101, South Beach, Oregon (☎ 541-867-6800): Stop for fish and chips. Open daily from 7 a.m. to 7 p.m.

» **Mo's,** 622 SW Bay Blvd., Newport, Oregon (☎ 541-265-2979): Mo's serves clam chowder in this original diner and others along the coast. Open daily from 11 a.m. to 8 p.m. and Saturdays to 9 p.m. If the line is long, visit Mo's Annex across the street.

» **Port Hole Café,** 29975 Harbor Way, Gold Beach, Oregon (☎ 541-247-7411): The café offers clam chowder, fresh seafood, chicken, steaks, and homemade pies. Open daily from 11 a.m. to 7 p.m.

OREGON CHEESE, PLEASE!

Although Oregon seafood, hazelnuts, wines, pears, and cranberries may be famous, few think of cheese as a major state food product. But Oregon is one cheesy state as the following list of cheese producers proves.

- **Blue Heron French Cheese Co.,** US 101, 1 mile north of Tillamook, Oregon (☎ 800-275-0639 or 503-842-8281; www.blueheronoregon.com): French-style brie and Camembert cheeses are specialties, but they also feature a wine-tasting room, children's petting corral, deli, espresso bar, and gift shop. Open daily in summer from 8 a.m. to 8 p.m. and in winter from 8 a.m. to 6 p.m.

- **Tillamook Cheese Visitors Center,** 4175 US 101, North Tillamook, Oregon (☎ 503-815-1300; https://www.tillamook.com/). You can take a self-guided tour through this huge factory. Enticements include free samples of cheese and recipes, a deli, an ice-cream bar selling Tillamook ice cream on waffle cones, and a gift shop with Oregon food products and plenty of cow kitsch. Open daily in summer from 8 a.m. to 8 p.m. Winter hours are 8 a.m. to 4 p.m.

» **The Ship Inn Restaurant and Pub,** 1 Second St., Astoria, Oregon (☎ 503-325-0033): Notable for English-style fish and chips and serves up other English food. Open daily from 11:30 a.m. to 9 p.m.

Regional specialties

Northwest tastes include artichokes, lemon meringue pie wine, oysters and more. In the list, discover what to look for and where to find it:

» **Artichokes:** Head to Bear Creek Artichokes, 1604 Fifth St., Tillamook, Oregon (☎ 503-398-5411), 11 miles south of Tillamook on US 101. Open daily from 9 a.m. to 5 p.m.

» **Boutique beer:** Check out Rogue Ales Public House, 748 SW Bay Blvd., Newport, Oregon (☎ 541-265-3188; https://www.rogue.com), serves brews from ales to porters, along with fish and chips. Turn right at the north side of the bridge. Open daily from 11 a.m. to 10 p.m.

Another option is Pelican Pub and Brewery, on the beach at 33180 Cape Kiwanda Dr., Pacific City, Oregon (☎ **503-965-7007;** http://pelicanbrewery.com). Try a Doryman's Dark Ale or Tsunami Stout with pub food. Open daily from 10 a.m. to 10 p.m. Sunday through Thursday; 10:30 a.m. to 11 p.m. Friday and Saturday.

» **Cranberry candy:** Try Cranberry Sweets Co., First Street and Chicago, Bandon, Oregon (☎ **541-347-9475;** https://cranberrysweets.com). Besides sampling cranberries, sample dozens of other sweets, from lemon meringue pie candy to cheddar-cheese fudge. Open daily from 10 a.m. to 5 p.m.

Or stop at the Cranberry Museum and Gift Shop, 2907 Pioneer Road, Long Beach, Washington (☎ **360-642-5553;** http://cranberrymuseum.com), to try local cranberry products and tour the farm. Open April through December Monday through Friday from noon to 5 p.m., Saturday and Sunday from 10 a.m. to 5 p.m.

» **Smoked salmon:** Swing by Bandon Fisheries, 250 SW First St., Bandon, Oregon (☎ **541-347-2851**), for fresh, frozen, and canned local seafood, including shrimp from April through September, Dungeness crab from December through July, and salmon from May through September. Open daily 10 a.m. to 5 p.m.

Also try Josephson's Smokehouse, 106 Marine Dr., Astoria, Oregon (☎ **503-325-2190;** www.josephsons.com), an old-fashioned store with fine smoked salmon. Open daily from 9 a.m. to 6 p.m. Friday, 9:30 a.m. to 6 p.m. Saturday, and 10 a.m. to 5:30 p.m. Sunday.

» **Weird wines:** Head to Shallon Winery, 1598 Duane St., Astoria, Oregon (☎ **503-325-5978;** www.shallon.com). A winemaker named Paul van der Veldt makes chocolate-orange wine, lemon meringue pie wine, and cran *au lait,* among other flavors. Unfortunately, he turns out only about 500 gallons a year. Open daily from 1 to 5:30 p.m.

>> **Willapa Bay oysters:** Stop at Oysterville Sea Farms, Oysterville, Washington (☎ **360-665-6585;** http://willabay.com/). Fresh oysters in the shell or in a jar and smoked oysters are for sale in this shingled cottage. Try some Oysterville Victorian cake mix or cranberry condiments, and preserves. Open daily 9:30 a.m. to 5 p.m.

Shopping along the Way

If you're an outlet fan, you may want to run your rig to Lincoln City, where you'll find factory outlets at milepost 115.6 on US 101.

For something unique to Oregon, look for products made from myrtle, a hardwood that grows only on the coast in the Coos Bay area. Myrtlewood Gallery, US 101, South Coos Bay (☎ **541-271-4222**). Open daily from 9 a.m. to 5 p.m.; closed major holidays.

Fast Facts

Area Code
The area codes for Oregon are **503** and **541**. Washington's area code is **360**.

Driving Laws
All RV occupants must wear seat belts in Oregon. The maximum speed limit on interstates is 70 mph. Speed limits are lower in urban areas.

Emergency
Call ☎ **911**.

Hospitals
Along the route, major hospitals are in Coos Bay, Florence, Reedsport, Seaside, and Astoria.

Information
Sources include Oregon Tourism Division, 775 Summer St. NE, Salem (☎ **800-547-7842**);

Oregon State Parks (☎ **800-551-6940** for information or 800-452-5687 for reservations; https://oregonstateparks.org); and **Oregon Department of Fish and Wildlife** (☎ **503-947-6000**; https://www.dfw.state.or.us).

Road and Weather Conditions
Call **511**, or the Oregon Department of Transportation at ☎ **800-977-6368** (available only in Oregon) or online at https://www.oregon.gov/ODOT.

Taxes
Oregon has no sales tax. The state gasoline tax is 25 cents per gallon.

Time Zone
Oregon is on Pacific Standard Time.

Chapter 21

California's Central Coast: Malibu to Monterey

The dramatic California coastline winds for 1,200 miles between Crescent City in the north and San Diego in the south, but the most scenic part is the Central Coast, one of the most beautiful places on Earth. This drive takes you down a stretch of highway that tourists and residents alike have been driving and enjoying since it was built.

The *natural* California is not the shops of Beverly Hills, the false-front glamour of studio back lots, San Francisco's hilly cable-car routes, or Sausalito's chic waterfront. The real California is green after winter rains, when wildflowers dot the hillsides, and then turns golden with the summer sun. You know it when you spot trail riders stirring up dust on horseback; strawberries and vegetables growing in long rows, moistened by the coastal fog; a solitary figure and two dogs walking a windswept beach; adobe walls sheltering the relics of 18th-century Spanish friars; and vineyards on hillsides of what was a spreading *Californio rancho*.

Choosing Your Route

Set out from the famous beachside community of Malibu, a few minutes north of Santa Monica. The drive follows SR 1, also called the Pacific Coast Highway ("the PCH," as locals call it), for 340 miles north to the Monterey Peninsula, which juts out into the Pacific about 100 miles south of San Francisco. The PCH sometimes joins up with wider, faster US 101 (from the Oxnard/Ventura area to Gaviota, north of Santa Barbara, and then again from Pismo Beach to San Luis Obispo); some days you find you and your RV are alone on the coastline. Expect to encounter surf pounding at the foot of the cliffs along the curving roadway. You drive from Malibu along the Central Coast, past world-famous Big Sur, to the Monterey Peninsula, a distance of 340 miles.

WARNING

Take your time driving along the Big Sur stretch of the coast, turning off into the pullouts (ones big enough to handle your rig, that is), and getting out to stretch and to photograph the scenery. However tempting some of the signs and side drives may be, before you enter, consider whether you can turn your RV around and get back out.

Also be wary of traffic on this two-lane highway. The restaurant Nepenthe, the most famous eatery along the way, is noted for its ambrosia burgers; expect a crowd on a sunny midday. Opt for a parking space along the roadway.

TIP

You can make a quick weekend run from Los Angeles to Monterey comfortably in one direction if you're bound for other areas, but don't try to make a round-trip. If you have a weekend, try driving from Los Angeles as far as Morro Bay, overnighting on the bay, and heading south again. Or drive from San Francisco along the Big Sur coast as far as Morro Bay and then return. You can catch the best of scenery, enjoy a seafood or Santa Maria barbecue meal, and take in a couple hours of antiques shopping, but you won't have time for the museums and the aquarium. If you're a shopper, this trip demands more of your time.

Planning Ahead

The Central Coast makes a splendid destination any season of the year, although summer fogs and winter rains can make driving a challenge, and rock- and mudslides triggered by the winter rains may close the Pacific Coast Highway at intervals. Be prepared with sweaters and jackets if you visit in summer; cool, dense fogs roll in during the night and hang on through the morning but usually burn off before midday. (Mark Twain remarked that the coldest winter he ever spent was a summer in San Francisco.) Warm, sunny days often occur along the route in February or March. September and October are often warm and clear; most summer visitors are gone by then.

WARNING

You always need campground reservations on weekends throughout the year. State parks often divide their sites into first-come, first-served sites and those that are reserved months ahead. The best commercial RV parks may be fully booked in summer and on holidays.

Take warm clothes, even in summer; hiking boots if you want to strike out on the trails and beaches; and binoculars. A camera is a must.

You can make the drive in two or three days, but you'll want more time to visit the area's must-see attractions. To enjoy the coast and its beaches, plan to spend several days camping in at least one serendipitous area that sings to you. Morro Bay is very popular. Allow at least seven to ten days for a perfect RV vacation.

SOLVANG: A LITTLE BIT OF DENMARK

Depending on your sugar capacity, not only for Danish pastries but also for cuddly sweet, you either love or hate Solvang, America's Danish community. Back in the 1960s, this town was a Scandinavian settlement that sold Danish souvenirs and hosted a mid-September festival, with *aebelskiver* (round apple pancakes cooked in a special pan) and sausage served to visitors. Today, Solvang is an attraction that fills the town with so many vehicles that only the most intrepid RVer would attempt to join them, although Solvang offers some edge-of-town RV parking.

Bakeries selling buttery pastries and cookies include **Danish Mill Bakery**, Inc., 1682 Copenhagen Dr. (☎ **805-688-5805**); Mortensen's Danish Bakery, 1588 Mission Dr. (☎ **805-688-8373**, www.mortensensbakery.com); **Olsen's Danish Village Bakery,** 1529 Mission Dr. (☎ **805-688-6314**, http://olsensdanishbakery.com); and **Solvang Bakery,** 460 Alisal Rd. (☎ **805-688-4939**, http://solvangbakery.com). Other local shops sell Danish china, chocolate candies, Danish costumes, leather-and-wood clogs, and European antiques. With so many great bakeries, this town is on the must-visit list!

THE MATING GAME ON THE BUTTERFLY COAST

The monarch butterfly is one of the most exotic visitors to the Central Coast, arriving in late October by the hundreds of thousands to 300 nesting sites within 2 miles of the ocean. Although the migration territory ranges from a golf course in San Leandro in the Bay area southward to the campus of the UC at San Diego, most sites are along the Central Coast.

Look for monarchs between mid-October and late February or early March at the following state parks and sanctuaries:

- **Monarch Grove Sanctuary,** Pacific Grove Museum of Natural History, Ridge Road near Lighthouse Avenue, Pacific Grove (☎ 831-648-5716)
- **San Simeon State Beach,** SR 1, 5 miles south of Hearst Castle (☎ 805-927-2035)
- **Morro Bay State Park,** State Park Road, off SR 1 south of Morro Bay (☎ 805-772-7434)

- **Pismo State Beach,** North Beach Campground, SR 1, ¼ mile south of Pismo Beach (☎ 805-489-1869)

- **El Capitan State Beach,** US 101, 17 miles west of Santa Barbara (☎ 805-968-1033)

- **Camino Real Park,** Dean Drive near Varsity Street, City of Ventura Parks (☎ 805-652-4594)

- **Point Mugu State Park,** 9000 W. SR 1, Malibu (☎ 805-488-5223)

Call ahead for directions and information.

Must-See Attractions

Getty Center
Los Angeles

BARGAIN ALERT

Allow most or all of a day to see this complex of galleries, gardens, gift stores, and restaurants. The gorgeously lit galleries display everything from Old Masters to Impressionists, sculpture and decorative arts to photography. The landscaped gardens invite strolling and contemplating a drop-dead view in all directions (smog permitting).

Travelers are told "You can't miss it," but if you head north on I-405 from I-10 toward US 101, you really *can't* miss the Getty Center. First, you see a huge stone complex crowning a hill to the west of I-405 as the highway climbs toward the crest at Mulholland Drive. Next, you see signage labeled *Getty Center and Getty Center Drive,* with arrows directing you to the garage. In a twist from the usual, the Getty charges for parking, but the museum is free. Allow a half to full day.

1200 Getty Center Dr., off I-405 near Brentwood. ☎ **310-440-7300.** *www.getty.edu. RV parking: Parking ($15 for cars) is by reservation only Tues–Fri (not needed Sat–Sun) in a parking garage that's not suitable for most RVs; park in the lot opposite the entrance, or use a car or public transportation (MTA bus no. 561 or Santa Monica bus no. 14). Admission: Free. Open: Tues–Fri and Sun 10 a.m.–5:30 p.m.,*

Sat 10 a.m.–9 p.m. Restaurant: Tues–Sat 11:30 a.m.–2:30 p.m., Fri–Sat 5–9 p.m., Sun noon to 3 p.m. Restaurant reservations ☎ 310-440-6810.

Hearst Castle
San Simeon

Arranging these must-see sights in alphabetical order under-scores the impact that captains of industry — J. Paul Getty in oil and international business, and William Randolph Hearst in publishing — have had on California culture. Getty's museum was a long-planned gift to the people of California, whereas Hearst's castle was his own opulent hideaway until his death in 1951. The Hearst estate endowed the castle to the state of California, and it became a state park in 1958.

Allow time to visit the artifacts rescued from storage and on view in the reception exhibit hall and to see the 40-minute film, *Building the Dream* ($8 adults, $6 ages 17 and under), as well as the tapestries in the theater lobby. Allow at least a half day or more if you're at the back of the line.

Hearst San Simeon State Historical Monument, 750 Hearst Castle Rd. (off SR 1 at the town of San Simeon, about halfway between Los Angeles and San Francisco). ☎ 800-444-4445 or 805-927-2020 for tour reservations. http://hearstcastle.org. *RV parking: Large lots at the visitor center, where all tours begin. Admission: Daytime tours $24 adults, $12 ages 6–17; evening tours $30 adults, $15 ages 6–17. Open: Daily. Day tours start at 8:20 a.m., with the last tour beginning at 3:20 p.m. Closed major holidays. Visitors have a choice of four-day tours, all of which require walking ½ mile and negotiat-ing 200 to 500 stairs. Evening tours with docents in period costume are scheduled on Fri and Sat beginning at 6:10 p.m. on some spring and fall dates. Visitors in wheelchairs need to schedule ten days in advance by calling ☎ 866-712-2286. Strollers, backpacks, camera bags, and flash photography are not permitted.*

Monterey Bay Aquarium
Monterey

Design magic and some $50 million turned the last remaining sardine factory on Monterey's Cannery Row into one of the world's top aquariums. Inside is pure enchantment, from the three-story kelp tank to a two-level sea-otter habitat. Hands-on exhibits let you touch anemones and bat rays, and you even find a corner that runs period films from the sardine-cannery days. Some 360,000 creatures are on-site, from jellyfish to sharks, and giant whale models hang overhead. The world's biggest window gives you a look into the Outer Bay exhibit, a million-gallon, human-made ocean populated by tuna, sunfish, sea turtles, and other denizens of the deep. Allow a half day.

886 Cannery Row. ☎ *831-648-4800.* https://www.monterey bayaquarium.org. *RV parking: In nearby lots (look for signage). Admission: $30 adults, $28 seniors, $18 kids 13–17, $11 people with disabilities and kids 3–12. Open: Daily 10 a.m.–6 p.m. Closed Christmas Day.*

National Steinbeck Center
Salinas

Although the inland city of Salinas is a few miles off the coastal route, the National Steinbeck Center, along with the surrounding pedestrian-friendly city center, makes this 16-mile detour more than worth the trip. The family will love exploring this hands-on museum.

Author John Steinbeck is familiar to RVers as a pioneer of the movement, as detailed in his popular *Travels with Charley.* This book tells the story of Steinbeck's 1961 ramblings around America with his French poodle, Charley, in a truck camper named Rocinante after Don Quixote's horse. From the people who read his book came many of today's RV aficionados. In the museum, you find the original Rocinante camper, along with walk-in galleries for each of his major books filled with touch, see, and smell exhibits. Film clips from movies made from Steinbeck books — including *Cannery Row, East of Eden,*

The Grapes of Wrath, Tortilla Flat, The Red Pony, and *Of Mice and Men* — play in each area.

The center looks at California agriculture from the human point of view, documenting the personal histories of farm workers in the Salinas Valley. Allow two to three hours.

1 Main St. (directly off US 101, 16 miles east of SR 1 via SR 68 from Monterey). ☎ *831-796-3833 or 831-775-4721.* www.steinbeck.org. *RV parking: Use the railway station lot across the street or street parking. Admission: $11 adults, $8.95 seniors, $7.95 ages 13–17, $5.95 ages 6–12, free for kids 5 and under. Open: Daily 10 a.m.–5 p.m.*

Point Lobos State Reserve
Carmel

You see the same Monterey cypress trees and fog-misted headlands in Point Lobos that you do on the 17-Mile Drive, except that instead of driving through posh suburbs, you're traveling through natural coastal scenery. Go as early in the morning so that you won't be tied up in a long row of cars that brake upon sightings of sea otters, sea lions, harbor seals, and seabirds. Explore 9 miles of hiking trails and 456 acres of reserve; carry binoculars to look for California gray whales during migration seasons, which occur in mid-January (southbound) and in April and early May (northbound). No dogs allowed, and no vehicles longer than 20 feet are allowed during the summer. You can park along the highway and walk in. Allow anywhere from an hour to a half day.

SR 1 south of Carmel. ☎ *831-624-4909.* https://www.pointlobos.org. *Admission: $9 per vehicle, $9 per vehicle with senior, $6 per vehicle with person with disability, $1 for a map. Open: Daily summer 9 a.m.–7 p.m., winter 9 a.m.–5 p.m. Limit of 150 vehicles at any time.*

La Purísima Mission State Historic Park
Lompoc

Locals pronounce the town *lom*-poke, not *lom*-pock, as comedian W. C. Fields pronounced it in his film *The Bank Dick,* shot here in 1940. The restored 1787 mission, now a state park, remains in a rural setting. Costumed guides, who carry on the original routines and demonstrate the crafts of the early 19th century, staff the site. The long, low adobe-and-wood buildings house chapels, a kitchen where candles are made, a museum of artifacts and photographs, Native American workshops, soldiers' barracks, and the small cells where the friars slept. Allow two hours for the visit or more for a hike or to go horseback riding (available on-site) on one of the trails around the mission.

TIP

The flower fields surrounding the mission start to bloom in June but are brightest in July and August. Take Ocean Avenue west from downtown and drive until you spot the first fields; then zigzag back and forth between Ocean and Central avenues on the connecting streets to enjoy a display of sweet peas, delphiniums, bachelor's buttons, marigolds, petunias, and zinnias. Also make sure to see Lompoc's 50 historical murals on public and private buildings in the middle of town, especially the temperance-minded lady smashing a whiskey keg with an ax.

2295 Purisima Rd. (3 miles northeast of town on SR 246 and Purisima Road, just off SR 1). ☎ *805-733-3713. www.lapurisimamission. org. RV parking: Large parking lot. Admission: $6 per vehicle. Open: Daily 9 a.m.–5 p.m. Closed major holidays.*

More Cool Things to See and Do

Although the scenery is spectacular along every mile of this drive, you may want to check out these other cool activities.

>> **Uncovering Egypt:** Movie fans who also are archaeology buffs love the **Nature Conservancy's Dunes Discovery Center,** 1055 Guadalupe St. (CA 1), Guadalupe (☎ **805-343-2455,** ext. 101;

http://dunescenter.org), combines hands-on exhibits about the landscape and creatures that live in the dunes, and artifacts of an excavation of a long-buried movie set depicting Egypt in the biblical era.

In 1923, on the Nipomo Dunes south of Guadalupe, Cecil B. DeMille built a movie set only slightly less ambitious than the Great Pyramids at Giza for *The Ten Commandments*. The production involved 1,600 laborers, 2,500 movie stars, and 110-foot walls flanked by four statues of Ramses II and 21 sphinxes. At the end, DeMille brought in a horse-drawn bulldozer and knocked down the set to keep a rival from coming in, shooting a picture, and releasing it first. The sands buried the set. Some 60 years later, a storm uncovered some of it, and documentarians preserved and cataloged items. The center offers docent-led hikes through the dunes that focus on the film, birdwatching, photography, and botanical and animal life. To visit on your own, drive west on the road by the cemetery to the parking lot right on the beach at Guadalupe Dunes Preserve. Alternatively, go 3 miles north and west 3 miles on Oso Flaco Lake Road to a parking lot ($4), and hike a trail and a boardwalk to the dunes; it's 2 miles round-trip. Allow two to three hours.

RV parking is available on the street. Admission is free. The center is open Wednesday through Sunday from 10 a.m. to 4:30 p.m.

» **Wine tasting 101:** Off US 101 in and near Los Olivos lies a sampling of Santa Barbara County wineries, including Firestone, Fess Parker, Zaca Mesa, Foxen Vineyard, and Gainey Vineyard.

Call **Santa Barbara County Vintner's Association** at ☎ **805-688-0881,** or go to https://www.sbcountywines.com for info and a detailed map of all the county's wineries.

» **Piering into the past:** Santa Monica Pier, Ocean and Colorado avenues, was slated to be the port of Los Angeles, the area lost out to San Pedro at the turn of the 20th century. Undeterred, the city built a sandy beach park and a playland pier, built between 1904 and 1921. A 1916 carousel that starred in the film *The Sting,* an arcade, and a Ferris wheel lend a Coney Island accent to this sunny pocket of Southern California. Allow two hours to a half day.

MONTEREY'S CANNERY ROW AND FISHERMAN'S WHARF

Cannery Row was, in the words of John Steinbeck, "a poem, a stink, a grating noise, a quality of light, a tone, a habit, a nostalgia, a dream." Today, the canneries are silent; regrettably, the smell of the sardines is long gone; and only the dream and nostalgia remain, along with a bustling commercial center aimed squarely at tourists.

The Monterey Bay Aquarium, 886 Cannery Row (☎ 831-648-4800; https://www. montereybayaquarium.org), is a must-see; when you're in the neighborhood with extra time, check out other attractions. If you know Steinbeck's novels — *Cannery Row* and *Tortilla Flat* — you'll recognize the landmarks, including Wing Chong Market (Lee Chong's Grocery), Ed Ricketts's Pacific Biological Laboratories (Western Biological), and Flora Wood's Lone Star Café (Bear Flag Restaurant). A marker in Cannery Row Memorial Park salutes the books' *Chicken Walk* and *Palace Flophouse*.

A 1905 Herschell-Spillman carousel whirls at 640 Wave St.; a playground named for Dennis the Menace, the comic-strip character created by resident Hank Ketchum that some will remember, calls out to all eager kids from Pearl Street. If you're in the mood, you can take advantage of Cannery Row's factory-outlet shops, wine tasting, fish restaurants, and shops.

Monterey State Historical Park and Fisherman's Wharf jut out into the bay a few blocks east of Cannery Row but with less-spacious parking, so plan to park in the Cannery Row area. The wharf is lined with takeout seafood places similar to Fisherman's Wharf in San Francisco; one local specialty is clam chowder served in hollowed-out loaves of sourdough bread. Forget the overpriced abalone; a former staple of coastal California, the delectable shellfish has been overfished, and that sold on the wharf today is imported. Instead, order the local calamari; it is delicious when fried.

Cannery Row, on the street named Cannery Row, is adjacent to Foam and Lighthouse streets in Monterey. A parking lot in the area is large enough for RVs; leave your vehicle in the lot and walk the six or so blocks to Fisherman's Wharf. For more information, go to https://canneryrow.com.

For more information on visiting the pier, contact the **Santa Monica Visitor Center**, 1920 Main St., Suite B (☎ **800-544-5319** or 310-319-6263; https://www.santamonica.com). RV parking is available in designated lots.

» **Shadowing Perry Mason:** The city of Ventura was the home of Erle Stanley Gardner, a lawyer and writer whose *Perry Mason* series began in 1933. Today, you can take a walking tour past Gardner's homes and offices in town. Allow a couple of hours.

For more information, contact the **Ventura Visitors & Convention Bureau,** 101 S. California St., Suite C (☎ **805-648-2075**; https://visitventuraca.com). The tour is available 9 a.m. to 4 p.m. Monday through Saturday and Sunday 10 a.m. to 4 p.m. RV parking is on the street. Some off-street lots are available, but avoid blocking private driveways.

Our Favorite Campgrounds

The Pacific Coast Highway (California 1, SR 1) is sprinkled with plenty of state park campgrounds where an RV can overnight (often without hookups) if you've made advance reservations or you arrive early on a weekday when other campers are checking out. Private campgrounds are more accommodating; you can make a call and leave a credit-card number to reserve an open site for as long as you want to stay. Altogether, nearly three dozen RV parks are located along the coastal route. The toll-free reservations numbers for the state parks listed are for a central reservations system that may involve a long wait on hold and much punching of numbers. I miss making a reservation with a person at the campground where you want a space, but those places are nearly extinct.

All campgrounds listed in this chapter are open year-round and have flush toilets, showers, and sanitary dump stations unless otherwise noted. Toll-free numbers, where listed, are for reservations only.

Malibu Beach RV Park
$$$$$ Malibu

If you ignore how near your next-door neighbor is parked and concentrate on the knockout view of the Pacific, you may like this close-to-L.A. campground, but be sure to reserve ahead. Going to the beach means walking downhill and carefully crossing SR 1. Activities include sitting in the sun outside your RV with binoculars, looking for passing whales or dolphins, or hiking in the Santa Monica Mountains. The park has six pull-throughs, so you may have to back into your cliff-top site.

25801 SR 1. (Take SR 1 from Santa Monica north to Malibu Canyon Road and Pepperdine University; continue west on SR 1 for 2 miles to the campground, uphill on the right.) ☎ **800-622-6052** *or* **310-456-6052**. https://www.maliburv.com. *Total of 142 sites with water and 30-amp electric, 82 full hookups, 6 pull-throughs. Laundry. Rates: $45–$119 per site, lower in winter. AE, DISC, MC, V.*

Marina Dunes RV Park
$$$$$ Marina

This landscaped park is 8 miles north of Monterey on the ocean, near dunes that are a short distance away via a sandy walkway. All sites are back-ins, not wide but framed by foliage for privacy.

3330 Dunes Dr. (Follow SR 1 for 6 miles north of Monterey; exit on Reservation Road and drive west a half-block to Dunes Drive. The campground is on the right.) ☎ **831-384-6914**. http://marinadunesrv.com. *Total of 88 sites with water and 30- and 50-amp electric, 84 with full hookups, no pull-throughs. CATV, data port, laundry. Rate: $65–$85 per site. MC, V.*

Morro Bay State Park

$$$$ Morro Bay

Located on the Morro Bay estuary, this charming state park provides great birdwatching, scenic camping, and a pretty 1-mile walk into town. From fall through early spring, the park is full of wintering monarch butterflies that sleep in the numerous eucalyptus trees in the campground. An 18-hole public golf course is adjacent. Kayak and canoe rentals are available across the road. Sites are spacious, most of them shaded and landscaped for privacy, with picnic tables, wooden food lockers, and stone fire pits/grills that look as though the Civilian Conservation Corps handmade them back in the 1930s. Some campsites can be reserved; otherwise, it's first come, first served.

State Park Road, off SR 1 at South Bay Boulevard and west on State Park Road to campground, on the right. ☎ *805-772-7434; for reservations only* ☎ *800-444-7275.* https://www.parks.ca.gov. *Total of 135 sites, 27 pull-throughs with water and 20- and 30-amp electric. Handicap accessible, pay showers, Wi-Fi. Rate: $34 per site. No credit cards.*

Morro Dunes

$$$$ Morro Bay

This clean, well-run campground is on the dunes by the sea in the fishing and tourist town of Morro Bay. Most campsites view Morro Rock and dramatic sunsets, and from the campground fence, the distance is ¼ mile to the beach, where shorebirds abound. To be close enough to hear the waves, get a back-in site, arranged like spokes of a wheel. If you like more space, book one of the pull-throughs at the back, still close to the beach but less noisy. Call for reservations any time of year; this campground is one of the most popular in California.

1700 Embarcadero. (From SR 1, take the SR 41 Atascadero exit and drive west ½ mile to the campground, on the left.) ☎ *805-772-2722.* https://morrodunes.com. *Total of 141 sites with water and 30-amp electric, 130 full hookups, 35 pull-throughs. CATV, data port, handicap accessible, laundry, Wi-Fi. Rates: $35–$50 per site. MC, V.*

Santa Cruz/Monterey Bay KOA

KID FRIENDLY

$$$$$ Watsonville

This well-kept resort offers special summer events for children, including softball games and cookouts (featuring hot dogs and s'mores), as well as year-round holiday observances, including a free champagne breakfast and roses for Mother's Day, an Easter-egg hunt, and Thanksgiving dinner. Other amusements include miniature golf, a heated pool, and bike rentals. Sites are wide, and the park is well landscaped. The ocean is less than a mile's walk. In spring and summer, Watsonville's strawberry fields are full of fruit; autumn brings the grape crush at nearby wineries.

1186 San Andreas Rd. (From SR 1, 5 miles north of Watsonville, take the San Andreas Road exit and drive west 3 miles to the campground, on the left.) ☎ **800-562-7701** *or 831-722-0551.* https://koa.com/campgrounds/santa-cruz. *Total of 177 sites with water and 30-amp electric, 140 full hookups, 7 pull-throughs. Data port, handicap access, laundry, pool, sauna, spa, Wi-Fi. Rates: $65–$110 per site; call to verify current seasonal rates and fees. AE, DISC, MC, V.*

Good Eats

Although chic, expensive restaurants line this route, some get uptight when they see a larger, longer RV drive up. I prefer friendly, down-home takeout spots and concentrate on local and regional cooking.

Santa Maria barbecue

After decades as cherished secret Central Coast cuisine, Santa Maria barbecue has reached national prominence because former L.A. residents and knowledgeable barbecue fans have edited major foodie journals. Some critics call this barbecue the best in the world, but I quibble there, because a fine piece of Texas brisket or Owensboro, Kentucky, mutton is also quite satisfying. Santa Maria barbecue places serve up unique side dishes of tiny, tasty *pinquito* beans, grown only in Santa Barbara County, and tasty salsa inherited from the *Californios*.

The Santa Maria style began more than a century ago with the hospitable *Californios*, Mexican ranch families who welcomed strangers with giant outdoor barbecues. Later, cattle roundups meant that local ranchers celebrated the end of the work by throwing hunks of beef onto flaming live-oak logs in a hand-dug pit and having a party. Then, in the 1950s, butchers in Santa Maria isolated the *tri-tip*, seasoned with salt, pepper, olive oil, garlic, and wine vinegar and tossed on the grill.

Today, you find Santa Maria barbecue in many restaurants along the Central Coast, along Broadway in Santa Maria on Saturdays, and Sundays between noon and 6 p.m. in parking lots where you see smoke rising from portable barbecues. You can also hit the Thursday-night street market in San Luis Obispo, where vendors with portable cookers clog Higuera Street and sell sandwiches or cooked barbecue. Or make this barbecue yourself by buying a tri-tip roast, already marinated, from a market like Spencer's Fresh Market in Morro Bay.

Besides *pinquito* beans and a salsa, other side dishes in a restaurant meal of Santa Maria barbecue include a relish dish of pickles, olives, carrot and celery sticks; shrimp cocktail; garlic bread; and a baked potato. When you buy from a roadside stand, consider taking in the flavor of whatever the stand is offering on the side.

The best Central Coast purveyors of Santa Maria–style beef barbecue are as follows:

» **Far Western Tavern,** 300 E. Clark, Orcutt (☎ **805-937-2211;** https://farwesterntavern.com): The owners prefer to use "bull's-eye" (ribeye) steaks up to 20 ounces cut from their own cattle but also offer "cowboy-cut" top sirloin cooked in the Santa Maria style, with *pinquito* beans and salsa on the side, as well as an appetizer of crisp mountain oysters with dipping sauce. (Called *calf fries,* they are *not* from the ocean but are part of a male calf's anatomy.) The restaurant is open Tuesday through Thursday from 11 a.m. to 8:30 p.m. and Friday through Sunday from 11 a.m. to 9 p.m. It's closed Monday.

- » **The Hitching Post,** 3325 Point Sal Road, Casmalia (☎ **805-937-6151**; https://hitchingpost1.com): The Hitching Post, north of Vandenburg Air Force Base, has been around since 1952. The meat is cooked in an open pit in the middle of the room. The restaurant is open Monday through Saturday from 4:30 to 9:30 p.m. and Sunday from 4 to 9 p.m. To find it, use SR 1, and take Black Rd. to Point Sal Rd.

- » **Jocko's,** 125 N. Thompson St., Nipomo (☎ **805-929-3686**; http://jockossteakhouse.com). Standing on the corner in Nipomo like a pool hall or burger joint, Jocko's is notable for Santa Maria barbecue and is open daily from 8 a.m. to 10 p.m.

Markets and meals

Instead of using a national chain store like Trader Joe's, fill your fridge with fresh fish and produce from some of many local spots listed next.

- » **Giovanni's Fish Market,** 1001 Front St., Morro Bay (☎ **805-772-2123**; https://www.giovannisfishmarket.com): This market has a crab tank and cooker outside; a takeout window for fish; and a fish market inside that sells seafood from cooked crab and shrimp to calamari salad and cod. The cooked crab is boxed with a tablecloth ready to eat on the tables overlooking the boats. The store is open daily from 9 a.m. to 6 p.m.; the kitchen, daily from 11 a.m. to 6 p.m.

- » **Morro Bay farmers' market,** 2650 N. Main St., Morro Bay (no phone): In the parking lot of Spencer's Fresh Market, find fresh fruits and vegetables, crafts, and cut flowers. Spencer's features European-style sausages; eggs from Cal Poly farms; and marinated tri-tip roasts. The market opens every Thursday afternoon from 3 to 5 p.m.

- » **San Luis Obispo's farmers' market,** Higuera Street downtown, San Luis Obispo (Convention and Visitors Bureau ☎ **800-634-1414**): You can chow down on hot Santa Maria barbecue sandwiches while you shop. The market runs year-round every Thursday from 6 to 9 p.m.

BARGAIN ALERT

» **La Super-Rica Taqueria,** 622 N. Milpas St. (take the Milpas turnoff from US 101), Santa Barbara (☎ **805-963-4940**): This taco stand is among America's most famous, thanks to a rave by the legendary food icon Julia Child. Instead of starting a fast-food franchise, owner Isodoro Gonzalez retained the same restaurant started in 1980, kept cooking what Julia liked, and adding specials. Recommendations include the Super-Rica, grilled tri-tip with poblano and the *pozole*. Open Thursday through Tuesday. from 11 a.m. to 9:30 p.m.

Fast Facts

Area Code

This chapter includes four area codes: **310** in the Los Angeles area, **805** south of San Luis Obispo, **831** north of San Luis Obispo, and **415** in San Francisco.

Driving Laws

All RV occupants must wear seat belts in California. The maximum speed limit on some interstates is 75 mph. Speed limits are lower in urban areas.

Emergency

Call ☎ **911.**

Hospitals

Hospitals along the route include French Hospital Medical Center, 1911 Johnson Ave., San Luis Obispo (☎ **805-543-5353**); and Arroyo Grande Community Hospital, 345 S. Halcyon Rd., Arroyo Grande (☎ **805-489-4261**). Major hospitals are also in San Francisco.

Information

Helpful sources include the California Office of Tourism (☎ **916-444-4429**; https://www.visitcalifornia.com), California State Parks reservations (☎ **800-444-7275**; https://www.parks.ca.gov), the California Travel Parks Association (☎ **888-STAY-CTPA [782-9287]**; https://www.camp-california.com), and the California Department of Fish and Game (☎ **916-445-0411**; https://www.wildlife.ca.gov).

Road and Weather Conditions

Call ☎ **800-427-7623.**

Taxes

Statewide sales tax is 7.25 percent. Some local taxes may raise that rate to 8.75 percent. The state gas tax is 58.2 cents per gallon, adding state and local sales taxes on top of that.

Time Zone

California is on Pacific Standard Time.

Chapter **22**

Route 66: OK to L.A.

J ohn Steinbeck called Route 66 "the mother road" in his classic novel *The Grapes of Wrath*. Whether it's being traversed by the book's dirt-poor Joad family in the 1930s, who headed for California with all their possessions tied to a broken-down truck, or the handsome hero-adventurers Tod and Buz in their shiny yellow Corvette in the 1960s TV series *Route 66*, this highway has sung its invitation to anyone who has a dream to travel the open road.

Route 66 is the highway that authenticated the age of the automobile, painting the image of footloose Americans as car travelers, proving that the going can be as rewarding as the getting there and that life can be lived on the road as joyfully as at home. To fill the needs of road-running explorers, enterprising Americans invented diners, tourist cabins, campgrounds, motels, and motor courts, which enabled travelers to park their vehicles beside their doors and see billboard teasers in comic-book colors advertising roadside attractions such as caged rattlesnakes and *jackalopes* (the imaginary, fast-moving offspring of jackrabbits and antelopes). Car-lovers even came up with drive-in restaurants, drive-in movies, and drive-in churches.

The original Route 66 ran "from Chicago to L.A." (as anyone who's heard the Bobby Troup song of the same name knows), but this drive travels only among Claremore, Oklahoma, and Los Angeles. More recently, the animated film *Cars,* which takes place in the fictional town of Radiator Springs (a fictional composite of towns along Route 66 such as Williams, Arizona), has focused more attention on the mother road. Not all the old roadway remains, so much of the time, this route follows I-40, which parallels and sometimes covers the old center line of old Route 66.

Choosing Your Route

Because Route 66 was also dedicated as Will Rogers Highway in 1952 to honor the famous humorist, the trip begins in his hometown of Claremore, Oklahoma, right on Route 66, and follows it all the way to Santa Monica, California, where a plaque in Pacific Palisades commemorates Rogers and the highway. Not far away is Will Rogers's beloved California ranch, now a state park and polo field.

WARNING

In Tulsa, take I-44 or I-244 to the west side of town to rejoin Route 66 at Exit 220. This section of the old route is well maintained. Because the turnpike charges a toll and has limited on and off access, you need to stay on Route 66 all the way to Oklahoma City if you don't want to miss any of the old landmarks along the way. One thing you might notice in Oklahoma is the tendency for the highway turns to be painted on the roadway lanes, making it easier for big RVs and trucks to deal with upcoming lane changes.

The distance from Claremore to Tulsa is only 20 miles on Route 66 and 105 more to Oklahoma City. From that city, follow a widened Route 66 out of town and through El Reno; then switch to I-40. Business Route 40, which also is old 66, detours through the towns of Weatherford, Clinton, Elk City, and Sayre, enabling you to drive segments of the original Route 66 (with more original miles in Oklahoma than in any other state) and I-40 all the way to Texas. In Texas, the route crosses the Panhandle through Amarillo, with more original Route 66 detours at Shamrock, McLean, Alanreed, Groom, Vega, and Adrian.

In New Mexico, the first major town is Tucumcari, followed by Moriarity. A few remnants of Route 66 remain in Albuquerque, so detour through the Nob Hill section near the University of New Mexico; then pick up a former stretch of Route 66 from Laguna to Cubero and from McCartys to Thoreau. The town of Gallup is filled with the spirit of Route 66 and makes a good place to camp overnight.

In Arizona, the Petrified Forest retains Route 66 connections; so do Holbrook, Joseph City, and Winslow. Rejoin I-40 to go on to Flagstaff without forgetting Winona, as the silky voice of Nat King Cole reminds us all in the song; then get off the interstate to explore more old Route 66 roadway. One of the longest, smoothest stretches of Route 66 that's still around runs from Ash Fork to Kingman, with another rewarding if narrower section from Kingman to Oatman.

In California, a turnoff at Needles travels north to Goffs and then south to Essex and Amboy before returning north to rejoin I-40 at Ludlow. Follow I-40 to Barstow, and take old 66 from Barstow through Hodge, Helendale, and Oro Grande to Victorville. At Victorville, take I-15 down the long grade to San Bernardino. Then, if you're in a hurry, take I-10 to the end of the road at Santa Monica. If you have time, poke along the 50 miles of Foothill Boulevard still numbered Route 66 between San Bernardino and Pasadena.

The basic distance is 1,453 miles; some of the detours onto old Route 66 add more miles to the worthwhile experience of seeing remnants of the America that was.

Planning Ahead

In general, this stretch of Route 66 can be traveled year-round, but in winter, generous amounts of snow may fall in the upper elevations of New Mexico and around Flagstaff. Conversely, midsummer can be quite hot along parts of the road in California, Arizona, and the Texas Panhandle. Spring can bring gusty winds to the Panhandle and the California and Arizona deserts. Overall, early spring and fall to late fall are the best times to travel.

Campground reservations aren't always necessary unless you have your heart set on a particular park. You can often decide by early to midafternoon how much farther you want to travel, figure how far you'll get, and call ahead to a campground in that area to reserve a spot (or at least find out what your odds are of getting a site that day).

When packing, take along hiking boots, rain gear, lightweight clothing for hot weather (even in winter), and warm clothing to layer up for cool days. Sunscreen, UPF (ultraviolet protection factor, UPF of 30 to 49 offers good protection) clothing, and sunglasses are essential in the bright desert sunlight of the Southwest. Make sure to take your binoculars and your camera.

Allow at least 9 days, preferably 10 to 14 or more, to make a leisurely tour of Route 66.

WHAT RHYMES WITH ALBUQUERQUE?

In Albuquerque, you can leave I-40 and take Central Avenue to retrace old Route 66, but the eastern end has little to attract you unless used-car dealerships and fast-food franchises make you nostalgic. The architectural scenery changes near the Nob Hill area by the University of New Mexico, where you get a reminder of the 1930s and 1940s.

Although the **Flying Star Cafe**, 3416 Central Ave. NE (☎ **505-255-6633**; https://www.flyingstarcafe.com), is known by locals by its former name, the Double Rainbow, it isn't from the 1930s. It sells great coffees and desserts, though.

KICKIN' BACK IN OATMAN

Oatman, founded in 1906, produced $36 million in gold before 1942, when the federal government decided that gold wasn't essential to the war effort. Before the 1930s Depression, Oatman had a population of 12,000; then the people all but disappeared. Today, resident numbers are growing again, but the town still is so small that wild burros roam the streets, seeking handouts from visitors.

Popular on the weekend RV circuit because of its nearness to Laughlin, Nevada, and Lake Havasu City, Arizona, Oatman hosts swap meets, antiques shops, old saloons, and a noontime Wild West shoot-out reenactment.

The best times to go are weekdays, because weekend parking can get tight in town, especially for RVs. To get there, take the evocative but narrow and winding part of the original Route 66 between Kingman and Oatman over the 3,652-foot Sitgreaves Pass. The best route to and from Oatman, if you're driving or towing a large RV or if narrow curvy roads make you nervous, is I-40 from Kingman to Topock on the Arizona/California border; then drive north on SR 95 to the Route 66 turnoff to Oatman.

Must-See Attractions

Acoma Pueblo

Acoma, New Mexico

Called Sky City, this hilltop pueblo is said to be the oldest continuously inhabited community in the United States, dating back to A.D. 1150. Constructed atop a 367-foot sandstone mesa near Grants, the village is open to visitors daily year-round by guided tour only. A dozen families still are in residence, although most tribal members have settled in the valley below. Visitors can purchase Acoma pottery and bread baked in the outdoor adobe ovens. Visitors aren't permitted to enter the *kiva* (sacred chamber) and need to expect certain restrictions, including paying a fee to use cameras or sketch pads. Allow one or two hours.

*66 miles west of Albuquerque. (From I-40, take Exit 102 or Exit 96, and follow the signs to the visitor center.) ☎ **800-747-0181** or 505-552-7861. http://www.acomaskycity.org/home.html. RV parking: In the designated lot in the village below Sky City. Tour: $25 adults, $22 seniors and veterans, $17 youth all ages. Open: Daily summer 9 a.m.–5 p.m., with the last tour starting at 3:30 p.m.; winter 8 a.m.–4 p.m., with the last tour starting at 3 p.m. Closed June 24–29, July 9–14 and 25, and December 1. No one can go beyond the parking lot in the village below the mesa without joining a tour.*

Calico Ghost Town
Calico, California

Extremely popular with European and Japanese Old West aficionados, Calico isn't a built-for-tourists ghost town that some people expect, but a real silver-mining town that thrived from 1881 to 1907 with a population of 3,500. Walter Knott of Knott's Berry Farm fame, who worked in the mines as a youth, restored and preserved the town, which is operated today by the San Bernardino County Park System. A modestly priced county RV park is adjacent to the town entrance; RVers camping on-site get free admission to the town. Original and reconstructed buildings, including a house made of glass bottles, sometimes serve as a backdrop for staged gunfights and other Western shenanigans on weekends and in summer. Allow a half-day or more.

*Calico exit from I-15 or I-40 east of Barstow. ☎ **760-254-2122**. http://cms.sbcounty.gov/parks/Parks/CalicoGhostTown.aspx. RV parking: Large parking lots at entrance. Admission: $8 adults, $5 ages 4–f11, free 3 and under. Open: Daily 9 a.m.–5 p.m.*

Grand Canyon Railway
Williams, Arizona

A steam train to the Grand Canyon leaves daily at 9 a.m. year-round from the restored 1908 train station in the town of Williams. Passengers ride the refurbished 1928 rail cars

65 miles north to the canyon, have a few hours for sightseeing, and return in late afternoon. The town has several nice campgrounds if you want to check in for the night. At the canyon, the train stops near El Tovar Hotel, where frequent shuttle departures set out for the South Rim.

Taking the train is a good idea, because Grand Canyon National Park now prohibits private vehicles from the entire South Rim from March to November — a policy started in 2004. The train doesn't run when heavy snow covers the tracks. In summer, adequate parking space isn't always available in the lots at the entrance, especially for RVs. Allow a full day.

233 N. Grand Canyon Blvd. (just off I-40; you can see the station from the highway). ☎ ***800-843-8724.*** *www.thetrain.com. RV parking: Lot by the station is big enough for any RV. Tickets: Coach to first class $67–$189 adults, $32–$153 ages 2–15; Dome car $189 for adults, $152 ages 2–15, children under 2 not allowed; Parlor Car $226 adults, children 15 and under not permitted. Prices don't include taxes and national park entrance fee. Discounts available for AAA members, military, and first responders. Departure: 9 a.m. Return: 6:15 p.m. Reservations recommended. Check with reservation desk for RV parking and camping.*

National Cowboy Hall of Fame and Western Heritage Center
Oklahoma City, Oklahoma

Framed by the windows at the end of the massive entry hall, James Earle Fraser's marble sculpture *End of the Trail* depicts an Indian warrior, his body slumped in exhaustion and defeat astride his horse, his lance drooping at the same angle as his horse's head. The subject represents the passing of the Old West. This excellent museum displays outstanding art and artifacts from both the old and new West. Galleries include the American Rodeo Gallery, Western Entertainment Gallery (with movie posters and film and video clips), and Prosperity Junction (a life-size replica of an Old West town). Allow two hours or more.

1700 NE 63rd St. (Take Exit 129 off I-44 west of the junction with I-35, and follow the signs.) ☎ **405-478-2250.** `https://nationalcowboymuseum.org.` *RV parking: Designated area in front of the museum. Admission: $10.75 adults, $9.25 seniors, $5 children 4–12, free 3 and under. Open: Mon—Sat 10 a.m.–5 p.m., Sun noon–5 p.m. Closed major holidays.*

Petrified Forest National Park and Painted Desert
I-40, northeastern Arizona

These two famous Route 66 landmarks lie across the highway from each other about 25 miles east of Holbrook. A loop road goes through both areas. Stop first at the visitor center near the entrance of the Petrified Forest to get a map and some idea of how this landscape was formed. In the time of the dinosaurs, 225 million years ago, a forest of trees fell into the water and gradually began to petrify, a process in which quartz replaces the organic cells of the trees. Allow a half-day.

WARNING

Tempting as it may be, picking up any pieces of the petrified wood is against the law. For those who want to acquire the wood legitimately, samples are for sale at the Crystal Forest Museum at the southern end of the area.

TIP

The Painted Desert is best seen early or late in the day, when the sunlight hits at an angle that makes the colors brighter. If you wear polarized sunglasses and photograph the desert with a polarizing filter, you get more dramatic colors. The park doesn't have campgrounds.

From Exit 311 on I-40, the Petrified Forest is to the south and the Painted Desert is to the north. ☎ **928-524-6228.** `https://www.nps.gov/pefo/index.htm.` *RV parking: At visitor center and at turnouts along the loop road. Admission: $20 per vehicle for 7-day pass; bike $10; motorcycle $15. Open: Daily 8 a.m.–6 p.m. Closed Christmas Day.*

Will Rogers Memorial Museum
Claremore, Oklahoma

This rather majestic memorial on the crest of hill is devoted to the life and times of the famous humorist and film star and to his final resting place. A theater shows clips from some of his 70 films, radio sets play excerpts from his popular radio show, and a children's interactive center makes finding out about him fun. A gift shop also is on the premises. Allow two hours or more.

1720 W. Will Rogers Blvd. ☎ 800-324-9455 or 918-341-0719. https://www.willrogers.com. RV parking: Large open parking lot. Admission: $7 adults, $5 seniors, $3 children 6–17, free 5 and under. Open: Daily 8 a.m.–5 p.m.; tours at 10 a.m. and 5 p.m.

ROUTE 66 MUSEUMS

All the museums along this route display artifacts, signs, and photographs of old Route 66 with varying degrees of sophistication. Museums feature displays of a re-creation of the highway decade by decade, a battered 1920 truck, a painted hippie van of the 1960s. Many displays of license plates, road signs, and a 1926 Dodge Touring Sedan, all items with connections to Route 66.

- **California Route 66 Museum,** 16825 D St. between Fifth and Sixth streets, Victorville, California (☎ **760-951-0436;** https://www.califrt66museum.org): RV parking is available in the designated lot or on the street. Admission is by donation. The museum is open Thursday through Monday from 10 a.m. to 4 p.m. and Sunday from 11 a.m. to 3 p.m. Allow one hour. Closed Easter, July 4, Veterans' Day, Thanksgiving, Christmas Day, and New Year's Day.

- **Devil's Rope Museum and Route 66 Museum,** Old Route 66 at 100 Kingsley St., McLean, Texas (☎ **806-779-2225;** https://www.barbwiremuseum.com): RV parking is available on the street. Admission is by donation. The museum is open March 1 to November 1 Monday through Saturday from 9 a.m. to 4 p.m. Allow one hour.

(continued)

(continued)

- **Mother Road Museum,** 681 N. First Ave., Barstow, California (☎ 760-255-1890; www.route66museum.org): RV parking is available in the designated lot or on the street. Admission is free. The museum is open Friday and Saturday from 10 a.m. to 4 p.m. and Sunday from 11 a.m. to 4 p.m. Allow one hour.

- **National Route 66 Museum,** Old Town Museum Complex, Route 66 and Pioneer Road, 2717 W. Highway 66, Elk City, Oklahoma (☎ 580-225-6266; http://www.elkcitychamber.com/main.aspx): RV parking is available in a large lot at the complex. Admission is $5 for adults, $4 for seniors and ages 6 to 16, and free for kids 5 and under. The museum is open Tuesday through Saturday from 9 a.m. to 5 p.m. and Sunday from 2 to 5 p.m.; it's closed on major holidays. Allow one hour.

- **Oklahoma Route 66 Museum,** 2229 Gary Blvd., Clinton, Oklahoma (☎ 580-323-7866; www.route66.org): RV parking is available in a small lot at the museum or on the street. Admission is $7 adults, $5 seniors, $4 ages 6 to 18. Free Children under 6, vets and active duty. An audio self-guided tour is available. The museum is open February through April Monday–Saturday 9 a.m. to 5 p.m., Sunday 1 p.m. to 5 p.m.; May through August daily from 9 a.m. to 7 p.m., Sunday 1 p.m. to 6 p.m.; September through November, Monday–Saturday 9 a.m. to 5 p.m., Sunday 1 p.m. to 5 p.m.; December to January, Tuesday through Saturday 9 a.m. to 5 p.m. Closed first week of January and all state holidays; call ahead. Allow two hours.

More Cool Things to See and Do

Some all-time-favorite attractions line Route 66:

BARGAIN ALERT

» **Burying the gas guzzlers:** At **Cadillac Ranch,** ten vintage tailfin Cadillacs are buried front-end down in an open field on a ranch just west of Amarillo, Texas, causing I-40 traffic to slow down and gaze. To pull over, take the Hope Road exit, which lets you pull off on a parking-permitted shoulder from and walk across some 1,500 feet of often-muddy field to get a closer look. The site is always open and always free. Allow 30 minutes if you stop.

» **Waking Andy Devine:** At the **Mohave Museum of History and Arts,** 400 W. Beale St., Kingman, Arizona (☎ **928-753-3195**; https://www.mohavemuseum.org), a casual, almost homemade museum, the city's favorite son is the main exhibit. He's the late film actor Andy Devine, who played comic sidekicks to various cowboy stars in countless classic movies and various TV series, such as *Wild Bill Hickok.* Movie posters, a replica of his dressing room, and costumes he wore fill his part of the museum. Elsewhere, you find everything from World War II airplane-nose art to displays of local turquoise jewelry. Route 66 souvenirs are for sale in the gift shop. Allow one hour or more.

RV parking is available in the designated lot or on the street. Admission is $4 for ages 13 to 59, $3 for seniors 60 and older, and free for ages 12 and under. The museum is open Monday through Friday from 9 a.m. to 5 p.m. and Saturday and Sunday from 1 to 5 p.m.

» **Digging for uranium.** Go into a simulated uranium mine, check out local tribal regalia, and eyeball geology exhibits in the **New Mexico Museum of Mining,** the world's only museum of uranium mining. 100 Iron St., Grants, New Mexico (☎ **800-748-2142** or 505-287-4802; http://www.grants.org/museums-galleries.aspx). Allow two hours.

RV parking is available in a medium-size off-street lot or on the street. Admission is $5 for adults and $3 for seniors and ages 7 to 18. The museum is open Monday through Saturday from 9 a.m. to 4 p.m. Closed Sundays.

» **Refueling at Bagdad Cafe:** Buses filled with French or German tourists pull up beside this undistinguished cafe on old Route 66 and pile out with cameras, saying "It's just like the movie." They're talking about a 1987 film called *Bagdad Café,* starring Jack Palance and Whoopi Goldberg. The movie didn't fare well in the United States but became a cult hit in Europe (hence the tourists yearning to have a Jack Palance burger or Bagdad omelet).

The Bagdad Cafe is located at 48548 Route 66, Newberry Springs, California (☎ **760-257-3101**), about 18 miles east of Barstow. It's open daily from 7 a.m. to 7 p.m.

Our Favorite Campgrounds

All campgrounds listed are open year-round and have public flush toilets, showers, and sanitary dump stations unless designated otherwise. Toll-free numbers, where listed, are for reservations only.

Bonelli Bluffs

$$$$$ San Dimas, California

This spacious, Good Sam–member campground has hilltop sites that get summer breezes and lakeside sites that are in a valley with fewer circulating breezes. Mature shade trees surround the grass-paved sites. My favorites are those beginning with the letter *B* on the bluff overlooking the Fairplex grounds and the local airport. Freshwater-lake fishing is available.

1440 Camper View Rd. (From I-10, take the Fairplex Drive exit and go north ½ mile, turn left on Via Verde, and turn right on Camper View Road; the campground is at the end of the road.) ☎ **909 599-8355.** https://www.bonellibluffsrv.com. *Total 190 sites with 30- and 50-amp electric, all full hookups, 15 pull-throughs. CATV, data port, laundry, pool. Rates: $61–$71 per site. DISC, MC, V.*

Calico Ghost Town Campground

KID FRIENDLY

$$–$$$ Yermo, California

Guests at this campground get free access to the colorful old ghost town of Calico. Although it's desert-hot on a summer's midday, late afternoons bring glowing sunsets that fill the old town with golden light. Reenactments of gunfights and other live shows take place, and shops and simple cafes line the main street. The weather is nice in winter unless a stiff wind is blowing from the desert. Weekends can be busy when a special event is scheduled, so call for reservations whenever possible.

Ghost Town Road. (Take the Ghost Town Road exit from I-15, and drive 3½ miles north to the campground, on left.) ☎ **760-254-2122.** http://cms.sbcounty.gov/parks/Parks/CalicoGhostTown.

aspx. Total 104 sites with 30- and 50-amp electric, 64 with water, 46 full hookups, 23 pull-throughs. Rates: $30–$40 per site. DISC, MC, V.

KID FRIENDLY

Circle Pines KOA

$$$$–$$$$$ Williams, Arizona

Circle Pines manages to be away from the I-40 traffic noise and downtown Williams, but it offers convenient connections to everything from van tours to the Grand Canyon to free shuttle service to the railway station in Williams if you want to take the steam train. Extras include an outdoor cafe serving breakfast and dinner, nightly movies in season, stables offering trail rides, an indoor pool and two spas, country-Western music in summer, and on-site rental cars.

1000 Circle Pines Rd. (From I-40, take Exit 167, Circle Pines Road, and drive ¾ mile to the campground, on left.) ☎ 800-562-9379 or 928-635-2626. https://koa.com. Total 120 sites with water and 30- and 50-amp electric, 81 full hookups, all pull-throughs. Bike rentals, data port, laundry, miniature golf, indoor heated pool, sauna, spas, Wi-Fi. Rates: $50.14–$105.84 per site. AE, DISC, MC, V.

Needles KOA

$$$–$$$$ Needles, California

The only celebrity resident of Needles that the world knows about is Spike, Snoopy's brother in the comic strip *Peanuts,* and in all fairness, this campground looks sort of like Spike's cactus-filled terrain. The location is especially nice in winter, when the weather is mild and birdwatching is good. A seasonal cafe operates November through April. Pull-throughs are large and shady.

5400 National Old Trails Hwy. (From I-40, take the West Broadway exit, and turn left on National Old Trails Highway; the campground is 1 mile down the road, on right.) ☎ 800-562-3407 or 760-326-4207. https://koa.com. Total 85 sites with water and 30-amp electric, 67 full hookups, 85 pull-throughs. Data port, laundry, pool, snack bar. Rates: $33.95–$36.95 per site. AE, DISC, MC, V.

Palo Duro Canyon State Park
$$$ Canyon, Texas

If you zip rapidly across the Texas Panhandle on I-40, you'll miss one of the most beautiful areas in the state: the spectacular Palo Duro Canyon, carved out of the red rocks by the Red River. The canyon is 120 miles long, 1,000 feet deep, and as much as 20 miles wide. You reach this campground in the canyon via a downhill road that crosses some dry washes. Sites are comfortably wide at 40 feet, and each has its own individual look. Some sites offer access for campers with disabilities.

11450 Park Road 5. (Take I-27 16 miles south of Amarillo to SR 217, and drive east 10 miles to the park.) ☎ *806-488-2227.* https://palodurocanyon.com. *Total 79 sites with water and 30- and 50-amp electric, no full hookups, 7 pull-throughs. Rates: $24–$26 per site. DISC, MC, V. 14-day maximum stay.*

Red Rock State Park
$$ Gallup, New Mexico

This park east of Gallup is where the Inter-Tribal Ceremonial (ITC), a gathering of Native American tribes, takes place every August; for details, visit https://gallupceremonial.com/home. In summer, traditional tribal dances take place in the amphitheater on the premises, and a museum nearby displays kachina dolls, rugs, pottery, silver, and turquoise jewelry. The campground has 103 extra-wide (50- to 55-foot) pull-throughs. The back-ins are narrower (30 to 40 feet) but still generous.

Off SR 566. (From Exit 26 on I-40 at SR 118, go east 3½ miles on 118 to SR 566, and travel north ½ mile to the campground, on left.) ☎ *505-722-3839. Total 245 sites with water and 30- and 50-amp electric, no full hookups, 150 pull-throughs. Rates: $22 per site. MC, V.*

El Reno West KOA

$$$–$$$$ El Reno, Oklahoma

This campground has a trading post with bargain-price moccasins and a live buffalo compound on the premises. The location is close to four restaurants that make the famous onion-fried burgers (see "Good Eats" later in this chapter). Other plusses are freshwater fishing, a pool, and a snack bar. On the downside, sites are narrow, and some hookups are side by side.

301 S. Walbaun Rd., 15 miles west of El Reno. (From I-40, take Exit 108, drive north on spur 281 some 300 feet to the Cherokee Trading Post, and turn right to the campground.) ☎ **800-562-5736** *or 405-884-2595.* https://koa.com. *Total 77 sites with water and 30- and 50-amp electric, 31 full hookups, 31 pull-throughs. Data port, laundry, pool. Rates: $36–$42 per site. DISC, MC, V.*

Good Eats

If it didn't actually invent the hamburger, Route 66 can take credit for making it popular. You find some historical claims on the mother road. On early drives across Route 66 beginning in the 1950s, big juicy hamburgers could be found everywhere, including chain restaurants. Following are a few of the best spots along old Route 66 that make old-fashioned burgers.

» **Classen Grill,** 5124 N. Classen Blvd., Oklahoma City, Oklahoma (☎ **405-842-0428**): A dozen toppings can crown the charcoal-grilled burgers, and the breakfasts are notable too. Open daily from 7 a.m. to 2 p.m.

» **Delgadillos Snow Cap Drive-In,** Route 66, Seligman, Arizona ☎ **928-422-3291:** Expect burgers served up with a sense of humor. Take advantage of a chance to chat with one of the founding fathers of the revitalized Route 66. Hours are Monday to Saturday from 10 a.m. to 6 p.m. and Sunday from 10 a.m. to 5 p.m.

» **El Reno's onion-fried burgers:** In El Reno, Oklahoma, three eateries grill burgers with thinly sliced onions, pressing them together as they cook so that the onion caramelizes, and then turning the burger and sizzling it some more. The whole business is popped on a bun and garnished with trimmings such as tomatoes, lettuce, mustard, mayonnaise, and sliced dill pickles. I confess, being partial to Robert's, the diner is tiny and colorful, and it was the first place that I tried the onion-grilled burger. Here's the skinny on the four restaurants:

- **Emma Jean's Holland Burger Cafe,** 17143 D St., Victorville, California (☎ **760-243-9938;** https://www.hollandburger.com): This diner, on old Route 66 in Victorville, serves up grilled burgers. Open Monday through Friday from 5 a.m. to 2:45 p.m. and Saturday from 6 a.m. to 12:30 p.m. Closed Sunday.

- **Johnnie's Grill,** 301 S. Rock Island Ave. (☎ **405-262-4721**): Open Monday through Saturday from 6 a.m. to 9 p.m. and Sunday from 11 a.m. to 8 p.m.

- **Robert's Grill,** 300 S. Bickford Ave. (☎ **405-262-1262**): Open Monday through Saturday from 6 a.m. to 9 p.m. and Sunday from 11 a.m. to 7 p.m.

- **Sid's Diner,** 300 S. Choctaw Ave. (☎ **405-262-7757**): Open Monday through Saturday from 7 a.m. to 8:30 p.m. Closed Sundays.

Looking for something other than a hamburger? You're in luck. Several options await:

» **Big Texan Steak Ranch,** 7701 I-40 East, Exit 75, Amarillo, Texas (☎ **806-372-6000;** https://www.bigtexan.com): The billboards promise a free 72-ounce steak, but you have to eat it *all,* and side dishes — shrimp cocktail, baked potato, roll, and green salad — in less than an hour. Otherwise, you pay $72. Many are called, but few can finish. The restaurant is open daily from 7 a.m. to 10:30 p.m.

» **Jigg's Smoke House,** at the Parkersburg Road exit on I-40 between Clinton and Elk City, Oklahoma (☎ **580-323-5641;** https://jiggssmokehouse.com): This rustic shack by the side of the road sells its own barbecued beef brisket chopped into sandwiches, along with beef jerky, sausages, ham, and bacon. It's open Tuesday through Friday from 11 a.m. to 7 p.m. and Saturday from 11 a.m. to 5 p.m. Closed Sunday.

» **Joseph's,** 865 Will Rogers Dr., Santa Rosa, New Mexico (☎ **575-472-3361**): One of the old-timey Route 66 stopovers, Joseph's boasts an adjoining gift shop of tacky souvenirs and a great breakfast menu that includes breakfast burritos and a spicy *carne adovado* (pork and red chilies) with eggs, refried beans, and flour tortillas. It's open Monday through Saturday from 11 a.m. to 10 p.m. and Sunday from 11 a.m. to 9 p.m.

Shopping along the Way

Although you'll come across numerous shops along Route 66, this one is notable:

» **Barstow Amtrak Station,** California Welcome Center, East Main Street off I-15, east of Barstow, California (☎ **760-256-8282**): Although the architecture of many McDonald's seems to be very cookie cutter, this one inside the station was created from vintage railroad cars and serves as the centerpiece of a tour bus stop and souvenir stand. Well, it's also more like the mother of all souvenir stands with items piled on the floors, hanging from the ceiling, and stacked on precarious shelves. Wonderfully tacky, the station offers howling, life-size plaster-of-Paris coyotes; plastic cacti 4 feet tall; Marilyn Monroe cookie jars; and personalized mugs for every Tom, Dick, and Lupe who happens by. RV parking is behind the station, where buses and trucks park. Open daily from 7 a.m. to 8 p.m.

Fast Facts

Area Code
The following area codes are in effect along Route 66: **928** in Arizona; **213, 310, 323, 626, 760,** and **909** in California; **405, 580,** and **918** in Oklahoma; **505** and **575** in New Mexico; and **806** in Texas.

Driving Laws
Seat belts must be worn in Arizona, Oklahoma, Texas, California, and New Mexico. The speed limit on interstate highways in Arizona, New Mexico, and Oklahoma is 75 mph and 80 mph on some highways. In Texas, the speed limit is 70 mph, and 85 mph on some designated highways. The California speed limit is 70 mph. In all states, speed limits are lower in urban areas.

Emergency
Dial ☎ **911** in all states. Cellphone users can call ☎ ***55** in Oklahoma and ☎ **800-525-5555** in Texas.

Hospitals
Major hospitals along the route are in Oklahoma City, Tulsa, Albuquerque, Gallup, Flagstaff, Barstow, San Bernardino, and Los Angeles.

Information
Sources include Arizona Office of Tourism (☎ **888-520-3434**; https://www.visitarizona.com/), California Department of Tourism (☎ **800-GO-CALIF** [462-2543]; https://www.visitcalifornia.com), New Mexico Department of Tourism (☎ **505-827-7400**; https://www.newmexico.org), Oklahoma Tourism and Recreation Department (☎ **800-652-6552**; https://www.travelok.com/), and Texas Department of Tourism (☎ **800-888-8839**; https://www.traveltexas.com).

Road Conditions
Call ☎ **888-411-ROAD** (7623) in Arizona, ☎ **916-445-1534** in California, ☎ **800-432-4269** in New Mexico, ☎ **405-425-2385** in Oklahoma, and ☎ **800-452-9292** in Texas.

Taxes
Arizona sales tax is 5.6 percent (local taxes can raise it to 10.1 percent); gas tax is 19 cents per gallon. California sales tax is 6 percent (local taxes can raise it an additional 3.5 percent); gas tax is 55.5 cents per gallon. New Mexico sales tax is 5.125 percent (city taxes can raise it to 8.938 percent and county rates can add another 2.188 percent); gas tax is 19 cents per gallon. Oklahoma sales tax is 4.5 percent (local taxes can add 6.5 percent); gas tax is 17 cents per gallon. Texas sales tax is 6.25 percent (local taxes can raise it to 8.25 percent); gas tax is 20 cents per gallon.

Time Zone
Oklahoma and Texas are on Central time. New Mexico and Arizona are on Mountain time, but Arizona doesn't observe Daylight Saving Time. California is on Pacific time.

Chapter **23**

ALCAN Trip: Seattle to Fairbanks

Historians aren't settled on the question of whether the first human occupants of North America came to North America via a costal route or an interior track. What's certain from DNA studies is that a small group succeeded in making the trek from Siberia between 13,000 and 15,000 years ago on foot.

This trip is certain to cross some of the same paths those early migrants saw as they made their way south and east to populate the Americas. It starts in Seattle (for Canadian travelers, from Hope) and goes along the Alaska–Canada Highway to Anchorage, at the top of the Cook Inlet of the Pacific Ocean. What you see on this trip is natural beauty amplified beyond measure by sheer vastness.

Mile after mile of green, blue water and abounding wildlife make this trip totally unique. As you go along some places you will both marvel and be in awe over the fact that roads were able to be built over this very challenging terrain. Getting to Alaska and crossing the wilds of Canada is thought of by some as the last place to escape cities, pollution, traffic, and the noise and lights of modern-day civilization. After making your visit you may feel exactly the same.

What's so amazing about western Canada and Alaska beyond the Northern Lights is the unspoiled natural landscape. Driving an RV, knowing that everything you need for comfort is on board and that the road ahead waits with an open invitation. On this trip enjoy wildlife, pristine campsites, fishing, and a never-ending array of scenes worthy of camera, watercolors, or oil on canvas. These scenes will replay in your mind long after you take this trip. You'll join an exclusive group of RV travelers who have made the trip to or from Alaska.

Choosing Your Route

From most places in the United States, Seattle is your starting point. Seattle has a lot to offer by way of attractions and points of interest, so you may want to take some of them in before heading north or save them for the return visit. Canadian travelers can begin this trip at a town called Hope, which is on the route.

A word or two about the trip: There are only four major routes to and from Alaska. Because of the terrain, route options and available roads are limited. You do have more choices for the return trip, however. One option to consider if you have plenty of time is to hug the Pacific Coast, using bridges and ferry boats for an adventurous but slower return. (This option is less inviting for larger class A motor homes.) Or reverse the trip route and maybe change your overnight campsites, keeping in mind that availability is limited.

The distance is nearly 2,500 miles in each direction, so your RV is likely to register well over 5,000 miles, with some side trips, before returning to Seattle. You'll be looking for an oil change when you return if you're driving a gas rig.

TIP

On a trip of this distance, I pull into what the U.S. Army calls "motor stables" every day, checking the oil levels, washer fluid, transmission fluid, and antifreeze daily, and checking tire pressure at least every two days. It's wise to carry spare fluids (motor oil, antifreeze, transmission fluid, and windshield-washer fluid) and whatever other maintenance items you have room and weight allowance for. Many RV folks consider it necessary to bring along a spare tire or two and many do due to the road conditions and distances without services.

TIP

This trip is a combination of many smaller trips. A weekend will never work for it.

» **Day 1:** From Seattle to Cache Creek, B.C., the drive is close to 283 miles on TC-1E. Canadian travelers make the 121-mile drive from Hope to Cache Creek.

» **Day 2:** From Cache Creek, the drive is 277 miles via Highway BC 97 to Prince George.

» **Day 3:** From Prince George, the drive is 253 miles again on Highway BC 97 to Dawson Creek.

» **Day 4:** From Dawson Creek, you make an easy 288-mile drive on BC 97 to Fort Nelson.

» **Day 5:** From Fort Nelson, the drive on Highway BC 97 is 321 miles. It takes a full day (seven to eight hours) of driving to get to Watson Lake after passing into the Yukon Territory.

» **Day 6:** The drive to Watson Lake to Haines Junction via the Alaska Highway is 369 miles.

» **Day 7:** From Haines Junction, on the Alaska Highway, cross the international border to the Alaskan town of town of Tok (290 miles total).

» **Day 8:** On the final leg of the journey, drive 321 miles on AK 1 to Anchorage.

TIP

If you decide to stay in the Anchorage area for a while, you can make interesting short trips if you have a tow car (consider a rental if you do not tow a car), such as watching bears in Katmai National Park or casting your eyes on a glacier at Portage Valley. The Alaska Railroad can take you on a one–day trip to Seward or all the way to the Spencer Glacier. At Kenai Fjords National Park, a cruise could yield sightings of whales, along with some of the most iconic landscapes in the state.

Planning Ahead

This trip takes a bit more than the average amount of planning and preparation. At approximately 2,500 miles (3,600 km) each way, it's longer than the average RV trip. Because you'll experience long distances, rough roads, challenging terrain, and elevation changes, it's helpful to have more than an average amount of tenacity.

The route has enough campgrounds, but reservations are highly advisable. Prices are high-moderate to moderate, and you should be prepared for unexpected repairs along the way. Be certain your tires are in enough condition for the trip; road service can be a long way off.

By far the best time to go is early summer. Late spring is all right if you can tolerate the possibility of snow and don't mind cooler temperatures. If you have an extended stay in mind, consider heading back by mid- to late September at latest; the weather can go south in a minute, and it takes close to 40 hours of driving over a week or more to get back to your starting point with during good weather conditions.

At 2,500-plus miles each way, allow about three to four weeks or more. With about 40 hours of driving it's a work week to get there with few stops along the way to bank some extra enjoyment from the miles driven. So, plan a full week to get there, another to get back; it is great to be able to spend more than a week exploring the sights, sounds, and lure of Anchorage area attractions.

The best time to take this drive is in late spring, summer, or early fall. In winter, snow closes many of the highways and sometimes with little warning, so late fall (October) is not a good time to begin unless your RV has winter tires and optional cold climate insulation packages.

TIP

Pack clothing for all kinds of weather. Rain gear is essential, as are hiking boots, jeans, jackets, and sweatshirts and/or sweaters, as well as winter coats, boots, gloves, and hats to wear in case of a cold snap. The days can get warm in summer. Average high/low Fahrenheit temperatures for Anchorage are May 60/38°, June 65/48°, July 70/52°, August 65/50°, and September 56/42°. By October, night temperatures can fall below freezing.

ALASKA: AMERICAN FRONTIER

The dual draw of gold at Willow Creek in 1896 and black gold (oil) at Nome in 1902 defined this state from a commercial perspective. Fishing and lumber played major roles as well. Today's visitors and homesteaders, however, come mostly for the pristine beauty of Alaska. Television reality shows such as *Ice Road Truckers* and *Mountain Men* add to the allure and attraction. The residents won't mind your visit if you're respectful of what enticed you to visit in the first place.

Must-See Attractions

Alaska Native Heritage Center
Anchorage, Alaska

This center displays the history and culture of 11 indigenous groups with a gathering place, a Hall of Cultures, and a movie theater. Professionally guided tours start at 10:15 a.m., 12:15 p.m., 2 p.m., and 3:30 p.m.

8800 Heritage Center Dr. ☎ **907-330-8000.** *https://www. alaskanative.net. Admission: Adults $24.95, seniors/military $21.15, children 7–16 $16.95, free ages 6 and under. Open daily mid-May to September 9 a.m. to 5 p.m., September to May 10 a.m. to 5. p.m.*

Alaska Wildlife Conservation Center
Portage, Alaska

Visitors can see animals here in 200 acres of natural habitat. Expect to see bears, bison, moose, wolves, birds of prey, and lynx. The center offers classes, programs, and tours. Allow a half-day to a full day for the entire complex.

WARNING

Never approach a wild animal on foot. Don't leave your vehicle when you see one. The bears are always hungry and/or just plain ornery. The ornery ones that are having a bad day don't fear humans.

Mile 79 Seward Highway. ☎ **907-783-0058.** `https://www.` `alaskawildlife.org`. *RV street parking is available. Admission: $16 adults, $11 ages 6 to 17, free 5 and under. Hours and days vary nearly every month so check the website before you plan your visit, or call. Tours are typically conducted between 10 a.m. to 4 p.m. on the days they are open. Closed holidays.*

Anchorage Museum
Anchorage, Alaska

This beautiful modern museum, designed by David Chipperfield and Kenneth Maynard, promotes all things Alaska. Kegginaqut YUP'IK Masks are must-see exhibits.

625 C St. ☎ **907-929-9200.** `https://www.anchoragemuseum.org`. Admission: $18 adults; $12 seniors, military, and students; $9 ages 3–12, free 2 and under. Open: May 1–Sept 30 daily 9 a.m.–6 p.m.; October 1 to May 30. Tuesday through Saturday 10 a.m.–6 p.m., Sunday noon–6 p.m.

Crow Creek Gold Mine
Girdwood, Alaska

This mine, less than an hour's drive from Anchorage, is the place to learn about the gold-rush days and do a little panning yourself. Some of the original buildings have been restored and display historic artifacts.

601 Crow Creek Rd. ☎ **907- 229-3105.** `http://www.crowcreekmine.com/`. *Admission: $24 adults; $20 seniors, military, Alaska residents; $15 ages 12 and under. Open: Daily June–Aug 9 a.m.–6 p.m.*

Cyrano's Theatre Company
Anchorage, Alaska

Check the company's website or phone in to see whether one of the plays might interest you. If not, consider going anyway for a little bit of contrast from outdoor attractions. This theater company has performed in Anchorage for 27 years.

3800 Debarr Rd. ☎ 907-274-2599. www.cyranos.org. Admission: $25 adults; $23 military, seniors, and students. Ticket are sold one hour before the show.

More Cool Things to See and Do

There's a lot to see in western Canada and Alaska. To find out more about the places you'll be traveling to and through, check the daily and weekly newspapers that serve the areas you visit. Don't miss out on taking a picture or a few of the Sign Post Forest at Watson Lake. Feel free to bring a sign from your own hometown to add to the collection.

Sightseeing abounds near Anchorage and along the way to get there with historic villages and towns, occasional quaint roadside stops such as Sasquatch Crossing at mile 147, Alaska Hwy., Pink Mountain, and the splendor of natural land formations that continue to delight the eye with each changing mile. Here are a few highlights to check out.

» **Alaska Center for the Performing Arts,** 621 W. 6th Street, Anchorage AK 99501 (☎ **907-263-ARTS,** or 907-263-2787; https://www.alaskapac.org): Great place to take in a play, show, or musical performance during your Anchorage visit.

» **Anchorage Market and Festival,** 225 E. Street Anchorage, AK 99501 (☎ **907-272-5634;** https://anchoragemarkets.com): This is a large open-air market, the largest in Alaska. Open mid-May 9 to mid-September. Hours: Saturdays 10 a.m. to 6 p.m. and Sundays 10 a.m. to 5 p.m. No admission fees. Plan about two hours. The festival days and hours are posted on the website.

KID FRIENDLY

» **Alaska Zoo,** 4731 O'Malley Road, Anchorage, AK 99507 (☎ **907-346-2133;** https://www.alaskazoo.org): This 25-acre zoo has been a popular attraction for tourists and locals since 1969, with birds you may never have seen before and dozens of other species, including Arctic animals. Stop and see the polar bears, which consider humans to be prey. Admission is $15 for adults, $10 for seniors and military, $7 for kids 3 to 17, and free for kids 2 and under.

Note: Safety is important, so an adult-to-youth ratio of 1 adult to 5 children is imposed for the safety of visitors and zoo animals.

» **Tony Knowles Coastal Trail** (https://anchoragecoastal trail.com): Multiple points access the trail; there is a trailhead at the northeast end of West 2nd Ave in Anchorage close to the railroad depot. This trail walk is free, is open day and night year around, and takes about two to four hours.

Our Favorite Campgrounds

Alaska and Canada are RV-friendly, with a good number of public and private campgrounds. Some rural areas have limited options largely due to a shortage of local users — camping families less than 50 miles from the campground who help subsidize the park when travelers aren't passing through in big numbers. When you're on a pass-through schedule, full-hookup sites aren't always necessary. State parks, national, and provincial campgrounds usually don't offer full hookups, but the scenery typically makes up for the day or two without them.

All campgrounds listed in this chapter have some sites with electric hookups, many limited to 30 amp. Some have flush toilets, shower houses, and sanitary dump stations. Prices are in US currency for the United States and Canadian currency for the Canadian provinces.

Brookside Campsite

$$$$–$$$$$ Cache Creek, British Columbia

The campground has well-maintained facilities and provides a relaxing stay. At this park, you meet RV folks from all parts of the world. This location is considered to be in the Canadian desert; midday temperatures can reach 104° F. in summer.

1621 Trans-Canada Hwy. (Minutes from the junction of Hwy #1 and Hwy #97 in the middle of Cache Creek). From Cache Creek, travel east on Hwy 1 and Hwy # 97 1.3 km to campsite.) ☎ **250-457-6633.** *https://brooksidecampsite.com. Total 90 sites with 15- and 30-amp electric, 58 pull-throughs. Wi-Fi, pool. Rates: $33–$41. MC, V. Open: May–Sept 1.*

Downtown RV Park

$$$–$$$$ Watson Lake, YT

This Good Sam park (discounts available for Good Sam members) is conveniently located in town. The sites have plenty of space for Class A motor homes. A nearby lake provides hiking opportunities and relaxing views. The park is quiet, which makes it a good place to sleep on your way to the next stop.

105 8th St. N. ☎ **867-536-2646.** *https://www.goodsam.com/ campgrounds-rv-parks/details/default.aspx?cgid= 890000760. Total 78 sites with water and 30- and 50-amp electric, some pull-throughs. Wi-Fi. Rates: $40–$58. AE, MC, V. Open: Apr 15–Oct 15.*

Mount Logan Lodge (not a campground)

$$$$–$$$$$$ Haines Junction, YT

Sometimes it is nice or necessary to take a break and splurge on accommodations. This is my recommendation for a stay in Hanes Junction, promoted as "your home in the mountains." You can stay in a classic yurt or a cabin or book the luxury suite in this characteristically classic lodge. Park the motor home for the night and enjoy all the classic comforts and a long hot shower. Head out the next day fully recharged from the experience for the rest of the trip.

KM 1587.5 Alaska Highway, Haines Junction, Yukon, Phone: ☎ *1 867-634-2817. https://mountloganlodge.com/lodge- accommodations. Parking for up to three motor homes at a time and just enough room to turn around. Call for and reservations; rates for accommodations range from $175 to $320 per night, all* *accommodations include a breakfast, and Eggs benedict is on the menu. AE, MC, V. Open: All year.*

Northern Experience RV Park

$$$–$$$$ Prince George, British Columbia

This campground is minutes from Prince George and close to shopping, restaurants, coffee shops, and grocery stores.

9180 Cariboo Hwy. ☎ **250-963-7577.** http://www.northernexpe riencerv.com/. *This location has Wi-Fi and full hookups available; there is a coin laundry on the premises. Pull -through sites require weekly rental. No extra fee for pets and a dog walk is available to guests only. Total 52 sites, some for tents. Rates: $33–$42. No credit cards. Open: May–Sept.*

Northern Lights RV Park

$$$$–$$$$$ Dawson Creek, British Columbia

Northern Lights RV Park has Wi-Fi and TV cable. It is locally owned and operated. There are new bathrooms and laundry as well as a meeting facility for larger groups and caravans.

9636 Friesen Subdivision. ☎ **1 250-782-9433.** https://nlrv.com/. *This park offers private washrooms, sites with water, sewer, electric, and TV, with 30- and 50-amp sites available. Both pull-through and back-in sites with room for slideouts. There is laundry and limited Wi-Fi. Location has 92 sites that are full hookups with P/W/S (30 and 50 AMP). Rates: $45–$50. DISC, MC, V. This campground is open year around.*

Ship Creek RV Park

$$–$$$ Anchorage, Alaska

This park, close to downtown, offers many conveniences and amenities, as well as easy access to many attractions. You can make tour reservations at the park and take advantage of clean restrooms and showers. Bring your fishing pole.

150 N. Ingra St. ☎ **907-277-0877.** https://www.alaskatravelad ventures.com/rv-park/anchorage-ship-creek-rv-park. *Total of over 100 sites with water and 30- and 50-amp electric; full hook-ups with sewer, spacious pull-throughs. Handicap accessible. Wi-Fi, laundry, showers, restrooms. Open to organized RV caravans so it can fill up fast. Rates: $39–$59. AE, D, MC, V. Open: May 1–Aug 1.*

Tok RV Village Campground and Cabins
$$–$$$ Tok, Alaska

A great place to rest up and enjoy the scenery before continuing your journey. Easy off the Alaxkan Highway, a place with fantastic views. There are a gas station, places to eat, and a grocery store.

1313.4 Alaska Hwy. ☎ **907-883-5877.** https://tokrv.net. *Over 100 sites with water and 30- and-50 amp electric; some full hook-ups with sewer; spacious pull-throughs. Wi-Fi, laundry, metered showers. This park offers Good Sam and AAA discounts. Open mid-April to mid-September. Rates: $48–$59 per night. MC, V.*

Triple G Hideaway
$$–$$$ Fort Nelson, British Columbia

Explore Fort Nelson or just hook up for a needed stop. The park has a gift shop and restaurant.

5651 50th Ave. (Old Alaska Hwy). ☎ **250-774-2340.** www. tripleghideaway.com. *Total 130 sites with water and 30-amp electric; full hookups; spacious pull-throughs. Wi-Fi at some sites, laundry, shower facilities, coin-operated RV wash. All sites priced the same at $47.25. Open year around, there is always a site or two available even in winter. MC, V.*

CAMPING IN THE WILDERNESS

Many campgrounds along this route are close to nature, which makes the trip attractive and memorable. But you should take a few extra precautions because of it.

- The wildlife, including bears, are hungry. Don't feed them.
- Avoid leaving food or grease-covered cooking items on the picnic table.
- Don't leave garbage bags outside. Deposit your trash in approved, ideally bear-proof trash containers at the campgrounds or follow the campground's rules for dealing with trash.
- To avoid surprises, look outside before you step outside.

Good Eats

Fortunately, on a long run like this one, you are equipped with your own kitchen and stocked refrigerator. When you stop for the night, take advantage of local offerings.

When it is time for dinner, the experience can include fresh salmon, pacific cod, halibut, crab, wild game, smoked meats, local jams and jellies, the chocolate delight found in Nanaimo bars, bannock, meat pies, and Canadian maple syrup on pancakes or waffles.

TIP

At the destination, I try to sample places recommended by others or look for an eatery with lots of cars with local license plates parked there at lunch time. Those kinds of places rarely disappoint.

» **49th State Brewing Company,** 717 W. 3rd Ave., Anchorage (☎ **907-277-7727**): There are three reasons to go to this establishment: the beer, the seafood, and the view. Consider taking a cab. The restaurant is open daily from 11 a.m. to 11 p.m.

» **Ginger,** 1425 W. 5th Ave., Anchorage (☎ **907-929-3680**): This popular restaurant says it's "not afraid to use spices." This is a great place to try out beers from regional micro-breweries and the latest in Pacific rim entrees and specialties. RV parking is available on the street. The restaurant is open for brunch Saturday and Sunday from 11 a.m. to 2:30 p.m., for lunch Monday to Friday from 11:30 a.m. to 3 p.m., and for dinner daily from 5 to 10 p.m.

» **Snow City Cafe,** 1034 W. 4th Ave., Anchorage (☎ **907-272-2489**): This cafe is open only for breakfast and lunch, and you need reservations. Enjoy the breakfast pancake of the month, quiche, a custom omelet, or one of the lunch specials. The cafe is open daily from 6:30 a.m. to 3 p.m.

Fast Facts

Area Code
The area codes are **907** in the Anchorage area, **604** in British Columbia, and **405** in Yukon Territory.

Driving Laws
All RV occupants must wear seat belts. The speed limit on interstates is 65 mph in Alaska, 120 kph in British Columbia, and 100 kph in Yukon Territory. Speed limits are lower in urban areas and at night.

Emergency
Call ☎ **911** in Alaska and Canada.

Hospitals
Along the route, major hospitals are in Prince George, Watson Lake, and Anchorage.

Information
Sources include Alaska (☎ No central phone number for Alaska); visit website for regional contacts: https://www.travelalaska.com.

British Columbia (☎ **604-682-2222**; https://thecanadaguide.com/places/canadian-tourism/british-columbia-tourism-information)

For Yukon tourist information call ☎ **800-661-0494,** or visit: https://www.travelyukon.com/.

Road and Weather Conditions
In Alaska, call ☎ **511**. In British Columbia, visit https://www.drivebc.ca. In the Yukon Territory, https://www.511yukon.ca/en/index.html.

Taxes
Alaska fuel tax is 12.75 cents per gallon. The sales tax rate in Alaska is 0%; however, cities and/or municipalities can collect sales taxes up to 7 percent.

Canadian fuel tax is 27.6 cents per liter. A federal sales tax (value added tax) is collected nationwide in Canada at 5 percent; provincial sales taxes range from 6 to 10 percent.

Time Zone
Alaska is one hour behind Pacific time. Most of British Columbia and the Yukon Territory are on Pacific time.

6 The Part of Tens

One unique attraction from each US state and Canadian province

The best RV travel gadgets to pack along

Chapter **24**

More than Ten Cool Places to Visit in the United States and Canada

I f you can't check out the world's largest ball of string or take a look at the corn palace while on an RV trip, when can you? Countless gems like that ball of string are located all over this continent. This chapter shares some of those places (one per each state or province you might visit by RV). Read about places to play, see, find adventure, just rest, learn something new, stay for a longer while, dine, or shop.

REMEMBER

Use the information about gadgets (such as GPS) provided in Chapter 25 to help plan your route to get to these places. Find that US/Canada road atlas to verify your route and set milestones and identify your required turns and merges ahead of time.

Alabama

High is very relative term. At the highest point in Alabama, set above what is now the Talladega National Forest, **Cheaha Mountain** is 2,407 feet above sea level from which you can view much of the surrounding countryside. At the Cheaha Mountain overlook, you'll find a tower that was built in 1948 by the Civilian Conservation Corps.

To get to Cheaha Mountain from Intestate 20, take Exit 191 south using US 431. Turn south to use the Talladega Scenic Byway, then use Route 281 South. Follow that along to Cheaha State Park. Drive the marked road up to Bunker Tower. I recommend visiting early in the morning or late in the evening. An enjoyable side trip unless the forecast calls for snow, rain, or lightning.

Alaska

As the economics changed in Alaska, native villages and totem were abandoned. In 1938, the US Forest Services began saving and restoring the totems at **Totem Bight State Historical Park.** It is a ferry ride to get there. Learn more at the ranger stations and on the website.

Ketchikan Ranger Station, 9883 N Tongass Highway, Ketchikan, AK 99901 ☎ 907-247-8574. http://dnr.alaska.gov/parks/units/totembgh.htm.

Arizona

Reputed to be the best cowboy bar in the west, **Big Nose Kate's Saloon** is an ideal place to dine and have a cool sarsaparilla. Park your RV somewhere safe on the back streets and walk through the town. If you pay to see the gunfight reenactment, you can get a free period newspaper down one of the side streets from the time of the famous gunfight. Receive a reprint of the 1881 Epitaph with the original Gunfight reports as part of your O.K. Corral admission ticket. Check out the gunfight reenactment at the OK Corral and the little boot hill cemetery on the edge of town while you are there if you have time.

Big Nose Kate's Saloon, 417 E. Allen Street, Tombstone, Arizona ☎ 520-457-3107. https://bignosekatestombstone.com/

Arkansas

Southern Tenant Farmers Museum is located on the Sunken Lands Cultural Roadway and is the trailhead for the Tour duh Sunken Lands annual cultural cycling event. Photographs, oral histories, and artifacts tell the history of sharecropping, tenant farming, and labor movements, featuring prominently the history of the Southern Tenant Farmers Union.

Southern Tenant Farmers Museum, 117 S. Main Street, Tyronza, AR 72386 ☎ 870-487-2909. Visit https://stfm.astate.edu/ or find out more at https://www.facebook.com/southerntenantfarmersmuseum.

California

Elmer liked glass and old things and put them together in very artistic ways. **Elmer's Bottle Tree Ranch** is a unique roadside stop that rivals many others, including the largest ball of twine and TP village. Please don't drive by this one without a stop and look-see.

Elmer's Bottle Tree Ranch, 24266 National Trails Hwy., Oro Grande, CA 92368. https://www.facebook.com/ElmersBottleTreeRanch.

Colorado

To complete a visit or simply find a reason to go to Colorado in the first place, take in a trail ride at **High Country Trails,** billed as the true adventure of the West. All ages from 7 years old and up and riding skill levels are accommodated. Select to go to the top of the mountain trail and overlook Granby, Hot Sulphur Springs, and Grand Lake off in the distance. Trail rides can take six hours and more.

Located at **Shadow Mountain Guest Ranch.** From Interstate 70 take Exit 232, take US 40 driving through Winter Park, Fraser, and Granby. Two miles west of Windy Gap take Colorado Highway 125 north for about 5.5 miles. Look for them on the right side of the highway.

High Country Trails next to 5043 CO-125, Granby, CO 80446 ☎ 970-887-8991 or 801-372-9868. http://www.highcountry-trails.com/.

Connecticut

Visit the **Glass House,** designed by Philip Johnson. Yes, that's correct — a house made mostly of glass. Those residents who should not throw stones! The house was built in 1948–49 on Ponus Ridge Road in New Canaan. The tour takes a bit over an hour. Tickets are required for admission and access to the home site is only via the paid tour. Advance reservations are required as tours often sell out.

Visitor Center + Design Store, 199 Elm Street, New Canaan, CT 06840. For tickets by phone, please call ☎ 866-811-4111. For more information call ☎ 203-594-9884; http://theglasshouse.org.

Delaware

It was a long walk, a bit of controversy, and a few lawsuits and good number of years to get from cast records to today's digital sound technology. Learn the beginnings of sound recording and history of the influential **Johnson Victrola Museum.** The museum features the achievements of Delaware's native son, Eldridge Reeves Johnson, founder of the Victor Talking Machine Company and an early pioneer of the sound-recording industry.

Johnson Victrola Museum, 375 S. New St. Dover, DE 19904. ☎ 302-739-3262. https://www.visitdelawarevillages.com/directory/johnson-victrola-museum.

Florida

The **Dora Canal Eco-tour** is a two-hour narrated tour by boat that will make you feel like you are starring in an *Indiana Jones* movie. The tour takes you into a Cypress Swamp that is chock-full of wildlife and ecological wonders. Among the 2,000-year-old trees, you see native herons, egrets, turtles, and alligators in their natural habitat.

After the tour, find some good eats at O'Keefe's Irish Pub & Restaurant, 115 S. Rockingham Ave., Tavares, FL 32778.

Premier Boat Tours, 100 N. Alexander Street, Mount Dora, FL 32757. Please call ahead for reservations; the boats can fill up fast on any given day. ☎ 352-434-8040. http://www.doracanaltour.com/twohour.php.

Georgia

Something everyone should see at least once even if you don't like trains. At the **Folkston funnel,** the train track is the route into Florida for eastern United States and east coast trains. From the platform, you can observe the trains pass and hear the engineers talk to each other and their company control centers as they negotiate their turn to pass through the "funnel." Great photo opportunity to get photos of the engines and graffiti street art that covers many of the box cars, and talk to people who are more into trains than one could even imagine. Here's a hint: The numbered engines actually have names!

Folkston funnel, 16 Oakwood Street, Folkston, GA 31537. For more information visit the county website at https://charltoncountyga.us/236/Folkston-Funnel.

Hawaii

At the center of Oahu, fairytale-like **Wahiawa Botanical Garden** is a picturesque, peaceful place. Home to a variety of plants and relaxing walking paths. Located on a high plateau in central Oahu between the Waianae and Ko'olau mountain ranges, the garden features native Hawaiian plants, including aroid plants, tree ferns, and epiphytic plants.

Wahiawa Botanical Garden, 1396 California Ave., Wahiawa, HI 96786. Get more information about the garden and its plants by calling ☎ **808-621-7321** or visit http://www.friendsofhonolulubotanicalgardens.com/Wahiawa.htm.

Idaho

The **Idaho Potato Museum** celebrates potatoes like no place else on earth. Open year-round from 9:30 a.m. to 5 p.m., and to 7 p.m. in June, July, and August. Plenty of room in the south parking lot for your RV. Learn the history and importance of potatoes and some of the early potato pioneers and their contribution, such as Russet Burbank. Pick up one of the recipe books while you are taking a walk through the gift shop.

The **Idaho Potato Museum,** 130 Northwest Main Street, Blackfoot, ID 83221. ☎ **208-785-2517.** https://idahopotatomuseum.com.

Illinois

General Ulysses S. Grant Home belongs to the state of Illinois. The gift of this home exemplified the appreciation of fellow residents of Galena, Illinois, to the General for his service in the Civil War. Designed by William Dennison, originally constructed in 1860 for Alexander J. Jackson. Thomas B. Hughlett, on behalf of only a small group of local citizens, bought the house for $2,500 in June 1865 and gifted it to General Grant. The home is attractive and furnished and is located on Bouthillier Street. The restored house is operated by the Illinois Historic Preservation Agency as the US Grant Home State Historic Site.

The Grant Home, 500 Bouthillier Street, Galena, IL 61036. ☎ 815-777-3310. https://www.granthome.com/.

Indiana

The town of Decatur, Indiana, yields two very meaningful visits for RV travelers. One is the American Coach/Fleetwood factory tour. The other is the juried metal sculpture art exhibit tour all around town every summer. Either one or both make the detour to Decatur worthwhile.

The sculpture tours are free and self-guided. Takes about 2 hours to walk the area, or you can drive block to block and park and walk. The factory tours are free and are available Tuesdays and Thursdays at 9:00 a.m. For current year information, visit the websites below:

https://www.fleetwoodrv.com/about/factory-tours

https://www.facebook.com/DecaturSculptureTour/

Iowa

Madison County is the Covered Bridge Capital of Iowa, perhaps of the world, and is home to a large group of covered bridges that exists in one small area of the Mississippi Valley. The tour to see the bridges inspired the book and then the movie, *The Bridges of Madison County.*

TIP

Madison County's bridges are on small roads, so you will want to pay to take the tour. **Madison County, Iowa, Chamber & Welcome Center,** 73 Jefferson St., Winterset, IA 50273. ☎ 515-462-1185. http://www.madisoncounty.com/tours.

Kansas

Prairie grass once covered 170 million acres of North America yet only about 4 percent remains, much of it in the Kansas Flint Hills area, where you can find the **Tallgrass Prairie National Preserve.** A few rare patches of these grasses remain in other areas of the country that are hard to find. This is the grass that fed the buffalo that fed the first to arrive Native tribes and later the early American settlers. Find out how large a role this grass played in the development and settlement of the west and why most of it was plowed under or burned away.

Visitor Center – Tallgrass Prairie National Preserve, 2480B KS Hwy. 177, Strong City, KS 66869. ☎ **620- 273-8494.** https://www.nps.gov/tapr/index.htm.

Kentucky

Need a costume, wig, or mask? Enjoy seeing things too odd to describe? **Caufield's Novelty** is the place for all that and more; they have something for every season, holiday, or event.

Caufield's Novelty, 1006 W. Main St., Louisville, KY 40202. ☎ **800-777-5653.** Big rig parking is rare, so this is a car or cab trip. Hours: 9:30 a.m. to 5:00 p.m., Monday through Friday; 10:30 a.m. to 4 p.m., Saturday; and closed on Sundays. Also closed November 1 for inventory. www.caufields.com.

Louisiana

Who doesn't love a rose garden? When **Gardens of the American Rose** is in bloom, it is one of the best. This is the largest (at 118 acres) park dedicated exclusively to roses. Also find sculptures and water fountains that also provide a focal point for the roses and more reasons to take pictures while you are visiting.

Gardens of the American Rose, 8877 Jefferson Paige Road, Shreveport, LA 71119. ☎ **318-938-5402.** https://www.rose.org/visit-public-gardens.

Maine

The **Kenneth E. Stoddard Shell Museum** is housed in a little covered bridge. There is mini golf, an ice-cream parlor, and an arcade nearby. The museum houses seashells from the Pacific Ocean that Kenneth, who was a US Navy sailor, collected from beaches and islands during World War II. Street parking is available. This museum is operated by Kenneth's son, Lee.

The **Kenneth E. Stoddard Shell Museum,** 510 Wiscasset Road, Boothbay, ME 04537. Open 10 a.m. to 10 p.m. mid-May to mid-September.

Maryland

Bel Air Armory is a historic Army National Guard armory located at Bel Air, Harford County, Maryland. It was constructed in 1915 of Port Deposit granite. Go just to see the building or get in on some of the events that happen here throughout the year. The building by itself is amazing, dating to 1915. Get to it by car or by cab; no nearby big rig RV parking.

Bel Air Armory, 37 N. Main St., Bel Air, MD 21014. ☎ **410-638-4506.** https://www.belairmd.org/493/Bel-Air-Armory.

Massachusetts

The Titanic Museum is run by the Titanic Historical Society, Inc., whose purpose is the preservation of the history of the famous ocean liner *RMS Titanic*, which sank by hitting an iceberg on its voyage to New York from England in 1912, one of the best-known losses in maritime history.

The Titanic Museum, 208 Main Street, Indian Orchard, MA. https://titanichistoricalsociety.org/titanic-museum.

Open: Monday to Friday 10 a.m. to 4 p.m., Saturday 10 a.m. to 3 p.m. Closed Sundays and holidays; admission: $4 adults, $2 children.

Michigan

Take in the Elk Ride Tour through the elk preserve and enjoy a great dinner in the Elk Antler Cabin halfway through the ride at **Thunder Bay Resort.** During the tour, Jack Matthias (the owner) or one of his docents will tell you everything you ever wanted to know about the Michigan elk herds, and you will see many elk in their natural Michigan habitat as you take the wagon tour pulled by draft horses or sleigh in the winter months.

Get there at least a day early and take in a round of golf, visit some of the local wineries, or get in on one of the shipwreck glass-bottom boat tours in Alpena. The RV park is the best in the area. Some of the nearby waters provide some of the best brown trout fishing in Michigan when in season. Plenty of rooms at the resort if you want to take a break from the RV for a few days or a week. Try one of the pizzas from the clubhouse to make this a no-cooking-needed visit. The pizza here is rated by some guests to be one of the top three in the nation, the second best in Michigan.

Getting a site at the campground is no problem usually, except for busy holiday weekends. Call ahead for elk ride and dinner reservations; this is a frequent stop for tour buses because it is so unique.

Thunder Bay Resort, 27800 M-32, Hillman, MI 49746. ☎ 800-729-9375. https://www.thunderbayresort.com.

Minnesota

Minnesota is reputed to have 10,000 lakes. The water is so clear in so many of them that you can see the bottom. Pick one to enjoy, as there are so many. A favorite for many travelers from the US and Canada is **Rainy Lake.** Go to fish, just enjoy the views, or take a boat ride. Rainy Lake is in Voyageurs National Park on the Canadian border. Rent a canoe or kayak with Voyageurs Outfitters in **International Falls.** International Falls is just across the river from Fort Frances, Ontario, so you might want to bring your passport.

International Falls, Rainy Lake and Ranier Convention and Visitors Bureau, 301 2nd Avenue, International Falls, MN 56649. ☎ 800-325-5766. https://www.rainylake.org/rainy-lake-map.html.

Mississippi

Erected in 1848, **Biloxi Lighthouse** was one of the first cast-iron lighthouses in the South.

The lighthouse is in the middle of US 90 at Porter Avenue, south of the new Biloxi Visitors Center, and just west of I-110 loop. ☎ 228-374-3105.

Missouri

Glore Psychiatric Museum, one of the St. Joseph Museums, ranks high on the list of unusual museums. This place chronicles the history of the state hospital's mental care and represents artifacts and information from a few hundred years' worth of mental health treatment. It is a *do not miss* for fans of the book, play, or movie *One Flew Over the Cuckoo's Nest.*

Glore Psychiatric Museum, 3406 Frederick Avenue, St. Joseph, MO 64506. ☎ 816-232-8471. https://www.stjosephmuseum.org/glore-psychiatric-museum.

Montana

With consideration for historical timing, **Frontier Gateway Museum** presents prehistoric times into the 21st century in seven buildings and outdoor displays in relevance to Montana involving Native Americans, early homesteaders, cattlemen, and railroad artifacts.

Frontier Gateway Museum, 201 State Street, Glendive, MT 59330. ☎ **406-377-8168.** https://frontiergatewaymuseum.org.

Nebraska

The **Joslyn Art Museum's** collection includes over 11,000 works featuring artists and cultures from ancient times to the present. Featuring temporary exhibits as well.

Joslyn Art Museum, 2200 Dodge Street, Omaha, NE 68102-1292. ☎ **402-342-3300.** https://www.joslyn.org.

Nevada

Forget the slot machines in Vegas; pan for gold here. **Rye Patch State Recreation Area** is a 2,400-acre state park when you can still pan for gold. Use the trails system to see wildlife such as eagles, owls, antelope, fox, and deer. The park also is a stopping-off place to go ghost town exploring and gold prospecting.

Rye Patch State Recreation Area, 2505 Rye Patch Reservoir Road, Lovelock, NV 89419. ☎ **775-538-7321.** http://parks.nv.gov/parks/rye-patch.

New Hampshire

The **Strawbery Banke District** is on the National Register of Historic Places. A living history museum, the Strawbery Banke District preserves the history of the area and people who lived there. Be sure to see the centuries of houses and there is much more to see.

Strawbery Banke Museum, 14 Hancock Street, Portsmouth, NH 03801. ☎ **603-433-1100.** http://www.strawberybanke.org/houses.cfm.

New Jersey

Thomas Edison National Historical Park contains multiple building preserves and celebrates much about the great inventor and industrialist. Thomas Edison's laboratory and residence, Glenmont, are in Llewellyn Park in West Orange in Essex County.

Thomas Edison National Historical Park, 211 Main Street West, Orange, NJ 07052. ☎ **973-736-0550** (choose extension 11, and leave a message). https://www.nps.gov/edis/index.htm.

New Mexico

In this tiny town on US 60 (about 70 miles south and east of Albuquerque) is the host town for seeing the ruins of the Salinas National Monument old mission ruins. Ruth and Kevin at the **Turner Inn and RV Park** (pet friendly) are excellent hosts and are always willing to chat with visitors about the area. Fees are $28 or $30 per night if you want to stay a while; there are weekly and monthly rates available. A few of many reasons folks stay a while is the opportunity to find precious gems on the public lands or collect wildflower seeds or to visit the ruins. There is also an active local artist community, Manzano Mountain Art Council, and a showroom (Cibola Arts Gallery, 217 W. Broadway, Mountainair) for the artists and artisans to display their amazing art works for sale in the quaint little downtown area.

Turner Inn & RV Park, 503 East Broadway, Mountainair, NM 87036. ☎ 505-847-0248. Visit the website at `https://www.turnerinnandrvpark.com/`.

See some comments about the art community at `https://www.facebook.com/Cibola-Arts-418026458254201/`; also see `https://www.nps.gov/sapu/index.htm` for information on the nearby Salinas Pueblo Missions National Monument ruins. The preferred "I don't want to cook" option in Mountainair is Alpine Alley, 210 N. Summit Avenue, Mountainair, NM.

New York

West of Canandaigua, the **Bloomfield Antique Country Mile** is a busy mile-long cluster of antiques shops along routes NY 5 and US 20 near Bloomfield. With plenty of shops lined up back-to-back, this cluster of shops is a terrific place for antique hunting. Keep a compartment empty for your finds.

`https://www.bloomfieldantiquemile.com`.

North Carolina

If your traveling though North Carolina and you have had enough fish and seafood dinners or just want to take a break from the salt-water sourced foods, then the ride up or down the coast is a way to New Bern, North Carolina, to check out a lunch or dinner at **Moore's Olde Tyme Barbeque.**

Moore's Olde Tyme Barbeque, 3621 Doctor M.L.K. Jr Boulevard, New Bern, NC 28562. ☎ **252-638-3937.** https://mooresoldetymebbq.com/.

If you have time, check out the nearby birthplace of Pepsi: **The Birthplace of Pepsi-Cola,** 256 Middle Street, New Bern, NC 28560. ☎ **252-636-5898.** http://www.pepsistore.com.

North Dakota

Scandinavian Heritage Park is an outdoor museum that showcases interesting artifacts from Denmark, Finland, Iceland, Norway, and Sweden. Features include a 240-year-old log house from Norway, a replica stabbur (storehouse), 27-foot-tall Swedish Dala horse, Gol Stave Church Museum, Finnish style sauna, and a Danish designed windmill, various statues, picnic shelter, walking trails, and gift shop.

Scandinavian Heritage Park, 1020 S. Broadway, Minot, ND 58702. ☎ **701-852-9161.** https://scandinavianheritage.org.

Ohio

Even if you never wanted to visit any place in Ohio, if you ever watched a *MASH* episode on TV or seen the play, this is the place to go for one or more **Tony Packo's Original Hot Dogs,** also known as the Hungarian Dog. "Corporal Maxwell Q. Klinger" played by Jamie Farr (who was born in Toledo in 1934), from the TV show *Mash,* set in Korea during the Korean conflict, talked about missing Packo Hot Dogs as his all-time favorite food from home. When you go there you can find memorabilia connected with the show and many of the actors.

Tony Packo's Restaurant, 1902 Front Street, Toledo, OH 43605. ☎ **419-691-6054.** www.tonypacko.com.

If you need another reason to go to Toledo, check out the Toledo Art Museum or the Toledo Zoo.

Oklahoma

Take the ride up and over to the far side of Mount Scott from near Lawton and Fort Sill to **Meer's Store and Restaurant** for a Longhorn burger and a slice of pie. Meer's doesn't serve just a burger; it serves a *Longhorn Burger.* To learn the difference, you just have to taste it.

Meer's Store and Restaurant, 26005 OK-115, Meers, OK 73057. ☎ **580-429-8051.** http://www.meersstore.com.

Oregon

Crater Lake National Park is home to the deepest lake in the United States. *Crater Lake* was created when a volcano blew its top. Learn about the many ecosystems found inside the park. Go to Rim Village first, then start your tour around the lake. The park is open year-round, 24 hours a day. State route 62 takes you there.

Crater Lake National Park Crater Lake, OR 97604. ☎ **541-594-3000.** https://nps.gov/crla/index.htm.

Pennsylvania

Want to see why maybe Einstein was so smart? **The Mütter Museum** is the place that houses slides of his brain tissue. The museum houses many permanent exhibitions, including the Soap Lady and a new Civil War medicine exhibition.

The Mütter Museum, 19 S. 22nd Street, Philadelphia, PA 19103. Call ahead: ☎ **215-560-8564.** http://muttermuseum.org.

Rhode Island

Open seasonally, **Green Animals Topiary Garden** is the oldest and most northern topiary garden in the United States.

Green Animals Topiary Garden, 380 Cory's Lane, Portsmouth, RI 02871. Call for ticket prices. ☎ 401- 847-1000. https://newportmansions. org/explore/green-animals-topiary-garden.

South Carolina

While in South Carolina, visit the **World's Smallest Police Station.** Dating back to 1940, this small (very small) police station functioned until 1990. This place is one of those places that you can miss in the blink of an eye, but it's worth seeing just for bragging rights.

World's Smallest Police Station, 170 S. Dogwood Ave., Ridgeway, SC 29130. http://ridgewaysc.org/worlds-smallest-police-station.

South Dakota

Museum of Geology features mounted skeletons of dinosaurs, mammals, marine reptiles, fish, and fossils from the White River area badlands.

South Dakota School of Mines & Technology, 501 E. Saint Joseph Street, Rapid City, SD 57701. ☎ 605-394-2467. https://sdsmt.edu/ Academics/Museum-of-Geology/Home.

Tennessee

Lane Motor Museum includes mostly foreign cars, cars, and more cars that qualify as cute, rare, classic, or antique, and also includes Mignet Aviation aircraft, bicycles, floating vehicles, and motorcycles. You may want to go more than one day.

Lane Motor Museum, 702 Murfreesboro Pike, Nashville, TN 37210. ☎ 615-742-7445. https://lanemotormuseum.org.

Texas

The Sixth Floor Museum at Dealey Plaza tells the story of a dark day in American History, when President John F. Kennedy was assassinated. A rifle was found on the 6th floor of the building shortly after the assassination.

The Sixth Floor Museum at Dealey Plaza, 411 Elm Street, Dallas, TX 75202. ☎ 214-747-6660. https://jfk.org.

Utah

Visit **Nine Mile Canyon, Carbon County,** to see "rock art" of Archaic, Fremont, and Ute peoples. In the canyon, you can find rock art, often called *petroglyphs*, dating back over a thousand years. There are also historical ranches and structures along the route, which is over 40 miles long.

Location: 20 miles north of Wellington, UT.

Vermont

Sugarbush Farm, Inc., is a 500-acre farm in central Vermont just beyond Woodstock. Visit the farm, and meet the maple trees that yield that ever so sweet syrup. Watch a movie about producing the syrup, and buy a bottle or two to take home.

Sugarbush Farm, Inc., 591 Sugarbush Farm Road, Woodstock, VT 05091. ☎ 800-281-1757. https://sugarbushfarm.com.

Virginia

The Flying Circus Airshow is hard to describe in modern terms. This airshow has a parachute jumper, a wing-walker, and super cool and classic aircraft winging their thing to amaze and amuse. The airshow runs every Sunday, May through October. It will not disappoint!

The Flying Circus Airshow, 5114 Ritchie Road (Route 644), Bealeton, VA 22712. ☎ **540-439-8661.** https://flyingcircusairshow.com.

Washington

Indianola Pier, hundreds of feet into the bay, is another great spot to test your fishing skills and to get out and enjoy a few hours or a day near the water. It is also notorious for star gazers to get a look at the night sky. If you're going to fish make sure you have season limits for each species of fish and license information.

Indianola Pier, 19839-19829 Indianola Rd NE, Indianola, WA 98342. https://wdfw.wa.gov/places-to-go/fishing-piers/indianola-pier.

West Virginia

There are many beautiful state capitol buildings around the nation, but the **West Virginia State Capitol Building** is particularly worth seeing. The building is built from marble from three states and was designed by Cass Gilbert from Zanesville, Ohio.

West Virginia Department of Arts, Culture and History, The Culture Center, Capitol Complex, 1900 Kanawha Boulevard, East Charleston, WV 25305-0300. ☎ **304-558-0220.** www.wvculture.org/agency/capitol.html.

Wisconsin

Kopp's Frozen Custard is a landmark in Wisconsin. Custard is 6% butterfat unlike ice cream, and it is rich, old-fashioned, and delicious. The Greenfield store location is modern and comfortable, and the flavors change daily. If you have every enjoyed an ice cream cone, you will love Kopp's frozen custard. Caution though — you might want to give up RVing and move nearby after your first taste.

Kopp's Frozen Custard, Greenfield Store, 7631 West Layton Avenue, Greenfield, WI 53220. ☎ 414-282-4312. Flavor-of-the-day hotline: ☎ 414-282-4080. www.kopps.com.

Wyoming

After or during a trip down Interstate 80, take Exit 68 to **Little America,** a respite from the road first opened in 1952. The Little America Hotel and Travel Center and Convenience Store are a welcoming and refreshing rest.

Little America, Interstate 80, Exit 68, Little America, WY, 82929. https://wyoming.littleamerica.com/travel-center.

Alberta, Canada

The **Icefields Parkway,** which is Hwy. 93 North between Banff and Jasper, yields fantastic views of the Alberta landscape and wildlife. https://icefieldsparkway.com.

British Columbia, Canada

Miniature World takes small to the extreme with over 85 amazing miniature dioramas and displays that let you immerse yourself in fact, fiction, and fantasy.

Miniature World, 649 Humboldt Street, Victoria, BC V8W 1A7. ☎ 250-385-9731. https://miniatureworld.com.

Manitoba, Canada

Heritage North Museum was established to preserve the heritage and history of Thompson and the surrounding area. Here on the site you will find two log buildings and blacksmith shop. Also find some of the First Nations' artifacts and those related to the early fur trade, fossils, and a woolly mammoth tusk. Blacksmith demonstrations occur during the summer.

Heritage North Museum, 162 Princeton Drive, Thompson, MB R8N 2A4. www.heritagenorthmuseum.ca.

New Brunswick, Canada

Imperial Theatre features performing arts of all sorts. The building is in itself a sight to see as well. Check the calendar on the website and find a show you want to see.

Imperial Theatre, 12 King Square South, Saint John, NB E2L 5B8. ☎ 800-323-SHOW (7469). https://imperialtheatre.ca.

Newfoundland and Labrador, Canada

L'Anse aux Meadows is by no means an easy drive but worth it if you're interested in Viking history. This site has yielded some of the first known evidence of a Viking/Norse presence over a thousand years ago.

L'Anse aux Meadows, St. Lunaire-Griquet NL A0K 2X0, is located on the tip of the Northern Peninsula, 433 km north of Deer Lake along the Viking Trail as Route 430. https://www.pc.gc.ca/en/lhn-nhs/nl/meadows/visit.

Nova Scotia, Canada

At the **Celtic Music Interpretive Centre**, you can enjoy live Celtic music seven days a week from May through October. The center promotes and hosts performances of traditional Celtic music of Cape Breton Island.

Celtic Music Interpretive Centre, 5471 Highway 19, Judique, NS BOE 1PO. ☎ **902-787-2708.** www.celticmusiccentre.com.

Ontario, Canada

CN Tower provides the most spectacular view in all of Toronto. Sky-Pod is the newest and the highest observation level and the view is breathtaking, not to mention the appreciation for modern glass building technology you will have after your visit. A must see and do when in Toronto.

CN Tower, 290 Bremner Boulevard, Toronto, ON M5V 3L9. ☎ **416-86-TOWER.** www.cntower.ca/en-ca/plan-your-visit/attractions/lookout.html.

Prince Edward Island, Canada

Anne of Green Gables Museum celebrates the book character that helped the world learn about Prince Edward Island. You can take the ferry in some RVs or make this a car trip from the mainland.

Anne of Green Gables Museum, 4542 Route 20, Park Corner, P.E.I., Canada. Email info@annemuseum.com for rates and reservations. www.annemuseum.com.

Quebec, Canada

Shrine of Saint-Anne-de-Beaupré is a marvelous structure on its own. The interiors of the church building amaze, and the St Anne's fountain is unlike any other. You may want to brush up on your French ahead of your visit.

Shrine of Saint-Anne-de-Beaupré, 10018 Avenue Royale, Sainte-Anne-de-Beaupré, QC G0A 3C0. ☎ **418-827-3782.** https://sanctuairesainteanne.org/en.

Saskatchewan, Canada

Galleries at **RCMP Heritage Centre** include a driving simulator, how Mounted Police are trained, and maintaining law and order in the west. Learn the many ways the Royal Canadian Mounted Police are professional and special and an impressive history and heritage.

RCMP Heritage Centre, 5907 Dewdney Avenue, Regina, SK S4T 0P4. (The Centre is located on the grounds of the RCMP Academy.) ☎ **866-567-7267.** https://rcmphc.com.

Chapter **25**

Ten Greatest Travel Gadgets

T he cool gadgets in this chapter will make your trip easier and remove many of the petty annoyances involved in getting where you're going.

Smartphone

As an RV traveler, you probably need to give up your flip phone. Smartphones and the apps that run on them can do just about anything but the laundry. You can use them to check Facebook, tweet, and pin; surf the web; text, message, or email; and play sweet games. And don't forget that they can make calls to other cell and landline phones from just about anywhere.

Some aspects of smartphones make them indispensable for RVers. They have navigation apps and phone service, and they can be used as Wi-Fi hotspots to connect other devices to the Internet.

» **Navigation apps.** All smartphones offer some form of navigation capability, often built into the phone's standard software and accessible by voice command or from within the web browser. Get accustomed to using these navigation apps by taking car trips to places you know and have gone to before, such as the grocery store or the mall, and listen to and follow the turn by turn directions to get there. This way, you will be familiar with how the apps work when you need them to lead the way.

There generally are settings in the apps to rule out road types, like secondary, and having to use a ferry boat to get there. Learn all the settings you can adjust so that you can tune the device to work its best for you.

WARNING

Study a paper map and know where you are going *before* you depart in your RV. Smartphone GPS navigation apps are generally programmed to direct a car, pickup truck, or SUV, or perhaps a semi-truck, not a motor home that needs 12 feet, 7 inches of overhead clearance or weighs in over 28,000 pounds. They also have a tendency to take you along the shortcut, not the big truck route by-pass you really need to use, so some knowledge of your desired routing is necessary so you know when to not "turn right here" as the app directs.

» **It's a phone, too.** No more hunting for the phone booth needed across 90 percent of the places you will travel in the U.S. and Canada. All the major carriers publish a map showing where they think they have coverage for voice and data.

TIP

When you shop for a smartphone, consider one with a large screen. Find a case or holder that keeps the phone firmly fixed near the driver's or navigator's seat. Also, find a hands-free Bluetooth earpiece or headset that lets you communicate with the phone if your motor home's radio isn't Bluetooth-capable.

Practice using the phone and its features when someone else is driving. If you're going to do the driving, set the navigation app before you start out. If the app fails, find a safe place to pull over and reset your routing on the application.

NOAA Weather Radio

The National Oceanic and Atmospheric Administration (NOAA) weather-radio channels may not cover *all* the areas you travel across or stay in, but having a NOAA radio is still essential for those times when it does. In most areas, a NOAA weather radio can keep you informed so that you can keep yourself and your family safe when the weather doesn't cooperate with your plans. A NOAA weather radio tunes to all seven VHF frequencies from 162.400 MHz to 162.550 MHz.

Here are where you can find NOAA coverage maps for the US and Canada:

» **USA NOAA coverage maps:** http://www.nws.noaa.gov/nwr/Maps

» **Canada coverage maps:** https://www.canada.ca/en/environment-climate-change/services/weatheradio/find-your-network.html

REMEMBER

Having a smartphone, radio, TV set, and weather radio on board increases your chances of staying connected to weather information and warnings, which can help you make safe travel decisions.

Dedicated Hotspot Device

A dedicated hotspot device can maintain an Internet connection for the kids or travel companions without interfering with what is happening on your smartphone. Most all of the major carriers sell a dedicated hotspot device that you can keep in the motor home to provide Internet connectivity for all those other devices you need these days.

Adding one of these devices to your cellphone plan will cost a bit more, but it can be well worth it to carry the convenience of Internet access with you on the road. It also provides the option to keep something in the RV connected to the Internet when you are on an errand or daytrip somewhere with the tow car or truck. You can also use the hotspot Wi-Fi device to connect some GPS models to the Internet for live weather and traffic information.

TIP

Consider buying one of the newer superfast 5G capable hotspot devices. Soon the nation will be covered with 5G capable towers giving superfast data speeds to meet your on-the-road connectivity needs. Also consider buying one that can connect to an external antenna. This will give you a more stable connection and increase the distance from which you can stay connected to a cell-phone tower.

RV-Specific GPS Device

This indispensable gadget helps you maintain turn-by-turn awareness, safety, and convenience while driving your RV. One big benefit of having a Global Positioning System (GPS) device specifically designed for RV use is that it can take into consideration your vehicle's characteristics, such as overhead clearance; it won't take you down a road with 10-foot overhead clearance when you need 12 feet, 8 inches.

Another great advantage of a GPS designed for RV use is lane-awareness and lane-change advice, which is particularly useful in large cities; many major highways and interstates require prompt lane changes.

RV-specific GPS devices are available in two different styles: a dedicated GPS function or a tablet with a GPS feature that will also do other things. Some models include bells and whistles such as a dashboard camera and trip recorder. As with any tech gadget, learn to use it before you need it. Consider favoring a larger viewing screen when you decide which model to buy.

TIP

Make sure that the device is in RV mode for height clearance and weight when you're pulling your fifth-wheel or driving your Class A or class B motor home down the highways and byways of North America.

REMEMBER

Some of the most useful features to look for include RV routing based on size and weight, phone connectivity for traffic updates, preloaded points of interest, voice-enabled command features, and preloaded information on campgrounds.

Digital Tire-Pressure Gauge

A small digital tire-pressure gauge is an indispensable tool for checking the tires of your RV, trailer, fifth-wheel, or tow car on a frequent basis. Knowing the recommended tire pressures for all vehicles and trailers and checking them frequently enables you to catch tire problems before they become big problems. It is good practice to always check your tire pressures first thing in the morning before leaving on the trip or your days travels.

Having one tire out of four or six running a pressure 10 percent or more below the other tires is a clue that it's time to get some service on that tire when you're near a service facility. If all tires' pressures are low by an equal amount after a big swing in outdoor temperatures, you may just have to add a little more air before getting on the road again. Your trailer, RV, or towed car performs best when all the tires are at recommended pressure.

A handy digital pressure gauge helps you keep tires in spec, improves gas mileage, and reduces uneven wear, extending the life of the tires while contributing to on-the-road safety.

Multimeter

This little electronic test meter helps you make sure that your RV's house or coach batteries are charging properly (13.8 to 14.7 volts DC) regardless of the source of charging current. The engine alternator, on-board generator, or the AC to DC converter when connected to campground AC power should all produce a charging current in that voltage range. You can also use this meter to check for adequate AC voltage in an outlet or camp power pedestal. A multimeter can also identify whether a house or clearance light bulb is burned out and whether a fuse is blown.

Learning how to use this testing tool and how your RV's electrical system operates can save you many service bills and trips to the dealership, and help keep your rig, lights, and devices properly powered.

Rechargeable Battery-Powered Vacuum Cleaner

Some big rigs and even class Cs have built-in vacuum cleaners. For the rest, you benefit from having a battery-powered handheld or standard-size rechargeable vacuum cleaner on board. From cleaning up beach sand to desert dust and pet hair to getting rid of angry unwelcome insects, a portable vacuum cleaner helps keep the RV clean and tidy. You can also use it to clean the carpets in the tow car or the pickup truck that pulls the trailer.

Charge the vacuum's battery every time you're hooked up to a campground power pedestal, and keep all the attachments in one place, such as a bag or toolbox.

CB Radio

Most folks consider a citizens' band (CB) radio to be "old-school," and it is. But old-school isn't no school. This radio can still be helpful; many over-the-road truckers and RVers have a CB turned on, monitoring channel 19 to hear what's happening up ahead as they roll down the road. Some police agencies monitor channel 9 (the help channel), so you can shout out to them if necessary.

TIP

Consider buying a pair of handheld CB portable units so that you can use them in and around the campsite to call the kids in for dinner or s'mores around the campfire.

Small Oil-Filled Electric Heater

Even though your RV is likely to be equipped with a propane furnace, heat pump, or resistance-heat-assisted air conditioner that can provide heat on cold nights, this gadget can help. You can use a small radiator-like liquid-filled electric heater to warm up the sleeping area or take the chill out of a bathroom. This type of heater is a low-cost alternative to draining the propane tank; also, it's quiet, giving light sleepers a bit of heat without the noise of the built-in heating alternatives.

TIP

When you need a little bit of heat in a small space without going over a 20- or 30-amp hookup limit, a small heater can fill the bill on chilly but not-quite-freezing nights.

Emergency Signs and Lights

RVers hope that they'll never have tire failures or mechanical breakdowns. If misfortune should strike, though, it's helpful to warn other travelers that your vehicle is disabled on the side of the road. Most states have move-over laws that require motorists to slow down or move over a lane away from stalled or disabled vehicles. Triangular warning signs and emergency warning lights placed behind your vehicle warn other motorists of your plight and keep you safe.

TIP

States that have move-over laws are listed at https:// drivinglaws.aaa.com/tag/move-over-law. As a courteous RV driver, however, you should always get over if you can safely do so.

WARNING

Some RVers carry railroad flares for night warnings, and using them is okay, but you should consider the flames and the risk to users. LED light kits are a safe alternative.

Appendix

Quick Concierge

Fast Facts

American Automobile Association (AAA)
For emergency road service, call ☎ 800-AAA-HELP (222-4357). To locate your nearest AAA office, go to https://www.aaa.com/stop/. Enter your zip code to be directed to the club for your local area.

ATM
Most highway rest stops and some campgrounds have ATMs. Cirrus (☎ 800-424-7787; www.mastercard.com) and PLUS (☎ 800-843-7587; www.visa.com) are the two popular networks in the United States.

Credit Cards
Visa's emergency number in case your card is lost or stolen is ☎ 800-847-2911. American Express cardholders and traveler's check holders can call ☎ 800-221-7282. MasterCard holders can call ☎ 800-307-7309.

Emergencies
Call ☎ 911.

Hospitals
Look for the blue highway signs with a white *H* signifying an exit for a hospital with emergency services. For a partial listing of hospitals along the drives in this book or in the urban areas we pass through, see the "Fast Facts" sections in Chapters 8 through 23.

Post Office
Some commercial campgrounds receive and send mail, sell stamps, and handle Federal Express and UPS deliveries for guests.

Road and Weather Conditions
Go online to www.fhwa.dot.gov/trafficinfo/index.htm for national weather and road advisories. For road and weather conditions along the drives in this book, see the "Fast Facts" sections in Chapters 8 through 23, or load the Weather Channel app on your smartphone.

Taxes
The federal tax on gasoline sales is 18.4¢ per gallon of gasoline and 24.4¢ per gallon for diesel fuel. For state gasoline taxes, see the "Fast Facts" sections in Chapters 8 through 23.

Toll-Free Numbers and Websites

RV associations

Recreation Vehicle Industry Association (RVIA)
☎ 703-620-6003
https://gorving.com/ or http://www.gocampingamerica.com/

RV rental agencies

Cruise America (Nationwide)
☎ 800-327-7799
https://www.cruiseamerica.com/

El Monte RV (Nationwide)
☎ 888-958-7959
https://www.elmonterv.com/

The Motor Home Xperts
☎ 800-232-8989
https://www.themotorhomexperts.com/article.php/77/moturis

Road Bear International Motorhome (Agoura Hills, California)
☎ 866-491-9853 or 818-865-2925
http://www.roadbearrv.com/en

Vintage Surfari Wagons (Mission Viejo, California)
☎ 714-585-7565
https://www.vwsurfari.com/

U.S. agencies

National Forest Service
☎ 800-832-1355
https://www.fs.fed.us/

National Parks Service
☎ 202-208-3818
https://www.nps.gov/index.htm

U.S. Bureau of Land Management
☎ 202-208-3801
https://www.blm.gov/

U.S. Department of Transportation
☎ 202-366-4000
https://www.fhwa.dot.gov/

Where to Get More Information

Numerous online and published resources exist for the curious RVer. Many are listed here.

Helpful websites

» `https://www.campingworld.com`: Supplies for the RV market.

» `https://www.gocampingamerica.com`: From the National Association of RV Parks and Campgrounds, camping information for more than 3,100 member properties.

» `https://www.gorving.com`: A comprehensive source of RV information by the Go RVing Coalition, a nonprofit organization.

» `https://www.koa.com`: Kampgrounds of America, operator of the KOA network of campgrounds.

» `https://www.rvamerica.com`: An RV sales and industry information site sponsored by *RV News Magazine*.

» `https://www.rvia.org`: A variety of information about manufacturers, retail shows, and clubs.

» `https://www.rvusa.com`: Find RV dealers, manufacturers, parts and accessory sources, rental units, and campgrounds.

Campground directories

Here are a few directories you may find helpful:

» **Bureau of Land Management:** 270 million acres of public land. Department of Interior–BLM, 1849 C St. NW, Room 5665, Washington, DC 20240 (☎ **202-208-3801;** `https://www.blm.gov/`). Free.

» **National Association of RV Parks and Campgrounds:** More than 3,000 RV parks and campgrounds. National ARVC, 113 Park Ave., Falls Church, VA 22046 (☎ **800-395-2267** or 703-241-8801; `http://www.gocampingamerica.com/`). Free.

- » **National Forest Service:** 4,000 campgrounds. U.S. Department of Agriculture Forest Service, Public Affairs Office, Box 96090, Washington, DC 20090-6090 (☎ **800-832-1355;** `https://www.fs.fed.us/`). Free.

- » **National Wildlife Refuges:** 488 refuges. U.S. Fish and Wildlife Services, Public Affairs Office, 1849 C St. NW, MS-5600/MIB, Washington, DC 20240 (☎ **800-344-WILD** [9453], or 202-452-5125; `http://refuges.fws.gov`). Free.

- » **U.S. Army Corps of Engineers:** 53,000 campsites near oceans, rivers, and lakes. U.S. Army Corps of Engineers, USACE Publications Depot, 2803 52nd Ave., Hyattsville, MD 20781-1102 (☎ **301-394-0081;** `https://www.usace.army.mil/`). Free.

Publications for campers and RV owners

- » *Camping Today:* Online magazine of Family Campers and RVers, 4804 Transit Rd., Building 2, Depew, NY 14043 (☎ **800-245-9755;** `https://fcrv.org/news/camping-today`)

- » *Motorhome Magazine:* TL Enterprises, 2575 Vista del Mar Dr., Ventura, CA 93001 (☎ **805-667-4484;** `http://www.motorhome.com`

- » *Trailer Life:* TL Enterprises, 2575 Vista del Mar Dr., Ventura, CA 93001 (☎ **805-667-4100;** `https://www.trailerlife.com`)

RV and Campground Lingo

In the same way that a potential home buyer must figure out the abbreviated language for real-estate listings — *6 rms riv vu* (six rooms with river view), for instance — an RVer should know certain terms that are peculiar to owning and operating recreation vehicles. Some of the more common ones are as follows:

- » **Auxiliary battery:** Extra battery to run 12-volt equipment.

- » **Basement model:** An RV with large storage areas underneath a raised chassis.

- » **Black water:** Wastewater from the toilet.

- » **Boondock:** To camp without electrical or other hookups.

- » **Cabover:** The part of a mini motor home that overlaps the top of the vehicle's cab, usually containing a sleeping area, storage unit, or entertainment center.

- » **Camper shell:** Removable unit to fit in the bed of a pickup truck.

- » **Curbside:** The side of the RV that's at the curb when parked.

- » **Diesel pusher:** A motor home with a rear diesel engine.

- » **Dual electrical system:** An RV system in which some lights and other electrical systems run on 12-volt battery power and others run on 110 AC electrical hookup.

- » **Dump station:** Also called sanitary dump or disposal station; where an RV empties the *gray water* (wastewater from sinks and shower) and *black water* (wastewater from toilet) from its holding tanks.

- » **Full hookup:** A campsite that provides connections for electricity, water, and sewage.

- » **Generator:** A component device that produces 110/220 AC electricity that is powered by a small piston engine fueled by gasoline, diesel, or propane that is built into many RVs but also available as a portable option.

- » **Gray water:** Wastewater from the sinks and shower.

- » **Hard-sided:** RV walls made of aluminum, composite, or another hard surface building material.

- » **Hitch:** The fastening unit that joins a movable vehicle, such as a towable RV or tow-car, to the vehicle that pulls it.

- » **Holding tanks:** Tanks that retain *black water* (wastewater from the toilet) and *gray water* (wastewater from sinks and the shower) when the RV unit isn't connected to a sewer.

» **Hookups:** The land connections at a campsite for electricity, water, and sewage. Sites that offer all three connections are called *full hookups;* sites that offer only one or two of three connections are called *partial hookups.*

» **Inverter:** A unit that changes 12 or 24 volt DC (direct current) from the coach batteries to 110-volt AC (alternating current) to enable operation of computers, TV sets, and other electrical devices, or AC appliances when an RV isn't hooked up to a source of electricity.

» **Leveling:** Positioning the RV in camp so the rig is level, using ramps (also called *levelers*) placed under the wheels, built-in scissors jacks, or automated power-leveling jacks.

» **Overflow area:** That part of a campground that can handle late arrivals when all the regular sites are filled or no one is in the registration office; the area usually is little more than a parking lot or open field.

» **Partial hookups:** Sites that offer one or two of the three land connections for electricity, water, and sewage.

» **Pop-up:** Foldout or raised additions to an RV that add height for standing room.

» **Propane:** Liquefied petroleum gas (LPG) used for heating, cooking, and refrigeration in RVs.

» **Pull-through:** A campground site that enables the driver to pull the RV forward into the site for camping and then drive out of the site on the other end to leave, without having to back up.

» **Self-contained:** An RV that needs no external connections to provide short-term cooking, bathing, and heating functions. Some campgrounds require self-contained RVs (no tents) because they do not have bathrooms or showers on site.

» **Shore cord:** (Power cord) The external electrical cord that connects the vehicle to a campground electrical hookup. There are three configurations, 20 amp, 30 amp, and 50 amp. The 50 amp is also 240 volt.

» **Slideout:** A portion of the vehicle that slides open when the RV is parked to expand the living and/or bedroom area. If the RV is parked in a narrow area or there is a tree in the way, you can keep the slideout tucked in or perhaps only open it partway.

» **Snowbird:** A resident of a cold climate who takes an RV and moves south to a warmer climate for all or most of the winter months.

» **Spirit level:** A device used for determining an even horizontal or vertical plane by centering a bubble in a slightly curved glass tube filled with a colored liquid. Some RVs come with built-in levels.

» **Soft sides:** Telescoping side panels on an RV that can be raised or lowered and are constructed of canvas or fabric.

» **Solar panels:** A collection of solar cells that convert photons from bright sunlight to direct-current electricity.

» **Street-side:** Side of the vehicle on the curb side when parked.

» **Telescoping:** Compacting from front to back and/or top to bottom to make the living unit smaller for towing and storage.

» **Three-way refrigerators:** An RV refrigerator/freezer that can operate on LPG, 110 Volt AC electrical hookup or generator, or 12-volt DC power from the RV batteries.

» **Tow car:** A car towed by an RV, also called TOAD, to be used as transportation when the RV is parked in a campground. There are two classifications: One tows with 4 wheels down the others require a tow dolly. Check your vehicle owner's manual.

» **Widebody:** Designs that stretch RVs from the traditional 96-inch width to 100 or 102 inches.

Index

About the Author

Dennis C. Brewer has a Bachelor of Science Degree in Business from Michigan Technological University and is the author of several books. A veteran who served in the US Navy, Chief Petty Officer (1968-1983) and US Army, Captain (1983-1995). As a self-described traveler and snowbird, Dennis is a lifelong camping and RV enthusiast; he and his wife Penny have visited 43 states in their Fleetwood Class A motor home so far.

Author's Acknowledgments

RV Vacations For Dummies, 6th edition, is assembled on a baseline of effort invested and work done by prior authors and researchers of five prior editions upon whose foundational work this volume is built. Thank you all.

There are hundreds of people at RV campgrounds and parks, destination attractions, and fine eating establishments across North America who kindly shared time, courtesy, and pertinent information with us over the phone and by email. Thank you for your contributions; very much appreciate the help, time, and information you shared for the benefit of the readers of this text.

Many thanks to my persevering wife, Penny R. Peterson, who helped tremendously to build this text, first by helping with the research and by allowing many of "our time" hours to be invested in this book.

High on that list of people to acknowledge and thank is James Weems, a full-time RV traveler, the technical editor who reviewed the entire text for accuracy. Thanks Jim.

As with every book, there is a team of people to thank and recognize and particularly those at the publisher who worked on this text. The Wiley editorial and production staff, as always, did a perfect job to bring this text into being and to you.

Thanks to Colleen Diamond, project mana......r understanding and excellent inputs and edits to improve this text. There are many others at Wiley, including Kathy Simpson, Jenny Vicenzi, Debbye Butler, and Mohammed Zafar Ali, all of whom deserve a great deal of credit and thanks for bringing this 6th edition to print.

A special thanks goes to Ashley Coffey, acquisitions editor at Wiley for two things. First, recognizing that this 6th edition of *RV Vacations For Dummies* needed to happen, and second, granting me the privilege of being able to become the author of a second *For Dummies* book.

Thanks also to Carole Jelen, VP of Tech Titles at Waterside Productions, for her support on this project and continued assistance as my agent.

Finally, I would like to thank you the reader, my fellow RV travelers, who will buy, read, and use this book all across North America.

Publisher's Acknowledgments

Acquisitions Editor: Ashley Coffey

Project Manager: Colleen Diamond

Development Editor: Colleen Diamond

Copy Editor: Kathy Simpson

Technical Editor: James Weems

Proofreader: Debbye Butler

Editorial Assistant: Matt Lowe

Sr. Editorial Assistant: Cherie Case

Production Editor: Mohammed Zafar Ali

Cover Photo: © dan_prat/iStock.com